PRAISE FOR DAVID KILEY AND *WHEEL HEAD*

"Dave Kiley was, at a young age, hit hard by one of those proverbial 'waves of life' that left him with a broken spirit and a paralyzed body. But like any true surfer who finds himself caught inside by a big set, he never gave up, kept paddling and worked his way back to a position in the lineup. Student first, learning what he wanted from this life… he became a fierce warrior, fighting to not only overcome his injury but climbing to the top of his chosen sports. Now he is the teacher who has lived the lessons and shares the knowledge so that others can understand that the power of one's own mind is a force to be reckoned with in any kind of adverse situation."

> – Gerry Lopez
> Surfer and Author

"Dave Kiley is a true American success story. In my life I've had the privilege of meeting hundreds of influential people. Dave is at the top of the list! His contribution to men, women and children with disabilities has been endless. Dave's 'no limits' attitude has allowed him to build innovative adaptive sport programs across the country… not to mention his gold medals in THREE sports!

The great lesson of getting through tough times and moving forward exemplifies what Dave is about. He has taken a bad break in life and turned it into a life mission of service. His selfless example is truly inspirational! His story is truly a compelling read.

The honor of knowing Dave for over 40 years has been a tremendous gift in my life. I hope people who get to hear his journey feel the same gift!"

> – Mike Scioscia
> LA Dodgers Catcher, World Series Champion;
> LA Angels Manager, World Series Champion

WHEEL HEAD

THE WHEEL PRINT OF DAVID KILEY

TOLD BY DAVID KILEY
WRITTEN BY MILES THOMPSON

WHEEL HEAD
The Wheel Print of David Kiley
Told by David Kiley
Written by Miles Thompson
Editor: Taylor Brien
Proofreader: Lyda Rose Haerle, Griff Mill
Cover Design: Nicole Wurtele
Interior Layout: Michael Nicloy

All images are courtesy of David Kiley

Paperback ISBN: 979-8-9913280-0-5
Hardcover ISBN: 979-8-9913280-1-2

PUBLISHED BY CG SPORTS PUBLISHING

AN IMPRINT OF
NICO 11 PUBLISHING & DESIGN
MUKWONAGO, WISCONSIN
MICHAEL NICLOY, PUBLISHER
www.nico11publishing.com

Quantity order requests can be emailed to:
mike@nico11publishing.com

Printed in The United States of America

This book of my life is dedicated to God and Sobriety. The primary person is my wife, Sandy, for all her love, sacrifice, and support. If there is no Sandy there is no DK.

Wheel Head is also dedicated to my children and my four magnificent grandchildren.

To my mother, a true lioness, and my siblings (especially my brother Tom).

To every single newly injured person young/old which I had the privilege of working with over my career; for the blessing of those moments. I had to give it away in order to keep it.

To all those in struggle with drugs and alcohol. There is a better life awaiting you.

To all my extended family and friends who have encouraged and supported me through good times and hard times over my lifetime as a "Wheel Head".

To my great friend, Miles Thompson who authored *Wheel Head*. Three years of blood on the pages.

Most of all, to my Queen, Sandy. You are with me always......

WHEEL HEAD

THE WHEEL PRINT OF DAVID KILEY

PART ONE

There is never a time in the future in which we will work out our salvation. The challenge is in the moment; the time is always now.
— James A. Baldwin

COSTA MESA

The art of life is to know how to enjoy
a little and to endure very much.

— William Hazlitt

We always compete.

    Who can spit farther, jump higher, throw to targets, and run the fastest?

Then come bikes beneath the tree—a glorious Christmas for sure. Jeff and I mount those 10-speeds like the hot-shit, little twerps we are. Tom doesn't get one, and to this day is bitter to receive my no gears, hand-me-down-turd of a bike. Yet, we ride the wind, cycling the neighborhood with a reckless fever. Freedom.

At nine, almost ten-years-old, I revel in the superiority of age and strength. My brothers are the lopsided proving ground. Advantage me.

My memory has me in the lead. Not good enough. Not then. Not now. Not ever. There's a difference between winning and the resignation of time and space slipping through the grasp of those willing to take me on.

The voice in my head rings clear, 'You can make it.'

A quick shoulder-check affirms they're a fair distance back. If I can get across the congested boulevard, they'll have to wait for traffic to clear. Winning.

The oncoming traffic barrels towards, bringing a blast of 1960s exhaust and artful design of chromed metal. Southern California in the mid-sixties, with its expansive car culture mindset and wide open boulevards, is a paved playground for anything with wheels.

'I can do it.' Already in high gear, I churn faster, harder, and bury my head beyond the handlebars.

Big Mistake.

The Chevy Apache pickup truck brakes but hits me flush and square. My books and lunch take flight. I feel them leaving before understanding why.

    My brother Tom remembers an orange rolling down the street. He thought it was my head.

1

David Kiley

Born in Sioux Falls, South Dakota, my first memories are of snow reaching higher than my younger brothers and me. There are faint memories of us digging snow caves. The Dakotas, with their frigid temperatures, drive the most full-bodied, burly men to fires and cedarwood barstools. Without knowing why, we're driven by the sun, boundless seasons, and the sound of mom calling us home for supper.

My mother, Mary Lou Kiley, has her hands full with myself and two younger brothers. The fourth sibling, Steve, is on the way and showing in her belly. I wouldn't call us trouble, but we're mischievous in a chaotic way that keeps her on high alert. Around the age of five or six, I begin to understand the advantages of weight and height. My brothers pay a certain price.

Mom mends our wounds, holds us accountable to time, feeds our faces, and bundles us in abundant, winter layers of clothing. She keeps us outside and healthy, all the while allowing her the needed elbow space for a mental recess and the tending of our home. She holds us responsible: finishing everything on our plates, washing dishes after meals, and because of her—all us boys are accountable for shovelling snow off the neighbor's sidewalk and driveways. She pays us a dime a piece for the job.

Early in their marriage, mom works at an insurance office. When the three of us come along, she works evenings as a waitress at a roadside cafe truck stop. She exemplifies a willingness to do the hard yards for her family and kids.

Mother, to this day, is a ninja bridge player. She will cut your heart out. She enters tournaments when time allows. These days, whilst pushing 90 years of age, she continues to play twice a week. If she gels with a partner, she will keep the team together building chemistry and ability.

She demands answers when her partner's play lacks a strategic purpose.

After a day of squaring off with 80-100 competitors, I ask her, how things went. If she and her partner place fourth or better but not quite capturing the prize, she replies in a ho-hum manner. If they win, which isn't uncommon, she becomes elated. I see her spark and passion. She lights up. This energy comes in the form of domination.

When the team comes up short, she doesn't mince words. Male or female, she gives them the business if their play is weak, wrong, or doesn't live up to her expectations. I feel bad for those at the wrong end of her displeasure. She does not. Her blood is my blood: then, now, and forever.

The competitive drive comes from Mom.

My parents both came from large, hardworking, salt-of-the-earth families. The credo around ours is simple: be on time, do your job at a high level, and respect those around you.

Dad, Paul Joseph Kiley, is the reason back then. A picture of strength, his hands speak of calluses, hard ridges, and long weathered lines.

I remember carrying his mitt to the ball field, around the corner from where we live in South Dakota. Looking back, those summer softball games draw me to the absolute beauty of ball and flight. Transfixed, I watch the ball from pitcher to batter. The crack of the bat. I began to tell by sound, the depth and danger of the ball meeting wood. Might it be caught? He hit that one higher than the trees. He's an easy out. This guy can hit it out—there it goes. With his speed, all he has to do is hit it on the ground. He can throw. He cannot. Best guy plays shortstop. The putz plays right field (no right field for me). The wind. An important variable. Which way is it blowing? Can the pitcher control the corners of the plate with placement?

Those softball games help create as keen a sporting insight as any six-year-old kid in the neighborhood. I begin looking for pick-up games: basketball, baseball, football—doesn't matter. Competition. The city blocks are full of athletes. I just have to find them.

There is also the accompanying beer after the softball affairs. I struggle understanding why dad acts differently, slurs his speech, and drinks a gully of water and milk straight from the carton many mornings.

I like being with dad, especially after a game, getting a soda and eating bar food. The commotion, wrestling with an edge of unknown danger, peculiar smells: stale keg beer, urine, and perfume. In a way I won't understand until generations later, I like his dive, lowly lit bars.

Mom, on the other hand, has her reservations.

There are arguments. They carry volume.

When you're a kid, things happen in a hurry.

The family is six strong with Steve, Tom, Jeff, myself, and folks. Dad goes ahead and scouts a place to live. Mom, not even thirty yet, sells the house and all our belongings on her own. She loads us on the California-bound train, departing from Omaha, Nebraska. She has the helpful hands of Grandpa and Aunt Joan in corralling us to everything California-bound.

Steve's an infant, wearing cloth diapers. Mom washes his stinkers in the train's restroom. Mothers at their mighty best. My grandmother makes fried chicken for the pilgrimage as we don't have the needed cash for train meals. Mom packs sacks of food that my brothers and I are constantly hand-grabbing. I imagine this is an enormously difficult time for my mom. Where my dad should have been, there were us boys and family substitutes. A blur of places, landscape, and folks. The journey west is a strong test of character and faith. Mom takes it on and soon we arrive—Costa Mesa, California.

Costa Mesa sits on the bluffs of Newport and Huntington Beach due west of Santa Ana and Irvine to the east.

The real estate squawk of "location, location, location" is yet to be the idiom it is today. Costa Mesa, in the early 60s is a fair shake—a fighting chance for a better life, and a pastoral, peaceful place in the sun.

We rent a duplex-style apartment in the beginning. Dad is growing and building the fabric of his craft. After working with Red's Cabinet shop, it isn't long before he opens his own business on Baker Street. He's his own boss. Dad is becoming a master of his trade. The cabinet business expands and grows, like the city itself.

Mom learns how to stretch a budget and becomes amazingly adept in the Southern California cuisine of Mexican food; tacos and burritos by the dozens like she has green chili salsa in her blood. The neighborhood "no goods" (my closest friends) often spend the night, lining up the next morning for the conveyor belt of mom's pancakes. We keep eating. She keeps producing.

My friends today still remember the tacos and pancakes. Simple, powerful memories.

I discover the Boys Club and its across the street, adjacent park. Major find. The acres of greenery not only provide baseball diamonds but valuable space

Our first Costa Mesa home. Bikes and skateboards ruled the day. Sharon is yet to be born to this Catholic family.

for kids like me to measure my speed and endurance against others. The club provides me with a clash of like-minded second graders scrambling for court time and the implicit "pairing off" that only competition brings. There are leagues: basketball, baseball, and flag football. My initial introduction to fair play, officiating, and the invaluable details of playing a game properly. Often, if you are not competing, you're asked to keep score or run the clock. Standings and stats are kept—constant talking points. Doesn't matter if you are a scrawny, undersized kid or one of many imposing teenagers at the club.

By the time I am in the third grade, we move into a house purchased by mom and dad. Off Baker and Fairview streets, our three-bedroom, single-level home is a commotion of activity. It isn't long before our Irish Catholic family grows, with my youngest brother Paul Junior (always PJ), and finally a sister, Sharon, joining the family. We cram our little slice of heaven with triple-bunk beds. We're living the Anglo dream.

Ever the tradesman, I watch dad build the Sistine Chapel of the neighborhood. Measured to exactly ten-foot and reinforced with the skillful pride of a proud, athletic father, our driveway is now the source of dreams—a perfect basketball goal. The stout hoop is built to regulation. Dad is a no-shortcut kind-of-guy, and at 8-9 years of age, shots leaving my fingertips are a vertical defiance of what's predictable and sturdy within the advanced years to come. There was no easing into it. Ten-foot is the standard from day one.

Weekends are a driveway frenzy of pick-up games, street tournaments, and HORSE competitions. HORSE games, legendary in parks, streets, and neighborhoods worldwide spark the creative relationship between myself and the ball. HORSE is about matching the shots of your opponent. If you miss, you gain a letter. If you spell HORSE—game over. I learn early on how to spin the ball off the backboard with reverses, baseline drives (from the grass to pavement), and no-look shots. I play into others' pedestrian relationships with the ball and spin to win many a HORSE game. If you can shoot, I enjoy testing myself and my half-grown jump shot against yours. A cute favorite is the straight-ahead bank shot, but if I get behind, you can count on reverse layups in bunches until you miss, and I win.

I fall in love with the ball. It needs to be with me—in my hands. I walk, dribble, jog, and sprint all over Costa Mesa in search of a court and the growing opportunities to prove myself. The constant is the ball.

I'm getting good and I know it. I have a blind faith, an inborn dedication to the game. The hows and whys are a blurry mystery, but the drive and need to be my best, so I can subsequently be better than everyone else, is non-stop. Away from the court, I'm timid, insecure, and unsure of myself. I need the game to build confidence and the ball to feel at home. This grounds me, and a work ethic takes over—a sanctuary from the disappointment I feel my father has with me.

Ours isn't the only driveway with a hoop. The Seymours, just around the corner, host many games. The Seymour brothers—friends to this day—along with my brothers, lay a competitive foundation within me that stirs.

The constant fallback, when no one is around, is to lace them up and play against my siblings. The games, once dishes and homework are done, take on an urgency that leads to arguments and hard fouls. It seems we never have the score right, and like many brothers before us, things brew and culminate until someone takes a punch or elbow.

The porch light gives us enough lighting to play into the night or until mom calls, "Time to come in."

"Just one more shot."

"In. Now."

"Okay, last one."

Ten to twenty shots later, I wash for bed.

The driveway is a great testing ground but I also need the lines, fullness, and complexity of the full court. I dribble a couple blocks to the local Killybrooke Elementary School to hoist up the thousands of needed shots. The solitary focus time allows me the needed space to pinpoint ball handling stutters, behind-the-back dribbles to clear space, and Harlem Globetrotter, Curly Neal, low-ball dribbles protecting the ball from bigger, more physical kids. Without exactly knowing, I begin to find my free-throw rhythm and routine. Muscle memory through volume shooting. A serving purpose strategy that plays throughout is spawned early in the desert landscape and solitude of Southern California.

It's the time of the transistor radio and live play by play action. Chick Hearn calling Lakers games. The incomparable Vin Scully's storytelling of the Dodgers. Dick Enberg describes the great UCLA basketball teams and the *Fearsome Foursome* of the LA Rams. Left to the imagination, everything seems possible.

The early proving ground is the open gym at the Costa Mesa Boys Club (now the Boys and Girls Club). A few of the older kids like my game, know I'll pass them the ball, and choose me for their team before others their own age. The small wins are mounting. I am driven. No one will ever take me off this perch.

The Boys Club puts me on my first team and league. Winners are given precious blue ribbons. We hang them on our shirts, shorts, bikes, and backpacks. The red and yellow—second and third place ribbons—are important and great for the growing collection, but it's the blue ones that carry the weight of the victor.

A determining arc in my progression as a player and young man is entrance into Saint John the Baptist Catholic School and introduction to grammar school basketball coach, Mike Campbell. He teaches me the nuances and details of the game and the importance of practice. Coach Campbell has a sweet baby sky hook. A shot more popular in the 60s than today. He sees my passion for this great game. I am a gym rat. I rebound his skyhook work outs and make myself available as a practice dummy for his older players. Unknown to me at the time, I'm searching for a father figure, be it Coach Campbell or my uncle Ted. They encourage and teach. I crave what they have to offer. Coach Campbell is someone I can count on. He is never not there.

Uncle Ted and I spend hours-at-a-time together. He shows valuable interest in other areas of my adolescence. He teaches me how to build *Hot Rod* model cars and paint them with patience, precision, and pride. Uncle Ted is my needed confidence booster. Uncle Ted teaches me how to race motocross. We traverse many of the local SoCal motos. Our bond deepens. I thank God for his influence in my young and turbulent life. Aunt Barbara and Uncle Ted always have a place for me to stay when things go sideways at home

I begin to realize I'm part of a fellowship. Within the neighborhood are so many Catholic brothers: the Clarks, Cloughs, and aforementioned Seymours. Strong and great friends to this day. All studs, and all after the same thing; athleticism in the name of sport. Kevin Clark is my best friend. His brother Bernie, the Seymours (John and Gary), and Billy and Scooter Clough form a meaningful band of sporting brothers. The "no goods"—as we are known—is a supernova of neighborhood athletes that are friends to this day. If it involves a ball, we play it. We chase fun with a fever of the pack we've become. There is a comradeship built through sport that transcends competition. Everyone plays to win. We are each other's prize to conquer, but the organic truce and treaties are powerful. The spirited recollection of the game just played becomes invaluable in developing all our juvenile personas. Not only is it important to story the scorers and playmakers but also the more workmanlike picks, rebounds, and hustle plays. Everyone gets a mention. This makes our pack its strongest

The strength found and accumulated within the hours and hours of competing with and against a fraternity of brothers begins to take me to new, and certainly more, grown-up places.

Friday nights become exhausting, sleepless endeavors in the anticipation of Saturday morning's 'open gym' at Costa Mesa High. I dribble walk/jog the short distance to the school and its hardwood dreamland.

During the morning traverse I'm Elgin Baylor/Jerry West preparing for battle against the hated Celtics.

Upon arrival, I stop and soak in awe-inspiring snapshots. The glass backboards. Visions of me kissing the ball off the glass, draining another. The heavy, colorful paint just beyond the end and side-lines, a brilliant reminder of what's too far, too much, and out of bounds. The stands atop the floor allow me to see greater versions of myself. As a kid, *massive* doesn't explain it. The all-time Costa Mesa High: scoring, assist, and rebound leaders etched upon the far wall are unknown world spirits. I don't know these super-jocks, but I imagine their path, and I'm on it.

These are moments I feel unstoppable. As undersized as I am to the mostly junior high and high school teenage athletes, I keep up. I like getting the ball to the dominant scorers. Big, superior, back-to-the-basket brutes with high percentage post moves, love the kid dishing them the ball consistently, when and where they want it. The rush of defending the ball like a bee chasing its honey. Annoying. Active. Pursuant.

Then there are the times I'm not picked to play. I sulk to the side-lines to watch or shoot out-of-the-way five-footers. Not competing, while others are, is the absolute worst. I wait for the studs to take lunch or for admiring girls to show up and distract the many chasing something else altogether. I am not to be denied and find my way onto many of the full-court, all day, Saturday basketball tug-of-wars.

Getting a ride home proves a dependable uncertainty and a stressful embarrassment. Almost always, I'm the last kid waiting for a ride. The sun has set. The coastal breeze cools to a chill, and there I sit, dribbling my ball waiting for dad to show. He slips, before eventually falling, into the ways of beer and the bottle. He's disappearing except for intermittent, severe stints of discipline. Mom pays the heaviest price, and her resolve in mothering our family never wanes. She instead continues at the highest, loving levels.

Be it the Boys Clubs of Costa Mesa/Harbor Area or the all-day Saturday pick-up, proving ground, throw downs—I'm just another youngster in need. Evenings are the curtain falling. I look for his approving nods and listening ear to the wonders of the day just passed. He built the basket, honing the skills of his athletic tribe, but none of the headlights are his. I wait and wait, hanging my head, only to rise again with the next set of lights approaching but dad is a continued, dubious no-show. Flustered and ashamed, I do my best to compose myself and walk the distances home in the dank and dark. The ball, again, my dogged and certain friend.

The choice is obvious.

I need to be on my bike more and more.

My Christmas 10-speed, an artful form of speed and independence, lays mangled and salted like a pretzel on the boulevard. The Chevy Apache, a confluence of American-made steel and design, shadows the scene like the behemoth it is, without a scratch.

The incoming sirens, a faraway reminder that things are serious.

The bones in both my knees are mince. As a ten-year-old, I'm unable to reflect that this accident and my shattered knees is anything more than a serious accident, a setback and physical imposition. I never think of not resuming my previous life and continuing my crusade to compete and have fun with my friends and brothers. The silver lining is the grace of youth. I don't project. I dream of the vision instead.

Sandy Koufax in his glory

It's 1963. John Wooden and the UCLA Bruins, led by Walt Hazzard and Gail Goodrich, go 30-0 and capture their first of ten national championships within the next 12 years. The Bruins implement a stifling full court, zone press transitioning into half-court, man-to-man defense. Their guard-heavy offense flows with speed, space, perimeter shooting, gutsy ball-

drives, and finishes at the rim. Hazzard is my guy: All American, Tournament MVP and takes on all comers even though he is often undersized.

That same year the Dodgers and Sandy Koufax sweep the Yankees in the World Series. Vin Scully, the Dodgers' play-by-play maestro, cements the fact: 1) There is much to be garnered by the examples of sport through sight and sound, and 2) I am in love with Los Angeles sports.

Three months in a Spica body cast is a prison term with its solitary thoughts and middle-of-the-night whimpers for mom (never dad) to adjust me and my tender areas. The hell of the Spica cast is the immobilization from basically the waist to knees. I have to crap laying down into a bedpan. Weird, difficult and humiliating. Peeing into a urinal, the impending mishaps and subsequent clean-ups draw me inward for periods longer than I like to admit.

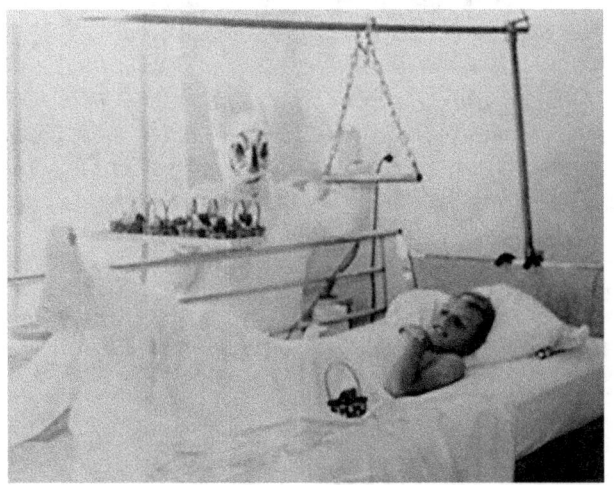

In the hospital after my accident riding my bike to school and my knees being shattered.

Recovering at home.

I take solace in the small, black and white TV (no remote). The great escape from the walls closing, descending on my underdeveloped thinker. Let me watch some Rifleman *or* UCLA *on the trusty box.*

Dad is on the edge. His barstool at The Huddle has his name on it and he is becoming more of a concept than an actual source of parenting. Mom, too often, is at the wrong end of his wrath and takes to wearing big, dark sunglasses as a way of covering the obvious.

I swear never to be like him, but deeper in the recess of my developing manhood, I understand he is a good man full of bad decisions. He never stops trying to quit.

Mom is forced to do the heavy lifting. Our Irish Catholic family of six kids is hers to manage. Not a complainer, she sacrifices mightily. During my time of convalescence, she works me onto the kitchen table and ties dumbbells to my feet with tube-socks and cracks the proverbial whip to lift, lift, and lift some more.

Occasionally, she organizes a front-yard outing. I am in essence given the human forklift to a blanket and the front yard. I am the mole out of his hole and into the sunshine. There are photos of me smiling, but it's complete misery. During this time, it is suggested over and again that I take up golf, taking the pressure and workload off my knees.

Rubbish.

Crap.

I'm a basketball player, and this is the course of my life.

PISTOL

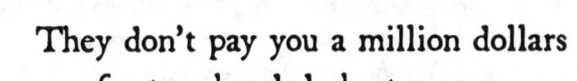

They don't pay you a million dollars
for two-handed chest passes.

— Pistol Pete Maravich

No one rises above the crowd without ego. Slippery slope.

Ego never tells the truth but following the herd as another nondescript face in the crowd bores me. The norm is for others. Getting lost in the garden-variety mix of commonplace or mediocre is to be regular and inconsistent. How can you be an agent-of-change without perpetually evolving?

What does it take to be consistently extreme, strong, and tectonic?

Muhammad Ali says, 'Don't count the days; make the days count.'

Years away from being a teenager, I begin a weighty rehabilitation regime. Once the casts are gone (I also broke my right arm in the Chevy Apache melee), I see the atrophy in my arms and skinny legs. My lower back is stiff, painful, and rigid, but I am up—and I am at 'em. I'm slight, but after the casts are removed, I feel puny.

It starts in the driveway, feeling the ridges of the ball on a dribble—leaving before returning to my welcoming mitts. The pop of the ball off the pavement feels and sounds like home. Behind-the-back passes (left- and right-handed) against the garage door—mom peeking from the kitchen counter with concern and stoic pride as I'm forced to move laterally on my new knees. Sprints to the rim with a variety of finishes: scoops, reverses, right-side, left-side, inside/outside hand, and elbow firm and away from ribs—clearing space finishes. Free-throws. Mid-wing, bank shots. End of the driveway heaves, just beating an imaginary clock on an invisible scoreboard.

Visualization begins young with me. I am constantly making game winning jumpers on my *Field of Dreams* home court.

I begin to see myself in the late-night sports reports chronicling the Los Angeles sports scene. Lucius Allen and Lew Alcindor are the present-day stalwarts winning national championships on television. The more I watch, the more I believe.

Closer to home, in fact—just down the road, Orange Coast College (OCC) has a great junior college team that I follow with my attendance and budding enjoyment of live sport. The OCC team inspires me.

John Vallely is the star player (he later transfers to UCLA and starts on two national championship teams). He's my local hero. He shoots the lights out and sets all the school scoring records; but unlike my heroes on television, he is blood, bone, and flesh before my eyes. I watch him in warm-ups. A factory of unchanging jump shots and pinpoint, exaggerated follow-through passes. In games, he's tough, but it's more subtle than in your face. He is a communicator and not overtly demanding as others. His game speaks for him. He is more the kind that will cut your throat, yet you don't know you're bleeding.

It's the mid-sixties, edging towards the seventies. There are more knee surgeries, another stint in a body cast, and the needed cortisone shots, kamikazed into the sides of my bony, developing knees.

I begin to understand how difficult normal is going to be.

My knees are bad in a way that as they develop and build, I feel the Apache truck's grill. Pain. I play through it all until another surgery slows me down, and I have to begin again. A twisted routine but one my stubbornness tackles head-on.

It's how it's going to be, and who I become.

Give me the damn ball and let's play.

The late-night sports reports are mounting. Mom has given up policing or limiting my intake. As long as I am on time for morning class and respectful of her chore list, I can watch the late news and impending sports report. Just past the weather and before Johnny Carson, at twenty past-the-hour; awaits seven minutes of sporting bliss. Way before the 24/7 of ESPN, the local news with its snappy sports guy is the source for millions like me.

This is where I met Pete Maravich.

Highlights pivot off him like no one else. He spins the ball off his finger, to head, to fist, and back to his finger before eyeing the camera with a cool cockiness never seen. Keeping the ball on his finger, he spins it through his legs, kicks the thing into the air, landing the ball on his opposite side, and finger. Easy. His ability to manipulate the ball on any appendage is bionic or the workings of a cyborg.

The personification of Pistol Pete is Pete Maravich. He manages the court more like a stage than the 94-feet of lines and boundaries that all else behold before entering.

I am 13 years old, and for the first time, I am watching someone brave enough to be different while simultaneously showing the world his authentic self.

I want to be just like him.

Pistol Pete averages 43.6 points a game his freshman year at Louisiana State University (LSU). With his floppy socks and Beatles' haircut, Pete has consistent range from 30 feet and, although he is scrawny and skinny (like me), he can hang in the air, clearing space from defenders, and knock down leaning jumpers. Undersized, he attacks the rim knowing his left is as strong and practiced as his right. Ball transfers are as common as the mounting LSU victories. His spectacular finishes are not the blind result of blessings, windfalls, and serendipity, but instead moments built through hard work, mastery of spins to backboard, and an undeniable work ethic that allows his ordinary to transcend into extraordinary.

I love his court vision and playmaking before all else. He escapes on-court traffic and double teams with behind-the-back dribbles. The space he creates leaves defenders the butt of cruel and repeated on-court jokes. Teammates know to fill lanes and expect the ball for easy buckets. Opponents, seeing something like never before are double faked into defending what never happens. What is happening is the blur of a phenomenon.

I particularly marvel at—then emulate—Pistol's between-the-leg bounce passes to post players; or on the fast-break to hustling teammates. He also likes to wave his hand over the ball when dribbling, only to slap the thing the opposite direction—with the other hand—to an LSU ally and an easy two.

Pistol Pete Maravich delves into my impressionable and vivid imagination. Through hard work he creates magic and an energy that I crave. Dare to be different. I don't have to play the game like everyone else. I want to dance, mesmerize, and deceive my opponents with the ball and use the type of theatrics Pete Maravich uses.

Nigerian playwright and poet Michael Bassey Johnson remarks, "Our talents are living things, we give birth to them, nourish them till they grow and become mortal."

His game is misunderstood. He is before his time by at least 20 years. He is showboating and labelled a hot dog by many opposing coaches and the press. Where compliments and praise should be showered, Maravich is questioned on his intentions and amazingly on his fundamentals. That's not how I see it. It's only through his fundamentals and absolute mastery of basketball's foundational essentials that he evolves into Pistol. He's art with imagination and creativity. Like none before. To ask Pistol Pete to play any other way is like telling Salvador Dali to paint between the lines.

Mom keeps us responsible. My brothers and I have paper routes for the local news-rag, *The Daily Pilot*. It's a 7-days-a-week gig: after school, on weekdays, and as the sun rises on Saturday and Sunday mornings. I pitch the bundled paper to doorsteps from my speeding 10-speed. I imagine myself as Sandy

Koufax, painting the black of home-plate each time the paper hits its mark. I am Pistol Pete delivering the ball perfectly to the outside hand of appreciative teammates.

Pete's father, Press Maravich, has everything to do with Pete's path of training and drills. It is said that Press forces a love of the game into Pete's soul. He once described himself as a basketball android. Pete Maravich averages between 43.6 and 46.6 points per game during his four-year collegiate career.

As much as I crave a father figure like Press Maravich in my athletic routine, I know different. Between dad's devotion to a burgeoning woodworking, cabinet business, and evermore seat at the bar, I hardly see the man.

Motivation comes in the form of organic love.

I love the ball, watching it in flight and what's possible with the thing in my hands.

My knees are compromised but I refuse to think of them as limiting. I can hardly jump, but I am quick and have the kind of court vision that coaches need for their teams to play at higher offensive levels. The hours, weeks, months, and years dribbling the ball are paying dividends. I don't need to see it. I feel it. There is a sizzle in my game that others don't have. Things are happening and the ball is better with me than with most.

It is high school. The gym is abuzz. Sport is king at our elite, private catholic school.

The ball is loose, close to the half-court line. One of those 50/50 balls that require toughness and determination to come up with. Another breathing, juncture of time to prove myself—to myself.

First to the ball, I find it between my legs. With no time to look, I reach for the leather of the ball and like a long-snapping, football center, I hike it 25-plus feet and hit my teammate in stride. He finishes.

My teammates are wide-eyed with disbelief. The bent smiles of teenage youth. Anything is possible at this specific moment in time. Anything at all.

The crowd erupts.

There's an energy to the next couple minutes of the game that carry the team to another level of competency. Our opponents are stymied, shellshocked. They're done.

I can feel their need to move on. Be anywhere but here.

Over five decades post my teenage years, I receive a Facebook message. I'm a grandfather and in the midst of an emotional end to an event attached to my name.

The message reads,

> *"I'm sure you don't remember this. One year (probably 1988 or '89) my Southwest State University team was playing an exhibition at halftime of your game in South Dakota."*

I remember the trip as there were many of my extended family in attendance.

I was watching your warm-ups and you made a behind the back 'scoop' type shot off the glass. I had never seen that and I gave a 'holy shit' when you did that. It was loud enough where you turned and looked at me. It was a combination of worry and embarrassment that I had offended you. Thanks for being great and giving us a great show.

        – Paul Nintz

Pistol Pete lives with and in me, throughout.

In 1974, NBA all-star, Peter 'Pistol Pete' Maravich tells a reporter, 'I don't want to play 10 years in the NBA, and then die of a heart attack at 40.' Maravich ends up playing 10 years in the NBA, and sadly, dies of a heart attack at the age of 40, during a pick-up game in a church gym in Pasadena, California.

Infinite abundance of talent comes with a price to pay. Sublime at first, with periods of extreme darkness in the fold of a settling dusk, 'Pistol Pete' Maravich is an example that I draw from throughout.

Self-destruction, adulation, and the elusive, lucid, stillness of one are the twist and two-step of a life-long dance on the athletic stage.

Long live the 'Pistol' and all that dare.

"Pistol"

Naismith Hall of Fame, Springfield, Massachusetts.

MOTHER OF GOD

"I'm learning to fly but I ain't got wings.
Comin' down is the hardest thing."

— Tom Petty

Alone, with my thoughts, I contemplate suicide. The .22 rifle is loaded and ready for the dastardly deed. Scared, the den is quieter than ever before. I'm the only one home. A teenager with no knowledge, experience, or inclination of such darkness.

Why?

Why not?

My right hand moves down the barrel, inching closer to the trigger.

An image of my father, half-drunk, bounding into the kitchen, concretes my desperation. An angry and physical drunk, he flexes his muscular, cabinetmaking forearms. He knows I'll hold my ground. I am the oldest of his tribe. He eyes me up. The alcohol concocting a recipe of angst and action. Steadfast in my resolve, I steer mom behind me and clench my fists. Something clicks within what's saturated. He backs off.

"Let's go hunting," he declares. The easily breakable code translates to, 'We're loading up the Bel-Air wagon to get good and drunk in the high desert valley.'

My breathing becomes exaggerated; then still and silent. Alone, the room carries more weight.

Mom pleads, "The boys need to stay. Don't drive. You are in no shape." This is a tipping point for her. A place she knows she cannot return to. She keeps my sister from the fray. The two will spend the weekend in a faraway and fuzzy mirage, away from their alcoholic husband and father.

A half-hour later we're carpooling with likeminded, beer-between-their-legs barroom cronies. It reminds me of ducks on the pond at the Orange County Fair but instead it's jackrabbits, canned beer, and live rounds in the desert.

Do I dare press the rifle's muzzle to my chin or am I looking to create attention? An impulsive, confused, and cowardly move. Chances are I won't die, but the dangerous act is serious and combustible enough for all to hear.

Either way the gun is loaded.

The room is darker than before.

17

In the summer of 1967 things begin to change.

We start making our way down to Newport Beach. Either hitch-hiking or riding bikes down Superior Hill, we find the peninsula of Newport a test of our increased athleticism. The summertime symmetry between body surfing and basketball works.

The salty coexistence between myself and Mother Ocean becomes a new worthy adventure. The stress and pounding on my arthritic, surgically repaired knees subside when dropping down the face of waves off the 56th street jetty or The Point at 17th street. I am a strong swimmer, and when aided by a pair of Duck Fins, a human water-torpedo in search of the next A-frame, foamy beast.

The south, summer swells of Newport take me in new directions. I revel in not knowing if I make and finish waves but instead in the knowledge that I'm not. I open my eyes to round, ocean water spinning, foaming, and spitting moments before entering the washing machine of the salty cylinder gloriously closing out, around, and then on me.

The breeze, like the sun off the dropping tide, is constant.

The sideshow of shapely females adds an intriguing layer that I plan on fully exploring. Hippie girls, straight girls, and the ones in the middle matter less than the possibilities of everything the beach has to offer.

I also begin playing pick-up basketball, coastal beach style for hours on end. Often, competing against grown men, I develop a depth of toughness and grit. Never one to back down, I learn to deal with a level of physicality I haven't seen or felt. Tuckered out, drained, and sweaty, I go catch some waves and recalibrate before heading home to afternoons of open gyms and summer leagues.

In its own way the beach adds a level of required discipline. The independence, decision making, and time management needed to live the duality of waves and hardwood (with its glass backboards proving ground) is a balance I'll always cherish.

St. John the Baptist, elementary and middle school, is my childhood haven. I'm a large fish in a small pond. The neighborhood friendships are deep-seeded and long lasting. We're all athletes. We compete in the Catholic Youth Organization (CYO) and the St John's boys are dominant competitors. Now and then, we're able to play in front of crowds at the bigger Orange County tourney for Catholics. For a young, string-bean wannabe like myself, this is the world I chose to chase with all I have.

The audience is mostly parents and competitors. The energy is nondescript with plenty of parental advice and cheering. I use my increasing visualisation tools. I'm what everyone is looking at. The assortment of eyes and opinions charge me. I'm a showman taming the lions with a burnt orange leather ball, accelerated pacing, and no-look passes.

This is me for the next four years.

Mater Dei High School is the big time.

The private Catholic school in Santa Ana attracts the best. Over ninety-five percent of its students are accepted to college. Its extensive athletic department is a feeder to the best California collegiate programs like USC, UCLA, Stanford, and Cal Berkeley. Pacific coast team sports like soccer, water polo, and volleyball are stalwart programs for the school's female and male students. The more individual sports such as cross country, golf, swimming, track and field, wrestling, and tennis excel yearly across the student body.

The Monarchs are a known football quantity. A few years before my arrival, John Huarte (class of '61) quarterbacked the Mater Dei program. In 1964, Huarte guides the Fighting Irish of Notre Dame to a 9-1 record and a top five national ranking. The same year he's awarded the Heisman trophy as the top collegiate football player in the country. Years later, Matt Leinart (Mater Dei class of 2001) captures the Heisman Trophy whilst leading the USC Trojans to an undefeated National Championship season.

Mater Dei is a destination school for many of the best in Southern California. You want to hit the right notes in the choir, split an atom in the lab, or pole vault onto the USA Olympic team: Mater Dei is the logical next step. Not all the neighborhood clan chose what's so obvious to the Kiley boys. The Seymours, who live just around the corner, decide on Servite, an all-boys high school rival of Mater Dei.

I'm taken aback by their decision. How could they?

The thousands of driveway battles. The ties that bind broken.

The countless sleepovers. Didn't the nights of shared adolescence, angst and a daydreamer's hope for the future matter? The Seymours to Servite takes a minute to swallow; we're supposed to be each other's outlet pass but once I put them in the rear-view mirror—they're the enemy—for now.

The Catholic school make-up of the Angelus League is ridiculously stacked: Bishop Amat, Servite, St. John Bosco, and Verbum Dei are top teams in any of the public-school leagues.

I live a stumble away from Costa Mesa High, an easy amble through the neighborhood. Take a left at Fairview and I'm there. At Mater Dei, I lose the leisure and comfort of what's familiar and around the corner. No cheeky walks home with the cutie from civics class. No rat-packs, side-stepping each other, cracking jackpots, and telling the whitest of lies. Instead, it's mom-carpool-rides alongside strawberry fields, past budding Latino businesses and housing. We head straight up Bristol Avenue—deeper into Santa Ana and the business of doing business in Orange County—before the A & W Root Beer shack and Mater Dei (Mother of God).

I awake before sunrise and dribble over to St. John's. I run the football field focusing on my breathing and endurance. The soul of these mornings speaks to me. The outdoor courts spring me to action. The roundness of the ball against the textured flatness of the schoolyard. I'm a spirit in motion, visualizing what isn't, yet always there. I make sure to salute the mornings; the long, artful trek of positive self-talk.

These simplest of times, repeated daily, on the sacred and trusted St. John the Baptist courts—before the carpool caravan to a school a few miles away—are the nuts and bolts that not only give me a chance at a proving ground like Mater Dei but is a foundational pillar throughout. You want something? Work hard to get it.

Knowing who I am or why I am, matters not. What matters is the routine and the dream. Without knowing exactly why it feels so right—I carry on. I don't need opponents, the eyes of coaches, school mates, or parents. I shoulder the solitude of the break-of-day sessions minus apprehension or care of what folks think but instead the knowledge, I'm exactly where I'm supposed to be.

John Wooden and his dominant UCLA basketball teams are a case worth studying. The program peaks my interest. Their crowds are raucous. You can see the stunned appreciation of what the audience is witnessing. Their best players: Gail Goodrich, Sidney Wicks, Lucius Allen, Henry Bibby and Marques Johnson are outspoken personalities. A college-aged Lew Alcindor partners with Muhammad Ali, Jim Brown, and Bill Russell and other prominent black athletes to speak out on the Vietnam War. Alcindor leads UCLA to three straight NCAA championships.

Steering the UCLA ship is John Wooden. The modest, soft spoken former English teacher is the head coach of the best team in the land. Without studying Wooden's 'Pyramid,' I begin to take on its core values. I watch it in action each Saturday on television as UCLA and the 'Wooden Effect' trounce another opponent into submission.

The cornerstones and foundational blocks of Wooden's Pyramid of Success are Industriousness and Enthusiasm.

I am the epitome of hard work and having a good time doing it.

I watch UCLA, with all its talent and bravado, buy into Wooden's discipline and life-affirming challenges. He puts it in ways we understand.

Wooden's explanation of Industriousness resonates with my core: "Success travels in the company of very hard work. There is no trick. No easy way."

His views on Enthusiasm, I carry with me: "Your energy and enjoyment, drive and dedication will stimulate and greatly inspire others."

I am a proponent of the Pyramid of Success the rest of my days. As an athlete, coach, husband, father, businessman, and lifeforce on earth, Wooden's Pyramid is a playbook for life.

UCLA three-time All American, NBA MVP, NBA Hall of Famer, and Grateful Dead enthusiast, Bill Walton puts it this way, "Coach Wooden taught us everything from how to put on our shoes and socks before a game to how to build a foundation for life based on human values and personal characteristics."

I ultimately study the Pyramid of Success intently.

Without question basketball is why I'm at Mater Dei. For Mom and Dad, it's the natural first step for the oldest in their Irish Catholic tribe. I get this. Unquestioned.

The CYO pits me against the best ballers in Orange County. My friends and I stand out as a great gang of competitors. I feel the colossal bond of teammates and friendship. A parochial fellowship of grind, hustle, and skill.

Mater Dei requires an entrance exam. I dread the thought of stillness, number-two pencils, and standardized testing. I remind myself the juice is worth the squeeze. Testing day forces me to miss a club team tournament game at the 29 Palms Air Force Base in the desert. Who's going to run the ball? I've been training all week. Why? To sit in a stuffy room and take an eight-hour test? Fuming, I look to fail the entrance exam. I mark many of the multiple-choice questions without reading things over. Doomed and waiting to meet with disaster, I'm shocked when I pass and am accepted into the major leagues of Mater Dei.

Looking back, did the athletic department make my time at Mater Dei possible by looking the other way? Maybe, maybe not?

Practice, training, and conditioning go great. What's difficult for others suits me. My body handles the suicides, line drills, and sprints. Surprisingly, I'm quicker than most on the team. My summer cross-training of waves and pick-up basketball helps with my breathing and endurance. The wear and tear on my knees is constant and the consistent ache of arthritis is a price I'm prepared to pay—and pay.

Through all my grammar school surgeries, my orthopedic doctor remains a repeated thread. Seems he always greets me with a needle directly into the bony side of my knees.

I'm willing to pay the price of pain.

Any price.

Any pain.

My sophomore year I begin to thrive. It's bittersweet. I belong on the varsity squad but my knees are in a constant state of recovery. Between doctors, trainers, and coaches, I feel caged. No one understands. I'm stronger than that day and that damned Apache truck.

I'm relegated to the Junior Varsity (JV) team.

I'm a playmaker that scores. It gets to a point where Coach Weihardt overloads the rest of the team on one side of the floor. He tells me to work "one on one" on the other side. I'm back at our driveway, dribbling between my legs. Should I wrap-around dribble behind my back to create a driving lane? Perhaps stop and pop. I look the defender in the eye—the dribble is a metronome to winning the moment. I'm in rhythm. His eyes lock with mine. Mistake. Head-fake left. Drive right. Strong side. Have him by half a step. He's quick and sprints to recover. I drive hard to the rim. He's looking to deny my right side. Seen it before. Muscle memory kicks in. Elevate off my right side. He loses his verticality leaning hard to my shooting hand. I've made this shot against myself thousands of times. Just get the ball to my left side. I hear the referee's whistle. Focus. The defender's body weight presses against my left hip. With my left hand, I excessively spin the ball off the lower left corner of the backboard. I feel the rush of teammates seeking rebound opportunities. My left hand pronates. I exaggerate the follow through. Off the backboard, the ball climbs towards its target. I'm knocked to the hardwood and land on the baseline. I look up. Pressing lightly off the front rim, the ball falls through the hoop. A teammate's outstretched hand helps me to my feet. The energy is charged. Enjoy it for a second. Only one. There's a free throw to make.

This is our offense for some games but not sustainable long term and not great for team morale. I corral a 44-point game against Salesian High School applying this tactic. Points like that bring pride and justification to the process but eliminates what I love most—passing the basketball.

During my four years of attending school, we look to be one of Orange County's best basketball programs.

It's my junior year. My life long relationship with the ball pays dividends. Teammates know my priority is the betterment of the team and the ball in my hands is precious and well looked after. Still, I must compete for the starting, point guard position on the varsity team.

Bobby Haupert is bigger and stronger. We've tangled before in the CYO league. Myself leading St. Johns and Haup leading Old Mission. Haup is the chosen one. He makes the varsity team as a sophomore and, more impressively, is the Monarch's starting quarterback the same year for the school's storied football team.

The team is at its best when Haup and I are on the floor simultaneously. The ball moves and turnovers are rare. I begin to rack up assists and lead all of Orange County in passing the ball for baskets my senior year. Haup motivates me to never let up, and while he's leading the football team in spring practices or competing in summer league quarterback/receiver competitions, I'm with the team and my teammates. I become more and more indispensable.

Game days are the best. Forced to wear a coat and tie (annoying), there's a game to play. After the student rally, the tie loosens a bit, and the afternoon transcends to a dense passing of people in the hall and classes full of noise.

One of the carpool moms drops me at home. I can finally get to my routine. Crosby, Stills, Nash & Young, Iron Butterfly, and Steppenwolf filter through the headphones. I see the court through wide angle lenses, each teammate's cut and outside hand is within my optics. The focus is perfection. Nash singing alongside Crosby—Stills' lead guitar, Young's power-chords making strange and perfect sense. I feel the details of the ball. Its ridges are the trigger to snap and follow through. Visualization isn't a thing yet. Coaches don't talk about it as a tool or valued technique, but it's what I do, and what I do for my entire career. Visualize greatness.

The Mater Dei Monarchs are a flourishing basketball force in a landscape usually dominated by the Los Angeles schools. We're beating teams that previously considered us a walkover. By the end of my two years of varsity ball the Monarchs qualify for the vaunted California Interscholastic Federation (CIF) playoffs.

Servite and the Seymour brothers are another competitive hurdle altogether. Neighborhood chums breaking bread, busting chops, and taking on the expansive world of growing up in a city doing the same.

The battles with Servite are legendary in the subculture of Southern California high school sports. My time at Mater Dei is no different. John Seymour (my age and grade) is a pure shooter. Leave him open and you will pay. I have the handles and full court vision. John wants the ball in space to lock, load, and shoot. He has a quick pull-up jumper that I willingly defend. I watch him develop the move in the driveways of his/my house. He takes the task of guarding me. I know how to beat him. Give me the rock.

Gary Seymour is a grade beneath John and me and is a spark off the Servite bench. His game is legitimate and personifies the team's rough and tumble style. My younger brother Jeff is a spark off our bench. Although shorter than I am, he's athletic and adds an important layer of physicality. Jeff makes us tougher, more likely to come up with 50/50 balls and is instrumental in the psychology of our overall toughness.

Brother Jeff's true calling is baseball. He's a catcher— the toughest spot on the field.

The Seymour brothers versus the Kiley brothers: Servite versus Mater Dei. Their driveway or ours. The shared experiences go deep. I feel the initial adult motivations and conflict of attempting to steamroll through and past good friends.

Sounds silly. It's not. It's everything.

For the record we split wins and losses. Servite and the Seymours beat us at ours, and we at theirs. The losses are heart-breaking and leave lasting scars.

It is the best of times—representing my school, teammates, and myself through basketball is a gift. One I understand completely. This is my life. See challenge, accept the confrontation, and live with the result. I'm wired for this. I stack the odds in my favor every time I take the court. The second or third time I see teams I have a competitive advantage. The butterflies in my stomach remind me of my strength, not apprehension. I not only love this game, but I understand it. To be a teenager and understand anything puts me in a rarefied time and space.

It is the worst of times—Head Coach Tardie is far from a leader having respect from the team or me. He is the hard-ass type that buries his knuckles deep into your chest if you don't meet his expectations. I refuse to let him see any weakness across my face. The team doesn't like playing for him, but we know we're at the crest of something extraordinary. The summer before senior year, Coach Tardie kicks me off the team. Someone saw me at a summer beach party with a beer in my hand and informed the coach. Minutes before a summer league game, Tardie pulls me over. He wants a word; I'm off the team.

Words blur and images appear. Then they fade. I'm in shock. It's a dreamscape sucker punch through my gut, landing across my chin. Breathing is strangled with each passing moment. Next to someone I love dying, this is the worst thing to possibly happen.

Tardie digs in deeper, "Son, your actions are…"

His words lose any meaning. I vow to destroy the rat bastard that drops such a devastating dime on me. Anger flips to desperation. I chase Tardie down. He refuses to waver. The jarring jolt of Tardie's bombshell is an earthquake within my nervous system. I squirm and am unable to find the words. A beer at the beach, and I'm done? There are no team rules. He never takes the time to care. A final look his way. He enjoys my hopelessness. I turn my back on the bastard.

Not wanting to get my ass beat by my ripe and ready father, I confide in mom. She reaches out to Tardie. Nothing. It's my turn to grovel. Tardie's office is cramped, tiny, and with paint-covering brick. The space is like Tardie himself: hemmed in, restricted, and lacking any thought or creativity. The room lacks the nuances you find in coaches' offices. Nothing to motivate the hungry teenage souls needing direction. He greets my uneasiness with a wry smile. There's not a particle of my being that trusts this guy. By the time he opens his mouth, I've checked out.

I look to transfer to Servite. The carpool to Anaheim involves traffic and freeways. Servite, like all high schools, requires athletes to sit out a year when transferring. No dice.

I hear the whispers, questions, and intrigue of classmates, teachers, and staff. Someone new runs the point for the varsity basketball team and another one circles the drain on the path to nowhere.

I can't do it.

I set the rifle down on the den's floor. Someone please help me. This thing surrounds me. I'm a fly in the web of a ravenous tarantula. If I can't play, I can't live. Who do I turn to?

I swallow a bottle of aspirin instead. A teenager with no knowledge or experience of the heart's darkness. I make my way to the curb of the Seymours' house and sit—not sure if I'm going to die, get sick, or pass out. The storm in my head is hurricane status. Sitting on the curb I understand how fragile I am without a real father figure.

Mater Dei and basketball are the great escapes from home. There's a consistent anticipation and anxiety of what may happen next. I am the buffer between mom and the fire-water induced rage of a man unable to father. Practices, workouts, and games keep me in a safe harbor. Basketball allows me to manage and sidestep the darkest and most persistent shadows dominating my psyche.

Basketball is high school.

High school is nothing else.

Never losing confidence in my game, I am in the midst of losing all confidence in myself.

I survive the dozens of aspirin down my gullet with the constitution and metabolism of a teenage athlete. Waves, workouts, and ego make me stronger than the Sandman nightmare of offing myself. On shaky legs, I make it to our front door and begin again.

Tardie calls me into his office. The warm, summer day adds to the anticipation and stink of this man making a move. His claustrophobic, turd of an office has me on edge. I mentally prepare my, *It's only one beer...please give me a chance* defense. Without access to the hardwood, I feel like an athlete with a serious injury. I've missed all of summer league and the invaluable on- and off-court connections with the boys.

Tardie eyes my uneasiness. He has me just where he wants me, squirming and under his thumb of authority. He lives for this. Me grovelling and begging for "*just a chance*" to prove myself. Tardie plays his role as the ever gracious and charitable coach.

I see through him. We all see through him.

Words are not enough for men like him and my father. Physical force, intimidation, and coercion—a diabolical cocktail of man-bullies getting theirs.

Tardie reinstates me back on the team. I promise him any and everything. He wants me to attend college. I agree. I'm obligated. Advantage Tardie. He never talks of landing spots and university again—much less any calls to collegiate coaches advocating for myself or any of my teammates. He's everything I know I'll never be in my impending adulthood.

I despise him, but I'm back on the team. I play despite him, not for him.

That evening, I celebrate with my mom. She's the first I tell the good news to. Let the weight of the world land on someone else's shoulders. I did my time. I have my life again.

Mater Dei High School Basketball.

John Seymour from our neighborhood gang shoots one over my defense—as the enemy from Servite.

FAMILY

What can you do to promote world peace?
Go home and love your family.

— Mother Theresa

Growing up, my brother Jeff and I are peanut butter and jelly.

I'm the pitcher. He's the catcher.

He's the grinding skateboarder. I'm the slippery body surfer.

Long and lanky, I work the angles with speed, vision, and efficiency. Jeff is power personified. His stout legs and core a base for the next explosive throw, offensive rebound, or full body skateboard carve.

Jeff falls in love with the sun and blossoming beaches of Southern California in the 70s. His darker features—like dad's—works well for him with the ladies.

There are dead-eye memories of Jeff, Tom, and I fishing off Newport Pier. Dad drops us off before work. We spend the day reeling in Bonita and whatever else we get to bite, crossing lines with like-minded enthusiasts before landing the strong, slippery, silvery haul. Later into the afternoon/evening dad eventually finds the time to fetch his sons. The times his beer-soaked remembrance lapses into having another, our friends' parents or mom picks us up and gets us home.

Jeff grows to despise our father for hardly being one.

Our family, my five brothers and sister, love one another but are slow to show it. Through the years our brushes with mortality velcro our needs to be cohesive and devoted.

In a crisis we turn up, contribute where needed, give freely of our time, and prioritize mom. Our strength in managing grief and loss towers the common day family traits of checking in and the need to hear or verbalize love.

Whilst the ink dries on this chapter of family, my brother PJ moves to the afterlife.

I get the call. It wakes me up. Where am I? This is not my bed. It quickly dawns on me. I'm somewhere else entirely. These walls aren't mine. These are walls of refuge. A place to finally rest. Sleep. There's a noble idea of editing, creating, and working together to better these pages before you. Nobility only goes so far. My brother, PJ, has been dying until just now and this phone call. His pain is finally over. I fear mine is just beginning.

I've been praying for him to pass. His intense pains are unrelenting. My two brothers, myself, and sister take shifts giving him morphine every two hours. At 2:15 a.m. on November 3rd, 2023, my youngest brother, PJ Kiley, passed away in Newport Beach.

Cancer.

In 2020, PJ catches COVID and suffers a mild, COVID-induced stroke. In recovery, he has unexplained pain in his lower back. Tests reveal he has urethral cancer and has his kidney removed in 2021. Cancer nodules remain in the surgical bed of his kidney. During this time, PJ suffers through the drama of a divorce with two boys in the wings: Kobe and Shane.

The adversity and weight of a world collapsing takes its toll on my youngest brother. Brothers Tom and Steve help with his pool business. They keep the company afloat. My sister, Sharon, is PJ's closest sibling. They're one year apart in age and have always had a strong and loving relationship. She's his needed download for all that's on him.

PJ is in regular chemotherapy treatments. There's also some radiation. There are signs of improvement. As anyone in the cancer world knows, you cannot let up or sleep on this disease.

Kylie, Sharon's daughter, takes over PJ's schedule. She keeps him informed and handles his company after Tom and Steve must pull back to keep a needed balance in their lives, marriages, and companies. Kylie is the enforcer—the bulldog gnawing at the many insurance and medical miscues. She is the lifeline to her beloved uncle. She's running his show. She makes calls and rallies his friends for rides to his many medical appointments.

Mom is all in and consistently calls us to action and support. She's 91 years-old. Mothers are not organically built to outlast any of their children. PJ is beat down. He's two-plus years into his chemo treatments and seriously underweight and malnourished. He has trouble eating. Can't keep it down. Yet, the latest CT scan shows the cancer is shrinking. Cancer's evil ways.

The family knows if PJ does not eat, PJ will die. My stubborn brother relents. He moves into the same assisted living center that mom lives in. In a month, he gains 22 pounds largely due to prepared meals provided by the facility. He looks so much better.

After a month, PJ decides to move back to his apartment. He's a man with a mind of his own. Always.

The move proves to be the beginning of the end.

He loses all the weight he's gained. Then some. The hospital and its pain management protocols prove to be too much. PJ despises hospitals. It's back to mom's assisted living center, Atria.

PJ knows. We all know. It will not be long.

Thank you for the hospice, Angels of Death.

They answer many questions.

There is a road map of gentle experience.

He is somewhat comfortable

His breathing is shallow.

He hangs on.

We're not prepared to all stare.

Are we to hope he stops breathing?

Afraid so.

Torturous.

Morbid.

There's a final ride. PJ's buddy, Matt, has the idea: "Let's go for a ride in PJ's truck." The Toyota TRD Pro is PJ's pride and joy. The bright orange, big motor, put your head back, lift package, beast of a truck is the personification of my brother. The thing stands out. He revels in its audacity and takes to telling strangers how much he loves his big, orange, fast truck.

PJ steps into the passenger seat. The funky, no foot-plate wheelchair stays behind. The ease of PJ's entry into his truck speaks. I selfishly fret if I can lift myself into this beast? I recently downsized my beloved Ford F-150 for a smaller SUV. The needed and strategic move helps my aged and ailing shoulders. Without any words, Matt lifts me and casually drops me onto the back seat.

Off we go.

The late October, early November Santa Ana winds are a picture frame to a perfect day. The air is pristine. The Pacific Ocean purrs with off-shores. The skin softens. The eyes see the almost forgotten grace of coastal Southern California. Matt jumps on it. Coast Highway and Newport Beach become distorted. The truck's throttle barks. PJ is chatty. It's good to hear his voice. He hits his vape. He takes a long pull from his coffee tumbler. Then another. We're living.

Around Crystal Cove, Laguna Beach, we turn the Toyota around and head back.

"Let's go to the restaurant at mom's," barks PJ. "I'm hungry."

It hits me. I never thought I'd ever hear my brother say those words again. Sobering.

PJ is younger, taller, and the most interactive of those living at the Atria. He takes to the underdogs. The lady with the most debilitating stroke. The ones that struggle verbalizing their diminished thoughts. He playfully flirts with another stroke victim. I love him for it. Her eyes light up as she describes the next beanie she's making for him.

We find mom. She struggles because her youngest son is in such pain. She plays bridge more these days as a diversion. The pain of PJ's demise is close to breaking her.

This moment in time is his. With his oldest brother and true friend, PJ orders a bagel, bacon, and another coffee. Things are lighter than previously. We feel the Santa Ana desert winds on our lips. PJ wants butter and cream cheese on his bagel. He crumbles up the bacon and drizzles it atop his build. Mom, ever reasonable, questions why he'd combine both butter and cream cheese. It doesn't make sense in her world. It makes perfect sense to him. He has the munchies.

PJ lifts his work of art to his mouth and bites in. He chews once before spitting it out. It's hard to watch but his show of determination resonates with me. He's his own man doing it his way, to the very end.

My father never tells his wife, Mary Lou, he loves her. A determined woman with 6 children, 11 grandchildren, and 12 great grandchildren, she certainly deserves more, but mom, to this day, wears it well. She's gracious, yet straight to the point; accommodating, yet sheepishly vulnerable as she trusts me with the hard truths of someone who lives life sincerely and on her terms.

We both have a love for my father (her husband), but neither of us can say we respect him—too many black eyes, living in fear, missed milestones, and fractured intentions. Mom reminds me that dad's boss is present as I'm on the surgery table having my spine fused. Any glimpse or hope of not being permanently disabled is to be known then. The severity of my lower back and the reality of function is in the eyes of the surgeons present. The horse pill of (my) life is swallowed whole.

Paul Kiley, father of six, his oldest son in a surgical fog, drinks belly-up at the Huddle Bar instead.

In 1974, mom divorces dad but keeps taking him back for reasons only she knows. He makes promises. She believes him. When lucid, he knows the beauty, function, and unequivocal influence of his blood into this family. At his core, he is a proud patriarch.

He climbs the ladder of his craft from laborer at the cabinet mill shop, to master cabinetmaker and business owner. Homes that currently run around million-plus are purchased for seventeen-and-a-half-thousand when we begin our Southern California journey in the mid-sixties.

He provides.

He bullies.

He steamrolls.

The fear of what begins as a verbal barrage quickly cascades into the physical. I'm the oldest. It's my fists that are clenched. My chin is a bullseye. I'm glad I'm there; mom and my brothers out of his sights, but what about the times I'm not? How many times has mom taken one in the chops unbeknownst to me? How many times has Jeff or Tom had to dig deep into their well of valor and bravery in the name of protecting our mother from the alcohol blazed version of the scary man down the hall?

What about Steve, PJ, or Sharon? The thought punches through my chest like the haymaker I'd like to give my father in his deep, noisy, alcoholic, passed-out slumber.

Things reach absurdity when dad purchases a liquor store just off Newport Boulevard. Talk about the mouse in charge of the cheese. The store is sandwiched between Wild Bill's Saloon and the Bay Cliff (no tell) Motel. Mom works the register whilst my brothers and I keep the place clean and shelves stocked.

Dad marries another.

Outlandish promises are made and mom takes him back as his ring finger silently makes promises to a different mistress but still, they endure, hanging on until the shelves of booze have voices. The bottles call, and he succumbs like never before. Mom pays a physical and emotional price that demands her exit from an idea she is beyond loyal to. Her belief in family is unparalleled but even Mary Lou, my valiant, competitive mother has enough.

Enough.

Enough.

I will always be his son, of his blood and bone, but his path is for cowards and a slippery slide that will follow me throughout, like a sweaty toothed, paint-peeling reminder of the darkness that he brings to us but also the capacity of what's inherently working and careening inside me.

After five boys, Sharon is born. Twelve years my junior, she's the last of the Kiley kids. Dad is a no-show at the birthing. Nothing surprises us anymore, but for mom (even with the absence of her birthing partner), the vision matches the reality.

She describes having a daughter after five boys, "Like having a dream."

Mom doesn't pine for a baby girl and wouldn't have been downhearted with a sixth boy, but with little Sharon, I sense a completion of our nuclear family bubble. Ozzie and Harriet we're not. Yet, on the surface, we're kids in the neighborhood, ball in hand, always looking for a game. We look like the product of cooperative, hand-in-hand, parents.

Sharon adds the dynamic of a daughter transitioning to schoolgirl. We put a ball in her hands and teach her to throw. She attends our games to befriend and mimic the moves of cheerleaders.

Sharon proves to be more than a girl playing house. She begins swimming and takes on coaching at five-years of age. That same year she set an Orange County record in the 50-yard backstroke. She wins all the time, in all the strokes. I love watching her compete and dominate. She grows into her swimmer body: long, broad shoulders, shredded and defined back with familiar swimmer's blonde/greenish chlorine hair. I think she's perfect. She has other

31

ideas and the routine of swimming ends around the beginning of her teenage years.

Like all of us, Sharon gravitates to the beach (52nd St./Newport) but uses the sand, salt, and wind off the ocean as a control center for friendship and socializing. We (the brothers) do the same but need the activities of fishing, surfing, and womanizing as the reason for our intrinsic reality.

I imagine mom enjoys these subtleties. Machismo and the constant pecking order of brothers certainly has its place, but the sharp elbows of us gut-chopping one another into submission varies in contrast to a mother and daughter sharing a perspective.

The hard truth is Sharon is to be the last of our tribe. Catholicism and birth control—or lack of it—can no longer counterpunch abuse, alcoholism, and absentee fatherhood. Mom makes the difficult, yet affirming, decision to use birth control as a counter-balance to the chaos of her marriage.

With over a decade between us, I miss most of Sharon's rite of passage years. Sure, I'm the cool oldest brother that influences an impressionable youngest sibling. Sharon has newspaper clippings of my sporting accomplishments in a corner of her room. She and PJ visit when I'm off to college hundreds of miles away. I make sure to look out and include her when I'm around but it would be decades later until I'm of true value to Sharon and her family.

Sharon's twenty-nine-year-old, beauty of a daughter, Kylie, suffers a devastating spinal stroke that leaves her an incomplete quadriplegic. These are dramatic times of physical and emotional tragedy for Kylie and the family.

Sharon remembers my words at the time, "Hey, Sis, this is my lane and you are not supposed to be in it."

Kylie spends eight weeks in a Neuro-Intensive Care Unit. It's too long. Speaking with Sharon and her husband Craig, we agree that the rehabilitation process is critical. My words to them are simple, "Sharon. Craig. She needs to move."

Navigating these critical times is something I've done and witnessed hundreds of others do. The times are dark, but the capabilities of the humanspirit are extraordinary. Kylie finds a familiar strength and her own deep, personalized capacity to deal with the hand she's been dealt.

Kylie and I are both the odd-shaped product of life within its terms. You find peace within yourself because if you do not, you will implode.

It's a few years later and the family is at a San Clemente restaurant celebrating mom's 80th birthday.

Kylie turns to me and Sharon: "The employees here must wonder if our family has a genetic defect."

Her words, poking light at our public display, amuse me. All within this fellowship know that life is stranger than fiction, and we best share a laugh at the illogicalness and long odds of what's directly before us.

I eye Kylie in her wheelchair whilst never overlooking the decades in mine.

Mom sits at the head of the long, chattering, busy table celebrating her birthday. My sister, Sharon, is opposite of Kylie.

Our mothers absorb our beast of burden and lighten the load with protective motherly intelligence and an attention to healing details that only mothers have the key to unlock. The absurd is worth a laugh only because they plough the hard, maternal yards for us.

The family business of choice is so Southern Cal.

Nothing competes with the salt of the ocean, but the ease of going for a dip in the backyard swimming pool meets SoCal's popular aquatic needs. This is a staple move for many Californians: backflips, belly flops, barbeques, swim races, diving for quarters, brutal water polo/basketball games, midnight skinny dips, slippery/wet kisses, holding your breath contests, meaningful (feet dangling in the pool) conversations, and revelations. The evening's backlit glow deep inside the pool's depths set many a mood.

Swimming pool maintenance and care, done well, is an agreeable choice with multiple revenue streams and consistent growth.

Sharon's husband, Craig, also works in the pool business and is an accomplice and motivating factor in all things aquatic. Sharon lends manual support in the beginning as Craig's initial employee in cleaning pools.

The brothers Kiley all lead a good, comfortable life. The kids are looked after. The cars are modern and there's a relaxation in our brotherly exchanges that speaks of hard working, honest contentment within living the American dream.

Working in sport and rehabilitation in my adult life is my chosen path. The story is constantly unfolding in revealing and pivotal ways. Memories are vivid and valued in the vault of my life's arc. They are precious and personal. It's who I am.

Whilst I built my global, regional, and local sporting resume and memories, my family steadfastly grows a budding lifetime business. Although each is their own boss and works their own territorial regions, the common denominator is chlorine, filters, and customer service.

I'm proud of them all.

Myself, Jeff, and Tom are the graduating classes of '71, '72, and '73 of Mater Dei High School. The three of us naturally travel in the same circles and share the subtle Shangri-la that is Costa Mesa and Orange County in the '60s and '70s.

Tom reminds me the 405-freeway ended at Harbor Boulevard in Costa Mesa/Santa Ana. In the '60s there's no city of Irvine, Mission Viejo, El Toro, or Laguna Niguel. There's nothing but celery fields, orange groves, and strawberry fields until the historic Mission in San Juan Capistrano. These days the toll roads, diamond lane bridges, and never-ending road work expansions are a daily reminder just how massive things have turned.

Tom's gift? He's the smartest guy in the room. His intelligence carries him throughout. We become closer after my injury. He is keen, full of empathy, insight, and asks poignant questions.

I know my siblings and I live a once-in-a-lifetime flight of simplified fancy in early Orange County. It's a time never to be repeated.

My brother Steve puts it this way, "I wish our children and grandchildren could have experienced the Orange County that we did."

Steve remembers the glory days, "It was nothing in those days to take the five-mile ride to the beach with friends. Heck, it was nothing to hitchhike there unless mom drove by and saw you. On the way home we'd stop at the Crab Cooker, get a bowl of clam chowder, and stuff as many free jawbreakers into our pockets as possible. We didn't seem to have the creeps back then, and parents didn't need to worry about their kids being abducted. I often wonder, what changed?"

Steve is a force in basketball. His size and determination naturally make him the enforcer in high school: outlet passes, screen and rolls, offensive board putbacks, and dirty work/pointy elbows make Steve hard to forget.

My youngest brother PJ: "I loved growing up in Orange County. It had everything I needed. We had the beach and surf, and the mountains with snow. We rode dirt bikes. We were water skiers. These were things I was interested in, and I was interested because of my family. They shared these experiences with me and I'm so grateful."

PJ begins surfing in grade school and is a standout volleyball player throughout high school. He goes on to play in junior college. PJ epitomizes why Southern California can be great. He's in it and he's on it. Having a great time.

The Boys Club, St. John the Baptist Middle School, Mater Dei, the beach, desert, mountains, lakes, and swimming pools. These are our fear-factor proving grounds.

Competitively, we're a proven commodity. We're capable of highlight-worthy clips, but, more and more, we're the subtleties of the game.

What we're really learning to do is win.

Within the circle is a definite hierarchy. Tom recalls, "We played games in the street or at the park. The sports rotated throughout the calendar year. Football in fall, basketball in winter, and baseball in summer. Dave's two years older than me, and Jeff a year, so I was close enough in age they'd let me play most of the time when they needed an extra guy. They also used me as the guy to chase the ball when it went down the street. They would count how long it took me to get back. I saw through this but wanted to be included, so I always went and got the ball."

My brothers and sister are the axis and orbit of my world in those days. Our job is to not only survive but prosper and better ourselves despite the rage of our father. That is what you did back then. Therapy, feelings, and reassuring hugs are not the way we operate. Happy pills and pharmaceuticals are decades in the making. Dealing with fear makes us (and this includes mom) stronger, more resilient, and tougher.

We're not bullies, but we take them on. If we take a punch—and we do—no one outside the circle sees the effects.

Our closeness is authentic but also a survival tactic.

We are strength in numbers personified.

We are love in one another's life.

Each sibling has an arm or finger in the make-up of the other.

We are the residual of a crossroad still to be travelled.

Decades removed from living in fear, I quietly begin forgiving my father. We speak on the phone more. At the end of certain conversations, I tell him "I love you." The awkwardness is massive and shifting like titanic icebergs.

Dad does his best to sidestep these farewells.

I'm reminded how much I love my kids and how I never tire of telling them.

In 2006, it's arranged for dad to visit us. We share our love of fishing in my double kayak. An evening fish fry with the family is the standard. I watch as my kids cherish the interplay with a grandfather they barely know.

Dad takes to our dogs: Magic and Barkley. The three of them are each other's shadows. I see joy in his walks to the pond. The dogs ambling ahead in their perfect rush to nowhere.

There's an ease in our words. Thoughts rambling into sentences without the pretence of who's more potent and powerful. The pond and lakes add a watery buffer. Conversations are of ripples and wind, bait and hooks. We are men on (and of) the surface, comfortable with one another for the first time as adults.

My dad with the catch of the day. A mess of crappie for the dinner table, in southern terms. My dad a good man with a bad disease. This was the last time I would see him alive and well...grateful.

35

Dad is sober his entire stay with us. The degree of difficulty has to be high. For this, I give him love and adoration.

As those in the program know, *an alcoholic alone is in bad company.*

I imagine him white-knuckling his desires in an isolated room, the walls slowly, yet assuredly, closing in on him. Alcohol fogging and numbing his pain.

I admire him for always wanting sobriety. These attempts litter his life in the circle of alcoholism, but the tides are constant and voices deeper than simply wanting positive change. You must humble yourself and find an honesty that involves humiliation.

A good man with a very bad disease.

I can only appreciate the difficulty, when I myself turn pro with King Alcohol in my fifties.

My brother, Jeffrey Allen Kiley, passes on August, 21st, 2007.

I remember the array of women at his service. There are hundreds in attendance on the bright south Orange County afternoon. Mom remembers the passing of her second son in a more pragmatic way: "The passing of Jeff got the family together. This family solves issues but I don't think it brought us close."

Dad passes five months previously. Full of drink and regret, the man still walked the earth for over 75 years. My Aunt Donna (my mom's sister) passes five weeks before dad. Three family services in a short six months leaves me contemplative and desiring more from our family dynamic.

Am I asking too much?

Should I demand more?

Maybe it's more than we can handle?

Peace activist and author, Norman Cousins, writes, "Death is not the greatest loss in life. The greatest loss is what dies inside us while we live."

A father of two cherished daughters—Lindsey and Amy—Jeff succumbs to years in the sun playing golf, driving convertibles, and long afternoons at the beach to the dreaded diagnosis of melanoma and skin cancer.

As kids we didn't concern ourselves with sunscreen, skincare, or shading strategies. Instead, we're one with the sun, not shielding but soaking of its magic—and for Jeff, its maladies. I've long understood that life isn't fair but to lose the strong, quiet vibe of my brother hits me in a way I cannot imagine.

I didn't get to know Jeff the way the rest of the family did.

It started in the mid-seventies. I'm earning my Associate Arts degree at Orange Coast College. Jeff, Tom, and I rent a three-bedroom house in Huntington Beach, behind the Edison Power Plant off Pacific Coast Highway. Still years away from careers in the pool business, Jeff and Tom both work at Supermarkets with good paying jobs. Mom is happy the three of us are together.

Our new living arrangement works great for Tom, and me. Jeff's a neat-freak whilst Tom and I have a party-house mentality. Jeff hates any kind of mess. He picks the wrong two roommates. We have parties; the kind of drugging, bad decision, cocktail-carousing, debauched blowouts that leave smells, stains, and burnt retina images.

Jeff knows early in his adulthood ascent that this is no way to live. Tom and I (of course) learn the hard way. Jeff is miserable with us and spends too many afternoons and evenings in his room without a hello or considerate word exchanged.

After earning my AA degree from OCC, I move to Northern California to continue my education. I regret I never get to know Jeff the way the rest of my siblings do. I chase the hardwood stages of basketball like rock stars chase fans on tour. The skills developed in our driveway and St John's the Baptist Middle School are all the rage in the subculture of wheelchair basketball in the 70s. I relish the competitive attention. It's new and revealing in a way I didn't know existed. Competitors want a piece of me and I'm more than happy to give it to them. Timing is everything and my time with Jeff—my brother/my teammate—dwindles.

He's good with me (even as I'm chasing a new life) but I'll always wish Jeff had a better big brother, than his memory of me—the slob roommate.

*Brothers Jeff
and PJ. RIP.*

Sharon, mom, Steve, PJ (RIP), Tom and myself.

RING OF HONOR

Being a role model is the most powerful form of educating.

— John Wooden

Ceremonial recognition in the form of awards, speeches, rubber-chicken meals, and costumed banquet halls have become a familiar habit over time.

In the early days, I'm the guy in the faraway corner, beer in hand, unaware that my name was just called for the all-tournament or Most Valuable Player (MVP) award. I awkwardly push through the masses or circle the entire hall for my moment under the lights. Finding the whole thing mystifying and bizarre, I simply want to fade beyond the lights and back to the corner normalcy of busting balls with the boys.

Over time *the boys* take a back seat to family, my wife, and the etiquette involved within the decorum of hosting or receiving an award. Corduroy trousers and printed shirts are replaced with suits, vests, and trending shoes. Beers transcend to wine, diet cokes, and water. The rubber-chicken is a constant.

In 2007, I get a call informing me I'm nominated for Mater Dei's Ring of Honor. A former classmate, Mariann Duane Dwyer, has taken the time to persuade me. We graduated together and share the valued memories of Mater Dei sporting life. Both playing our spirited roles as cheerleader and basketballer point guard.

I don't know what to say or where the Mater Dei Ring of Honor lands in my psyche and recognition hierarchy. I do know Mater Dei is one of the most recognized high schools in the nation. I can be in Tel Aviv, Israel, or Sydney, Australia, with a blessed *USA Today* sports page by my side, only to see the Mater Dei Monarchs as the top ranked high school football program in the country. Mater Dei is so much more than football. Pridefulness with a dash of self-satisfaction simmer within, as I am one of many Mater Dei alumni that lay the bricks of a framework slowly rising to superstructure status.

The Ring of Honor is not about how many points, assists, and wins one helps put in the annuals and record books. The Ring of Honor is about the depth and deeds for others. Throughout my playing days, my competitiveness and absolute desire to be better than everyone, drove me to the brink of what's accepted as opposed to what's over the line. As a teammate, the expectations are excellence and effort. Winning has high costs. Can you maintain the profound intensity and standard set by me? If so, come aboard. If not, I'll see you down the road and question what could have been.

This is a vastly different night. My wife, Sandy, and I travel from our adopted home of Mooresville, North Carolina, to my original home of Orange County and Mater Dei. I'm shocked and amazed how many classmates and friends are in attendance. Total surprise. The unwavering family support, as always led by our matriarchal mother, reminds me that without them this place isn't home.

These are the moments that matter. These are the proud accomplishments that define me in God's eyes.

What do I do for others?

Do I make a difference in others' lives?

A Ring of Honor recipient is to be an agent for change. A priest and a nun are also inducted. My decades working in disability sport as competitor, administrator, facilitator, coach, and mentor have led me here. I'm the only Wheel Head (person with a disability requiring a wheelchair) in the room—and I like it.

I'm reconnecting with my able-bodied life.

I'm grateful. It feels like a place I haven't visited in far too long.

One of my best friends, Joe Kapsch, introduces me. The undersized, back-to-the-basket lefty, jokes he's a southpaw version of Kareem Abdul Jabbar. Joe accompanied me to a speaking engagement in Italy a few years back. We talk a lot of smack. The laughs flow.

Joe takes my breath away describing how he apologetically felt following my spinal cord injury at the age of nineteen. Joe was with me that day and struggles with survivor's guilt for far too many days and nights. I appreciate and love the guy. His words, like my own acceptance speech, are a blur of impassioned honor and joy.

I allow myself to eliminate the bravado. I soak it in instead of eyeing the fire escape exits. I am the son of a proud mother. I am a dutiful husband to my beautiful wife. I am a father leading by example. I am a spoke in the wheel of change. The eyes surrounding me, the same ones I grew up with, are here tonight. There's a depth to our shared gazes, an extra pinkie squeeze to the many proud, manly handshakes, and a sincerity to the abundant, time-worn embraces of a memory lane evening.

The intention is to feel big—empowered, but in the midst of reconnecting with my able-bodied life (a place I like to be, by the way), I feel humble, smaller, yet stronger than before.

Am I disabled? Yes, but damn less than most.

It's not my intention to be what society has in mind for me. I play the cards I'm dealt. My spinal cord injury inspires me to search and be different. It provides me with the motivation to rock my world but more importantly those of kids with disabilities and those newly injured. I'm not a survivor. I'm a searcher. I accept life on life's terms.

The Ring of Honor evening is a confluence of who I was, who I am, and who I am supposed to be.

Throughout the room are the many high school peers, fellow athletes, and fans. I leave my wheel print throughout. They are the better for it as I am the better for friends and family encouraging or stepping aside as I steadfastly do it my own and uncharted way.

We share the experience of growing up a Monarch. We're the stepping-stones leading to the cathedral that is present day Mater Dei.

It's unspoken but we know.

Ring of Honor at Mater Dei High School with wife Sandy. Proud to be a Monarch

PART TWO

The best journeys answer questions that
in the beginning you didn't even think to ask

— Yvon Chouinard, Patagonia

GAME CHANGER

We are all broken—that's how the light gets in.

— Ernest Hemingway

Change is all around. It's a year-plus since graduating Mater Dei. I have no clear direction with 'ball or college. The University of Gonzaga shows interest, but left to my own devices, I lack the maturity and focus to complete forms, keep appointments, much less make life-affirming, college-of-choice, on- or off-campus decisions.

I need help and there is none from Tardie or my father.

I slip into the half-baked world of survival and partying. Crap jobs, like working as a grunt in dad's cabinet shop, have me not only questioning life choices but leapfrog me into the quicksand of bad decisions and detrimental behavior.

I move in with my neighborhood and good buddy Billy Clough and a guy named Mike Lacey in a weathered, ranch-style rental in Santa Ana. As wayward as I feel, living large in my own place in perfect Southern Cal, I am also bulletproof in a nineteen-year-old, devil-may-care kind of way.

Work.

Party.

Girls.

The trifecta of vitality keeps my basketball reflections more in my subconscious than on the tricky and narrow plank of regret.

My days of thieving begin in high school. I get popped stealing an album from the White Front Store on the corner of Bristol and Paularino: Santana's debut album entitled, *Santana.* The album hosts an angry, cross-eyed lion's face, full of teeth and rage. It needs to be mine. My folks get the call from the store itself. The police are involved. I'm in a world of trouble. My choices remain that of a delinquent until years later.

Just out of high school, I backpack, bodysurf, and hitchhike my way around the Hawaiian Islands of Oahu, Kauai, Maui, and the Big Island. The adventure lifts my spirits exactly like the enchanted, breathtaking Polynesian gods intended to. Yet, as I look back, I remember the ease and excitement of stealing a backpack from the local sporting goods store—The *Pineapple Split* trip.

I take to robbing beer trucks full of cases of exposed and unattended nectar. Whilst the drivers manage their hand trucks into liquor stores and supermarkets, I'm quick with a couple cases into an awaiting ride. The slippery slope of debauchery and binge drinking awaits.

The most brazen and extreme thrill of thieving is entering a major department store inside the massive South Coast Plaza Mall. I hoist a Persian rug, twice my size, over my shoulder before calmly walking down the escalator and straight out the door.

These are not proud times. These are the times of a lost teenager trying to be a big shot.

The scheme actualizes in a matter of moments. Amongst the clanking of drunken toasts, keg beer guzzling, and Deep Purple's "Smoke on the Water" rebounding from speakers into soaked membranes, I have an idea. I turn to Joe Kapsch. He's my boy and usually up for anything.

"Joe, let's head to the mountains in the morning," I suggest. "Katie Dolan and Margie Dowling are in. How 'bout you?"

Joe's a quick yes. We throw another one back. The Friday night house party roars in the background.

On the morning of January 29, 1973, we load up Margie Dowling's Datsun station wagon with the required beer to get to the base of Big Bear Mountain.

Big Bear is the Southern California equivalency of nothing else in the world. Turn west and I'm in the waves of Newport or Huntington Beach in a matter of minutes. Redirect east and, in just under two hours, I'm skiing the slopes of Snow Summit or Snow Valley.

We have a different plan: innertubes and whatever hill shows itself first.

I'm wearing my trusty Woody's Wharf t-shirt with cut-off sleeves. There are warmer clothes in my backpack but the sun's out. That's all I need.

As the oldest, I volunteer to drive Margie's wagon. My third beer into the four-beer drive, I begin to see the San Bernardino National Forest. At that moment, I love my life. Four friends working a morning buzz, cracking jackpots while easing down the road. Somewhere around the base of the National Forest we pull into a welcoming liquor store. The plan is for the girls and Joe to buy orange juice and Galliano. I go ahead and appropriate (down my pants) the needed vodka, in the creation of the popular seventies' concoction— Harvey Wallbangers.

Up the mountain we go.

The backseat is mixing cocktails like we're moments away from the opening chords of Led Zeppelin's *Houses of the Holy* live on stage. We are strength and ignorance within each drawn breath. We are players on the path of each other's destiny, but we have no idea why we're really here or what this trip into the forest will ultimately mean.

I take a long pull from my impromptu Wallbanger before downshifting into the sharp, mountainous turn.

My buddy, Joe Kapsch remembers, "The car was filled with beers, a big bottle of Galliano, and vodka. We were ready to go—indestructible—nothing was going to stop us from having a great day. We drank like there was no tomorrow."

The final twenty-minutes, ascending the mountain is a blur as the increased altitude and effects of Mr. Booze take control of my dexterity and decision making.

After the rental of innertubes, I take a final pull off our concoction of ignorance.

The plan is to freefall down a steep hill. It's 1973 and just like we didn't think twice about not wearing seatbelts or drinking and driving, the powers that be have no organized, public inner-tubing strategies or safety protocols in place. Find a slope and spin 360s down the fall line, incurring maximum speed is the move.

We spot a handful of like-minded knuckleheads, inner-tubing down a break in the trees. Right at the cusp of blackout drunk, I scurry up the hill, ten to twenty feet higher than the rest. Liquid Courage personified.

The weather has turned. Snow begins to fall.

Joe Kapsch recalls, "We got out of the car, grabbed our tubes and hit the run. I went down first. Nothing spectacular. It was fun and fast. Dave was next and he went higher up the hill. About halfway down, his innertube spun out of the regular route and was out of control."

I remember only a snippet of the speed. The Disneyland, Mad Hatter, Teacup-like ride that has me spiralling like a top. There's a faraway hissing sound innertubes make cascading downhill. The skimming of rubber against snow creates a glide that hums like a crisp northern wind and a tea kettle just before it's about to blow.

Any tranquility I'm feeling is quickly interrupted as I collide with two strangers—girls veering on their own path and outside the narrow run surrounded by trees. Their wayward speed-drift now becomes mine. Knocked off course, my newest pathway involves an immovable, massive Evergreen tree. I vaguely remember the sensation of spinning.

Things are dark and uncharted.

I stop spinning. Impact. I immediately go into shock. I'm stupid drunk. A seismic and dreadful unconsciousness begins to grab me. I'm concussed. My brain searches for a time just moments ago. Pain. The Wallbangers have me edging towards full black-out. If I black-out, will I die? I scream in pain instead.

I'm alive. That's all I know.

"The sound of a body hitting a tree—the thud sound is indescribable. It's a dead sound," recounts Joe, first on the scene. "Get up Dave. Get up. Get up," he repeats. "You're Dave Kiley. Get up. Get up."

It continues to snow.

I can't get up.

Do I hear voices calling for an ambulance?

Is that Margie and Katie standing over me in horror and fear?

Voices again.

Real or subconscious?

The beer, Wallbangers, and mountain elevation have me in a sleeper hold.

The ambulance arrives.

Moments?

Minutes?

Hours?

Immense pain.

I scream like a wolf at the moon.

Are those fingers across my face?

Mine?

Can I move my arms?

Get up then.

Step away from this.

I'm here instead.

Is that the sun?

Is that the light?

From what I'm told, it takes hours to get down the mountain with mounting snow and skier traffic. The paramedics can't give me anything for the pain, the beer and Wallbangers see to that.

I can't remember the ambulance ride or arriving at the San Bernardino County Hospital. I left my friends in a helpless and horrible space of the unknown. Joe and Katie, after all is said and done, remain the closest of friends to this day and a source of encouragement.

I wake up in a Stryker frame, strapped down like in an asylum and flipped regularly like fundraiser flapjacks. A Stryker bed frame is an evil contraption. I'm on a stretcher, yet there's a stretcher on top of me. The straps are everywhere: arms, head, legs, pelvis, chest, feet, and back, pressing the stretchers together with me sandwiched in between. All I can see is the ceiling. I eye the cracks and water marks of the weathered, county facility. The Stryker frame keeps my spine immobilized in an iron lung kind of way. Primitive. Frightening.

A couple hours later, two nurses (out of a Hitchcock film) grab the bed-length rails above my head and flip the Stryker frame 180 degrees on its horizontal axis. I'm now staring at the floor. It feels as if I'm going to plummet and crash. I don't, but the sensation is one of a kind, a dizzying loss of control amongst absolute helplessness.

I know how to do this, I think to myself. I recovered from the Chevy Apache in 4th grade. The Stryker frame is another go-between on my certain path— running the beaches of Newport, bare feet and toes gripping particles of sand with each piston-like kick of my stronger-than-ever bottom half.

I do what I always did. Visualize. Overcome.

I'm switched to a circular Stryker frame. I now look and feel like a carnival attraction. The thing has the ability to rotate on any axis. Instead of being flipped from ceiling to floor, I am now stood up on this circle of doom before being placed face down.

A steady morphine drip continues through my veins and into my consciousness. The room feels dark with too many unattended corners.

It's not long before friends begin to show. They sit cross-legged, necks arching up whilst looking up at me from the floor. It's a cruel comedy but nonetheless pure Stryker frame dark humor.

The family begins to deal with the uncertainty.

My sister Sharon recalls, "I was in second grade. Mom was making PJ and I pancakes. The phone rang. Mom began crying uncontrollably. She hung up the phone and told us Dave had an accident. I will never forget how scared I was seeing him in that contraption. I didn't understand. He was in jail with all those bars around his bed. I peered through the door hesitantly. My brother was on his stomach and his arms were on this moving roller tray. He told me to come in and not be afraid, with a smile on his face. I will never forget that moment."

I have surgery right away. They fuse the vertebrae of my spinal cord and place Teflon rods along the spine to strengthen the fusion. The multiple, post-surgery drips into my vein eases the discomfort and distress but my thinker is on tilt. I'm not adverse to the sensations: the incumbent time-released warmth bathes my fear and pain. I struggle lining up my thoughts and images properly in my overriding need to make sense of things.

I'm unable to see myself but it's beginning to feel heavier than the Chevy Apache bicycle crash. I'm prepared to give what is required but what are the obstacles? Where are the booby traps? Who has the answers? What are my questions?

Somewhere in my morphine, filmy fog, I hear 'paralyzed.' I'm unable to dismiss, disavow, or rationalize the words. I know it doesn't sound good.

Can I walk again?

An orderly or nurse's assistant enters the room. I'm not sure which. He's a low man on the totem pole. It's not the time, but my need to know outweighs all else. I ask him the question. The four words that will define my life:

"Can I walk again?"

"No," he answers. "You're paralyzed from the waist down."

My father, ever the mediator, overhears our exchange. He less than politely asks the orderly for a word. Just outside the front door of my room, I watch dad pin this poor, misguided sap to the wall; all the while reminding him how this type of delicate information best comes from a doctor or therapist, certainly not from him.

The news drives me inward. I clam up. My walls are Green Monster high and not to be recessed.

The moment hangs for hours and hours. The world is on its side, reminding me with its straps, nurses, and dimness how colossal my beast of strength needs to be. Is this the bell I need to answer? The—I can't walk, dig deep whilst looking everyone in the ass—bell of inequity. Will this smother, shape, and mold me? Dad. Decades of drinking and there he stands: firm and strong. A few Wallbangers and I'm the personification of: paralyzed, assistance, adaptions, and indwelling.

A couple yesterday's ago, I swam like a dolphin, ran like the breeze, and fearlessly took what I needed. Today, I'm strapped to the Stryker, alone with my paralyzed thoughts.

Time stands still (or at best crawls uphill) when convalescing from a calamity. Is the term *paralyzed* my new moniker? Deep and dastardly thoughts begin to ping against the walls of my noggin. My focus thankfully shifts with increased talks of acute care and pain management. I'm in need of better surroundings and expertise.

So long, San Bernardino County Hospital.

I take a helicopter to Newport Beach's Hoag Hospital. Hoag sits atop Superior Hill. Just below is the peninsula of Newport, and its jetty breaks of 44th and 56th Street. In the afternoon, the onshore breeze wisps its ocean's scent up the hill, into the westside of Costa Mesa and the exposed rooms of Hoag Hospital.

The production from bed to gurney to helicopter proves annoying and agonizing. Movement equates to pain. Pain increases the morphine.

The wind howls atop the rooftop. The bird and its blades are loud. Can't talk. Can't hear. Dad hustles along beside me. Another ride in silence. In the family station wagon or medical helicopter, the song remains the same.

We land as soon as we take off. My deep-dive memories take me back to Hoag and the Chevy Apache. A kid then. A man now. It doesn't matter. I need this place. It's as close to home as I know right now.

I'm smothered in good care and visits from friends and family. The environment puts me more at ease. When I ring the call-bell, nurses appear. I find myself laughing again. Not a Richard Pryor, Saturday night gut-wrencher, but enough to rekindle exchanges and stay engaged. The private room and afternoon airflow off the coast, call to mind possibilities and promise.

I'm jacked up. I know it. The gravity of my spinal cord and what does or doesn't function is an hourly, daily bender of a road unimagined, but the days in Hoag soften the blow.

The cruel joke, that is the partner of any serious injury, is a cushiony and familiar place to land. I find solace on the bluffs of Newport Beach, alongside my hometown of Costa Mesa.

Joe Kapsch and me shortly after injury. While going to Sac State, we attend a Seals and Crofts concert at Chico State. Every picture tells a story!

RANCHO

You don't lose if you get knocked down;
you lose if you stay down.

— Muhammad Ali

Rehabilitation is a constant, twisting road into the unknown. It tests your capacity.

In many vital ways, I'm the same fourth-grader that defied odds almost a decade ago. As strange as it sounds, I have fond memories recouping from the Chevy Apache. The first ever assault on my body. I not only recovered—I excelled. Hoag Hospital ties me to family and friends. At Hoag, I'm not overwhelmed by my paralysis. I'm hopeful, even happy.

I have high anxiety about leaving here, just like I did when I was 10 years old.

Rancho Los Amigos Rehabilitation Hospital is the next logical place for me. It's a county facility. It's where I'm to spend the next four months, at least. The ambulance ride unnerves me. Less than an hour away, Downey, California is a ride into the unknown from my sheltered, Orange County, coastal life. I'm not impressed with the view from the ambulance's many windows. Downey, and its main thoroughfare, Imperial Highway, is a hustler's jungle gym. Taco stands, muffler shops, and corner neon liquor stores line the streets. Saddened, I check out. Everything morphs to a blur.

There's a stoutness and vulnerability as they lower, then raise the ambulance gurney from vehicle to pavement. I feel the familiar warmth of the desert sun. Optimism—the bright side. I accept the challenge. They raise the arms of the gurney. There's a click, locking things in place. Instantly, it's real.

I'm escorted down a long corridor. Another prisoner serving his sentence.

It smells. The disinfectant is strong but does little to mask the stench of the afflicted.

In my room are four other paralyzed souls of what used to be. My eyes open. What the hell have I gotten myself into? The room sleeps six. I'm lifted into bed. There are five inhabitants. Where's the sixth? I can only imagine.

A sign above my head is posted. It reads, **_Log Roll._**

Immediately, I am dosed with an overriding concern for my life. A matter-of-fact nurse asks me the last time I've had a bowel movement. I can't remember. Minutes later my first enema and indwelling catheter are systematically placed inside of me.

Lying in bed with wheelchairs all around me, I eye my immediate future.

I try to move my toes. I ask my brothers to be my eyes. Nothing. I can't stop touching my legs, trying to feel something. Nothing.

I have no sensation of the catheter inside me. It must hurt.

A collection of urine bags hangs from each bed in the room. This petrifies me. Quadriplegics and paraplegics make no sense. From my bed, I eye them rolling the hall en route to physical, occupational, and recreational therapy. I'm living in another world on a faraway planet.

Two nights a week is suppository night. A literal shit-show. The darkness reeks of in-bed, body bombs. One after the other. I begin to understand humiliation and embarrassment as a routine. Nurses and aides administering this sinister but necessary act.

My bladder and bowels are hijacked from my body. This is paralyzing more than not moving my legs. So much personal invasion by strangers, whose job is to keep me pissing and shitting. I obsess over what's being done to me. I project the worst, all the time and every day.

Please, no visitors, I constantly think to myself. Nights are the worst in this joint.

I finally fall asleep until I'm rustled awake. I'm reminded who I am and where I'm at. The nurse raises my aching shoulder before gesturing towards the sign above my bed in thick magic marker. She then pushes lower on my back, resting the majority of pressure and weight on the opposite hip and shoulder. I sense another pair of hands repositioning my legs.

Thinking things can't get worse, I'm reminded they will.

"We'll log roll him again at daybreak," the one says to the other.

"Don't forget the bedpan from bed three."

First, I'm paralyzed, and now I'm a log. The days are dark. The night is the abyss. I have another month in bed. My surgical wounds and restructured spine are healing.

Mom understands no one is to visit on bowel nights, but, during the day, the visits from friends and family are constant. I do my best to present an outward positivity. Mom visits every day. On weekends my bed is pushed into the courtyard just outside our room. My crew smuggles in beer and a joint or two. My mood changes. It enhances the moments. I feel the breeze. We're slicker than the staff and refuse to get caught. I hold onto some of the weekend weed and during one particularly frustrating night, I take a big hit off the reefer. I blow it as far away from my bed as possible, swallowing the rest and destroying any evidence. There's five of us in the room. They'll never know who to point the finger at.

The next day my entire small dresser and bed are inspected and searched. In the early 70s, recreational drug use is not for the clumsy and incompetent. Those I hang with (especially myself) are experts and polished, in the trade of leaving no trails.

I do what I always do—deny, deny, deny.

Life in the bed makes for long, miserable days. I find it close to impossible to convey what it's like to be 19 years old, where everything is new, different, and difficult to comprehend. My body from the waist down has morphed into an atrophied, paralyzed world of the unknown. Everything my body does naturally is now a recipe for disaster and humiliation.

Closing in on a month of my stay at Rancho, the visitors dwindle. I get it. Downey, and Rancho in particular, is what those living on the coast despise: traffic, busy boulevards, concrete, exhaust, heat, and stale air.

Throughout, my brother Tom's visits never waver.

Tom explains, "It was about a 40-minute drive to Rancho from our home in Costa Mesa. I visited Dave two to three times a week. He was told he will be paralyzed from the waist down for the rest of his life. He told me he won't be able to have sexual intercourse—a devastating prognosis. He was down and depressed when I would visit. One day I told him, 'It's a long drive to see you and your mood isn't much fun once I get here. Maybe I shouldn't come anymore?'"

There are sparks. Things are slowly evolving into a new normal.

"On my next visit, I walked into his room and Dave had a huge smile. This was something I hadn't seen in a long time. I asked why he's so happy? His reply, 'I got a boner,'" Tom adds.

My always knocking-on-the-door crisis of not fathering children contains a speck of hope. Many hills to climb before I cross that bridge.

I'm introduced to the body jacket. The jacket allows me to sit up (out of this asylum of a bed) and begin the long path of living life on my ass. At first, the dizzying effects of sitting upright can only be dealt with in small doses and limited increments of time. I build stamina. The chair becomes more a play toy, a vehicle to be. I'm told to get in the bed. I roll the chair out of sight instead, finding a freedom I didn't imagine. I take the armrests off the Everest & Jennings wheelchair assigned to me. They're of no use and add weight.

I have a knack of landing in the underbelly of most environments. I'm the hippie-type in search of the next. Before I'm allowed any precious weekend passes home, I push the sprawling hospital grounds. I feel every section of the sidewalk, each crack like the sound of a train towards its destination. I can feel the day against my skin. I'm in it again. I add more hand-speed to the push-rim and tire. Faster. Harder. I like the solo sojourn.

Without knowing how or why, I stumble onto a ward of decubitus ulcer or pressure sore patients—most are Vietnam Veterans. They're all lying prone on gurneys with big wheels and push-rims in front so they can get around unassisted. Perhaps, I should delve and explore into their tragic, numerous, and humorous war stories, but I want to simply hang instead. Around these guys, I don't think about loss and regret. These long hair dudes like me. They want me in their tribe. They explain (while they pass another joint) what happens to your skin when you don't take care of yourself.

It's ordained for me to witness their demise—six months to a year on their stomachs. No thanks. No way. From that day on I'm acutely aware of the entirety of me. If I can feel it or not.

How did I end up here? This situation and body are not mine but the instinctual journey is both personal and profound.

This cannot be where I'm supposed to be?

Learn? Refuse to learn? What am I? Who am I going to be?

No fucking idea.

God and his cruel sense of humor has all of my attention and intentions.

I drive a souped-up '67 Volkswagen bug. It's modified to run with Porsches. It's mean: custom paint, SS headers, Zenith carburetor, 88mm pistons, Hurst shifter, and sporty Porsche hub caps. The 8-track is booming glorious, heavy back-beat, classic rock and roll. The bug runs fast, loud, and looks first-class.

My brothers and I decide to sell the manual transmission Volkswagen. To add insult to injury, we also put my Spanish made, Bultaco dirt bike up for sale.

I love both these vehicles.

The warden psychiatrist was in earlier. He wants me to talk to the sex doctor.

The nerve pain in my left leg (commonly referred to as phantom pain) has become real and constant. I feel the agony of a thousand shards of glass into my lower left side.

The physical therapy department puts me onto this stretchy table to combat my discomfort. It's a torture rack from a Fright Night skit. The pain does not subside. The pain intensifies.

I'm in survival mode. The onslaught of warped newness never wavers.

What will tomorrow bring?

I am full of deep, personal, fox-hole prayers to a God I don't understand, yet find a strange and misguided comfort in.

I need a sign, a friend—a reason.

ED

I almost cut my hair
But I didn't and wonder why
I feel like letting my freak flag fly
And I feel like I owe it to someone.

— Crosby, Stills, Nash & Young,
"Almost Cut My Hair"

He limps into my room. His beard speaks to my seventies' sensibilities. The thing trails to the middle of his chest. In this brief cusp of time, I can't take my eyes off his bristly, hard-earned facial growth. Ed has polio, but it doesn't minimize his six-foot, ten-inch frame. His thick, dark, geeky glasses and pulled back, shoulder length hair give him an intellectual/giant look that speaks more to peace than fight.

Ed, my recreation therapist, mentor, and NWBA Hall of Famer.

He's heard of my basketball reputation.

I want to melt away and avoid this conversation with all I am. I'm a real baller and want nothing to do with this guy.

He introduces himself, peering over my bed like an eclipse of the sun, "My name is Ed Owen."

I grunt a disrespectful response.

He spews about wheelchair basketball.

Angered, I focus on my half-eaten lunch. Processed mystery meat jailed next to canned vegetables and stale white bread.

Ed's easy-going nature isn't swayed by my abrupt rudeness. He instead finds a chair next to the wall and makes himself at home.

At six-foot, two inches tall, I'm commonly the tallest in the room. After meeting Ed Owen, I realize those days are long gone.

He finally leaves.

Weekends at Rancho are *hard time.* It's more a prison term than a rehabilitation facility: my body jacket, a straight jacket for the healing and gimped-up. Even in the jacket, I know I need to move: push the expanse of this place, chasing a version of me that no longer exists; getting from one painted line to the other quicker, faster and with an internal need that only makes sense to me.

I hate it all but repeat until figuring newer, more isolated ways to chase something that isn't there. The repetition builds muscle memory, hand-speed, and turning technique. Tight turns have myself and the body jacket almost tumbling sideways out of the chair, but I'm learning where the line is. I pick and choose the precise moments to cross-over towards a chase; a hustle and velocity that has me right on the edge of road rash and disapproving, head-tilted warnings from therapists, doctors, and unimpressed nurses.

Then, I see him through a window leading to the courtyard and makeshift hoop.

He's in a wheelchair this time. The giant in my room, speaking nonsense about wheelchair basketball.

Sitting down does nothing to diminish his length of torso and reach. As he pushes forward his chest bends like an accordion to his pointy knees. Nose over toes, his core and athleticism have him back to the ready position. He grabs more wheel by lifting his elbows above his push rim. His head lifts, arching his back, before his inertia and might repeat and perform. He creates a down-force that literally shakes his chair. His speed increases immediately.

Now he has a basketball. He holds it in his hands like others hold a baseball. Alone on the court, he's into his routine. This I understand. His chair spins like a top, kissing shots off the glass with dominant and non-dominant hand, post shots.

He seldom misses.

Thinking he might see me, I lean back hidden, like a shadow.

He moves to the free-throw line—one after the other—a careful loft and arc finding its target. I'm taken by the quickness and ease of his movement to the ball. He presses the ball next to his wheel, and the circular motion brings the ball back to his shooting hand. At the free-throw line, he gives the ball a mighty bounce, spins his chair to square his shoulders to the rim, and fires another effortless shot.

I'm in awe but my ego (ever developing) feels dwarfed compared to the revelation of what I'm witnessing.

In silence. In hiding. My world is changed—forever.

The days following involve finding the backbone to become a part of what big Ed is selling. I'm not sure exactly why, but I find the process daunting. I'm humbled and unprepared. Starting at the bottom, in a game I know so well, carries a weight I need to shed.

At a time when purpose and decidedness are beyond my control, I make a decision. I find Ed Owen.

He's the Recreation Therapist of the spinal ward at Rancho. In his reserved way, he sees my potential. His consistent calm allows me to work through my frustrations. The ball, the court, and Ed help me escape the mundane hours of physical and occupational therapy. I dodge psychologist sessions and instead use the court as my mental/physical proving ground.

Ed instructs me on the relationship between the ball and the chair. The body jacket doesn't allow me to bend, and I routinely bounce the ball off my wheels learning various dribbles: high, low, hard, and cross-over.

I make my first shot. It's like medicine. I stay reserved as I'm still unsure of myself and this bearded fascination next to me. More and more I want to escape to my safe haven—the basketball court. The lurking stage, just beyond my shared room, has me gazing, visualizing, and contemplating its lines and spaces. The court is becoming my comfort zone, again.

Time passes. The days get shorter. Ed begins the arduous task of toughening me up. He routinely slaps the ball from my lap. His massive hands, like bear claws, coming down hard and careening the ball off the many sharp angles of my cumbersome hospital wheelchair.

He's relentless.

"Go get it."

The ball rests on the grass behind the end-line and rim.

"Keep your dribble," he insists. "Get it off your lap."

Frustration. Anger.

"Use your dribble to keep space from the defender."

Finally at the ball, I rifle a baseball pass back to him. I push through the grass with ego and purpose. Back on the court, I'm determined to not let big Ed swipe the ball from me.

I come at him with the ball. I veer to my strong side (the right). He's way ahead of me and blocks my path before I can build momentum. He stops me—thus stopping the ball—a defensive standard. I bounce the ball and simultaneously free my hands to turn away from him. I gather the ball, successfully creating a bit of space to restart my attack. He teaches me this. Seeing an opening, I put the ball on my lap and accelerate.

I might have him.

Can I finish at the rim?

I begin to bring the ball to my outside hand (the left). Before I can, I feel Ed's claws and condor-like wingspan knocking the ball from my lap, up my chest, and off my outstretched arm.

We both know I need to keep my dribble and use my outside hand far more. This allows me to create space away from defenders with my inside hand, thus sneaking an accelerating push with both hands whilst executing a speed dribble.

I know what's coming next.

Ed doesn't disappoint.

With a calm so opposite of his actions, I hear the three familiar words, "Go get it."

DARKEST BEFORE DAWN

Keep my mind from constant turning
towards the things I cannot see

— Jesse Colin Young

I have a rare weekend pass.

I'm high. My girl can't handle the wheelchair, much less the body jacket strangling my core. She jumps ship. I don't blame her. I take another pull—another drink.

The blur of my new life begins to transition to a necessary numb.

A nifty blonde approaches. For whatever reason she's chasing her own blurry version of numb. Her breath smells like a house party, keg beer. She's teetering. Maybe we're a fit?

"Dave, I don't know how you do it," she stammers before resting her hand on my shoulder. "I think I'd probably kill myself."

Four months pass. I'm facing discharge. I'm consumed with fear over leaving what's become shockingly comfortable. I'm safe. How can I stay longer? Dad's hedging towards inevitable divorce. I tell mom, I'm 'okay' staying longer. The day comes. Jailbreak. Maybe they've lost the keys. I'm lesser than I feel. I'm overtly self-conscious. I'm dependent on others. Am I a freak? I look handicapped. I am disabled. I eye Rancho in the rear view. I keep thinking, *now what. Now what?* I sink deeper and deeper as each mile passes. The wheels spiral east to west. I fall deeper into what's darker.

I watch my legs atrophy. Disgust. Humiliation. I'm a fourth-grader again. Bedpans and urinals the tools of recovery.

I sit in my parent's home, looking out the back window. Sleeping has become a task full of pain and haunting distractions. I have six weeks left in this body jacket. God knows how long before I drive. What are my limits? Drive what? I have no ride. My brothers sold my car. What is money if I'm stuck?

I am fading. There is absence of light.

These are the forces of darkness.

Sitting in my parents' home after discharge from Rancho and rehab…lost in my thoughts, unsure and fearful.

WHEELS

Life is like a wheel. Sooner or later
it comes around to where you started.

— Stephen King

Leaving Rancho means many things. Grace, grit, and graciousness are in demand. The act of appearing comfortable, confident—even when inside churns frustration and angst—has me in a foreign and counterproductive mindset. Transitioning thoughts into words and meaning is sobering. I'm a stranger in the most familiar of settings. Confidence is crucial. I have some. I need more.

One of my Rancho roommates has a chair for sale. Recovering from a severe neck injury, he's one of the rare chosen ones that leaves Rancho walking. I buy his Stainless Wheelchair for fifty bucks.

As the legs continue to atrophy, the body jacket finally comes off. My spine is robust, strong, and able to absorb rotations, twists, and the teeth-rattling, side-to-side contact of on-court competition.

My core needs help. The months in the body jacket necessitate surgical fusion healing. My unused mid-section is dramatically weakened.

The rare moments of bliss are subtle but lasting. To finally feel a favorite, perfectly worn, cotton t-shirt is a luxury fully appreciated and cherished. It's the little things.

I turn to the boys in the neighborhood to chop my new chair. First to go are the removable side guards. Then we chop the push handles. I do not need any unwanted pity or help. Gone. We take a hacksaw to the seat, back-posts. Gone. I have only a few inches of back support. Less is more. Less looks tougher. Less strengthens my core.

I eye the revamped Stainless.

My wheels are a statement of personality and independence. She's streamlined, tough looking, and more in line with my shifting self.

The more I start to move, the more things begin to change.

I push the prolonged boardwalks of Newport and Huntington Beach. Tanned, shirtless, and with hair halfway down my back, the distances travelled became an inner-game of chase. I inwardly revel when passing joggers, find increased hand-speed when overtaken by balloon-tired, beach-cruising, bikini babes, and nod approvingly to the gawkers downing pints of beer.

The surfers give respect. The jocks a stunned, questioning, trying-to-put-it-together silence. Girls smile this wondering glance that speaks of bravery I've yet, but will soon, find.

Minus the confines of the body jacket, I'm free to discover the details of pushing, coasting, accelerating, tight-turning, and, most importantly, stopping. The sun off my shoulders reminds me I am in it. I am making this time mine.

Southern California is the epitome of car culture society. There's tremendous pride in brand, size motor, custom paint, and tires. It's 1973 and American steel is king.

After a month of bumming rides, pushing hundreds of coastal miles and yearning for freedom, dad takes me to the local Dodge dealer. It's the dad thing to do: accommodating, good-hearted, and compassionate. On the flipside, it's the most turbulent time of my parents' marriage. His drinking is followed by more drinking until the eventual nightly drama creates a scene of ugliness and regret.

We careen down Harbor Boulevard to the dealer. These days dad is driving an Oldsmobile Toronado. A statement and direction away from marriage and family.

Dad's been drinking. He immediately gets into it with the manager. He's a slick, salesman-type that irritates. Concoct this with my drunk-since-noon old man, and the sparks are destined to fly.

They do.

My dad moves on the guy.

He's not having it and reaches for his coffee.

This is where dad makes people pay.

Not today.

He's too deep into Mr. Booze.

The coffee hits him flush in the face.

Dad brushes the heat and coffee stain off his smirking mug.

He's in no condition to reply.

I'm so embarrassed.

I feel paralyzed.

Nonetheless, I pick it up a couple days later.

It's mine: a '73, fire orange, Dodge panel van.

The Flaherty brothers, Kevin and Brian, from the neighborhood, are the next piece of the puzzle. They convert this empty shell of a van into a cozy, comfortable bedroom on wheels.

First, they build cabinets over the wheel wells on both sides for needed storage. Then, they cut knotty, dark wood to panel the side and back doors and hang a tapestry covering the ceiling.

I don't know if we burnt one too many joints or I'm living in blind faith. I give the go ahead to cut a hole in the back roof and insert a small air-vent. I open and close the vent with a rotating handle.

It's the seventies, and orange vans require gold and shag carpeting. We lay four-inches of foam beneath the shag for extra cushion on my tush. A nod of the cap to my Vietnam brothers riding gurneys whilst waiting for their sores to heal.

Not me. Not me. Not me. Never me.

Next, the legendary, Irish Catholic brothers lay a piece of plywood in the back, off the floor, behind the storage cabinets and wheel wells. A raised bed is created with a four-inch mattress and fitted sheet. My sleeping bag stows in the cabinets nicely as well as my big, zebra-striped pillows.

There's only the driver's and passenger seat. I add a bean bag for more seating and comfort. The bed is another passenger option. Safety and seat belts—forget it.

The boys add tangerine, island-friendly curtains, covering the side and back windows. Then, a sun roof.

The Flaherty brothers are confident, cocky even. They tear into the roof of my new van with a saw that sounds like a thousand dogs barking off-key. I watch in terror. It all works. A window of plexiglass is hinged into place. To open the sunroof, I must unhinge the window and bring it inside.

Black lights and lava lamps; a hippie home on wheels.

I have it all.

My love, peace, and happiness van with Mater Dei High School friends.

THE GIANT MENTOR

They call him the Great One.
— The Peanut Gallery

With Ed there is no task too small. His philosophy requires a stamina to go-over-again a skill-set until it's routine.

Opponents do not take the ball from me. I don't allow it. Ed teaches me this.

No one contributes more to wheelchair basketball than Ed Owen.

Many today don't know who Ed Owen is. Memories of the greats of his time die with those of the time he played.

It's a travesty but also true of the genuine, gentle gift of Ed.

Michael Jordan, Diana Taurasi, and Wilt Chamberlain are all-time greats and celebrated with shrines in the Hall of Fame, but more importantly, they're a product of leagues, publicists, and a revenue stream that broadcasts their achievements for prosperity and profit.

My game statistics last as long as the scorebooks kept by wives and little brothers are tossed in the trash bin. Once the production of sport-specific wheelchairs becomes profitable, there are image and financial opportunities. Wheelchair basketball never grasps the urgency and historical importance of its numbers in explaining its greatest performers.

Ed puts up big numbers, but more than everything, he's a teacher. This separates him from other greats in the game. He dominates any time he pleases. He defends and scores in the post but just as easily runs the ball at the point. I marvel at his athleticism. I then am enraged as Ed takes time from the action. He's giving pointers to an opponent on how to better set a pick or the defensive angles needed not to get picked.

I'm driven to demolish and win at any cost.

It's not until decades later that I understand Ed's level of care for a game he so loves. Only by making those around him better does the product progress into something greater. Ed inherently knows this.

I can never fully emulate his unique on-court gifts during the tug and war of competition. I'm just not wired that way. I want those involved to feel, hear, fear and memorize me dominating the game.

Ed's example of compassion and caring for others is a constant reminder to be a more grateful warrior and competitor. Ed is in me. I'm better for it.

I'm not mature enough to fully understand the layers of sport and life that Ed is introducing me to. I'm having fun and more importantly distracted from the dark, twisted, and dominating thoughts still circling.

The electric motor and gears of the lift ascend me up and into the rear of the hospital van. Ed then straps my wheels to the tie-downs before using a pulley and ratchet system to sturdy the chair.

Feels demeaning, gimpy, and small.

I hate it.

Ed's team, the Santa Ana Raiders, is competing against the Los Angeles Stars.

It's my first time beyond Rancho. There might have been an occupational therapy trip to the market, but that's Rancho extending its walls into the adjoining community. We're headed into the pulse of Los Angeles.

We pull into the parking lot. Ed tosses me a jersey. Instantly the competitive vibe is recognizable.

I have no idea what I'm in for. Still in the body jacket, never practiced with anyone but Ed, and in absolute awe of a world beyond Rancho, I push towards the familiar sounds of whistles, buzzers, frenzied communication and action of the game.

Widney High School is the home of the Stars. A cracker box court just off a parking lot full of custom-painted vans, chromed sedans, and Detroit-made, American-designed, early seventies, hard and true steel.

First impression on entering: speed, more speed, lots of speed, and afros. The Stars, with David Efferson, Calvin Young, and sharp shooting Manny Villa, execute with an urgency and pace that highlights athleticism and a touch of arrogant brashness.

The Stars' boisterous fans are either brown or black.

The power of sport personified. I'm in.

The sharp-dressed brother always observing, taking studious notes, is Hall of Famer, Leroy Ransom. Throughout my playing days, I often observe what we call "Leroy sightings." If I'm competing abroad or up the coast in Oakland, Leroy is either coaching the Stars to championship games or up in the rafters at USA competitions. Leroy loves basketball.

Late in the game, Ed puts me in.

It's a simpler time. There are no complaints about playing against a guy in a body jacket. I don't think I'm even on the official roster.

I'm Ed's boy and that's all the collateral I need.

Memory is a funny thing through the decades. There are certain and succinct moments that last a lifetime.

It's my only shot attempt in the game.

I receive the ball in a crowd.

No time to think.

There's traffic but also space.

I let the mid-range fly, like a million times before.

It drops.

The kid in me wants to celebrate but I sense this is the first of many clashes with and against these men.

I play it cool and hustle back on defense.

First road trip: 1974. One-year-post from the Harvey Wallbangers, multiple bad decisions, and snow tubing debacle. Ed's riding shotgun. My new van is orange and screams of misdeeds, but allows me to pull my chair in whole, before climbing into the driver's seat.

The Denver team is good but we're really good. Ed, Bobby Murdoch, Steve Javier, and myself have the Santa Ana Raiders on the proverbial map. We're building momentum each time we take the court. We handle business and beat the Denver boys on the Saturday of a two-game trip. That evening is my first night in a hotel. Way cool. The rest of the team gathers in our room and the adjoining room.

We party.

Ed disappears.

Ed is not a drinker and is known for drinking litres of Pepsi in a single setting. Tonight, he drinks a bottle of wine to himself.

I can't find him. I'm in the hall. I check the lobby. He's my roommate. I search the parking garage. Nothing.

Out of ideas, I check the bathroom. There he is.

The Great One, as he is known by the boys on the team, is laid out in a bathtub unable to maintain his 6' 10" frame.

I know I need to be compassionate, thoughtful, and kind to this man that has done so much for me. Instead, I call in the boys. We laugh until our eyes take on salt and our sides hurt. Ed and I are in the minority of a team filled with Vietnam vets. I feel the brotherhood of a group that has a doctrine on the subject.

Basketball on the road is special like that. Everything I'm experiencing is through a new, more profound lens. Ed and the Vets know I have the skills to help the team win more games than previously known. I know Ed and the Vets are teaching me, through glorious and ridiculous examples, how to be a man.

Ed is a motorcycle guy.

There's no reason not for him to ride one—except that he uses a wheelchair to play basketball. Your basketball chair is your everyday chair and vice-versa in the 1970s. The days of sports chairs are decades away.

Ed rides a BMW bike. His adaptations include a mini sissy-bar behind the bench seat. Welded on, the sissy-bar is a hook big enough for a folded wheelchair. It's decided there's room for a second.

I know all I have to do is ask.

Ed lives on the peninsula of Newport Beach, directly across from Balboa Island and its ferry. His apartment is up a healthy flight of stairs. I climb the wooden steps often. Anyone that lives in Southern California knows, a friend with a place in Newport is a friend indeed. We traverse the numerous outdoor courts: working on skills, adding shooting range, battling one-one-one, and often just hanging out. Other times I break away and enjoy the beach's boardwalk and numerous watering holes.

There's chatter of a pick-up game at the Long Beach Veterans Administration (VA). Most recently, Ed's added a fabricated camber block to my stainless frame. The block adds about two-degrees of camber, increasing stability and turning radius.

The Long Beach Flying Wheels are a top team and legendary program. I'm up for all takers and challenges.

"How 'bout I ride with you?" I ask.

"To Long Beach?"

Ed nods his approval.

I want the experience because it's with Ed.

My feet rest comfortably on a small platform instead of pegs. We load a second chair—my chair—on the sissy bar.

Ed hits the throttle. I hang on to him with a bear hug. We wear helmets even though it's not the law of the time. My initial and overriding thought? *Whatever you do, don't fall off. Stay on the bike. Stay on the bike.*

Ed and I at his wedding in Vermont in the '70s, and I am proudly his best man.

Here I am, close to a year post, on the back of this BMW. What would mom think?

Ed's conservative with speed. After winding through Newport and Costa Mesa we hit the entrance of Interstate 405 heading north. Ed keeps it in the slow lane. I'm fine with the strategy. As I begin to finally look up, I'm able to take in the shock and awe of those sharing the freeway with us.

Folks know Vietnam permanently injured too many, but any disability awareness or accessibility advancements are non-existent. I understand completely this is a defining moment.

I puff out my skinny-ass chest in elation. I can do anything. I wish Ed would go faster.

It's 1976. I'm living, and going to college at Cal State–Sacramento, earning a degree in Therapeutic Recreation. I love my time in Sacramento. I'm beginning to figure my place in the order of things.

Sacramento—its rivers (the American and Sacramento) flow through the capital city with an ease that calms. Tractors and farmers regularly slow traffic whilst crop dusters work the low-bearing horizon.

I have near free reign of the college's gym for shooting and chair skill sessions. Ed and I make the Paralympic team. The games are in Toronto. I'm 22-years old and playing in my first games. It's hard to imagine that a mere three years ago my world was tossed upside down, landing me on these wheels that I'm slowly learning to be at peace with.

We drive/road trip from California to Eastern Canada. My orange, 1973 Dodge panel van: side windows and curtains, sunroof, padded shag carpet, and a bed built on top of cabinets is the custom build needed for such a pilgrimage.

I garner the needed help in building a two-wheel trailer to store gear and create space in the van. The trailer is rough in construction but strong in character. *California to Canada or Bust* is painted on each side. We're comfortable and cheerful in my burnt orange, "peace and love" van. We take turns sleeping on the platform bed in the back whilst the other drives the miles.

The road and its intersecting highways are a glimpse into the decades to come, churning the expanse of a country—the world, chasing competition.

We have "ball on the brain," talking strategies and details throughout the trip. Somewhere around the Rocky Mountains, I realize Ed has taught me every important fundamental the game has to offer.

I look back at his long frame sleeping in the back and hit the gas.

We head due east for Detroit.

There's a stop in Denver and a night in Sioux Falls, South Dakota, with my grandparents.

Finally, in Detroit, we stay with Hall of Fame coach, Bud Rumple. He's the coach of Team USA and winner of seven national championships. The Detroit Sparks' coach opens his home to us. We train outdoors in the neighborhoods of Detroit for close to a week. Some courts have rims with no nets. Others have the chain nets. It's rough. It's Detroit.

Close friends Joe Thorn and Vince Edson road-trip the country to meet us in Detroit. The two feed their own addiction to the game. Afterwards they follow us into Toronto as fans, friends, and support system.

The street battles with Joe, Vince, and an assortment of Sparks players is the sublime preparation needed. I burn through tires I can't afford to replace but it's a freeing time to just be in the moment. I'm with dudes who need only a ball, hoop, and an afternoon.

Perfection is where you find it.

It's time to point the van towards Toronto. The unknown of crossing the border and navigating a thriving metro like Toronto is a pending and daunting adventure. Joe and Vince follow us beyond the border.

We pull into the basketball venue. The games are branded as the Toronto Olympiad for the Physically Disabled and the first Paralympic Games to be held in the Americas.

We're driving home from Toronto. It's been a good trip.

Ed and I lead the USA in scoring in the final against Israel. Baruch Hagai, along with Ed, are the best players in the world. Baruch is a heady player with a deadly touch. He carries the Israeli squad to the gold medal game. I take a charge from Baruch late in the game. It's his fifth. He's gone. We never look back. Gold Medal. Best in the world.

U.S.A. 59, ISRAEL, 49
By Bill Dampier

The two U.S. basketball stars in action. Ed Owen (left) and his protege David Kiley. Between them hey scored two-thirds of the U.S. teams total points.

I also compete on the track during the Toronto games. It's a crazy ride, as I've entered four events: the 100 & 800 meters and two relays with some very fast California boys. I'm constantly shuttling between the track and hardwood.

I'm too young to understand the meaning of things. I'm just doing my thing.

I'm fast on the track and lucky enough to be influenced by some of the greatest: Gary Kerr, Rod Williams, and Steve Kerr. We compete in the Cal Games and Nationals leading up to the Paralympic Games. Our relays are legendary. Two golds.

In the 100 meters, I'm head-to-head with the fastest man alive, Ray Lewandowski. Ray hadn't lost a 100-meter race in over a year. He has beat me throughout the season. I use the first chair with smaller push rings in the event.

In the final, Ray tears off the line for the lead. My top-end speed kicks in around the 50-meter mark, and I pass him to set a world record. I'm the fastest in the world.

Five paralympic events. Five gold medals.

It's my turn to drive.

Ed pulls the van over.

I think of all my new world goals. Somehow, somewhere the door to it all springs, wide open.

"Thanks," I say.

Ed grabs his Pepsi litre.

"Thanks for everything."

Ed is tired. He retires to the platform bed.

I careen my orange Dodge back onto the highway.

The Great One sleeps in hard-earned peace.

SACTO

The beginning is always today.
– Mary Shelley

Southern California is a true love.

A place I'll always return to.

A place that is family and home.

I bask in its unabashed sunlight. The times of routine or mundane are persistently outweighed in the sublime of light, wind, and waves off the Pacific, the eye-popping clarity of snow atop Mount Baldy on a crisp, clean winter's day and the simple neighborhood stroll past palm trees, desert cacti, and healing, swollen Aloe Vera blooms.

Ninety-five times out of a hundred, these snapshots of time pass unnoticed. We're on our way to what's next. We're in a hurry without knowing exactly why. There's also the five times per hundred where time settles. I'm able to feel and see my surroundings.

I'm as brown as the wood of the many tendered fences. Stubbornness, perseverance, and discovering a newer, authentic sense of self allow freedom of thought—free will. I begin to make good decisions to combat the impulsive ones. Today, my thoughts are not of what others think or perceive.

I am slowly healing.

I finish my time at Orange Coast Community College with an Associate of Arts degree. The two-year program fulfils most of my core class obligations to any four-year university across the country. I remember watching the great John Vallely shoot the lights out of the OCC gym as a kid. Vallely transferred to a tremendous academic and sporting career at UCLA.

What am I capable of?

What is my capacity?

My time with the Raiders is brilliant. During my first season we finish the regular season undefeated, only to lose in the national championship game to Curtis Bell (much more on him later) and the Indianapolis Mustangs in an excruciating overtime.

Santa Ana and the Raiders is a gravitational pull that drives. Basketball is life as a high-schooler. I traverse the streets of Santa Ana and the halls of Mater Dei like only a teenage athlete can. Then to meet the *Great One*. For a while we are invincible: Ed, myself, and the Vietnam Veterans. The Santa Ana Raiders reignites a spark to a game I was moving away from. The wheels beneath my ass are less a sentence of time and choices. They're a vehicle. I'm a defining competitor. I'm a willing passenger.

It's during this time with the Raiders that I also meet Bob and Sharon Murdock. I'm at the cusp of my teenage years and am needing to be more of a man than a grown kid. Bob, one of the many Vietnam veterans in my life, is rendered a paraplegic in the conflict. He's a seasoned and quality baller with an approachable and fun-loving side. His wife, Sharon, is a redheaded firecracker. Quick with witty retorts, I learn early on it's best to stay on her good side.

Without fully understanding why, I lean into them to better understand the many facets of life in the chair. Their marriage is playful and affectionate. Sharon's love for Bob is transparent. She wants the world to see he is her man. Their big, ranch style home in Villa Park becomes my second home. A peaceful place to rest and be. They clear a room for me. It becomes my room. There is a feeling of belonging. A coveted space to ask, pry, and question the dump-truck of thoughts surrounding this new life upon me.

Their daughter, Toni and I, are friends to this day. Toni goes on and marries Gerry Lopez, the King of the Pipeline. The most influential surfer of his time and a legend. Bob and Sharon pass before their time. Toni, and I, reminisce the precious memories of them with laughter, delight, and a sadness that eventually transcends to joy. The stories continue. The time Bob and I caravan down to Mazatlán, Mexico, on a guy's trip. Our friends in both our custom vans either hanging out of windows or sun roofs, full of questionable ideas and misguided intentions.

The drive down the sunshine coast of California and Mexico is a crystal memory typical of Bob's independent choices without limits.

Bob and Sharon Murdock are a distinct spark that drive me towards what the world has on offer.

It's all bigger than me.

I am my own compass.

It's time for the next move.

The move to Sacramento is logical. California State University of Sacramento (Sac State) offers a degree in Therapeutic Recreation. Their Recreation curriculum is recognized nationwide. I look to do for others what Ed did for me. Couple that with two competitive, wheelchair basketball teams in the capital city and I am a man making a move.

Any good-byes are dwarfed in the anticipation of riding into the unknown.

Costa Mesa to Sacramento is a seven-to-eight hour ride up Highway 99. Once you're up and over the engine-boiling Grapevine and begin careening down its backside, you are leaving Southern California and that way of life behind you. If you make a left towards San Luis Obispo and San Francisco, the days and nights remain familiar in the ocean, nightlife, and culture. Stay in the valley and you're living in dust, combines, and trucker-tans. The Central and Northern California valley remind me just how big and diversified the state is. Past Bakersfield and headed north, things expand: ranchers, cattle, slaughter houses, garlic fields, orange groves, rice farms, cantaloupe orchards, and vegetable crops offer honest pay and laborious days.

I am an example of a wing and a prayer. Not sure where to live initially, I sack out in a teammate's spare room. This has his wife less than thrilled. The night I bring home a dog seals my fate. I begin looking for new accommodations.

Enter the Aguilera family and Vietnam Vet, David Aguilera. The Aguilera family is a big reason I chose to play for the Capital Cagers instead of the more established (and proven winner) Sacramento Athletic Club. David's father is the team's General Manager and offers up his house as an introductory solution. There are nights I sleep with David in the family's California King size bed. There are also many nights I choose to sleep in my van or on the couch of any willing teammate.

There's a failed attempt to live in the Aguileras' back yard in a small trailer. There's an outdoor shower and bathroom for my most primitive needs. It doesn't work out.

Yet, I love my time in Sacramento.

My teammates are predominantly Latino or Black. They're tough and from the streets. Again, I am amongst a variety of Vietnam Vets. They accept me—the new hippie, white-boy kid that can play. We become tight and these just-tell-me-what-to-do, role playing teammates love to play ball. No job is too small or too dirty. I teach them what I know. The things I learned from the Great One.

More than a few of the Cagers are gunshot victims. They are also familiar with guns themselves. During one game and fracas, teammate Gus hits the floor after a sturdy hit from an opponent. From under his cushion a gun falls and slides across the half-court line. Once things are tidied up, the game proceeds. I am not in lily-white, Costa Mesa anymore.

They tell stories of nights in their custom, conversion vans where they fire shots over the top of their rival's vehicles.

"Pow."

"Pow."

"Pow," says Big G, mimicking his pistol with his thumb and gun-finger.

It's exciting being with this team/crowd. It stretches me in ways I hadn't anticipated.

An in-town rivalry quickly develops between us and the Sacramento Athletic Club. The all-white Athletic Club are used to chalking up wins against the Cagers. They are none too happy the long-haired hippie and his dark-skinned brothers/amigos are challenging them for turf rights and league honors. The games are rough, smack-talking throw-downs in front of boisterous, home-cooking crowds that are decent in size and large in volume. I grow to love these games.

I begin to understand Sacramento with all its beauty and allure. I start salmon fishing on the American River. I drive the hour and a half to San Francisco for the sights and smells of a city and its cultural jackpots. I spend days at a time in Lake Tahoe to ponder the depths of an unexplainable lake and its high-altitude peaks and summits.

A professor calls me into her office. I've missed a few classes and she wants an answer. I'm mature enough (in an immature way) to tell her, "I learn by doing. I live it." I pass her class and all the others to earn my degree.

I use the university's basketball courts as my personal work space. The long hours with the ball, in such a rarefied, personal space remind me of home and Saint John's the Baptist. Volume shooting, long hours visualizing success through repetition and preparation. I'm an original. I revel in the knowledge and growth of being unique, but I'm also grounded in the truth of success. *Coach John Wooden calls it Industriousness. The first foundational block in his pyramid of success.*

I call it hard, damn work.

I enjoy getting away from the city lights, and venturing into the foothills of the Sierra Nevada. Quirky, country towns like Auburn, Applegate, Meadow Vista, and Grass Valley offer quiet and solitude. These towns pitch a backdrop of hippies, cowboys, red-necks, and peace pipes. Folks get along because within their differences is the commonality of working the land for crops, family, and community. They do it well. They do it with respect for one another.

When I head east from Sacramento, it's easy to access off-road trails just off Highway 50. I eventually find a cabin in Diamond Springs to live in. My new home is in the foothills of Placerville. Although the trek to school and practice is close to an hour, the serenity of living *away from it all* is something I begin to cherish. Living outside the city limits of Sacramento also puts me in range of Lake Tahoe. A one-of-a-kind blessing.

After my first year up north, I sell my custom orange Dodge van to aforementioned Gary Kerr and I purchase a 4-wheel drive Plymouth Trail Duster. The red and white beast sits me high above what's below. I'm able to stand, lift my chair above the tailgate, load in the rear, before bracing myself against the truck, and steadfastly side-shuffling to the driver's side to my seat. This is a new move and one I'll consistently use throughout my days. Most importantly, the Trail Duster is big and bold. The gold rush foothills become my playground, and essential reset time.

I'm not a rookie anymore. I'm leading a team and program. In our first year the wins mount but the losses are predictable. Passion, hustle, and heart are integral but also have limits. We need a big man with a nasty side that can defend and score. We need additional talent.

Like myself, Joe Thorn is taught by Ed Owen. A student of the game's fundamentals, Joe's sublime moves in the post help generate the needed space to score consistently. Most importantly Joe is tough, big, and enjoys flexing his muscles inside. Joe Thorn is also a well drilled marksman at the free-throw line. He fits in perfectly with a team that prides itself on a recipe of intimidation, unity, and performance. He is welcomed to the Cagers with open arms.

The Cagers take over the turf war in Sacramento. The Athletic Club cannot keep up with us. Joe gives us the needed easy looks at the rim. The percentages of upsetting us are slim to none. The boys know how to get Joe to his post spots. I drop the ball to him on a dime from all angles and depths from anywhere on the court.

We begin to travel across state lines to compete. The Aguileras barnstorm the community for support: car washes, tamale and garage sales, cookie and cake bakes. Mamma Aguilera makes her own tortillas—deliciousness. Her kitchen intrigues me, and she teaches me the basics in the making of menudo soup. The Mexican concoction of protein, vegetables, and beans become a staple in my diet.

Within our newfound travels we befriend the Mexican National Team. We meet up with them in Sacramento and Southern California. The games are lively, Spanish speaking affairs. Elbows are sharp, pointy, and full of defying glares. When the games are over, I often ride the Mexican team bus working on my broken Spanish. I love this time together. We laugh, reliving highlights of games and pivotal plays. We toast one another with the knowledge that when we're between the lines—it's all business.

The first year playing with Joe is memorable.

Our sectional and final four qualifying tournament is at De Anza Junior College in Cupertino, California. The Cagers are a wild card. We're a team with a fighter's chance but not much else. The Los Angeles Stars have speed, size, and sharpshooters. They are heavy favorites to advance from the western sectional to Cleveland and the final four.

The Stars lose in the semi-final to a young, Albert Campos led, Long Beach Flying Wheels. We haven't beaten the Stars all year and to see them lose gives myself and my upstart teammates a kick of confidence to do what only we imagined.

We're quicker than the Flying Wheels and play with an aggressive balance of post and perimeter play. Joe and I get hot early. My guys don't allow me to get double-teamed with constant cross picks and rubs. Whenever Long Beach starts to build momentum, Joe hits a mid-range, a pair of free-throws, or one of his patented post-ups. I knock down some daggers from deep at pivotal points and use my dribble-drive to get to the rim in transition.

We win a tight one.

I remember Long Beach coach, Bill Johnson, lambasting his troops—with volume and anger, "You just got beat by three monkeys, a gorilla, and one real player."

We revel in his shocking displeasure.

The National Wheelchair Basketball Association (NWBA) has to recognize us: the Capital Cagers. We upset the best in the west and are a final four contender.

The Aguilera family works double-time in raising funds to get us airfare and lodging for Cleveland and the final four. It's a beg, borrow, and steal approach that looks more like Girl Scouts selling cookies than an elite sports team looking to make history. Yet, in a mere two weeks the funds are raised.

We open against the Richmond Rim Riders. Tom Brown is one of the best shooters the game has ever seen. Carl Cash, Pat Killeen, and Jimmy May round out a super-four lineup. All are future Hall of Fame awardees.

The strategy is to shut down Cash, Killeen, and May. Tom Brown will get his, but if we can minimize opportunities for others, we'll be able to wear them down. Our Cager soldiers work the game plan, never stretching their limits. They know their roles and do their jobs.

Joe Thorn blasts off with double-digit rebounds and a 33-point effort. I stuff the stat sheet with a triple-double (double-digit numbers in points, rebounds, and assists). We stay the path and play with a trust of one another that is years beyond our time together. The Cagers are in the final.

Music City (Nashville) advances in the other semi-final, beating the Detroit Sparks. Bud Rumples' Sparks are yearly favorites to take the title. Beating Long Beach in the round previous has us confident and ready to perform. The titans of the time are not advancing like in the years previous.

Is this our time?

Are we a titan?

Music City is formidable. They're led by Roger Davis, a long-range shooter without peer and fellow Hall of Fame teammates, Willie Buchanan, Dickie Bryant, and Norman McGee. The depth coming off the benches is dramatically different. Music City substitutes really good players with playoff experience whilst our bench only goes a couple deep with willing but inexperienced warriors.

The day before, Joe Thorn is the probable MVP choice of the tournament with his 33-point game. Twenty-four hours later, Willie Buchanan and the depth of Music City does a number on Joe. He finishes the championship game with 2 points. Without brother Joe's numbers, I pick up the slack with added shots, possessions, and points. We're in it midway through the second half but the Nashville squad begins to pull away. We lose the game. Music City is crowned the national champions.

Pain. Anguish. Misery. Torment.

I love playing with Joe and feel his highs and lows like they are my own.

Three final-fours in the past four years and no championships. The previous two against Hall of Famer Curtis Bell and the Indianapolis Mustangs. This one is more difficult to take. The Aguileras, Joe, and the gritty toughness of the Sacto boys makes an authentic group. The yellow brick road is aligned for us but still we come up short. There's an overbearing weight on my competitive spirit that only time can heal.

The celebration continues. Music City, and its Nashville tribe, clanging cowbells and cutting down nets. The time is theirs.

I look away from my teammates long enough to eye (again) the pretty girl. She's ringing her cowbell, just like she did during my free throws. After my second make(s), I chose not to give her the *take that* look— that's a trademark for anyone who has the nit-witted gall to think they can distract me from my objective.

Who is this girl?

Capitol Cagers upset their way to the National Championship game. I met the scorekeeper who became my wife shortly after. I'm riding a square tubed welded chair I had made. The wheelchair revolution was just around the corner.

My home boys.

81

THE PRIZE

Once in a blue moon someone like you comes along.

— Van Morrison

I'm the new kid on the block. I've just marked my turf in front of a discerning old guard, less than thrilled, or willing, to recognize what's next. To them, I'm a head-band and blonde long-hair more than a progressive, next-generation talent. The younger crowd supports me. They see in me, a version of themselves. Vietnam has done a number on our country. We're far from the saviours of the great wars previous. Guys looking like me personify change. Guys looking like me, that can play, transform programs, and do it all with statements and flare. I'm reframing what folks hold dear. It's a wow moment, but also a breaking of traditional norms that carries the weight of change.

The NWBA awards banquet is the first time I cross paths with Tim Nugent. The large room is filled with Wheel Heads, friends, families, and coaches. There's a sublime chatter/buzz filling the air. Tim and his wife Jeanette introduce themselves.

It won't be until years later that I fully understand Tim Nugent's ground-breaking contributions to accessibility and disability sport.

Tim Nugent introduced disabled World War II veterans to higher learning at the University of Illinois. He used the GI bill and government-assistance programs to cover their academic expenses. In David Davis' book, *Wheel of Courage,* Nugent says, "I realized very quickly…that they needed more than clinical therapy and more than counselling—they needed an opportunity to be alive and to sense a feeling of achievement and belongingness. Sports helped them to overcome self-consciousness and it helped to develop self-confidence on the part of the individual with a disability. Why have a bicep if there is no use for it?"

The Nugents are warm and respectful. I think they see in me a positive change to what I now understand is the resolute, and life-changing game of basketball on wheels.

I exit the periphery of the Nugent's; I'm exiting a source of history and knowledge.

There she is. The cowbell girl.

I'm enamoured with her looks from my Cager's table of hoodlums and teammates. I attempt to find her gaze at the Music City table. Nothing as of yet. I take a good pull from the bottle—old school liquid courage — and move towards what was the enemy lines just hours previous. Without talking to her directly yet, I learn more about her. Her brother is Mitch Stephens, from the Nashville team. Interesting.

She's the scorekeeper for the team.

I probe further with an official (but awkward) introduction.

"Hi," I stammer trying to remain somehow cool. "I'm Dave."

"Sandy," she responds.

We exchange words.

Her smile is perfect. She has a sense of humor. Sexy.

Minutes, hours, or moments later, the evening moves to the awards segment. Time is lost. I'm forced to retreat back to my boys and the Cager table. We're called on stage for second place recognition. My brothers in arms hit the stage. I'm proud to be their comrade, and seeing them on the stage reminds me just how much we've achieved—but bottom-line, second place sucks.

The national champs are announced and called to the stage.

She's with them.

Her eyes lock on mine. We share a smile/smirk.

The night continues. I want first team all-tournament. Always have. Always will. I think of all the hours training with Joe. All the neighborhoods—the rough ones more memorable in sight and sounds. We shot free throws for hours in our attempts to make a hundred in a row. I chase the goal for decades. It's not until I'm 60 years old that I knock down a hundred straight. The game has its own sense of humor.

My name is called. I'm first team all-tourney. Yes.

MVP is next. I wonder which member of Music City will pick up the award? My name is called instead. I head back to the stage to collect this surprise award. It's not that I don't feel I deserve it, but we lost. They won.

I take a couple photos. I again look her way. I give her my best cheeky, *cowbell* look.

She smiles straight into me.

The evening loosens its grip. No more awards, vegetables next to meat, or distant gazes. Combatants become drinking buddies, and coaches mingle amongst one another. I fit in many of these expanding circles but not tonight.

The band thumps the sounds of the late seventies, lots of Boston, Aerosmith and Steely Dan. The wheel-heads are dancing. Weird and uncomfortable. Still, I make my way to her and ask for a dance. It's a slow one. Even weirder.

She sits on my lap. Both the Cagers and Music City look on.

Dickie Bryant from Nashville likens himself to a ball-hawking Cupid. He's annoying, comical, and boisterous simultaneously.

All the feelings are floating in my head. I go with it. I'm a glorious passenger. She seems to take in the world with a glance.

The band stops.

I accompany her to her room. She sits on my lap. The first kiss. Some more—and then some more. I desperately want into her room. Not going to happen. She plays it as cool as it's supposed to be.

One more parting kiss. Her smile and eyes melt.

I stop for a second, look at her for a beat, just in case she changes her mind.

Doesn't happen.

I roll away and down the long corridor, planning my next move. Psyched but sad.

We're headed in opposite directions. Nashville to Sacramento is separated by the Grand Canyon, Rocky Mountains, and Mississippi River.

I'm living a country western song.

Sandy after Cleveland Final Four and prior to proposing in 1978.

BETWEEN HELLO AND GOODBYE

Once we accept our limits, we can surpass them.

— Albert Einstein

A plan's motion is afoot.

John Chambers is a can't miss finisher, dead-eye perimeter marksman, and an early, outspoken advocate for disability rights. A conversation with John easily swings from politics, to baseball (and his beloved Dodgers), to the details of wheelchair basketball: chair positioning, holding and releasing off picks, shooting techniques, and drawing fouls. A bearded charmer, John's sharp banter is accompanied with quick and numerous pulls of cold beer.

John Chambers is a kindred spirit and a quality baller. The plan is for him to join the Cagers. Towards the end of our unlikely run to the championship game, John begins the move from southern to Northern California. During the off-season John moves in. The cabin in Diamond Springs suits him.

We take to a local place—*Poor Reds*. The rib-joint/bar is rustic and tiny. The owners take to us. Chairs are stacked and tables rearranged. We down their *gold rush* specialties—*Gold Cadillacs* with an easy anticipation. It feels good to be a regular within this hard-working, festive, and genuine community.

That summer, John and I put together a four-week adaptive sports camp on the Sac State campus. I pitch the adaptive camp to work alongside the National Youth Sports Camp (NYSC). The NYSC camp is a long-standing camp for able-bodied kids. Why not piggyback an adaptive camp? Inclusion in the name of sport. Perfect.

Things are in place: insurance meetings, curriculum, staffing, accessibility, meals, fees, emergency contacts, heat protocols, facilities, and transportation.

We are preparing (for what I believe is) a first-of-its-kind, junior, adaptive sports camp.

One of John's superpowers is overcoming obstacles. He does this his entire life for folks with disabilities. Across his career as a Recreation Specialist, he fights for accessibility long before George Bush, Sr. enacts the Americans with Disabilities Act and mandates nationwide accessibility in 1990.

During the summer of 1978, Californians vote in record numbers to pass Proposition 13. Prop. 13 lowers property taxes for homeowners. The state has been leaning on home owners for over a decade in the funding of schools, fire, police, and public transport. Folks are fed up. Property taxes double/triple as their housing values do the same. A modern-day gold rush but with a heavy cost. The collateral damage of it all—government services take a massive, seven-billion-dollar hit.

Half way through our four-week, ground breaking camp, public transportation bus drivers go on strike. They see the writing on the wall. Jobs and salaries are destined to be cut.

John and I scramble for a solution. Most of our kids are getting to camp via the city bus line. A tenderfoot at leading noteworthy events, I know enough to know panic is futile.

Leading by persistent representation and an inner desire is the John Chambers way. I'm a quick study. Without knowing it at the time, we're making history. Our camp is busting down the proverbial door.

Bus drivers, as much as I understand their frustration, are not going to deny these kids the possibilities that sport and our camp offers.

With some quick/jive talking, we hire transportation to collect the kids that are unable to get rides. The cost is substantial. We haggle for lower prices. We find the needed funds through budget shifting and tough decision cuts.

The camp doesn't miss a beat. We push limits and tap into the raw potential of our junior athletes.

John Chambers, an NWBA Hall of Fame Member, goes on to serve as the Governor's Council of Developmental Disabilities in Nevada. He serves on the boards of the California Wheelchair Athletic Association, the National Recreation and Park Association and the National Therapeutic Recreation Society.

John's example of service is not lost on me. I serve on the California Governor's Council on Disability in the nineties. I work alongside future Governor Arnold Schwarzenegger who is representing the Special Olympics, and Olympic decathlon gold medalist Rafer Johnson.

My mind is no match for my heart when it comes to the cowbell girl, Sandy Stephens.

I call her on rotary dial phones relentlessly. The three-hour time distance from Northern California to Tennessee often finds her father answering my after-dark, meddlesome calls. I'm the thin-necked, need-to-be-close-to-your-daughter, left coast protagonist that I fear this man has been waiting his entire days to pummel, embarrass, and ultimately dismiss.

Phone conversations aren't tracked by time but instead a measure of how accurately and completely I am able to convey my interest. I have an overbearing need to be in a place that is collectively ours.

Calls are tracked by duration back then. My phone bills are massive.

The summer following our initial awards night banquet flirtations and first kiss, I'm due to attend the National Wheelchair Games in Virginia. Western Virginia borders Tennessee. I fly to Nashville to meet her family. The two of us will then drive to Virginia and the National games.

Sandy's brother, Mitch Stephens (a champion table tennis competitor) and his gal Helen, also attend the games. Mitch and Helen go on to become husband and wife.

Time to meet her father.

A lightning bolt of fear hits me as I enter the downstairs entrance. I eye the family photos adjacent to the entrance. There he is. A head shot of Grover Stephens in his Army uniform. He personifies every would-be boyfriend's worst nightmare. In the photo he's stoic, serious, and unsmiling. Worse even, he's just around the corner.

Mr. Stephens is a mountain of a man, chiselled, and with a flat-top crew-cut. We shake hands.

Meet strength with strength. His shake is firm, as is mine. He looks me in the eye. I do my best—I'm pretending to be strong but inside I'm fading— approving nod. I return his look with one of my own.

There's a moment of silence. *Should I say something? I got nothing. Survive and advance. Survive and advance.*

He breaks the awkwardness, "Want a beer?"

My relief overflows. I look at Sandy. The reason. She understands the moment and meets it with a subtle grace I forever admire.

The rest of the family and siblings are straightforward, uncomplicated, and welcoming. Sandy's mother, Madonna, is as sweet as can be: Southern hospitality personified.

The next day's drive to Virginia is full of agreeable surprises. We take Sandy's BMW. She asks me to take the wheel. Driving her car is amazing. I realize, it's who's in the passenger seat, but after years of driving above-ground beasts of vehicles—to drive this reactive, German, road-hugging gem transforms. I captain the entire trip.

The games themselves are a bit of a blurry distraction from our time together.

I'm there to push the track. I'm entered in the 100-, 400-, 800- and 1,500- yard races. I'm also entered in a couple relays. It is the national games after all. I know I take home medals and enough of them are gold, but it's all secondary. The adoration of others is hazy, indistinct, and vague. Clarity and meaning are under construction continuously. It has nothing to do with how fast I can push a chair.

I'm taken aback and humbled at the event's banquet when I receive a recognition award. The junior camp that John and I create ripples enough wind of change to reach Virginia and the National games.

Our four-week camp is too long, takes an unfathomable amount of planning and energy and doesn't make its workers any money. It's full of drama but more than anything, we did it. At its highest levels, we're a stepping stone for the next generation's elite, adaptive athletes. In an everyday sense, we've helped build a bridge for youths into the world beyond bedroom walls and over supportive relatives.

Awards can be lip service but to be recognized at the National Wheelchair Games for the Sac State NYSP Junior Adaptive Camp exceeds. The levels are new. John and I work our tails off. To sit in that moment and share with Sandy my surprise and joy has a meaning not known before.

Grazing the guardrail with my Plymouth TrailDuster is a tell-tale sign.

The 4-wheel-drive truck absorbs the graze like a suggestive and handsome scar. No big deal. Yet, I'm distracted. She has my attention and focus. I'm lucky if I can laser in on anything when she's riding shotgun.

After Virginia, Sandy flies west for a nine-day whirlwind road trip/romance.

I show her Lake Tahoe (site of guard rail incident). It's a true wonder of the world. It needs to be shared, gawked at, respected, and is a shockingly stunning backdrop for intrigue and pleasure. I want her to see and feel the absolute best of my state.

Next is Yosemite National Park. Giant, ancient sequoia trees backdrop the granite cliffs of El Capitan and Half Dome. We take trails that literally have us amongst the clouds. We camp, creating fires as a source for cooking and warmth. Some nights we sleep under the stars whilst others we take to a makeshift bed in the back of the Trail Duster.

We then head south to meet my family and friends. Sandy comes from a large family and is able to absorb mine seamlessly. Mom approves, and my sister Sharon sees in Sandy a sister she's never had.

Even though, *this thing,* this love tornado is operating within its own torrent pace—as I'm showing off this southern beauty to everyone I can—time slows when we're *in it* together.

Heading into San Diego, we make our way to my aunt and uncle's. They live in Fallbrook. Avocado groves everywhere. Barb and Ted have always been such a positive influence in my life. I want them to see this version of me. Their connection is an example of togetherness. They welcome Sandy and me into their home for a meal. It's simple. It's warm. It's truly special.

Time to head north and back to Diamond Springs.

The central coast of California speaks to me. It's easy driving. Why exceed the speed limit? Time is a favor. Don't rush it. There's an ease to its wide-open spaces: farmers, cowboys/girls, surfers, hikers, wineries, and fishermen easily share what's massive, tranquil, and untamed. Morro Bay, Monterey, Carmel, and the giant Redwoods add to where I'm at and what I previously have only hoped to experience.

It's love.

I've rehearsed the question repeatedly.
Nauseous, nervous energy consumes.
Fear of rejection.
Real possibility.
Not a straightforward task.
Is anything these days?
Resolve.
Carry on.
I tell her I'm not sure I can have children.
I remember the doctor's voice like my own.
Family.
Paramount.
She sits on my bed.
My humble, rustic cabin fits.
Dark seasoned oak.
Warming quilts.
She reassures me.
She loves me.
I know it.
Enough already.
Say it.
Ask it.
A quick prayer.
I say the words.

I ask her to marry me.

There is an awkward silence. Thirty seconds is an eternity when time is electric and moves at a supersonic pace. I'm steering a breakneck fast-break with my point-guard heart. Her *"yes"* melts me with joy and then responsibility. Within an instant a new plan forms and begins.

Overwhelmed but ecstatic; joyful but fearful—I watch her board her plane back to Nashville, Tennessee. I have to get my act together.

I have to tell John and Joe.

John Chambers has just arrived with the vision of teaming with Joe and me. After our final four championship game, the future beams bright for the Capital Cagers. John is the pivotal missing piece. He's a big-minute player and looks to give the Cagers some much needed depth.

He's an easy find. All I have to do is open the door of our Diamond Springs cabin. Boxes and belongings surround his space.

I blurt out my plans for Tennessee and Sandy.

I can hear his thoughts. *You just met her. What about us? What about the Cagers?*

There's no clear answer. This man—this brother of the cause—moves his life to join this *thing* happening in the valley of Northern California. It's sad, an absolute plunder in his eyes, but I'm filled with an uncontrollable joy. My infectious/contagious, overriding elation begins to soften the blow.

John is eventually happy for me.

We speak more. We both know mighty Joe Thorn will be a tougher sell and more difficult situation all together.

Joe and I bond like kin and teammates throughout 1977 and '78. Our time together and on-court training is legendary. Two like-minded (I refuse to get outworked) fanatics looking for competitive advantages. Our one-on-one games are steamroller contests with the consistent question—*are you ready to quit?* Neither of us ever do.

We spend hours and hours talking about strategy, shooting technique, and the potential of ourselves and rivals. We trek up and down Highway 99 from Sacramento to Orange County and San Diego in Joe's 4-wheel drive, tank-like vehicle. We travel with rations and half-gallons of water. Joe doesn't like cold water. He drinks it hot with only the windows to manage temperature in his extreme rig. I never get behind the warm water but Joe's a chiselled Vietnam Veteran who doesn't need the creature comforts that I spoil myself with.

How do I tell him?

How will he take it?

I'm nervous. *Could things get volatile?*

I ask John to help me break the news.

The hour journey to Joe and his wife Vicky's house in urban Sacramento gives me more than enough time to ponder and confuse the situation. Joe wants to redeem himself. His finals performance just weeks ago is below his standards. I'm about to tell him I'm getting married and playing for the Nashville team that shut him down.

I'm about to break my closest friend's heart. There's no easy way. We arrive.

No small talk. I just say it.

I see the air releasing from his lungs. Not many words are spoken. His look of disdain speaks louder than anything else.

Our eyes meet. He's such a great friend but at the moment his look speaks clearly—*I hope you know what you're doing.*

Life is stranger than fiction.

Less than 16 months after meeting Sandy we're living back in Northern California. I'm chasing the beginning of a lifelong career as a Recreation Therapist.

Sandy and I are living in Walnut Creek. She's the bread girl working the bakery at the local Alpha Beta grocery store. I'm working at the Ralph K. Davies Medical Center in downtown San Francisco. I'm taking newly injured, spinal cord patients to ball games like the *Great One* did for me. I'm starting my initial job/art-form of combining sport and disability.

The ceiling is high. My office overlooks the San Francisco Bay. In one breath, it's the perfect beginning. In the next, I'm continuously sitting in the Bay Area bumper-to-bumper, urban sprawl congestion. Something will need to give.

We're both working laborious days but the nights are ours. It's a shared time. Not yet 25 years old, I'm half the partnership of a full-blown, full-fledged, grown-up, husband and wife relationship.

She tells me she's pregnant.

"I just love babies," she shrieks.

We're both ecstatic. We're newlyweds. There are no anxious or burdensome doubts. We're going to figure it all out.

The biggest question mark of my being is answered. I am a father.

The love circle of any Wheel Head is a bender: the intimidation of intimacy in the early days, learning my body all over again, finding the grace to be truthful, honest, and exposed. I understand the training and knowledge of my body and its functions—trial and error, humility within the errors, and finesse within each small win.

My universe changes the night we first meet. Sandy is by my side the next five-plus decades. Her pregnancy within the first few months of marriage amazes and confirms. The circle of life screams to be heard with our first-born Justin and then four years later, daughter Danielle. Both are married today (Bethany and Randy) and are loving parents to our four grandchildren: Cruz, Lucas, Lily, and Jace.

Plant a seed.

Watch it grow.

The Kiley Tribe at a gathering at Mimi and Pop's house.

COMING HOME

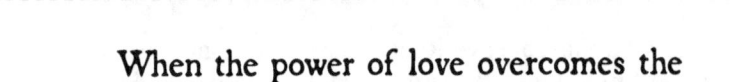

When the power of love overcomes the
love of power, the world will know peace.

— Jimi Hendrix

Sex. Disability. Vietnam War. The 1970s.

I first met Jon Voight in the fall of 1977. The actor lands the lead role as Luke Martin in the upcoming film, *Coming Home*. Voight's a method actor and his livelihood depends on playing roles—but what separates a method actor is his/her decision to immerse themselves into the most minute details of those they characterize.

Voight is all in.

Coming Home is the story of Vietnam veterans returning home. Voight's character is wheelchair bound due to a spinal cord injury obtained in battle. His rival in the film, Bob Hyde (played by Bruce Dern), is a Captain in the United States Marine Corps and is about to be deployed into the conflict. Hyde sees the deployment as a career opportunity. He returns home with a self-inflicted, gunshot wound to this lower leg. Hyde suffers from post-traumatic stress disorder with fits of rage. He is a displacement within society.

Voight first came on the scene whilst I'm playing with Ed and the Santa Ana Raiders. The team is made up of war veterans.

What I didn't understand fully at the time is the fascinating, look-through-the microscope our group is; Voight did. The movie has a scene with Voight playing wheelchair basketball. There's a joyful toughness as the veterans mix it up on the court. Voight is chasing authenticity.

For a spell, he's a regular at our practices. We take to one another. We're also the same size, blonde, with similar builds. I'm in the midst of emerging as a personality and a stand-out performer. I have no problem verbally bobbing and weaving my way through scrimmages. Voight digs the vibrato.

Voight takes his time in the chair seriously. He wants to understand transfers. He asks good questions. He watches with a keen interest. His on-screen transfers are believable. There is no cringe factor.

When the movie shoots, I'm away in college. A producer calls and asks me to be an extra in the therapy pool scene. Any influx of cash piques my interest. I'm the starving student personified and have no problem driving the central valley—and seven hours—to Southern California.

Many scenes are filmed on location at Rancho Los Amigos Rehabilitation facility.

I remember not wanting to leave Rancho. Now, I'm an extra in a Hollywood movie production filming there. I pause, chuckle, and exhale before entering the spinal cord injury ward.

Voight is there during the therapy pool shoot. I eye him and one of the producers heading my way. He has a wry, devilish grin to him.

"I have a love scene with Jane Fonda," he says. "We're thinking you'd make a great body double. What do you think?"

"I gotta get to class up north."

The producer jumps in. "We'll give you plenty of time to get back. You'll be getting paid."

"I'll do it," I answer.

I'm as nervous as I've ever been.

The set is dark and closed for the nude scene.

Voight's character, Luke, falls for Sally, a volunteer at the local Veterans Administration Hospital. Sally, played by Jane Fonda, is married to a Captain in the Marine Corps. He is serving in Vietnam when Luke and Sally meet. Sally and Luke befriend one another before becoming lovers.

I sit on the bed in a skin-colored bikini brief awaiting Jane Fonda.

She enters the set nude.

The script has Sally reaching her first-ever orgasm with Luke.

I can barely look. I'm consumed with fear.

She's not yet in bed. I hear her steps approaching. I sneak a second peek. It's not Jane. It's a body double. A cruel, yet lusty twist of fate. The double is simmering hot with a lean and gleaming body.

What have I got myself into?

This is a big step in Luke's new life. He is confronting his fears by sharing them with someone else. Their relationship transforms Sally into a newer, less conservative, version of herself.

The cameras roll. Our steamy scene begins. My fear overrides any thoughts of pleasure.

The sensual scene continues. The cameras continue their invasive probe into my own insecurities. I close my eyes whenever possible.

Coming Home is a hit.

My sex scene (as they say) ends up on the cutting room floor. My own twisted turn of anxiety is never to be seen. Just as well. The story is a lifelong folklore tale, filled with a self-deprecating mix of humility and what could have been.

Voight goes on to win an Oscar as the year's best actor. At the end of his acceptance speech he thanks, "…the men who gave me all their experience to deal with. All the men in chairs. The Veterans, the civilians, the walkers that are so strongly represented in what I call 'my work.'"

Fonda also wins an Academy Award as best actress. She is the driving force behind the film. Her production company, Indochina Peace Campaign (IPC), conceives and executes the project from beginning to end.

The film ends with Martin (Voight's character) speaking to young men about his misinformed experience in Vietnam, whilst Hyde (Dern's character and husband to Sally) places his Marine dress uniform on a Los Angeles beach lifeguard station, takes off his wedding ring, and swims naked into the ocean as his final gesture.

DISABILITY/ABILITY

Let my life reflect the infinite abilities within each of us.

— Robert Hensel

I've never liked the term *incomplete injury.*

It sounds suspicious.

What muscle function is he hiding?

I saw him stand up at the urinal the other day.

He puts his chair in the back of his truck.

Can he walk?

Wheel Heads gossip with the best of them. It makes sense. Traumatic
and tragic injuries have folks consistently looking at those that are better off.
Muscle function and ability are a constant topic of conversation amongst spinal
cord injuries. Those with less function envy those with more, and the ones with
more envy the amputees who seemingly have everything.

The snow tube debacle leaves me mostly paralyzed at the T12/L1 vertebrae.
I'm basically a bit of a broken mess from the waist down. The immediate
and noticeable loss of mass in my legs stuns and depresses me. My legs keep
shrinking. It doesn't take long to understand a miracle isn't around the corner
of well-meaning prayers and a distant phenomenon made for others. My upper
body expands like Popeye, spinach, and Olive Oyl. I am the tale of two halves:
top and bottom.

By the time I leave Rancho, I'm wearing an ankle foot orthodox (AFO), short
leg brace on my right side, and a long leg brace on my left.

There's some return in my right-side quad muscle. I also have a small use of
that hamstring. It's not much but enough to stand with the aid of the AFO.

My left leg has less function and requires a long leg brace. There is a bit of
usage in my hip with minimal quadricep return.

With the two leg braces (short and long), I am able to waddle along with
forearm crutches. My swing-through method of ambling on crutches only
works because the muscle to body mass portion of my top half, exceeds the
crippled aspects of my bottom half. Stubbornness, hard work, and my reaching
need to not be the guy "always stuck in his chair," has me upright enough to
reach for the sugar on the top shelf or easily stand and lean on the bleachers
after a long practice or game. The ability to stand allows a more balanced
head space. The blood flows. Pressure is relieved off my ass, and I enjoy the

simple—yet precious—exercise of looking folks, standing next to me, in the eye.

There is also a price to pay. My left side has severe and debilitating nerve pain. During the simplest conversation, alone drinking my morning coffee, or at the absolute most inopportune moment, my left leg nerve pain has me systematically reaching for my knee in a contraction of indescribable pain. I urgently look to stop what drastically feels like a thousand knives jabbing my nerves. People notice, and ask, "Are you alright?" When driving, I routinely ask a friend to 'grab the steering wheel' as I convulse in this relentless pain. Night time is always the worst. I never sleep through the night as the pain seeks to torment without conscience.

The issue of chronic pain suffered through a spinal cord injury is burdensome. It has the capacity to drown the strongest of us into a sinking sea of darkness. It seems nonsensical and virtual, as the affliction originates below my injury level, but I (and many paraplegics before and since) will tell you—the agony is real.

The price of admission is steep. Wheelchair basketball is a collective of colorful, resolute personalities. All with a story and most with a devil-may-care pridefulness that walks the thin line between foolish, honorable, and glorified.

I'm no different. What's dark fades. The light and grace of day supersedes. I get so good, so fast, it intoxicates. The acceleration in talent, form, and execution is a massive ego boost. It also pisses off the old guard. They figure my double-time climb up the talent ladder is somehow suspicious. I distribute the ball with a flare and sizzle that is not uncommon in today's game but in the late seventies is explosive and a shock to the norm.

I revel in it all. Others sneer. I'm taking what used to be theirs. I'm constantly searching for ways to play the game faster. I play with an authentic athleticism that transcends disability and wheelchairs.

I make half court, behind-the-back passes because I can. It elevates me, fans, and teammates, but more importantly—the game itself.

Classification of athletes within wheelchair basketball is an evolutionary process.

In the beginning, athletes were classified as either *complete* or *incomplete.* In 1966, the Stoke Mandeville Games in England began classifying players in three different categories. Athletes are worth one point, two points, or three points according to their disability and function. Teams are allowed twelve points for the five players competing on the floor.

In a twelve-point system, the ones with the most function (amputees, post-polios and those able to fully rotate) are class threes. A person like myself—a spinal cord injury at the waist down (or double above-the-knee amputees with limited rotation) are class twos. Spinal cord injuries around the chest levels are class ones.

The intention is for those who have less limitations to not take over the sport, leaving others with more disabling conditions spectators. How does this get applied? How does the game excel whilst also maintaining an equitable share for those permanently in wheelchairs?

Classifiers are an integral aspect of what we do. In my early days, classifiers are mostly physical and occupational therapists. Their method is a medical one. Observations are not on the court/between the lines but instead in sterile rooms. They observe you in your chair and out. I remember catching medicine balls, sitting on an elevated mat, reaching to my left and right side; the classifiers searching for my rotational limits.

Classification (in theory) works. The intention is pure.

Then there's the human, competitive condition—do whatever it takes to win.

It's common for teams and players to sandbag, leading to lower classifications. The medical method allows for fake wobbles when reaching right/left or above your head. Motivation comes with increased court time and visibility. The backfire effect of the sandbagger's play is that keen eyes know. Competitors and peers dismiss the sandbagger into the abyss of fraudster or con artist.

Then there's the orthopedic injuries affecting: joints, tendons, muscles, bones, or any other related tissues. Is their injury significant enough to even qualify for disability sport? Often spectators are irritated by the obvious nature of someone competing who doesn't use a wheelchair on a regular basis.

It's confusing to Joe Public, the fan, when a player stands after being knocked to the floor. The rules' intention is to be inclusive. If player A is unable to compete in the able-bodied version of that sport, then player A should qualify for wheelchair basketball.

Was this abused by teams?

Absolutely.

A protest process is established to have players reviewed, reclassed, and even disqualified.

I never paid it much attention. I'm good enough to be on the floor at any class. There are classification conflicts—trust me. Because I can use crutches and stand, even take steps while holding onto something sturdy, my classification gets questioned repeatedly. My ability and capacity for incremental gains through hard work, sparks the flame of the suspicious, and more succinctly—the lazy.

You want to beat me? Outwork me.

Still, there are those that take exception. I am at the center of a number of classification protests. It's ludicrous. The reality is, to consider me the same as a below-the-knee amputee that can walk out of the gym is nonsensical.

It's a farce to consider but yet they try. It's a dirty game as teams and coaches know if they can change my class our team suffers. I imagine the psychological play is for myself and teammates to lose focus on the goal at task.

It's all bush-league.

I play my entire career as a class two within the twelve-point system.

Screw all of you who try to change my classification with worthless protests.

World Championships and the Paralympic Games use a 14-point classification system. The International Wheelchair Basketball Federation (IWBF) model is functional. The European countries are the driving force behind the 14-point, functional system. They have professional leagues with the best worldwide players making serviceable wages.

Within the functional system are pivotal considerations for strapping.

Low-point athletes with balance issues often strap a waist band around their mid-section. Mostly attached by Velcro, the stretchy, gut-strap allows for added side-to-side and forward stability. Feet, hips, and knees are routinely strapped to the chair with either Velcro or snowboard-like click straps. The chair, mind, and body respond as one.

Placement of knees, feet, and specific sitting cushions, allow mid-pointers like myself the opportunity to maximize our core and pendulum (up/down) pushing motion. The tiniest tweaks create noticeable changes in sitting positions, turning radius, and top-end speed. Mid-pointers are constantly tightening or loosening straps in the hopes of finding their optimal balance points.

Amputees build cusps or custom straps for their nubs, creating greater connectivity to the chair and cheeky, almost unobtainable ways of detecting their ass lifting from their cushion. The move is illegal but rarely gets called. High-pointers can dominate games with size, speed, and the ability to tilt their chairs. *Tilting*, an extremely athletic move, creates expanded spacing for shots, post defense, and rebounding. Those that *tilt,* put all their weight on their left- or right-side wheels, with the opposite side wheels elevated and spinning in the air. The art is to not over rotate and end up on the floor.

It's not uncommon for specialized strapping to increase an athlete's classification by half a point in the functional classification system.

Functional classifiers observe athletes in their element: at training and during games. It's rarer for functional classifiers to follow the medical model and see athletes out of their chair.

I play as a class 3.0 throughout my international journey. It makes sense. It's justified. The 14-point system classifies athletes from 1.0 to 4.5. The half-point increments—in theory—are a practical way to pinpoint an athlete's true level of function.

Doug Garner, a Hall of Fame coach at the University of Texas, Arlington, and IWBF *Gold* Classifier since 2005, compares the medical and functional system this way, "I think the medical system allows more functional capacity on the floor and in some opinions leads to better basketball. I think the inclusiveness of the medical system led us (USA) to not developing our low-point players. The functional system is more inclusive to all levels and values all levels of function. It's fun to see and appreciate the inclusion of the whole spectrum."

Always an educator, Garner continues, "Some say the functional system limits the 'high performance' level of the sport, which in turn, some believe, limit how people see the sport as true athletics. To me, this illustrates the systematic 'ableism' of a society and is something that can/should be addressed in education and awareness."

The NWBA switches to the functional 14-point classification system in the early 2000s.

My team, the Casa Colina Condors, are knee deep in another championship run. I hear, second-hand, that Detroit Sparks' Bud Rumple has filed a classification protest. Next, I hear the protest concerns me.

It's tiring.

Here we go again.

I go through the routine. The protest has me out of my chair, on a mat, leaning left, then right. I bend forward before working myself upright.

If Bud thinks this is going to distract me from the goal, he's wrong. I've been through this before. Doesn't work.

The review comes in. My classification changes to a three. I throw a fit. One expletive, after another, followed by another.

More anger.

A day away from the semi-finals of the Final Four, Championship Tournament.

My fury does not subside.

I find the tournament organizer. I threaten to leave—with my team—and not play in the championship tournament.

"See how your Final Four goes without four teams," I scream, without punching something or someone, but I'm close.

I search and find the classifier. "I've been a class-two for over ten years. You're going to change me to a three—and now? A day before the semi-finals." I ask him what he's been smoking lately and if this is a way for him to make a name for himself. I suspect it is.

It's best, I tell my teammates what's happened. I've threatened to pull our team from the event for goodness' sake. In classic form they have my back.

Calmer heads prevail. We lodge an appeal to the protest. Paperwork and a few shillings later we await the decision.

By rule the classifier that has upped my classification cannot be a part of the appeal process. Sweet relief.

It's overturned.
I play as a class 2.
We beat Detroit for the national championship.

PART THREE

Life is a succession of lessons which
must be lived to be understood.

All is a riddle,

and the key to a riddle is...another riddle.

– Ralph Waldo Emerson

FRANK

Fan the sinking flame of hilarity with the
wing of friendship; and pass the rosy wine.

— Charles Dickens

*"If we are to succeed, we have to enjoy what we do," John Wooden explains
in his book on the Pyramid of Success. "If we enjoy what we do, we will be
enthusiastic about it. Enthusiasm thereby enables us to push for as long as
we need to push to achieve our best."*

Frank Burns is enthusiastic. He's the windy city of Chicago blowing you
off your proverbial feet with one-liners, deep-dive basketball knowledge, and
a mid-west engagement that sucks you into his swirling, semi-deranged, and
brilliant vortex.

I first met Frank when I'm with the Capital Cagers. We're competing in
the Bluegrass Invitational in Lexington, Kentucky. The tournament draws the
top teams in the country. I'm in the midst of 'blowing up' as a personality and
worthy rival in the wheelchair basketball world. Players and coaches introduce
themselves to me regularly. It's consuming and weird. I'm not used to this kind
of attention. Awkward.

Frank's approach is one of legend. He connects through sports. Right
away you know he's all Chicago. The Bears and Bulls will be talking points
throughout. His humor puts me at ease and helps tear down the walls of moving
on to something or someone else because I'm uncomfortable.

Frank's a graduate of the University of Whitewater, Wisconsin, and working
his way through his master's degree at the University of Kentucky. Kentucky is
a basketball-crazed campus with storied victories and national championships.

We make plans that night to hang out and take in the collegiate nightlife.

We make the rounds: frat bars, a dive bar, pulsating clubs, and a guy with an
acoustic guitar joint. At 1 a.m., Frank offers to show me around campus. The
beers and cocktails have us in need of a leak. The bushes are our only option.

We navigate to our spots and the campus police pull up. They hit the blue
and red lights. My low-profile in the chair has me close to invisible to the cops.
Frank stands tall. He's on the front-line of things. He tells me to stay hidden.

I continue to piss in the tucked position and before the cops exit their cruiser.
I holler back at Frank, "Tell the cops you're a botanist."

Our drunken laughter fills the still, night air.

The footsteps of the cops approaches.

We are straight-face and keep it together. I remain hidden.

The more outrageous the situation, the greater Frank is. He adores the attention and comes from a theatre background. I hear him share a laugh with the cops. They remind him that urinating in public is a crime.

He assures them it will never happen again.

There's the obligatory warning from the men in blue.

We belly laugh the instant they're out of sight. Frank loves the botanist reference. It's a running joke the rest of our time. This is the beginning of hundreds of comedic, athletic, and life-altering stories that Frank and I will share over the decades of our friendship.

Fate is a tricky one. It changes your life.

Frank and I are a product of fate—with a healthy ingredient of faith.

Sandy's pregnant, and the world is a spinning top of possibilities. The problem is my job in San Francisco. The Ralph K. Davies Medical Center is driven by policy and a robust risk management strategy. The view out my office is of the bay and Pacific Ocean, but the reality is my style of community-based exploration for the newly injured doesn't jibe with the suits at Ralph K. Davies.

All rehab is to be done in-house. Six months pass. It's time to roll the dice.

I call Frank. He's working at Casa Colina Centers for Rehabilitation.

As fate would have it, I'm offered Frank's job the year before but turned it down as I'm living in Nashville with my new bride in her hometown and near her family.

In Nashville, I work for the Federal Government within Affirmative Action. It's a coat and tie, 9 to 5, get a haircut, turn on the sprinklers, clock watching, water the plants, jock job—that is mine because I can play ball. Work is long, boring, and unfulfilling.

I thank Casa Colina and tell them I cannot accept their generous offer, but they should consider Frank Burns for the role. Frank just completed his master's degree from the University of Kentucky in Therapeutic Recreation.

Lenore Hersch, Head of Casa's Recreation Department hires Frank. He immediately establishes the Casa Colina Condors wheelchair basketball team.

Frank's legacy is being there first and implementing programs of significance. The guy is a shuck-and-jive maestro, a trailblazer in the name of disability sport, with a screenwriter's mindset for problem solving and creating content and product. His dreams and visions are the largest in the room.

I tell Frank of my professional woes. The Bay Area of Northern California isn't working for us, and with Sandy pregnant, the uncertainty of career, home, and unborn child leaves us tense and restless. Frank promises he can get me a job within the Casa Colina Recreation department. Problem is, there's no job currently available.

On a leap of faith, Sandy and I pack the vehicles and head south down Highway 5, traversing the same onion, garlic, and cantaloupe fields that Joe Thorn and I drove years previous to tournaments and competitions. The adventure is constant.

There's a slight tightening and reassurance in our grip when we hold hands and grasp onto one another. Sandy believes in me, next level. I'm outwardly confident and carefree but the sharp, jagged edges of anxiety lay in wait, in my thoughts and in my gazes into everything unknown. I have dragged this lovely creature of a woman (my wife), across our expansive country on a promise. I must deliver.

My brother, Jeff, agrees to house us. He's living in the upstart, pre-planned community of Irvine in Orange County. His welcome is appreciated but also comes with a side of reluctance as he likes the solitude within his carefully woven environment. Jeff's neatness is obsessive. My domestic skills are still in their infancy. Sandy saves the day on this front.

I pick up odd jobs working as a classroom assistant for the developmentally disabled. I clean mountainous, restaurant coffee pots on the weekends. I'm paid per pot.

Sandy helps at mom's liquor store (she takes ownership of the store in the divorce settlement with dad) on the bluffs of Newport Beach. My pregnant wife is in the midst of a robbery in the store. She's told to empty the register. She eyes her assailant.

"That's no gun," she says. "That's your finger."

She grabs his finger beneath his windbreaker. The supposed gun collapses at his thumb and index finger.

"No money for you."

With a glare (*get the hell out of here*) and the threat of a shove, the wannabe thief hits the bricks and exits out the door.

Despite the obstacles and unpredictability of the time, I am at peace. I'm not stressing. The restlessness of living in the Bay Area is gone.

I get the call.

Frank is on the other end. He delivers.

I'm meeting Lenore Hersch about my new job as the newest Casa Colina Wheelchair Sports Programmer and Recreation Therapist. I'm working with inpatients on navigating the tragedy of paralysis and acclimating themselves step by step (so to speak) back into the community.

My Community Adjustment Trips (CATS) programming into the neighborhoods is similar to the outings Ed Owen took me on as a bewildered, new spinal cord injury patient. The tasks involve crossing railroad tracks, using a public bathroom, popping your first curb, or pushing to the tavern and having your first beer (I have to answer for this one). The outings are under my supervision and watch.

My primary role is inpatient Recreation Therapist. It's the early days of the 80s and Casa Colina has figured how to bill patients through Medi-Cal/ MediCare for my services. I write notes reflecting functional outcomes similar to Occupational and Physical Therapy. This new billing practice opens doors for Recreation Therapists. We can be hired within departments that are willing to pay for practicable services.

Casa Colina is in Pomona. Pomona is only thirty miles from Huntington Beach but also sits at the base of the San Gabriel Mountains. It's right next to the Inland Empire of Riverside and San Bernardino. It's a comfortable, sleepy community of higher learning with Harvey Mudd, Pitzer, Cal Poly Pomona, and Claremont McKenna Colleges.

Sandy and I move to neighboring Claremont. We find a two-bedroom apartment. Our street is lined with shady, trusted, and sturdy trees. There's plenty of porches and friendly folks ready with a gesturing, benevolent wave.

Living behind us is a friend and therapist that catches Frank's eye. I see him passing in the night, up her stairs.

January 21st, 1980, is a monumental day.

When we have noble goals, we prioritize our greatest dreams.

My beautiful wife is overdue to deliver our first child. The third day of no trips to the maternity ward has my world levelling off to life and work responsibilities. It's understood, I am to let Sandy know my whereabouts at all times (no cell phones).

Work has me in Long Beach getting hand-controls installed on the hospital work van. My job responsibilities are quickly mushrooming. The need to transport patients into the community is a testimony to my increasing role in things.

The hand-controls shop is a spit away from the Long Beach VA. There's time to kill. I check in on the many veterans I know working, playing ball, and simply hanging out. As expected, there's some action on the courts. A few pick-up games later, I realize it's been a few hours since I've arrived. I head back to the shop.

The frenzied installer locks eyes on me down the street, and hollers, "Is your wife having a baby?"

I answer, "Oh shit. Yes."

"You gotta go," he barks. "We will settle up later."

The new hand-controls get put through the test. The VA, to the ever-present Hoag Hospital, is a 30-mile drive. I hammer down the 405 heading south. I can make up some time if I get off on Brookhurst (a side-street boulevard) and drive parallel to the coast. There are traffic lights to navigate—a bunch of them.

I look both ways and continue to bust through each red light I encounter. The new hand controls feel sturdy and responsive.

My eyes constantly scan for cops.

'I can't be late for the birth of my first born. I can't.'

I screech into the hospital parking lot like Steve McQueen.

I sprint to the delivery rooms. They're rolling Sandy to the birthing area. She sees me, just before I see her.

If looks can kill—I'm a dead man. Sandy's mother intensifies things with a double-down glare of her own. *"Don't they know what I did to get here?'* Think I'll leave out the part about the pick-up basketball games.

The nurses gown me up.

The doctor is the father of one of my schoolyard friends. His son PJ is an outstanding athlete and buddy. There's a familiarity within my untrained but highly anticipated dance into fatherhood and family man.

Our son enters into the world. He literally pops out. He's a human ball of energy within his first seconds of life. He thinks he can fly. Dr. Santangelo grabs our new born son by the leg before he face-plants into the sterile, tiled hospital floor.

The clock on the wall reads 3:49 p.m.—Pacific Standard Time.

The day before, the Los Angeles Rams lose a tough one in Superbowl XIV against the Pittsburgh Steelers. I can't help myself, "The Rams could have used you yesterday, Doc," I say.

Justin is born. Sandy and I cannot be happier. My beautiful bride and myself, the world's newest mother and father.

Prayer request answered.

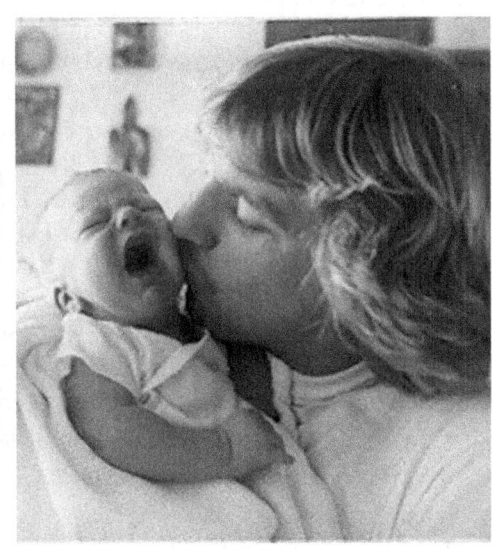

Justin, after birth, grows into a fixture on my lap.

The best moment in my life, and Frank is right there. His magnanimous, cock-eyed grin greets me in the waiting area. This cements our lifelong, fraternal brotherhood.

We talk of middle names. Frank, of course, recommends "Justin Time" or perhaps "Justin Case." We instead introduce Justin David Kiley into the world and all it has to offer.

Later in the evening, Frank and I pick up a bottle of Yukon Jack and head over to my brother's nearby place. A few pops later, I'm standing on my braces, side-by-side, up against the fence with Frank and taking, yes, another leak. Frank eyes me up. I am so happy. He knows it. He sees it.

"You're a dad. MOFO KY (use your imagination), you are a dad," he says.

We laugh out loud into the perfect fall night and take another pop.

Coach John Wooden and the UCLA Bruins basketball teams win 10 NCAA championships in 12 years between the years of 1963 and 1975. In that span, the Bruins win 88 games in a row. Their decade plus of greatness is built on a stifling man-to-man defense, superior athleticism, and a home court advantage that transforms the laid back, coastal community and student body into a boisterous and constant full house.

The UCLA brand colors are baby blue and gold. The blue represents the ocean and local wildflowers. The gold speaks to our golden state and sunsets.

One of Frank's initial decisions is to replicate the uniform colors of the Casa Colina Condors, the same as UCLA's. A subtle, yet enlightened move.

Frank's first season with the Condors goes well. I'm not with the squad but the wins come in bunches for the upstart team. The stalwart and legendary Southern California programs, Long Beach Flying Wheels and Los Angeles Stars, are put on notice; there's a new contender in town looking to take what's been theirs for decades.

There's a nucleus of talent in Albert Campos, Calvin Young, and Curtis Bell. The three, high class players do the majority of their work in the post and finishing high speed, spinning layups. Frank's initial version of the Condors has some serviceable mid-pointers in Bill Bowness, Steve Hamilton, and Ron Scanlon but there's a definite fit for a ball handling, ball hawk, mid-point baller like myself.

In strategy, the fit is impeccable and immediate. Right away, I know we have something—something special. Still, there are hurdles to clear. Relationships to build on and get right. Personal bridges to construct.

Frank pulls me aside. He asks me to *shoot less.*

What? This is my first year with the team?

Where is this coming from?

This doesn't sit well with me. I question Frank as a coach and motivator.

The game in 1980 is more about game plans than the Xs and Os of pick and roll techniques, defensive line shadows disallowing the needed angles for said picks or non-dominant hand passing and shooting through daily practice.

During this time there's an emphasis and fascination on new lightweight, aluminium chairs and using this newfound glide/explosion of hand-speed and torque to beat your opponent with physicality and technique.

It's a one-on-one game—on and off the ball.

This is my wheelhouse. My will and effectiveness within this paradigm are unmatched. There's no controlling the *sizzle* within my game. I know where players need the ball to be effective and I get it to them when they need it. I also use that same sizzle to shoot from deep, attack the rim, and score clutch baskets that win games.

Shoot less?

I take good, high percentage shots as it is.

I take a deeper look. I begin to understand Frank's desire for me to be a pass first, point guard. Besides Curtis and Albert in the post, there are quality shooters in Jim Worth, Domingo Melendez, and my ole buddy and class one legend, John Chambers.

There's a depth surrounding me that needs to be fed. Athletic egos are built on individualised hours, visualized through repetitive drills and a drive to not only be your personal best but a dominant presence within the strongest of competitors.

Frank and I come to an understanding built on respect. I'm the distributor, but I am also the proven commodity when the game is tight.

Albert Campos and Curtis Bell are Hall of Fame performers.

Albert has a multitude of finishing-at-the-rim skills, quick/strong hands that take what he wants. He has a defensive mindset that spreads throughout the team and a willingness to do the dirty work that all great teams must have.

Curtis is a showman/scorer. He fills the scorebook with baskets and free-throw attempts. Curtis has an uncanny ability to rise in chair—like he's squeezing his butt cheeks—and come down with the ball, be it rebounds or my arching passes into the post. He's a proven champion and is built to dominate segments of games. I learn to love the art of getting him the ball. He makes me famous, so does Albert.

We are three teammates that are former rivals. At certain times of contests one of us is the strongest force on the floor. Mistakes still happen and when they do there's verbal jabs, negative body language, or a sideways dagger glare. No one backs down.

The growing pains between the three of us rise to the surface. More than once the threat of *"taking it outside"* looms during practices and scrimmages. These times are often tougher than our conference games. Yes, at times, it gets heated.

Frank's concern is obvious but also laced with a city street knowledge that these things tend to figure themselves out over time and with repeated victories. The fact that we don't always like each other on the floor in practice is secondary to the bonding time together figuring it out.

We beat the Long Beach Flying Wheels in resounding fashion. We travel into the heart of Los Angeles and handle the LA Stars. Momentum is building.

Every game, Frank is in a coat and tie, adding a needed legitimacy and proven look to the more subcultural, casually attired game of wheelchair basketball. Frank pulls folks into our games. His midwestern humor is always on display—his gift is his welcoming nature. We build a base of support. Fans and employees of Casa begin to attend in droves, filling the middle school venue with a home court vibe that's welcoming but also territorial in maintaining a level of showmanship and defeats of those willing to enter.

During the week, Frank's chosen attire is his classic 80s style coaching shorts: thick elastic band, nut hugging, belly popping, butt grabbing, upper thigh showing, catastrophe of a look. There's a whistle round his neck and a shirt of one of his beloved Chicago sports teams or the newest Frank Burns designed Casa Colina Condor Basketball golf shirts around his shoulders.

The man is a force.

In our first season together the Casa Colina Condors take it all.

The Final Four tournament in Charlotte, North Carolina—as chance would have it—goes surprisingly easy. At halftime of the championship game, we're up 42-18 on the Chicago Sidewinders with Don Vandello, Vince Caputo, and Randy Wix. We coast to victory.

With three minutes left our role and secondary players are in the game. The celebration begins. Albert, Curtis, and I have long forgotten our flare-ups and heated battles in practice.

We are in the precise and exact moments of victory: dignity, distinction, and triumph take form in nods and grins. These acts take a second but are timeless.

Basketball is a poetic game, masked within inflated egos and the indisputable fact that there's only one ball; and multitudes in need, creating a potential confluence of conflict. We work through it. We reach a higher and better level of self.

I look towards the front-end of our bench. Frank's still coaching it up. The bench guys on the floor deserve his best. It doesn't matter the score. These three minutes are what matters. There's a need to contribute: a rebound, steal, assist, stop, or hoop. It's great cheering for the guys usually cheering us. The championship is a few possessions away.

Our victory celebration defies description. We're out of our chairs, on the floor. Frank's bear hugging all-comers. Teammates lifting themselves or getting lifted to the rim and cutting down the net. Wives, girlfriends, and moms cradling one another. There's a shared zeal with all involved that the juice is indeed worth the squeeze.

The party moves to the school bus, and we ride to our uptown Charlotte hotel. There's a visible concern across the forlorn grill of our Southern Baptist, volunteer bus driver. We're a melting pot team with a ringleader coach. His concern is legit.

We need beer. We need it now. There's a chant throughout the bus. We subside. Frank approaches the driver. He's not into it. The chant is back. It fades. We plead. Frank has a couple more words with the guy. The bus pulls off the congested street into the liquor store parking lot. There's an eruption. The driver stands up. He's speaking to all of us.

"Y'all have to promise to not pop any of these beers on the bus. Am I clear?"

"Yes, sir."

"Of course not."

"Never happen," we respond.

Frank and the walking amputees return with cases of beer. The beer is loaded on the back bench of the yellow school bus. Mistake. One by one the cool cans are passed around. One pops. Then another. The driver scans his rectangle mirror. Too late. In unison another dozen canned beers pop open. The unmistakable opening of canned beer is omnipresent. Beers go down our throats. Beers are poured over the top of teammate's heads. Beers atop our own heads. It's on.

We arrive. There's beer all over the bus as we exit. I look the driver in the eye and tell him, "We are sorry." His silence speaks louder than any words. Collateral damage. I look behind me. Teammates, arm in arm, shot-gunning beer.

Inside the lobby of the Sheraton hotel the chug-a-lugging continues.

We stuff ourselves in the elevator. With cases of beer on our laps we pop another. Our rooms are close to the top floor. The elevator door opens. There's the bright idea of shaking an unopened brew and fire hosing each other. Laughter. Euphoria. The elevator door opens next floor up. We fire hose unexpected souls wanting and waiting for an elevator ride. The door closes. We fire hose at each other again. The absurdity continues every time the elevator door opens. Ladies in evening gowns. Couples on a night out. Guys on the prowl. Doesn't matter. All get dosed with grade-A American brew.

The elevator door opens. It's security. They're not amused. The shenanigans come to a grinding halt.

This is the greatest feeling in the world.

I wouldn't change a thing.

Winning a championship: most amazing feeling of joy and laughter ever.

When any Condors get together, we always talk of the bus ride and elevator chaos.

Earthquake.

It's not long after our initial championship run. Frank pulls me into his office. He drops a bomb.

His role is changing from creating high quality, disability sport programming into fundraising. He's not into it. He's already taken a job at the University of Whitewater–Wisconsin, as their newest Head Coach.

I'm stunned.

Shocked.

Sad.

He continues.

He has recommended that I be hired as the new Director of Wheelchair Sports at Casa Colina Hospital.

I'm trying to process.

I have no experience in fundraising.

I can't be intimidated.

I have family responsibilities.

Can I do this without Frank?

Sadness again.

Excitement.

I'm going to lead an adaptive sports program.

Wait until Sandy hears.

Silence.

Things fade to white.

Frank's crooked grin grabs my eye.

I realize Frank Burns has teed it up for me.

He has set the tone for the greatest opportunity to become who I am intended to be.

Coach Frank Burns takes me to the ground as we celebrate our first National Championship.

Frank inducts me to NWBA HOF class of 2000.

Arm and arm in our young days.

Frank, RIP.

DK likes #1.

FOLLOW THE MONEY

If it's only about money, we are hopeless.
If it's about people we are hopeful.

— Maxime Lagace

I can't sleep. Toss. Turn.

It's early. The sun is yet to break through the darkness of night.

Nervous energy has me making coffee. Sandy and Juice (Justin's earned nickname) sleep. A newly purchased coat rests next to the chosen tie. It feels like the coat is mocking me. It's questioning if I'm up to the task. It knows my fidgeting is an edgy tell.

I need to become someone I never dreamt of becoming: fear, distress, and angst maintain their invasion of my thinking and course of action. I tell myself again, *I am the Director of Wheelchair Sports at Casa Colina Centers for Rehabilitation. I can do this.*

The submerged jitters of the moment mimic those of my first championship attempt. I've never done this.

Doesn't matter.

I'm not schooled for this.

Doesn't matter.

What matters?

I cannot fail. I must get this done.

In the parking lot, I eye myself in the rearview mirror, adjust and tighten my tie. I brush any fluff off my new (and dissimilar) jacket, run my fingers through my most current/tight haircut, and exhale deeply.

I understand the strategy. I'm the typecast Southern California, jock blonde. Within my sporting successes, I've acquired an antenna for reading the room and correctly verbalizing the appropriate "thanks" to corporate types and long-term sponsors. I learn by doing.

Entering the room, I'm introduced to Fred. Fred goes on to become a future board member for Casa Colina Wheelchair Sports, but today he's the guy I need to sell myself to. Like the rest of the surrounding community, Fred knows Casa Colina but doesn't know me or wheelchair sports. Fred knows beer. His distributorship is booming. There's a collage of dozens of different beers throughout his office wall shelves.

We've done the small talk. It's time to step up.

"Our fundraising golf tournament is in need of a $10,000 sponsorship," I say. "Your business is a great fit."

Fred takes a minute. He processes the ask. He excuses himself.

"Give me a moment," he says.

He leaves the room. I have a good feeling.

I catch my breath. Once Fred is out of sight, I give myself a clenched fist. Tension morphs to warmth. Fred returns with a check for the full ten grand.

Ten grand in the early 80s is a significant amount. Positive financial sponsorship relationships greenlight disability sport during this integral time. The term *disability sport* has yet to be coined. In the 80s everything was wheelchair this, wheelchair that.

The ride home feels like knocking down a big shot and winning an important game. I replay our exchanges. Fred appreciates sport. Was an athlete once himself. Understanding this, I make sure to reference our recent championship—the Lakers—and how game changing they are with Magic Johnson pushing the ball; the Dodgers and Fernando-mania; but the punch that really lands is when we speak of the newly injured—adults and kids in search of some sort of spark. I tell Fred that sport can be the emerging flicker. Casa Colina is the foundation for them to rebuild the rest of their lives. I'm the conduit. I'm the living, breathing example.

I instantly learn the art of relationship building.

I realize I'll need to be into the surrounding communities, rubbing elbows with the wealthy, successful corporations and sporting celebrities. It's time for me to comprehend the utter life-changing capabilities that are now at my fingertips. I have the platform. Sport, recreation, and wheelchairs all shine brighter with the almighty dollar riding shotgun.

Frank Burns gives me the keys. I'm the driver of the fundraising bus. It's my job to create and host a flagship event.

We put on a smallish celebrity golf tournament. A good first step, but we need a sports celebrity to lend his/her name to the event.

Sandy takes a job as a dental hygienist. Her boss is Dr. John McGwire, father of baseball slugger Mark McGwire. It's early in Mark's storied career, and the McGwire family resides in Pomona. We think hard about asking Mark McGwire to lend his name to the event. It's early in his career, and he's yet to be characterized as one of the Oakland A's beloved "Bash Brothers" with teammate Jose Canseco. Mark McGwire is a home-grown talent with a massive upside.

The other sports celebrity in consideration is Mike Scioscia. Mike lives in neighboring Glendora and is the starting catcher for the Los Angeles Dodgers. The Dodgers have a legendary fan base and a colorful core of standout performers, such as: (Manager) Tommy Lasorda, Orel Hershiser, and Fernando Valenzuela. Scioscia is a blue collar, no-nonsense, salt-of-the-earth guy. Dodger Stadium draws close to 50,000 fans a game when they're competitive—and they're in the hunt almost all the time.

It's decided Scioscia is our guy. Mike graciously accepts our request.

I didn't realize at the time but this decision is an absolute game-changer in the landscape of physical rehabilitation, relating to sport and recreation. We're legitimate.

Within a couple years, our celebrity golf tournament blows up. With Mike Scioscia's name to the event, and an influential, volunteer community-based committee, we expanded to a larger facility. We move the event from the Redhill Country Club to the Industry Hills Golf Club and its expansive two golf courses—the Eisenhower (Ike) and the Zaharias (Babe)—at the Pacific Palms Resort. We fill both courses with 144 golfers per course. There's a celebrity in each group.

The event becomes a well-oiled machine. Mike uses his influence to recruit the majority of his Dodgers teammates and coaches.

Mark McGwire goes on to win the American League Rookie of the Year Award. He continues to lend his time and face to the event. Actors and actresses converge on our fundraiser, bringing with them the glamor and glitz of Hollywood.

Mike Scioscia is a different breed when it comes to being a celebrity. He works closely with me without being asked. He calls me as much as I call him. To this day, we text or call one another.

Mike goes on and hits arguably the second most important home run in Dodgers team history. With the great Doc Gooden on the mound and trailing the New York Mets two games to one, Mike Scioscia comes to bat. The Dodgers are down 4-2, to the heavily favored Mets, in the top of the ninth. The first batter, John Shelby, walks. ABC broadcaster, Tim McCarver says, "That could be a very, very big walk."

Al Michaels calls the play, "Scioscia at the plate. Hernandez playing back of the runner at first…and that's ripped to right field and deep. Strawberry goes back. She's gone. Mike Scioscia with 35 home runs in eight-and-a-half years in the major leagues. We talked about him throughout the series, big and strong but really a contact hitter. A man who doesn't strike out a lot and who doesn't have a lot of home runs, averaging about four per season…hits the biggest home run of his career."

With that the Dodgers win the game in 12 innings on a home run by Kirk Gibson and a dramatic save by starting pitcher, Orel Hershiser.

It's a season of dreams for the underdog 1988 Dodgers. Kirk Gibson goes on and hits the most dramatic home run (in major league history) as a gimpy, injured, ninth inning, pinch hitter. His unlikely blast beats the bash brothers of Mark McGwire and Oakland Athletics in game one of the 1988 World Series. Furthermore, Gibson's historic bomb comes against Hall of Fame reliever, Dennis Eckersley.

The Dodgers and Mike go on to win one of the most unlikely World Series in the history of the game.

After his Dodger days, Mike stays in the game and excels. As manager for the California/Anaheim/Los Angeles Angels, Mike wins 1,650 games, with a winning percentage of .536 in his 19 years. With Scioscia at the helm, the Angels win their first (and only) World Series title in 2002. The same year he is named baseball's manager of the year.

Mike and I, stay at it and grow the tournament each year. We find presenting sponsors, like local banks, to put their name on the tournament next to Mike's and Casa Colina. We pound the pavement asking for in-kind and financial contributions: Howard's Appliance, Bushnell Optics, Brunswick Bowling and Billiards, the National Hot Rod Association (NHRA) Drag Strip and International Raceway all commit to us.

As the event continues to build, I have the idea to use disabled golfers as celebrities. Massive success. Groups rave about the amputee golfer that beats their scores. Brad Parks (a spinal cord injury), known for his tennis accomplishments, plays the course on his crutches. With his one-arm swing he eagles a par 5.

The event raises needed funds but also, just as important, flaunts the ability and grit of the disabled athlete. The financial importance of country club types and celebrities seeing, first hand, the feats of our disabled golfers, raises the bar even higher.

The high-end products that Mike and I procure, feed our silent auctions the night of the event. Wealthy golfers bidding against celebrities is a proven formula. We execute this strategy and at its peak our celebrity golf tournament raises a quarter-of-a-million dollars. These funds pay my salary, and allow me to hire others with disabilities to run programs. The first junior program is established with its own leaders and employees: Paul Haugen and Jim Miller. Self-defense is taught by black belt enthusiast Ron Scanlon. His exhibitions and classes (taught from his wheelchair) translate to those in chairs and the able bodied. It's transformative. We implement an Outdoor Adventure component to our programming: fishing, camping, climbing, snow skiing, white water rafting, water skiing, and hiking are all on offer. This helps connect families and loved ones to the weather-friendly California National Parks.

We're blowing up.

One afternoon, close to home, I look up and eye a large, rectangular billboard with myself and the family pasted for the world to see. Our bank is a presenting sponsor for our next fundraising event.

I shake my head in amused disbelief and take a left turn towards home.

The relationship with Mike Scioscia continues to bloom. Mike secures a billiards sponsorship. Next thing I know, I'm face to face with Willie Mosconi.

His legendary battles with Minnesota Fats are tales of mythological proportions. We create a fundraising pool tournament. The Vietnam Veterans show up in droves. Another success. Willie Mosconi gives me a signed cue stick that I still have as a treasured piece of memorabilia.

Willie Mosconi, a legend of legends, helps me raise funds for my sports program.

The momentum builds.

We deliver community-based programs in wheelchair tennis, track and field, 10K and marathon racing, quad rugby, a junior wheelchair basketball team, and three adult basketball teams. We employ the largest number of Recreation Therapists and Wheelchair Sports Specialists in the country.

I think of Frank Burns and the opportunity he creates for me. I'd never guess how successful we've become at raising funds. I, alongside with Mike, venture into and add important recreational layers to the disabled population. It comes full circle as a former patient of mine and friend, Robert Duncan, becomes Chairman of the Wheelchair Sports Board. The bonding agent in our financial creation is Casa Colina President, Dale Eazell. Dale gives me the green light at every juncture. Grateful. I greatly understand Dale's business savvy in my own day-to-day life.

We tap into what's local.

The NHRA headquarters is in our backyard. A golf committee member is the connection. The Pomona International Raceway and Drag Strip are within a stone's throw from Casa Colina. From our backyard you can hear the top fuel and funny car dragsters. The roar and rumble of the dragsters echoes for miles and is louder than you can imagine. I'm invited and given VIP seating. The packed grandstands erupts with cheers for favorites John Force, Ed 'the Ace' McCulloch, and the one-and-only Shirley 'Cha Cha' Muldowney. I have an idea.

Can we put on *'Wheelchair Drags?'* The classic Christmas tree lights descend to begin a wheelchair drag race. These long, three-wheeled racing frames sprinting side by side, down the same strip where dragster legends race, intrigues me. I invite the eight fastest sprint racers I know, and create a money purse. The NHRA is in for the demo at the prestigious Winter Nationals. The event is on. More notoriety. More publicity.

Ed McCulloch becomes a yearly donor. Shirley 'Cha Cha' Muldowney (the first female to drive a top fuel dragster) takes tours of Casa Colina and becomes an advocate. We bring the press along. They eat it up.

Recognition.

I receive the Jerry Buss Humanitarian award. Jerry Buss is the owner of the 80s dominant Los Angeles Lakers. We create a brand before brands become a vogue and a fruitful business strategy. Lakers Coach, Pat Riley, and fan favorite, Kurt Rambis, attends the NWBA Final Four hosted by Casa Colina at Cal Poly, Pomona. The Lakers Girls dance. The place is packed. We're connected to everything in Southern California.

The presenter of the Humanitarian Award is Magic Johnson. I am in awe. My hero.

I eye him before the ceremony. He's chatting up aspiring actress Holly Robinson. Robinson goes on to marry USC and NFL quarterback, Rodney Peete. Heavyweight champion George Foreman lurks in the background, along with James Worthy, Kareem Abdul Jabbar, and the rest of the Lakers.

I catch Magic's eye. He exits from the actress.

"You're my point guard idol," I say. "Would you mind signing a few things?" My backpack is full of Magic gear.

Magic and I share some one-on-one time, two ballers talking a common language whilst all around the world spins and glamorizes itself. I know this night amongst celebrities at the Century Plaza Hotel is about an acknowledgement and realization. The moment lasts. This is the time I take with me. Forever.

Noble intentions often become afterthoughts without the snowball effect of relationships. The commonality of strength as everyone pulls from the same side of the rope. I've always known this through sport. Now, I know this through business and finance.

Money changes things. Always has. Always will.

Mike Scioscia and I on the field at Chavez Ravine with my son Justin.

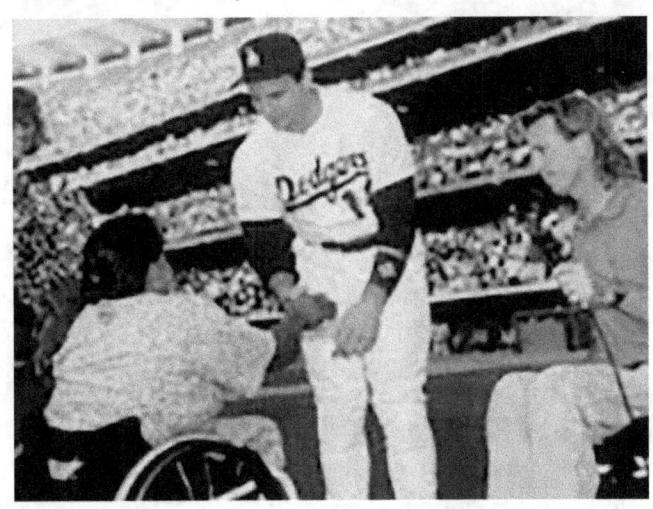

One of my junior athletes Tony Lara (RIP) and Mike's wife Anne. This happened a lot over time being involved with the Dodgers and Mike Scioscia.

I encountered Tommy Lasorda often because of Mike Scioscia.

*Magic Johnson at Sports Star Awards Dinner. Magic, along with
George Foreman, presented me with the Jerry Buss Humanitarian
Award for my work in adaptive sports with Casa Colina.*

A SECOND TASTE

There are always new, grander challenges to confront,
a true winner will embrace each one.

— Mia Hamm

In Southern California they're easy to spot. You see it in their eyes. Their spark ignites the next *Go,* and speaks to the glorious, dues paid. They're the ease in the chaos. It's not that they're enlightened. In fact, their knowledge base is more singular. They stand out. The width of their shoulders carries the payload and eliminates the unnecessary stress of pondering the opinions of others. Without knowing it, they're constantly recovering. Replenishing the protein, nutrients, and vitamins to begin again the chase of excelling. They're the swimmers and divers on dryland amongst the pedestrians, hair almost dry, loading up on lunch and needed caloric intake to sustain until dinner. They're the wrestlers, cauliflower ears gnawed from taking hits, stout legs a base to the next explosive move, eyes casually piercing their immediate surroundings. They're the lanky volleyball players, just off the beach or back from a full team scrimmage, drinks in hand—they're a consistent hydration to the art of jumping higher and reaching farther. They're the water polo and soccer players smoothly entering the situation. Their grace of movement is practiced until it's not, and becomes unrehearsed—a secondary nature. You don't know they're there until you keep stealing a second look. They're the sailors with the sunscreen and wind burn, eyeing the breeze and taking in what's bigger. They're the runners, reaching for coffee; their limbs a habit of movement and acceleration.

They're everywhere in Southern California, but they're also just another subplot. Southern California glorifies the rapid rise. In contrast, the indifference of what's *daily* and *regular* make up the majority of its inhabitants. These good folks are part of a larger grind. Their happiness comes in the form of paying the mortgage (rent), raising healthy families, and a sense of community. There's a lot of folks here and it takes all kinds.

The athletes you see in line at the market are mostly existing on a shoestring, living on: parents', the government's, or their partner's dime. They're chasing a vision of themselves created through television, bedroom posters and affirming brushes with greatness. The struggle is admirable. It has its own currency in the form of handsome hook-ups, beach bods and the comradery/community of all the other So Cal athletes and dream-chasers.

It's the early 80s. The same handsome gaze of the sun-drenched jock is growing in numbers. People are taking notice. The double-take is the wheels.

They're the basketball team, tossing a couple back after practice: boisterous, cocky, ball-busting, and communicative. Their fellowship is deep. They're a like-minded tribe chasing wins, championships, and a potential legacy. They're the doubles partners, rising in the rankings and making plans. A quick lunch and it's up Coast Highway to the next match. They're the road racers, loading their gear into the back of vans and trucks. Their trek up and down the numerous Southern California river trails, draws the approving nod and awe of a running community about to take serious notice. They're the Blister Bowl in the parking lot just off the sands of Santa Barbara: spirals, hits, road rash, returns, interceptions, and touchdown spikes drawing eyes away from the latest bathing suit cuts and post-surf flirtations. They're the San Diego downhillers. Jack Murphy Stadium hosting the wobbly, on-the-verge-of-death, downhill races of its devil-may-care southland residents. The after-parties in Ocean Beach are legendary in length, consumption and locals' interplay. They're the Long Beach Harbor water skiers skimming the surface on knee boards. On their knees or bellies, their need for speed has the attention of all expecting another tranquil harbor swim and read of the latest crime thriller. They're the surfers traversing the sand in home-made rickshaws. Their friends dump them into the Pacific Ocean to prone surf Newport or Huntington Beach. They taste the salt of the Pacific in every wave they punch through, paddle over, drop-in, and wipe out on. The sand sticks to their tires like paste, but it matters not. They're caught in the faraway buzz of remembering that set wave, the drop, and choosing the line to a favorable exit.

It's the early 80s, disability sport is mushrooming, and Southern California is the epicenter.

They're the ones you see in the world. Their far-and-wide, contented stare, not just for the young, tribal, able-bodied, scholarship types. They are the Wheel Heads; bronze and strong—taking a needed break and prepping for the next session.

It's an inspired time for wheelchair sporting men and women and although they're miles apart from their able-bodied peers in recognition and support, they're breaking ground—and for the first time travelling beneath the same stars.

The greatest addition to the 1980-81 version of the Condors is the influx of funding. There are no out-of-pocket expenses. Flights to major tournaments are covered, as are hotel expenses and meals. The only tournament we drive to is the yearly, preseason, warm-up affair in Balboa Park, San Diego. Mileage is covered.

The LA Stars and Long Beach Flying Wheels remain our local rivals but the tone has shifted. They, like the rest of Southern California, want nothing to do with us. Teams take their medicine that we're more than happy to deliver. There's a respect for all opponents, but there's also a heavy-handed confidence that any successes garnered against our team—the Casa Colina Condors—is to be squashed in our next counterattack. If you score on us. We score the next three times on you. If you try to run clock and stall the game (no shot clock during this time), we counter with a chair stopping press with passing lane takeaways from the long reaches of Albert, Curtis, and me.

There are still growing pains.

I'm the de facto player/coach. I don't like the job. I'm the gatekeeper of everyone's minutes on the floor. I don't like coming out of games. The person playing behind me wants in the game. The conflict is elementary. I'm also dealing with egos: big and strong whilst also sensitive and unstable.

It's a big tournament game. Albert has missed a couple bunny layups in a row. I pull him. It's a simple decision. Cool down. Refocus. Wait your turn. We go on and win the game.

There's a knock on my hotel room door.

It's Campos. I can tell Albert's knocked a few back. He's confrontational. I know why.

He threatens to do a number on me. I love the guy, but I'm not going to back down. I also understand. We quickly apprehend the potential calamity of any punches landed.

I close the door on my down-trodden teammate. This isn't what I signed up for.

Turning my back to the door, I exhale. Full of rage and relief simultaneously is a strange, hard-to-swallow pill. I decide then about my future as the team's player/coach.

I gotta get out of this role. It sucks.

In March of the 1981 season, the Casa Colina Condors are in the Final Four championship game against the North Florida Renegades. The Westland, Michigan, event looks like it's teed up for the Detroit Sparks for another strong tourney run. The Renegades have other plans and dismiss the Sparks in the semis.

The Renegades are led by Johnny Johnston, a ridiculously good mid-range shooter. His repeated shots off the glass is a lesson in old school fundamentals. A Vietnam Vet, Johnston surrounds himself with size, accomplished skill-sets, and like-minded warrior -ough, Vietnam Veteran teammates.

Bill Richardson, a lanky 6'6", double amputee, sprints the floor and lacks no confidence defending Curtis in the post and between the free throw lines. Their transition battles and the need to establish and deny position is physical and a pure battle of wills. Mike Gabriel and Bob Patterson, both single leg amputees, are solid defenders, scorers, and play with a length that's built to intimidate. Rick Helms, a national team class one, secures the starting five.

The North Florida Renegades are leathery good. They're tough as nails but ultimately don't have the intangibles it takes to beat us. It takes superlative effort and execution to hang with us. To beat us takes an in-the-moment greatness that oversteps actual ability. Pundits call it "the zone."

We beat North Florida 61-49. They're formidable. As brothers of the cause, they have my full respect but it's our time. Curtis has a great weekend and is the championship tournament's Most Valuable Player.

The Casa Colina Condors are back-to-back champions.

The second taste is as sweet as the first.

PART FOUR

Everyone wants to live on top of the mountain
but all the happiness and growth
occurs while you're climbing it.
— Andy Rooney

REVOLUTION AND EVOLUTION

Don't ya Know?
They're talking about a revolution
It sounds like a whisper
Poor people gonna rise up and get their share
Poor people gonna rise up and take what's theirs.

— Tracy Chapman

Eric Walls, or 'Flea,' and Brad Parks doing Quadra moves well before their time.

The uprising begins with a determined ripple.

It's the late 70s. A Southern California crew of athletes gear up to take on the pompous, corporate attitude of lumbering, stagnant wheelchair designers and builders, and start assembling a lightweight performance wheelchair revolution in the garage of Jeff Minnebraker.

137

Jeff is the founder of the first custom-manufactured aluminium, rigid, sport, and everyday chair.

There are two national companies that dominate the manufacturing of wheelchairs: Everest & Jennings (E&J) and Stainless Medical (referred to as Stainless). E&J is the big dog and rules the market. The Stainless ride is a bit sportier. They add a second axle post, moving the center of gravity forward an inch. The shorter wheelbase allows the chair to turn quicker. It's still pure, indefensible crap.

Both dubious manufacturers use grade-8 bolts as axles. This nut and bolt system breaks on a regular basis. The mayhem of competing often has its competitors stuck in quicksand (so to speak) as they await able-bodied help to leave the floor on 3 wheels. The 10- to -15-minute fix demands spare axles, tools, and timely elbow grease to enter back into the game. Distracting. Frustrating.

The big company attitude is, *We don't have to change. We own the market. We're all you've got.*

I remember bringing my Lazy Boy of a recliner home after my discharge from Rancho: push handles—hacksawed away, backrest (I seek the freedom to turn and rotate unencumbered), and a leather belt with the inscription, "Make Love Not War," fastened at the seat-post to tighten up the upholstery and add lumbar support.

The modification is also a statement that I'm different. I'm in search of what's beyond being handicapped. I am (like many 1970s compatriots) in search of *cool.*

In the mid-1930s chairs weighed close to 150 pounds and were made entirely of wood. The things didn't fit through most standard doorways. Around this time, a fed-up Herbert Everest tires of convalescing after a coal mining accident. Everest fractures his spine and needs a better form of mobility.

Everest partners with Harry Jennings to change the landscape for returning World War II veterans. War is a catastrophe. Within catastrophes are plenty of spinal cord injuries.

David Davis wrote in his book, *Wheels of Courage,* "He (Everest) enlisted the assistance of Harry Jennings, a non-disabled mechanical engineer, and a solution soon emerged that revolutionized mobility for people with paraplegia. Working together out of Jennings's garage in Southern California, they fashioned a comfortable, foldable wheelchair made of chromium-plated steel tubing."

A mere 30-plus years later, I'm in a Southern California garage. Jeff Minnebraker tells me to take a spin in his aluminum, low back, chair. I experience his, "chair-like-a-skateboard," firsthand.   A limitless spirit overwhelms. An inventive, athletic profoundness takes hold.

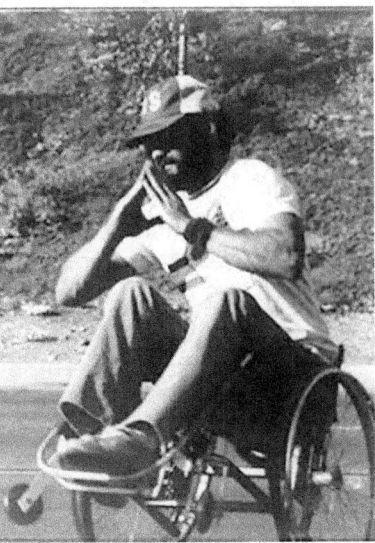

Jeff Minnebraker, the founder, pushed his own limits all the time to gain the perspective of possible, not impossible.

Jeff in my backyard hangout, San Dimas.

"My chair, I streamline it as much as possible, and look at it more in the way of a sports car. It's something that will perform—something that will really function and do the job," says Jeff Minnebraker.

The quote is taken from the movie, *Get it Together.* Its opening scenes show Minnebraker navigating a Southern California river trail: descending, sprinting, wheeling across water, and spinning wheelie 360s. The twenty-minute and fifty-four second film debuts in 1976 and draws the attendance of Jane Fonda and Jon Voight at its initial screening. Their Academy Award winning movie, *Coming Home,* is yet to be released.

Minnebraker continues, *"I want my chair to be something that will turn really quick."*

Raised in Santa Monica, Jeff takes to the region's waves as a surfer and the streets as a skateboarder. As a kid, Jeff's father instills in him a workmanlike approach that lasts.

Jeff asks his father to buy him a skateboard.

"Dad brought me up, if I wanted it, I needed to make it," says Jeff. "From there, I built my first skateboard."

Jeff went on to become a Makaha Skateboard Team rider: *"I loved doing 360s. I could do 8 to 10 at a time."*

Jeff began to challenge everything to do with hospital issued relics. Their limited options keep those with spinal-cord injuries stuck in a yesterday of needing help, more than a tomorrow of promise—and reaching a potential that a quality, custom fitted ride presents.

The word *wheelchair* connotes a very real, negative reaction in society. Add to that, the 1970s are the dark ages of accessibility and disability rights. Minnebraker wants more. He takes to his garage and begins one build after another.

"I wanted these chairs to be sit down skateboards," says Jeff.

Little did he know how his obsession would change the world of mobility for generations to come. Those nights, mornings, and hours in the 'garage,' Jeff built prototypes—one at a time—that shifted the landscape of disability transport (for the better) —and forever.

During the late 70s, I'm indifferent to the history being forged in Jeff's garage. I'm away in college in Northern California. I come home to Southern California often though, and it doesn't take too many trips to converge on Jeff's garage. The first moment I sit in one of his aluminium, shorter wheel-based chair/skateboard/bike, tricked out rides, I'm sold.

The backrest is only 6 to 8 inches high. The thought of flipping backwards pings through my membrane. I have quick learning skills. Talent. Get past it. I do. Freedom of movement overwhelms my senses. I imagine veering left. All it takes is a shoulder turn and look. Astounding. The ride does the same to the right. I throw my shoulders back. My hands are off the wheels. The front-end lifts. Caster wheels leave the ground. I quickly grab the wheels to stay upright. I eye Jeff. He smirks knowingly. I'm out of the garage. I'm on the road letting it rip. I grab the big wheels behind the backrest and hammer down. A full push has my hands almost scraping the pavement. Repeat. Hand-speed. My thing. I'm gone. I turn behind me to look at Jeff. His diminishing silhouette is a testimony to his craft. I turn back. The shorter backrest allows freedom of rotation. I'm forced to stop. I don't want to. The cul-de-sac dead-ends. I throw my hands onto the tires. My shoulders lunge forward. Speed, gravity, and inertia doing its thing. The caster wheels lift. I spin a wheelie 360. Another. I'm a continuous, spinning blur. Astonishing. Dizzying. I take long hard pushes back to the garage. I'm gliding. Fifty feet is covered between pushes. Whoa. I see Jeff. He's full size again. He looks like a dad. I feel giant and small. Like a kid learning to ride a bike.

"What do you think?" he asks.

Words leave me. It's like when you first connect bat to ball. A stunned silence and admiration of the ball in flight. Words lessen the feat.

"Looks like you were moving pretty good."

I shake and nod my head approvingly.

Jeff sees the future. Aluminium is a superior product to stainless steel in weight and performance. Quick-release axles are also a major lifestyle improvement. No more broken axles and the chore of making things right. These axles don't break. Jeff's rigid frames weigh-in around 20 pounds. Ground breaking and less than twice the weight of an E&J or Stainless Super Sport. The quick-release axles allow folks to load in and out of their cars much easier. The process of pushing a button at the center of each wheel's hub, frees the wheel from its axle plate and in a matter of seconds both wheels are loaded into sedans as well as trucks and stylish sports cars.

As an innovator, Jeff's moving away from the negativity that's associated with the term "wheelchair." He looks at his designs as a new form of passage. A better way to get from one point to another. Pure, clean and simple—the calm before the deluge—it's an enchanting time, full of possibility.

This is the guy leading the revolution.

I'm in.

Rip it!

Every band leader needs strong players.

Jeff, follows the Great One, Ed Owen as the Recreation Therapist at Rancho Los Amigos, Rehabilitation Hospital. He doesn't have to look far to find his rhythm section. Former patients, Eric Walls and Brad Parks, come on board.

Walls, a surfer out of Huntington Beach, is a mid-level spinal cord injury. He's a workhorse and Jeff's go-to guy. Eric, nicknamed Flea, burns up the Los Angeles basin freeways finding the needed parts to set up shop. Eric is pivotal. As a T-8 injury (paralyzed a couple inches below his chest), he shows the lightweight, custom rides are not just for lower-level injuries like Jeff, Brad, and myself. Eric is the first I've seen throw his chair on two wheels and ride with both a big wheel and caster wheel spinning freely in the air whilst he steers holding the opposite caster. The move is a statement. The cool factor is steep.

*Eric Walls throwing it on two wheels. A defining and
radical move not seen since the Quadra days*

Eric Walls is a salt-of-the-earth guy. His loyalty factor to Jeff, and the creation of lightweight, performance chairs has him sleeping on the shop's cold, cement floors. Perpetually worn out, Eric sees the future of life-altering, custom chairs throughout the world but also is the personification of perseverance, commitment to the task, and hard work.

Every shop needs an Eric.

Brad Parks, from Laguna Beach, has the looks and brawn. A next level skier, Parks reaches too far, and too high, one critical afternoon. He takes to the air doing a competitive backflip, over-rotates and crashes back to earth with a life-changing spinal cord injury. Always a charger, Brad returns to adaptive snow skiing years later an outstanding and passionate skier.

One of Brad's initial introductions to sport is through Jeff as an inpatient at Rancho. There's a key scene in the award-winning documentary, *"Get it Together,"* with Jeff and Brad hitting tennis balls.

Parks remembers, "Jeff was helping me learn to play wheelchair tennis and there was an instant bond. We became buddies during that day of shooting."

Bob Vogel, writing for new mobility magazine, described a snippet of Parks' and Minnebraker's relationship: "Parks is attending the University of Santa Barbara and stops by Minnebraker's house in Woodland Hills on the way home from school. Parks asks if he can sit in Minnebraker's chair. "The chair feels incredibly light and quick compared to my slow bulky chair," says Parks. "Jeff transfers into my chair, and when I look over at him, I'm shocked! He looks so handicapped. I say, *'Is this the way I look?'"*

The initial members of the band are in place.

Jeff knows his new product is a departure from the mainstream. To do this he must be all-in. He quits his job at Rancho with its benefits, health insurance, and stability.

He sells his house for start-up capital.

He initially names his venture Quadra Transports. It's no mistake the word wheelchair is none-to-be-found in the company's title. After listening to others, Jeff realizes his ground-breaking product needs to be clarified as a "wheelchair." It's the first in a line of philosophical compromises that chip away at the striking independence of the start-up business and its colorful characters. Quadra Wheelchairs goes on to never be referred to by its full name but always Quadra.

Enter Mary Wilson (now Mary Wilson Boegel). Another Recreation Therapist working at the same Ralph K. Davies Hospital in San Francisco. Mary is pivotal in procuring my short-lived gig at the same San Francisco Hospital.

She wants in on the revolution. She leaves the (still affordable) comforts of what's on both sides of the Golden Gate Bridge and enters the shop life of Quadra. She is the Stevie Nicks of the band. Wild at heart, superior at reading people, and with a welcoming smile. Mary is the office gatekeeper. She interacts with an impatient public wanting in on what they've seen and heard about.

With a low-level, incomplete spinal cord injury, Mary embodies the grace and ease of a Quadra in motion.

The boys in the shop hunt speed, turning radius, and durability under the most extreme conditions. They call it Research and Development. Jeff's taken to spinning wheelie 360s with such force that he's able to remove his hands from the wheels and press them together as if he's praying. There's a mounting energy presiding over the move that allows his chair to continue to spin on its two big wheels until he begins to recalibrate the move into another twirling derby. He throws his weight forward and the trick subsides on all four wheels spinning.

Watching Mary in her chair is to see the relationship between athleticism, style, refinement, and a womanly self-assurance. Mary brings out the sexy in the lines and cuts of the chair.

Me, Mary, and Jeff at Century Plaza Hotel, where I received the Tribute to Courage Award from Casa Colina Hospital.

Mary Wilson was the perfect balance to all the Quadra dudes from its beginning.

We all go through Mary to see where our order is in line. She seldom has the answers we're in search of, but still, we feel better nonetheless.

Quadra is piling up firsts in the world of transport for the disabled. Eric Walls puts it this way…Quadra is:

"First production on non-steel, ultra-light, aluminium, manual wheelchairs. Frames are heliarc-welded by hand. 60-61, T6.

First to integrate custom, anodized frames to particular needs: rims, frame and components.

First to source and use removable ½-inch, PIP PINS or QUICK PINS. Now called quick release wheel axles for easy disassembly.

First to outsource the Quadra custom Quick Pins.

First to create multi-adjustable rear axle plates with 16 different axle positions.

First to have aluminium wheel rims with hard anodized, hand rims, with stainless mounting hardware. First to lace using only stainless-steel spokes to aluminium, Bullseye hubs.

First to use high quality sealed bearings on back wheels and front castors.

First to make extruded Aluminium Castor Forks with multi axle holes for large and small castor wheels. Anodized to your color preference.

First to use Urethane front Castors—Power Paw, with sealed bearings—lighter and narrower profile.

First to use stainless-steel and titanium for fastening hardware on all hardware points.

First to have waterproof seating upholstery."

By 1979, the garage is bursting at the seams. The team secures a small shop in Westlake Village, just north of Los Angeles.

It's around this time I see a shiny, electric green, 10-speed bike soaring past me. It's stunning. An impression is made. A few minutes later, I see the same bike parked at a convenience store. I pull over. Eye the thing up. The green speaks to speed. That's it. I want a green Quadra. Jeff says, "No problem," and makes me one at no cost.

I'm part of a movement.

I begin to visit the Quadra shop more and more.

Chairs are stacked and hung across one wall of the shop with a rainbow of colorful frames. It's like looking into a world that isn't actualized yet. It's black and white versus color movies and television. It's knowing one-hundred-percent that outside these walls, the world for the disabled population is on course to change for the better.

Conversations begin. I use my name recognition to penetrate the largest athlete market—wheelchair basketball.

I'm part of team Quadra. Jeff, Eric, Mary, and Brad are the heavy lifters, but I'm the test pilot—the influencer—using my reputation and growing relationships across the sporting country to help sell chairs.

In my first Quadra chair, creating influence of sales in basketball, vs Joe Sutika of the Sparks, and in HOF.

On the track. In this track photo, Jim Knaub, me, and Brad Parks are all heavy hitters in the sport.

Will to win.

A new look and attitude are ready to hit the streets.

The new shop not only gives the crew a proper workspace, but also a heightened realization that a prosperous future is just around the bend.

University programs and community based basketball teams are ordering chairs a dozen at a time. A team in Illinois has their chairs ready to ship against one of the shop's walls. There's a statement of personality and sporting fellowship happening.

"Suddenly, there were groups of red, blue, and green chairs going out the doors, and teams were looking like real teams. Not this hodgepodge of wheelchairs," recalls Jeff.

A Quadra movement that begins at a subcultural level in Southern California garners momentum throughout the United States and then globally. Wheel Heads, the one's with such limited choices for generations, are now choosing colors, urethane or pneumatic (inflated) caster wheels, brakes or no brakes (most athletes choosing no brakes at all), and a first ever, shortened wheel-base allowing others to mimic the aforementioned radical skills of the Quadra Crew.

Everything today that we take for granted and makes everyday life and elite sport better, begins with Jeff Minnebraker and Quadra. The use of lightweight aluminum. Anodized frames give the Wheel Head user a first ever splash of needed color. The quick-release axle simplifies taking wheels off and on in split seconds. Sealed bearings eliminate dirt, grime, and rust. The chair glides smooth and free on skateboard-like urethane wheels. The center of gravity adjustment allows users a turning radius never known.

It's a great time to ride a Quadra.

Quadra is spoiling me to my core. If I want it, they hand it over and more. Besides basketball, I'm traversing Southern California playing tennis, football, and pushing track. Old and dear friend John Chambers hosts the first ever wheelchair tennis tournament in Los Angeles' Griffith Park. I make it to the finals against Brad Parks. My exploits as an athlete are taking shape. The Condors are on a roll and I'm winning most individual events.

Just before the Quadra explosion, Brad Parks and I compete in the first-ever wheelchair tennis tournament played at Griffith Park in LA; organized by John Chambers.

Brad gets the win in the final. This is where the competition began.

My job at Casa Colina also extends my reach for Quadra.

I'm a proud Quadra rider. There's a movement. Quadra, doing what's never been done before, peaks and keeps my full attention.

Quadra takes on an investor. We'll call him The Investor. I'm neither here nor there, on the move. I trust everything Jeff and the crew decide.

I get a call.

It's a company out of Ohio named Invacare. They want to fly me out and discuss a paid sponsorship deal to ride their chair.

I'm intrigued and hop a flight to Cleveland.

That night, belly up in the bedroom of a swanky hotel, I can't shake this feeling in my gut. *What about Quadra? Is this the right move?*

The morning comes and I'm full of anxiety (the good kind if there is such a thing). I'm picked up and taken to Invacare headquarters. During the ride, I'm thinking, *Invacare, Invacare, Invacare.* Sounds a lot like invalid. *What kind of name is that?*

I'm inside the executive office. First class. Corporate. Commercial.

This is new territory. It's new terrain for any wheelchair athlete at the time. I do my best to take things in stride. Inside, I'm churning.

I'm offered $17,000 a year to ride in their new, forthcoming chair. It's 1980, and 17K is a brick-ton of cash. I think about the family. The influx of cash eases things mightily. I do the math. My Casa Colina salary and this sponsorship? My heart says, *yes, yes, yes.* I keep cool as best I can.

It hits me.

What about Quadra? What about my crew? What about Jeff? The guy's my friend. This is not going to go well.

I get back to Southern California. Sandy and I powwow. There's a tempered excitement. The additional income is a relief and a spark in the same breath. If we're blessed enough to have another child the resources are there.

We both know the impending awkwardness must be dealt with.

I make the forty-five-minute drive to Westlake Village and the Quadra shop. How's this going to go over with Jeff? The Investor seems to be taking on a larger role and is a part of the meeting. I'm in the shop's office. I let it out.

"I have an offer…"

Jeff hangs his head. He's disappointed—on the verge of being pissed off. His tone confirms my take.

Squirming inside, I defend my decision. Looking just at Jeff, "Jeff, brother, I have a family. I can't turn down something as big as this."

There's an uncomfortable beat.

"I can stay on with you and Quadra. "

Another beat.

Jeff asks how I see this happening?

"I'm hoping you can better their offer by a couple grand, so I don't have to switch everything up and leave this relationship with people I love—and equipment I worship."

The Investor owns the moment, "All right, we'll give you $20,000 per year to stay with us and influence sales."

With both sets of eyes staring through me like precision lasers, I reply, "Hell, yeah."

I owe Jeff, Eric, Brad, and Mary. They're the ones in the warehouse pumping out products. Chairs are out the door to basketball players constantly. My job is easy: work my trade, perform at an elite level, and be genuine with folks when they "lay eyes" on me, in my colorful, bold, big-attitude Quadra.

Before The Investor comes on board, I remember Jeff making the short trek to Ventura County and the city of Camarillo to meet with Everest & Jennings Wheelchairs. All I know is the meeting doesn't go to plan. As much as everyone—on the athletic side—of mobility knows, E&Js are a diminishing and out-of-date product. Quadra shows them the future. They're not interested. A move, to this day, I'm sure they regret.

"We paved the way for ultralight chairs. No one wanted to accept this except the athletes discovering just how fabulous that kind of mobility is," says Mary Wilson Boegel.

I finalize my sponsorship deal with Quadra and get it in writing. A professional, performance, and influence-based contract is in place.

I am an elite athlete. I am a performer and, for the first time in adaptive sport history, I am the first paid and sponsored athlete. It's hard to wipe the perpetual smile off my face.

For a year, everything is golden. The early in-my-career relationship with Quadra sets the tone for decades to come. Stay close to those loyal to you but also realize that loyalty only goes so far. In business, as in all facets of the human experience, the truth predicts outcomes.

I talk with Jeff and Eric about building a race chair. We explore all the means of making the thing lighter, faster, and durable. The answer is titanium.

California is full of monsters on the track. The simplicity of going fast, take a left, and come-on-back has a meaty collection of heroes: Jim Knaub, mighty Brad Parks, Jim Martinson, Gary Kerr, John Rudolf, and Texan Randy Snow are all capable of winning a variety of races. My need to beat the best peaks my drive to take them on.

Quadra strips away pounds of weight from my previous track chairs. I take my feather-light, titanium-built Maserati for its initial spin. I feel like a cheetah chasing prey. Soon, the combination of training, chair, and an overriding desire to win—to be superlative—allows me to beat the fastest guys in the country. I don't dominate but I can push the track with anyone. In a race, I use drafting strategies and a finishing kick to win.

Jim Knaub, me, John Rudolph, Jim Martinson, Gary Kerr, and Unknown in 1500 meters at Washington Huskie Stadium at National Championships. I draft my way to a win with finishing kick.

Jeff designs and builds a Tower Chair. I'm in. I look at him in his. He's 4 to 5 inches taller than when in his 'normal' chair. He has 27-inch wheels beneath him. The thing is all attitude. It says, *I'm your equal. I will look eye-to-eye with those that previously looked down on me.*

It's the middle finger to everyone.

It's clear to me, Jeff has enough of living in a world with his neck craned to eye what's above him. My first week in mine, I revel in my newfound height. I look men in the eye. A subtle, yet powerful realization that simple things matter. I rub shoulders with Sandy. We chuckle at how fresh and playful the move is.

I enter the president's office at Casa Colina.

I'm in the Tower Chair.

He double-takes like there's a gnawing at his ankles. I look down at him sitting at his desk.

"You, in that chair, make me uncomfortable," he says.

I remember Jeff's line and reason for creating the Tower Chair, "It's a walking world out there."

Staying in rhythm like a drummer in time, "Now you know how it feels to always look up at someone," I answer. "It sucks. Right?"

Jeff's intention is clear. Flip daily experiences on its ear. Challenge pre-existing notions with shock and awe. Control moments that have previously controlled you. Make people uncomfortable through athleticism, design, and sheer will—before they're comfortable with who you actually are: a person far more profound than tragedy and recovery.

A tale of folklore—the kind where witnesses are larger than fact—begins to be shared concerning Quadra and breakability. Stories begin to be told of Jeff, Eric, Brad, and myself successfully dropping from loading docks without breaking axles and sticking the landings. We also find giant curbs and have contests of who can jump the gnarliest ones. I take on the biggest with success.

Photos of the boys tilting their chairs downhill begin to be spoken of: *radical, out-there, gnarly, hairy, and renegade* are terms thrown around.

The tale that tops all others can only be told by someone who was there.

Eric Walls begins, "Close to Quadra's shop, we did a crash test using a stretch of paved road adjacent to Highway 101 North. There was a dirt culvert (an open drain beneath a road or highway) about 3 to 4 feet in depth. The road was seldom used. I don't think it even had a name. We used it as a shortcut to a great, little deli on the southbound side of Highway 101."

I remember the place. Great turkey sandwiches with baklava and ice tea.

"It was summer. It was hot. We opened the sliding door of Jeff's 70s Chevy panel van. I (Eric) was driving with Jeff, Mary, and Brad all sitting in the back. We were keeping pace with the northbound, freeway traffic. Jeff says, 'Hold on' and flings **his** chair out the open slider much like an Army Airborne paratrooper launching out of the doorway.'"

I remember the chair doing cartwheels over and beyond itself as the mad scientists look on. Each impact and ricocheting bounce drawing distinctive gasps. The ride back to the chair simmers things. It's that moment before something extraordinary happens. We all eye the thing before staring at one another.

"We circled back and picked up his chair thinking it's completely toast. [But no] just a few scratches on the hand-rims."

I'm not in the van because Eric tells me so, but in an indestructible way we're all in the van. Wheel Head's tired of unserviceable, antiquated, heavy, and always breaking detachable-bullshit, all have reason to rejoice.

The word spreads. The Quadra crew is on to something big.

It's not long after The Investor comes on board that I begin to see less of Brad and Mary. The severity of it all doesn't hit me at first. Life is large. I'm certain Brad and Mary have their reasons. I don't give it much thought.

The need for an investor is logical and in-step with the growth of the company—and the group's dream. Things begin to happen in the dark. Jeff

Minnebraker, the innovator and primary owner, trusts the wrong dude. There's disharmony in the shop.

"I lived in the factory with Jeff and Eric for two years," adds Mary. "We liquidated everything for Quadra. I ended up moving in with a gal that ran the local coffee shop and starting commuting in. I go to open things up and the keys don't work. He (the Investor) had changed the locks."

"I brought in an investor that ended up being Frankenstein," says Jeff. "There were cargo containers (full of chairs) going to Norway. I never saw the money."

Jeff loses majority ownership and doesn't quite know how.

There's a move to squeeze Eric out. He's the constant. He's the day-one guy. It's only a matter of time and when.

I become collateral damage. My contract ceases to be honored. The Investor is stiffing me. I hear nothing.

The Quadra crew and I are angry. The dream is disintegrating before our eyes. I retaliate the only way I know how and secure pro bono counsel from an attorney on the Casa Colina board. He goes Pitbull on the breaker of all promises. We hit him between the eyes. My contract is in writing. The Investor is forced into a legal corner. He has no options but to pay me retroactively. I get a check for what I'm owed. Vindication.

Jeff's left to salvage what we can. He has to hang on within a bad situation and attempt to get what is due. It never happens. The Investor uses the business like his personal ATM. It's crooked. What is the aspiration of hope, now smells of a slow, burning decay.

The Quadra era ends. It's a short three-year run. Heroic and distressing.

Eric, the closest to Jeff then and now, is a trusted partner, teammate, and workhorse when Jeff and Quadra need it the most. With a clever knack for design, he is often the first to test drive and push the boundaries of the father of invention, Jeff Minnebraker.

Walls falls victim to broken trust. He is moved out the Quadra door by the dastardly deeds of a villainous character. A partner no longer, he watches Jeff try to hang on to what is rightfully theirs. Business is often a swindle. A hard lesson not lost on Eric.

After Quadra, Walls moves to Hawaii. This is where a quiet legend comes to life. The Maui locals take to him as a wave charger and friend of the aloha lifeforce. His rickshaw innovations of getting in and out of the water are another testimony to his design and fabrication capacities. Made with lightweight, PVC piping, balloon tires and a kitesurfing harness for a seat, Eric's rickshaw is easy for someone to push and pull him in and out of the ocean.

In his early teens, Eric busts his back climbing a backyard tree to check the surf. He falls. There's a live wire, electric shock involved. Boom. Life changing, spinal cord injury. Eric never loses his stoke for the ocean and returns to her riding waves on his belly and in the prone position. Even as a teenager he's way before his time.

Eric Walls is a boundless surfer. He likes the big ones. He takes on gnarly, rocky breaks where losing your board takes on very real consequences. Filmers and photographers have plenty of content of the-guy-on-his-belly charging the Polynesian paradise of waves.

Not one to enter contests, he surfs for the dream, leaving the dusty trophies for others to tend and polish. I've never once heard Eric toot his own horn— never.

I know Eric will never choose an easier, softer way. He is the essence of 'Go Big or Go Home.'

Eric shared with me a message he received from Jeff during the construction of the words upon these pages. I imagine revisiting the scar tissue of Quadra is scratchy and still raw for both.

The message from Jeff to Eric reads, "You were number one. First employee of Quadra. I know that. Thanks."

'Flea,' a living legend in Hawaii captures some of the greatest waves ever recorded! Eric Walls, the best lay down adaptive surfer of all time.

Brad Parks lives a grateful life. With his lovely wife, Wendy, by his side he enjoys the fruits of his labor. Brad's perch atop what he's built is a testimony to hard work, smarts, and dedication to his craft. His twin daughters, Maiyah and Sarah, are the spark that drives his purpose.

Brad parlays his start-up time with Jeff on the tennis courts into a worldwide personality in the sport as a competitor, administrator, and founder.

In 1980, Brad creates the National Foundation of Wheelchair Tennis. He takes on the role of Billie Jean King for the sport. He creates awareness, a pool of competitors, clinics for the generations to come, a tournament schedule, a ranking system, pivotal relationships with the United States Tennis Association (USTA), Kids Camps, celebrity up/down (a doubles match with a player in a chair and an able-bodied partner) exhibition matches, a national championship tournament, and the resources to fund an office in upscale Irvine, California. Perhaps, most importantly, the USTA adopts the official rule that wheelchair tennis players receive an additional second bounce when needed.

Brad is the sport's voice, personality, and greatest advocate.

Today, wheelchair tennis is internationally renowned with handsome event earnings. There's a wheelchair division at all four grand slam events.

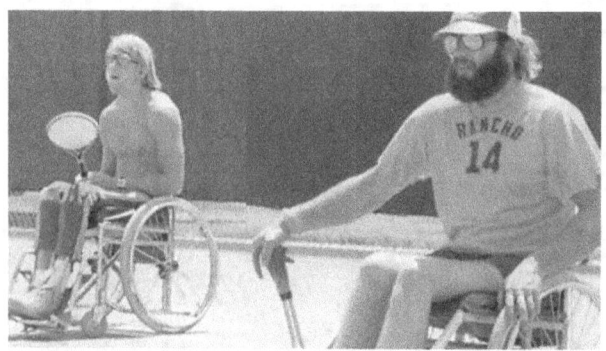

Brad's trademark tongue hanging out, is in this moment with Jeff Minnebraker. Jeff was Brad's Recreation Therapist at Rancho. Who knew tennis would forever grow to worldwide acceptance and play. A powerful moment in history.

Who would have thought: first, Jeff and I rallying tennis balls with a second bounce allowance, then Jeff and Brad slapping the ball around in 1976-77 on the public courts of Southern California. We're all the first to use the two-bounce rule and now there's disabled kids in Japan, Australia, or Peru with dreams of one day playing in Wimbledon or the French Open.

In 2010, Brad Parks is inducted into the International Tennis Hall of Fame. He's the first Wheel Head to be inducted with the likes of John McEnroe, Arthur Ashe, John Newcombe, Chris Evert, and Billie Jean King.

Brad Parks, with family, friends, and dignitaries, displays his International Tennis Federation Hall of Fame in Newport, RI. Brad is the founder of organized wheelchair tennis... 'The Godfather' of the sport–for wheelchair tennis being accepted in all Grand Slams.

Brad's the best player of the game's early generation, with three US Open singles championships and a Paralympic Doubles gold medal at the 1992 games in Barcelona, teaming with Randy Snow.

These days Brad and Wendy own a home overlooking the Pacific Ocean in San Clemente and another in scenic Utah. An avid surfer and snow skier, Brad introduces me to "WaveSki" surfing at "Old Man's" beach at historic San Onofre. Just outside his home in Utah, Brad also introduces me to adaptive mountain bike riding. We traverse the trails, at times with speed and gusto and at other times with an eye on the astronomical beauty of God's creation.

Brad's a big part of the Quadra creation and mindset. Sometimes, I think success, or lack of prolonged success, is less important to the outlook, attitude, and mentality those days instilled in the make-up of its characters.

Brad's an example of living a life of his own choosing.

Success isn't a destiny, but a skill set for Mary Wilson Boegel.

She admits, "It was a very difficult transition for me psychologically. We knew Quadra was having this global impact, but after two years we were pretty strung out—pretty fried. He (the Investor) comes in and sets us off into different levels of mental health issues."

In 1984, Mary met Bruce Boegel. They begin building Standing Frames for children and adults with physical disabilities. Thirty-nine years later, Prime Engineering continues as a family run business and corporation out of Fresno, California.

Prime Engineering's 'Kid Walk' allows kids the option to rise from their chairs and explore their world as participants. The invention is ground breaking within learning environments as kids now have the length to access blackboards, surfaces, and most importantly, friends.

Mary remembers her first ride in her Quadra, "I felt like I wasn't grounded. When I merged with the chair my disability went away."

Mary is a grandmother of three these days, although her extended nest is even larger with family and neighborhood youngsters constantly under her care. Kids are "the light in this chapter of my life," and they're all family to Mary.

Quadra is a horse-pill of an experience for Mary to swallow. She holds onto the fact that things end unfulfilled, begrudgingly, and without dignity but she talks with reverence and love for its characters.

"I don't regret it. I can't," she says.

It's difficult and unfair to not only witness but to be an authentic, valuable member of a team changing the landscape of something that's so overdue. From 1979 to 1982, that transformation is high performance, lightweight wheelchairs. The change is Quadra.

"A true labor of love."

In her seventies (the oldest of the Quadra crew), Mary stays philosophical: "There are no books for aging with a spinal cord injury."

A moment passes.

"So once again, I'm here trailblazing what happens next."

Mary continues to change the world in precious ways—infinitesimal ways, but always the change.

Jeff Minnebraker lives a life without rules. East, west, north, or south are daily choices. Travelling in a Nissan camper van, Jeff travels throughout the National Parks of California, the Northwest, and western United States.

He lays his head wherever he wants and is led by his own spirit. No one tells him what to do, when to be there, which direction to go or why he needs to be there.

His freedom to do so is well earned.

Jeff's solo lifestyle is decision based. Decades ago, he lost Quadra—his dream. In essence, it's his life's work given for the advancement of others. Noble. Tough to swallow. The end of Quadra is a stinger. Jeff's creativity was on display at a time when our subculture needs it the most. His crew worked their jobs and were critically involved in manufacturing a lifestyle chair never seen before. I look at the best, most modern, sleekest chairs of today and see the Minnebraker/Quadra influence.

Trust is a derivative of truth. When it works it's an enchanting magic-carpet ride—when it doesn't the pain never really subsides but instead gets shoved into a dark, sleepy corner of a festering memory.

Being ahead of your time is a burden. Ask Pete Maravich. Ask Jeff Minnebraker. People want to touch, feel, and be in the vicinity of what they've never seen before. It becomes too much at times.

Jeff earns his commercial pilot's license, works in the aeronautical industry, and then (for the fun of it) attains his sea plane rating. He flies amphibious airplanes, jets, and helicopters. "It got me away—away from money and greed," Jeff says.

He drives the highways like a Bob Dylan chorus. With tunes thumping and his mind most undoubtedly still working toward invention and improvement. Jeff carries on. I imagine he dreams of what could have been. I would. His innovations of design have created freedom, personality, and convenience for a population so underserved.

Decades later, I can testify, without hesitation, that my first ride in a Quadra Transport is a game changer. Moves are fluid. I feel a sense of freedom I've never associated with a wheelchair. For the first time, I like the way my chair looks. It's suggestive.

These days, my friend is not the biggest fan of people. He keeps his small circle of friends close and doesn't let many in as he travels to the next National Park sunrise and thoughtful sunset. Jeff lives off the grid. He's checked out and does whatever he damn well pleases. In one breath, it sounds great. In another, I envision a lot of loneliness in this genuine, great man.

I'm lucky to break through, and with the help of Eric, have a phone conversation with Jeff. We talk of the Great One, Ed Owen, and his impact on us both.

"Bigger than life. An amazingly fit person."

"If you had the foundation of Ed Owen you're going to be just fine," I answer.

It's two old Recreation Therapists sharing memories. It's easy. We ping pong on a variety of topics. We both realize we did solid work.

"You were instrumental, and affected a lot of people for the good. I did the same job because it helps people," he says.

"Amen."

I tell him, I'd like to nominate him for the NWBA, Hall of Fame as a contributor. Quadra makes the game faster, more athletic, and better.

Silence. Subject change. More Ed Owen banter.

I throw out some more Hall of Fame talk. He deserves to be inducted and recognized for his contributions. He deflects. There's another hush to the conversation.

Jeff ends the building awkwardness, "I'd rather go out with a whimper instead of a bang."

While under contract with Quadra, a new company out of Clover/Fresno begins pursuing me. Quickie or Motion Designs already has my great friend Randy Snow under contract. The Texan is a powerful personality, life-force and mentions to me (more than once) that Quickie wheelchairs are here to stay and work well. He wants to know where I'm at and if I might want in.

I'm true to Quadra. They're my team. They inspire me.

The Investor changes things. Towards the end of 1982, I find myself with no chair/equipment sponsor. Jeff is hanging on. He is owed. The rest are gone.

"Loyalty" is another of Coach John Wooden's foundational blocks in his Pyramid of Success. Wooden writes, "Loyalty is the foundational quality that gets us through hard times. Will we compromise our integrity when temptation is great or the going gets rough? Or will we remain loyal to our beliefs and core values."

There's a sadness, where before there was such hope and life affirming change coming from the Quadra shop/factory. The capitalistic gift of ideas into production and fair market trade loses all traction as greed supersedes.

Loyalty has vanished.

Sad but true.

In the summer of 2024, I receive a message from Mary. I've been pestering her for some photos of the Quadra crew back in the day. She of course delivers.

Mary then delivers groundbreaking news, "Jeff and Quadra are being credited for starting the Complex Rehab Technology (CRT) industry! This is huge! CRT is a large and invaluable industry of products that are the most innovative and directly enhance and improve the lives of folks with physical disabilities. We would not be nearly as active, productive or happy were it not for Jeff and CRT. I know all of us have known this for a long time, but finally Jeff in particular and Quadra overall are getting the much deserved recognition, so everyone around the world is clear on who is the founder of this incredibly important technology. Can you imagine!! Starting an entire (huge and lucrative) industry that continues to live on and innovate to improve lives today and in the future!!! This recognition is just "breaking news" globally, with more coverage to come. There are several books in the works acknowledging this too. I am so thrilled that Jeff is recognized as the "Father of CRT" and personally so grateful to have been close to his brilliance all those years ago."

Mary's words on the screen take a moment-and-a-half to swallow whole.

I swell with emotion and a prideful sense of being on the ground floor with such an extraordinary group.

Bottom line. Jeff Minnebraker and his Quadra crew did it first. Period.

I'm at the National Wheelchair Games in Seattle pushing track. All the heavy hitters are there. I'm in my late-twenties, athletic prime, but I'm also more thoughtful and strategic with finishing bursts. I don't win them all, but I win enough to be a logical bet in any mile, half-mile, or relay race.

Randy Snow and I are competing (as always). Continuously a contender and often a champion, Randy is fierce. Away from the battles, he's casual and relaxed. He loves his Stevie Ray Vaughan Texas-based blues, is philosophical in thought and conversation, and is a creature of the night. His humor and desire to laugh is contagious and legendary. We get on well.

In Seattle, I meet Marilyn Hamilton on a deeper level. Injured in a hang-gliding accident, she becomes a force in disability sport. She recruits Jim Akimoto and Don Hellman—fellow hang-gliding enthusiasts and forms Quickie Wheelchairs. We had spoken in the past about Quickie and the possibilities—but Quadra has my heart and devotion. With Quadra, my performance levels are on-point. I'm also not crazy about the name Quickie. It's silly. Little did I know their slogans, "Nothing Beats a Quickie" and "Get Out There" would translate into successful worldwide sales pitches.

Marilyn Hamilton is a bit of a human bulldozer in business and in life. If something is immovable, she digs deeper until the obstacle is a memory. She goes on to capture the 1983 US Open Tennis Singles title. Her day-glow yellow chair and wheels match her yellow belt and gloves. The bold colors go on to become an 80s signature, the neon of pink, green, blue, and orange, an audacious standard of the time. Hamilton also becomes an expert sit/adaptive ski racer. She competes in the 1998 Innsbruck Winter Paralympics and brings home a silver medal in women's slalom. I am learning to snow ski and race when Marilyn is in her prime.

She finds me in the elevator of the event's luxury Seattle hotel.

I'm still riding my Quadra but there's no sponsorship.

There's a pause.

I'm listening.

She wastes no time.

The elevator climbs.

Her pitch is strong.

I explain what it's going to take.

Before we get to where we're going, a deal is struck.

I find Randy and tell him the news. He's elated. Little did both of us know Hamilton and Quickie will go on and make us two of the most recognizable and high-profile duos in the world. Quickie is able to capitalize on the demise of Quadra. With deeper pockets than their predecessor, Marilyn and her squad create Team Quickie. The country's, and then the world's, best athletes are sponsored with chairs and products.

Randy and I are living the sporting dream. We're obscenely sponsored and taken care of: airfare, hotels, rental vehicles, food, and extras are all covered expenses. We have it all. Through the hard work of Brad Parks and the National Foundation of Wheelchair Tennis, a professionalized tour takes shape. Randy dominates. He's spanking opponents in opening rounds. He isn't stretched until the semi-finals or finals. He goes on to win a record 10 US Opens. I create a formidable obstacle for him in some hard-fought semis and finals. I use my athleticism and chair-skills to maintain a top five ranking for over a decade and ultimately rise to a worldwide ranking of 3 in the world. Randy adds an element of incredible shot making to win the biggest of matches. My first love, basketball, is where I plant my flag. The Condors go on to win 8 National Championships. Randy and I begin living large when we're on the road.

After a tennis tournament, we have a rental car provided by Quickie. We're late for the airport (as usual). We decide to just leave the rental on the curb of the departure gate. We race to catch our flight and never think of the rental car again.

Pretty much always late, we have a routine when we get to the gate.

The gate agent is stressed, seeing the two of us in chairs, hustling towards her. Randy digs deep into his Texas charm and drawl, "If you want to save time, you can switch us to first class and we can wheel into our seats. Wham. Bam. Easy."

If not, the gate agents will need to call for assistance and aisle chairs. Valuable time lost. Travellers silently simmer and wonder why the airline is departing late.

"Mr. Snow. Mr. Kiley. Here are your first-class boarding passes."

We agree to take turns with our first-class hustle. Others watch us as if we're on stage. We revel at our twisted skill sets, almost as much as we relish our first-class seats and lifestyle.

Spoiled and irresponsible—absolutely. We're out of control. We imagine we're "rock stars" living in a crazy, excessive, and sport induced time. In our entitled minds we have it all going on.

As ballers, Randy and I are peanut butter and jelly. Randy is a NWBA MVP. We're rivals, but when we play together on USA national teams it's poetry. He's a solid finisher and mid-range shooter. I find him with every type of Pistol Pete pass in my arsenal. He handles them all. He makes me look great. I make him look great.

As doubles partners, we win back-to-back US Opens. Randy's an extraordinary shot-maker, and opponents tend to hit to my side of the court more often. Our strategy is for me to advance to the net on any type of opening and use my length to finish off points. If teams try to hit away from my imposing net game, Randy slices his backhand low and hard to set me up for bunny overheads. He drives his forehand for angle and down-the-line winners. Often when he's serving, I press up to the net. Randy's cannon service game is weapon enough, but with me picking off weak, lack-of-direction, service returns, I can't remember losing a game on his serve.

I'm at the net, my head ducked low, and Randy reels off four straight aces. A couple are struck with pure, overriding heat, and a couple with elite spin, stretching the returner into the outer fence.

For the next 25 to 30 years, Randy and I are the faces of Team Quickie and all its promotions, competitions, events, trade shows, and public relations.

We do a lot of good. We share endless laughs. We're taken care of.

Randy and I remain tight throughout. We check in with one another over the phone. Our conversations always close with the same two words, "Stay alive."

The Quickie explosion is heard around the world. A campaign, and advanced marketing scheme allows the company to run a *fast break* to success. More international tennis players begin playing in the ever-growing wheelchair tennis tour across the United States. Quickie begins to make a push internationally. Marilyn Hamilton is proving a marketing superstar.

Quickie puts people in place that not only have passion but have a professionalism that translates way beyond the world of the disabled. Quickie speaks the language of business—supply and demand, quarterly profits, and public relations.

Wayne Kunishige, a trailblazing, stoic, behind-the-scenes achiever, takes on an increasing role. His expertise helps in the expansion of Quickie.

Quickie adds Jim Black to the mix. Jim's a standout regular on the wheelchair tennis circuit. He hits a wicked top-spin backhand and a slick slice forehand. Jim understands design and is quick to the burgeoning technology of the times. Add to that the guy is a born salesman, and it's hard not to find Jim either in conversation or brainstorming the next big Quickie reveal. Jim and I have a direct and consistent line of communication on topics of new technology and sales over the years. It's a critical relationship to the "process."

Jim Black eventually moves from Global Sales to a new position of Director of Quickie Sports and Team Quickie.

Marilyn is the lioness of the company. She hunts first-time experiences and marketing directions until Quickie is undoubtedly the worldwide leader in its field. After many years of leading the cause, Marilyn Hamilton eventually leaves Quickie. The company is purchased by Sunrise Medical, and like many founders and creators before her, there are tensions, philosophical differences, and power battles leading to her exit.

More change and transition. Jim Black hires Ryan Webb to head up Team Quickie. It looks and feels like Quickie is set to rule the world.

The Quickie Marketing Department proposes a poster idea to me. I listen sheepishly, knowing I'm solid with the project. Who doesn't want a poster of themselves? Judy Hirigoyen, now the Marketing Director, is the magnetic pull. She drives the project forward with an infectious belief. I'm in.

Judy organizes the photo shoot at Fairfax High School. On the border of West Hollywood, the school has a legendary, old Hollywood feel. There are ghosts in the rafters. I know the historic gym has been the backdrop for numerous advertising campaigns.

The day comes. I appreciate the respect given. Without seeing the finished product, I know this is a big deal. There's a natural light on the opposite side of the gym. It's a shadowy light that speaks of a far-away world. The semi-circle of windowed glow off the far wall has a 1950s, Hoosiers, set-shot sensation.

My job is to shoot free throws all morning. One attempt after another until they get the right *shot.* I'm dressed in a practice reversible, gym shorts (the longer the better), white (halfway up the knee) socks, and nondescript shoes. The mood and atmosphere are workmanlike.

I shoot another free throw.

Any player who's serious about the game—their game—knows that free throws are critical to winning or losing games. It's a given. Elite players improve their free throw percentage as part of the process. I'm elite, and because of that, I'm at the line hundreds of times with the game in doubt. Nothing about that process is free. Wins are earned. There is a price to pay.

From day one as a youth in the driveway, I take the time to shoot as many free throws as possible. I imagine I'm Pistol Pete Maravich. My goal is to make a hundred in a row.

The legend of Larry Bird has him swishing 100 free throws in a row in order for him to be done with his shooting workout. Tough to comprehend. Most legends are.

I'm up to 50 or 60 in a row.

I keep trying throughout my career. The muscle memory of the free throw is built through decades of frequency and routine. Breathing. Vision. Extension. This never changes. I'm wired to hit, repeat and repeat.

My shooting workout consists of 300 shots. I record 30 spots. Makes and misses. I have a numbered goal per workout that I record ahead of time. Pressure. My 30 spots consist of inside bunnies to out beyond the three-point line. Ten each. All recorded.

I'm in the corner of my local YMCA gym. I have a hoop to myself. I appreciate rebounding help during shooting workouts. The thankless job mostly goes unanswered. My headphones are on with good vibes in my ears. I'm 62 years old, still chasing the elusive 100 free throws in a row.

I begin.
I retrieve my ball after each make.
I'm in the zone without understanding why.
Past experience tells me the zone is fleeting.
Don't give it any recognition.
Ride it.
Distraction is the enemy.
Shoot.
Repeat.
Shoot.
Repeat.
Ten.
Twenty.
Forty.
Sixty.
Eighty in a row.
Shoot.
Repeat.
Shoot.
Repeat.
Ninety.
Ninety-five.
Shoot.
Repeat.
Shoot.
Repeat.
A hundred.
A hundred and four.

A ball speeds past me. It feels like a bowling ball whistling towards its target. I turn behind me to the direction of the speeding ball. It's a weightlifting buddy. He tries to hit me like he's picking up a ten-pin spare. He's off target. He has no idea of the moment, the internal place. I finally have made a 100 in a row.

Zone and focus gone, I miss the very next shot.

It takes most of my lifetime to hit a hundred in a row. I'm proud of my old ass getting it done whilst most my age have laid the ball down for the couch.

There's nothing free about a free throw.

The poster is a hit and the things are big.
Literally.

A typical concert poster is 24" X 36". The movie poster is 27" X 40". My poster is bigger. The thing is ginormous. It dwarfs any poster I've put on my walls. The angular shot shows the ball in flight. The rim and net are in the frame. The slogan reads:

I WILL DRIVE THE LANE.
I WILL DRAIN THE THREE.
I WILL FINGER ROLL.
BUT THE ONE THING I WON'T
DO IS FADE AWAY.

It's a dramatic photograph, with ghostly, midnight tones and ninety-degree window panes. My right hand pronates the follow through. The indirect lighting lifts the ball to its target.

A giant pallet of posters arrives at the house. I am to sign them all. There are five-to-seven feet of posters on top of each other. I plan out the process. I employ my kids to help. We create an assembly line of sorts. With each signature, the kids move the poster to the growing "finished" pile. It takes both of them to successfully lift and place each poster. Several thousand signatures later we call it a day. That day with the kids (moving each poster in unison), with Sandy playing garage foreman, is a distinct memory I'll always hold onto.

The poster is all the rage at the popular trade shows. Retailers take them for their shops. Parents want one for their kids. Kids want one for their room. You need wall space, as these things are immense. I still get remarks

The Fade Away Quickie poster could be found all around the world.

from folks remembering the poster for their daughter or son. They tell me they're grown now, but back then—they wanted to be just like me.

Humbling.

Jim Black is Quickie Sports Director, with ties to Team Quickie.

Jim notices James Coughlin (Arkansas Razorbacks basketball big man) using anti-tip casters off the back of his chair to lean away from defenders and not flip backwards. Jim thinks this is brilliant. A spark is fanned. A mass market, fifth-wheel concept is born.

He combines the center of gravity adjustment, with the integral fifth-wheel protruding from the back of the chair. Athletes move their center of gravity forward, and the thing turns like never before. The shorter wheelbase (or increased center of gravity) has the chair wanting to flip backwards with sudden movements or sharp/fast turns. The fifth-wheel keeps all wheels on the ground. Gamechanger.

It's also important that during this time (the mid-nineties), Jim is a top ranked, worldwide tennis player. When serving, the fifth-wheel allows Jim to reach back—even farther, creating greater spin, without any wheels coming off the ground.

He engineers the center of gravity adjustment that's built into the frame. His fifth-wheel technology is a design still prevalent in today's tennis, basketball, and quad rugby chairs.

Jim is also in touch with a snowboard company that produces ratchet ankle straps. He sends me some. We have ideas but neither of us know the full potential of secure strapping. My buddy Jeff Dills happens to be in my office when they arrive. We start playing with the idea of using the ratchet straps as a waist/pelvis strap on our basketball chairs. You have a buckle strap attached on one side of your frame at your waist. On the other side is the attaching strap. You feed the strap into the buckle and tighten. For the first time ever, we are strapped/secured to our chairs, our hips firmly in place, eliminating any wasted movement or recovery time. No more projectiles. I've experienced, and seen too many basketball players flying out of their chairs like flying squirrels. No more. It's a supreme moment of innovation. "One with the chair" translates into better function in specific ways for specific needs.

I tell Jim it won't be long before the entire world is using this kind of strapping for seating and positioning in adaptive sport.

Strapping is a subtle, yet profound change that moves adaptive sports forward. Its use is extended to other sports like alpine, Nordic skiing, and handcycling.

This is where it begins. We talk of transforming basketball chairs to a new and better performance level through increased technology. These conversations with Jim are similar to the ones I had with the Quadra crew over a decade ago. The Quickie All-Court hits the market, and I'm proud to be part of such a profound change.

Global Product Manager.   Head of Quickie Sports. Director of Team Quickie.

He did it all when the sports movement needed it the most.

Jim Black.

In 1997, Jim Black presents me with the idea of having my own signature basketball chair. They also pitch the idea to Randy Snow. His signature tennis chair hits the market a couple years later.

My name on a chair. My handwriting across the bottom tubing. An absolute first. I'm excited beyond belief. I see it as a testimony to the amount of value and respect the company has for my influence and accomplishments. I've spent over twenty years on the court and I feel I am appreciated by my peers.

Jim's engineering and forward thinking are the foundation to this needed and fully adjustable basketball ride.

It's a great time to be me. It's a great time for disability sports and basketball. Team Quickie has the giants of the game: Pat Anderson, Randy Snow, Matt Scott, Mike Schlappi, Jeff Glasbrenner, and Dutch tennis standouts Monique Kaulkman, and Esther Vergeer. My job is to find the best, the next generation of ballers and put them in one of my signature chairs. My judgement is trusted. I reward Jim and all of Quickie with sales, sales, sales.

The Dave Kiley signature Quickie All-Court chair becomes the number one selling basketball chair in the world. Its rise to the top is rapid. Jim draws up a royalty program and contract to benefit me. I sign the mutually agreed upon contract for each and every chair sold worldwide for the next twenty years. I have no idea how things will pan out.

I make a lot of money. Quickie makes millions.

Each quarter, a check shows in the mail from Quickie/Sunrise Medical. Sandy and I open each with apprehension, nervousness, and joy. We're never disappointed. My biggest quarterly payment is north of twenty-grand.

I feel like a pro athlete promoting his signature shoe.

I'm Michael Jordan minus the zeros.

The Quickie affiliation lasts for 36 years from 1982 to 2018. Quickie morphs into Sunrise Medical and seeks to be every person's chair for every imaginable disability. It's not uncommon to see Quickies in hospitals and airports as stock rides. They make power chairs, power assist devices, and pediatric strollers.

It's the evolution of a disabled population wanting and needing more bespoke products. Quickie answers the call, rings the bell, and cashes the check. The reach is wide. In doing so, there's less and less of them on the courts. The

Germans, Japanese, Aussies, Chinese, and British are all making their own; and they're quality. American companies, Top-end, Colours, and Per4max all stake claim as premium fabricators.

I begin to hear plenty on Sunrise Medical and only a scattering of Quickie news. The emphasis of founder Marilyn Hamilton, specializing in sport and sleek everyday chairs, changes. My relationship with Quickie diminishes. The new folks at Sunrise Medical don't know me. The contract and royalties end without a personal call.

Another sad truth.

In 2015, Sunrise Medical purchases RGK. RGK is named after the first names of its original co-founders Russel Simmons, Greg Eden and Keith Bolesworth. Based in the United Kingdom, RGK makes custom fitted chairs for everyday and sport. Industry icon Jim Black lands with Sunrise Medical—after years away—as Director of Strategic Accounts and Business Development for RGK. The RGK brand rules the British market. Great Britain's Paralympic sports are funded through their national lottery. Plenty of RGK chairs across basketball, tennis, and quad rugby are purchased through lottery funding. RGK parlays their successes in the United Kingdom and spreads its reach (and sales) across Europe.

Sunrise Medical is now RGK, which isn't Quickie.

These days I ride and am sponsored by Per4max. Longtime friend Willie Hernandez is the founder and designer. These days he's a small business owner, NWBA Hall of Fame recipient, and winner of 19 national championships within the NWBA.

Knowing Willie for multiple decades (since he was nine years old), our conversations are seamless and connected. The Per4max vibe and culture is unique by today's standards. They don't want all the disabled dollars. Their focus is dominated by streamlined, high-performance rides. I have a custom titanium frame with carbon fiber, Spinergy Wheels with titanium hand rings. The lightest chair I've ever owned. Willie personally designed and built my rolling sanctuary. After multiple shoulder surgeries, cutting weight off my OG (old guy) lifestyle is critical.

Willie, and business partner Chris Kommer, appreciate my influence and wheel print on all of adaptive sport over the years. I feel welcomed to be part of their team. Willie and Chris are two of my best friends today. I also revel in knowing—for over five decades—I've never paid for a chair.

I ride the wave of wheels. It pays. What company is the rage one day is history the next. I'm able to not only keep up but lead. My name on things is part of a prospering process. There's a sustainability and legacy that attracts others into our sporting world more and more. Ad executives take sincere notice. The chair is more like a skateboard than ever before.

Somewhere, there's a guy in his garage, torch in hand. He's cracked some design code. He thinks he's different from us. The enlightened concoction of trial and error. He cocks his head back. His welding mask props open. There's a cock-eyed grin. He knows. This is going to work.

Where he leads, I follow.

PART FIVE

Yes, I love to eat honey but there is that moment
just before I begin
That is so much better.
— Winnie the Pooh

DUSTY OLE ROAD

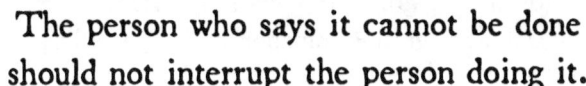

> The person who says it cannot be done
> should not interrupt the person doing it.
>
> — Chinese Proverb

Michael 'Shorty' Powers is a personality. He's a cross between a caricature, a riverboat gambler, and stand-up comedian. His cheeky grin and thick Texas drawl are constant. A fast-talking, fun-loving storyteller, you never know how you're about to be persuaded. You just know it's coming and you know it's going to be a wild ride.

I meet Shorty through basketball. It's tournament time. Winners move on. Losers go home. California versus Texas. Typical and characteristic of the time. If it's tennis or basketball there's an edgy, leave-it-all-on-the-court battle between what's east and west of the Rio Grande. Shorty introduces himself to me post-game.

I'm in victory mode. I listen.

He eases into things with compliments on my game and team's fight. Shorty's gift of gab begins to rev up. He likes chasing adventure: hunting, kayaking, fishing, and hiking. He's putting together a climb this summer which is only a couple months away.

Sounds like a worthwhile challenge but also a bit rushed. What do I know of climbing a mountain?

I'm 28 years old. I'm as strong as I'll ever be. My physicality is unmatched. This is my mandated mindset as an increasing number of Wheel Head warriors want my scalp on their totem pole of conquests. It's also the truth.

The climb takes on the tallest mountain in Texas—Guadalupe Peak. High winds are the norm, as are extreme temperatures, and fifteen to thirty percent grades in parts. We're to ascend three-thousand vertical feet. It's beginning to sound like something society says can't be done. That overriding thought ping pongs in my thinker. A couple days later I tell Shorty, "I'm in."

He's excited like he just landed a monster fish.

What have I just said yes to?

My go-with-my-gut, blind faith approach intoxicates, but also overlaps with undercooked corners of everything unknown.

What's comforting (amongst my apprehension), is Shorty understands the healing powers of the outdoors. He wants everyone, no matter one's ability or immobility, to be part of the outdoor adventure world. This attracts me.

After numerous lengthy calls, a date for the excursion is set. I learn more about Shorty's outdoor adventure program—Paraplegics on Independent Nature Trails (POINT).

My relationship with POINT lasts to this day and is a glorious one. Its name these days transforms to Turning Point.

I ask Shorty, "How are we going to pay for all this?"

There are airlines, hotels, ground transportation, specialized chairs, and talk of a film crew. Film crew? This sounds pricey.

Pay for it?

In Shorty Powers' world the climb will work at a profit. He might not know exactly how just yet but a call here, a nudge there, and a favor or two will get the climb where it needs to be.

"You leave that all up to me," he says with a cock-sure grin.

His confidence, his can-do slant on things, takes me on a five-plus-decade friendship ride. Shorty teaches me more than I ever imagined. The great outdoors is the constant in our ever growing friendship.

Shorty hits the phones.

A film crew and support team are in place. It's made abundantly clear that the support team will in no way be helping us with any physical assistance. We can help one another. That's it. West Texas Rehab is donating a motorhome for our use and comfort. We'll use the home (on wheels) to transport to Guadalupe Peak and use it as a command center for the climb.

Shorty has experience with hikes and climbs. We agree six is a good number for the Guadalupe ascent.

Donnie Rogers' name is mentioned. He lives in Houston and is moving to Dallas to work with POINT. Donnie is lean, strong, and has some function in lower extremities. He has experience with climbs and offers up a casual but determined mindset. He's keen to get it done. Check.

Joe Moss, a Vietnam veteran, isn't a climber but is a bull of a man. Joe is leading a group of soldiers traversing the Vietnam jungle and steps on a landmine, losing both legs above the knees. Having Joe along reminds me of the quality and quantity of Vietnam Vets in my life. I think of the influential Vietnam Vets I've met along the way. Joe Moss, indeed. Check.

Shorty recruits John Galland from Mound, Minnesota. John has extensive experience in climbing, and I hear he's an outdoor adventure "guru." I recommend a friend of mine from North Carolina, Bobby Leyes. Bobby moves from Raleigh to play with the Condors for the 1980-81 season. He earns a national championship and moves back to North Carolina. I like Bobby and feel he can handle the extreme adventure. Check. Check.

Five paraplegics and a double amputee. The super-six team is in place.

We need specialized chairs for the climb. Still the Quadra test pilot (or is it crash test dummy in this case), I put in a call to good friend, Jeff Minnebraker. Always a "cutting edge" catalyst of design, he quickly says yes.

Donnie Rogers specifically outlines a chair design. His design includes needed attachments: big knobby tires, balloon tires on the front, a sewn-in-the-upholstery backpack, and a plexiglass box connected to the frame underneath the seat to store our gear.

The chairs skip to the front of Quadra's production line. They're fast-tracked as our ever-approaching deadline/climb approaches.

Quadra custom chair, referred to on the climb as 'Mountain Mama.'

I ask Shorty again, "How are we paying for all this?"

"Just leave it up to me."

Enter Jack Grimm. Grimm is an oil man from Abilene, Texas. His wealth is absolute. A pure, everything is bigger in Texas exaggeration. Jack Grimm personifies the 10-gallon Stetson hat, snakeskin cowboy boots, expansive belt-buckle, and regional bolo tie atop his western shirt and beneath a custom sport coat. A man of adventure, Grimm funds ocean searches for Noah's Ark, as well as an attempt to find and raise the Titanic. His local affiliation with the West Texas Rehabilitation Center in Abilene has Jack Grimm in step with the locals. He's a big fish in all the ponds.

He's the richest person I've met.

I'm awestruck how linked Shorty is to connected people. Never one to reveal his hand fully, there's a mystery to his ways, but one thing is for sure—if you need it, Shorty Powers can find it.

Shorty is a gambler. A Wild Bill Hickok, Doc Holliday, lays-it-on-the-line kind of bets that separate grown men from posers. I learn early not to bet against Shorty. I don't like losing money. More importantly, I educate myself beyond his charm and stories. Beneath his everyman's banter and wit is a guy wanting better things for folks. We talk on the phone all the time. Plans and ideas are a constant over the years. We're both at times outrageous. Work past that and we're kindred in our outreach to our beloved subculture.

It's a Friday night. I'm beginning to understand Shorty's bravado when it comes to the required cash needed for our climb. It's the night of the fundraiser for the West Texas Rehabilitation Center at the Abilene Civic. Crooner Andy Williams is the entertainment for the night. Bob Hope has hosted the shindig the previous years. The goal for the evening is to raise $750,000 for the rehab center. The room is packed. Tickets are $125, $150, and $200. The Fire Chief must be a paying customer as capacity is way beyond fire safety standards.

We're told contributors are donating up to ten cents for every foot we climb.

I eye Shorty, cocktail in one hand, the other flailing above his hairline, describing something larger than life. He's reeling another one in. I look around the room and realize how underdressed I (like the rest of my crew) are.

This is no Bud and Sissy, *Urban Cowboy*, mechanical bull kind of night. When it comes to hair, hats, diamonds, and lipstick smiles, everything is bigger in Texas. The ladies are proud, proper, gracious, and welcoming.

There's a hush to the proceedings. That precious moment before the pop of a champagne cork.

Andy Williams breaks into his standard, "Moon River." A 30-piece orchestra follows in beat. I begin to understand the money needed for our climb is but a drop in the bucket comparatively to what's happening tonight.

Alan Shepard, the first ever American astronaut to enter space, and the fifth to walk on the moon, introduces himself to me. Big Jack Grimm slaps me on the back, asking how long I think it'll take to get up Guadalupe?

Shorty enters the circle.

To Shepard and Grimm, he's a trusted Texas compadre. I'm sure they have things to discuss.

I see an opening.

Exit.

Work my way to the open bar.

Sweet relief.

I need to see Guadalupe. Put eyes on her.

It's a five- to six-hour drive to the base of our mountain destination outside Carlsbad, New Mexico. The Guadalupe peak is in Texas, but the closest town is in southern New Mexico.

After some Texas storytelling on the previous night's festivities, we all take intermittent naps. Our gear is packed into the vans and pickup trucks of our support crew. Our upscale, cush motorhome eases down the road. It's comfortable. I nod in and out. Peaceful.

I awake anxiously. Last night at the fundraiser the term "crippled" is repeatedly used among the West Texas social elite. Either on the microphone or in conversation, the term is thrown around effortlessly. This doesn't anger me. It's just weird. Makes me cringe.

I sit up. Eye the boys. There's a weighty silence.

We all see Mt. Guadalupe against the late afternoon sun.

"Holy Shit," is all I can think to say.

I hold it in. Take a deeper breath. Show no fear.

We land in the upper parking lot and campground of Guadalupe National Park. It doesn't take long for Shorty to get into it with a cluster of park officials and rangers. There's a rule. No camping on the trail. This is Shorty's wheelhouse. Give and take until he gets exactly what he wants. The principal talking points are safety and camping issues. The park personnel warm to the six of us and the continued negotiations with Shorty are a back and forth. Close to sunset Shorty brings us together.

"We're all good. Let's get some rest. Tomorrow, we will pack our gear. Monday, we're up this thing."

Onsite District Ranger Jon Jarvis recalls, "I had the responsibility for campground operations, search and rescue, law enforcement, and horse patrol in this amazing desert and mountain park. Every day was an adventure and the POINT climb was the absolute highlight of my time as District Ranger."

Jarvis continues, "I discussed the plan with my supervisors and in true National Park Service (NPS) approach to public use, as long as this activity would not harm the resource or significantly impact other users, we were going to be supportive. I personally worried about the safety of the men on the trail due to the narrow trail, cliff edges, and all the desert hazards that include cactus, scorpions, rattlesnakes, and heat."

Open, starry skies are my best sleeping pill. It's July. It's high desert hot. We all sleep beneath the galaxy.

Crack. Loud. Flash. Lightning. My heart races. The power of mother nature overwhelms. The others have plastic tarps covering themselves and sleeping bags. Motorhome is too hot. Not an option. I roll myself and my gear beneath the motorhome. The rain falls hard and sounds like hail on a tin roof.

I'm dry. I sleep well.

Sunday is *get-your-act-together* day.

We all begin packing our Mountain Mamma, Quadra trail chairs. It's a complicated process. I bring the essentials to get up the mountain: a lightweight goose-down sleeping bag in my under-chair compartment, a rolled-up ground pad in my backpack peeking out of one corner, a t-shirt, a Turning Point baseball t-shirt, a Casa Colina tank top, a UCLA hat, and one pair of pocketed, olive pants. Water, instant oatmeal, nondescript snack nutrients, and a bit of sugared treats go into the custom backpack sewn onto the billy goat chair. This song and dance go on for hours. I reposition and eliminate anything I don't need to cut weight. I understand that everything I take adds to the physical challenge in front of us. A red bandana and pair of rounded, eighties sunglasses complete the look.

We all stop and stare at her. She's mocking us with her verticality, crevices, loose rocks, and scarred, sweaty fangs. Guadalupe isn't majestic. Guadalupe is a sun blistered, uninhabitable, dirt sandwich teasing us to take bigger bites. She's road rash and blisters, dehydration and dust.

I feel her eyes on all of us like a bully wanting our lunch money.

She's in my bloodstream. Pulsing. Throbbing. I rubberneck up and towards her. We put eyes on one another. For the first time I understand just how far fetched our intentions are.

There's a hand on my shoulder. I'm snapped back into the moment. It's Shorty.

"Just a dusty ole road," he says. "Let's huddle up. Pete has some Polaroids of the trail."

Pete Sevy is our lead support. He knows Guadalupe. He offers up photographs of the trail so we can strategize our ascent. Some are helpful. Too many are fearful. Several look like carbon copies.

"I'm not sure these guys can make it," says Sevy to the *Carlsbad Current-Argus* newspaper. Luckily none of us see the downer quote until after the climb.

The six of us have come together through good intentions. No doubt. Prepared? No way. Expeditions like this (in the able-bodied world) involve a preparedness of details, time, bench marks, and gear. Not this crew. We have a sketchy strategy, and at the top of our playbook—in big, bold letters—is the title, *Wing It*.

I awake every couple of hours through the night. *Is it time? Is it now?* I'm Ahab before leaving the dock. The whale awaits.

We're all awake by sunrise. Nervous Wheel Heads making last minute adjustments to gear that's been monkeyed with numerous times already.

John Galland has a urinary tract infection(UTI) and removes himself from the trip. UTIs are kryptonite to any of us five, spinal-cord injury types: dramatic body temperatures, increasingly sweaty and clammy in weird places like ears, elbows, and eye-balls, piss that smells of ammonia and looks like soup. Less than an inch into the climb, Guadalupe has us down a man. Ominous.

After the obligatory photos we get to the getting.

We leave the pavement and access the trail. Initially, it's easy. Shorty inherently takes the lead. His enthusiasm is a testimony of doing the unthinkable. He is our leader (for the meantime) and why we are here.

We find ourselves in a rock garden. The gulch, or dried up riverbed, is a series of ups and downs. Our first real test. Bobby, Shorty, and Joe all take early tumbles out of their chairs. The sideways falls are a by-product of narrowness, loose rocks, and steep decline. I navigate the section successfully, giving thanks to Minnebraker and the Quadra crew. The curb jumping sessions, downhill races, and sideway wheelies all valuable context for this exact moment.

Day 1: We begin five-strong.

Next one down is Donnie Rogers. Unafraid of anything the mountain has on offer, Donnie takes a slanted segment of the trail with too much speed. Light, strong, and with partial functioning, lower extremity muscles, he pops back into his chair quickly. I see this and understand, if we are to get to the peak, Donnie will be by my side.

The flip side of the coin is Shorty. A higher-level injury, with no function from his abdomen down, he struggles considerably more getting back into his chair when falling. His energy expenditure is twice ours. Double-down, Shorty's devil-may-care lifestyle has Guadalupe smirking. She increases doubt. She intends to teach.

The downhills begin to take a toll on Shorty's hands. The oversized knobby tires require an expanded grip. Shorty can ride a wheelie with the best of them. His backrest nearly dragging on the ground and his caster wheels and foot plate nearing vertical, he gets down the steepest of grades. His hands pay a price. He's also the only one not to wear gloves. His digits feel every rock and pebble.

Around hour five of the climb, Shorty is facing real difficulties. He's in pain. It's his wrist. He carries on—for a while.

It's obvious. Shorty needs to pull out. We're all shaken. Bummed out. The heft of Guadalupe takes down our leader.

She's a heartless bitch.

We finally leave the rock garden. Six hours. We haven't gone far. We begin to take on more of an incline.

I'm the lead dog of the pack now. One thrust/push after another. There are times I feel like I'm clinging to an anvil in the middle of the ocean. I fight through by taking the next push. Another inch in the progression.

I come upon an obstacle. Looks ruggedly manicured and in place for a reason. Not sure what to make of it. I call out to Donnie at the rear of the pack. He informs us about water bars. Water bars keep heavy rains from eroding the trail. The diagonal rock formation acts like a wall or dam and impedes water from becoming a stream or brook. Sounds great for the trail. A pain in the ass for us.

Donnie demos and pops his front end over the water bar. He rests there and begins leaning forward. He moves his seating position forward and does a hop or aggressive rock of his chair. His big wheels make their way over the bar. Impressive. I will try. It works.

Staying in the chair is a pivotal goal. We obviously need to save valuable energy. Also, the group's success will be determined if we can take care of the skin on our atrophied, spinal-cord injured asses.

We experience hikers on the trail. They're encouraging. We wonder out loud what they really think, taking in an inching parade of Wheel Heads bound by more muscles than brains.

The day ends. It needs to. We haven't begun to seriously elevate yet. I can't stop my mind from racing and visualizing the extreme actions of tomorrow. I don't allow myself to dwell on Shorty, as difficult as that is. I have to lean into the hopeful, expectant, and triumphant times ahead. It feels like a stretch.

Camp for the night is set.

I hear voices from our base camp. Evidence we haven't gone far. Shocking.

The night turns perfect. The galaxy offers hope.

A blissful sleep beneath a celestial blanket.

We awake to Guadalupe's glow. The calm before the looming struggle. Her sunrise service stirs and helps tranquil the moment. We hear the rustle of base camp making breakfast. A dispiriting reminder of where we are. Still, we savour the serene moment.

Our single-burner stove boils up our main menu item—Quaker Instant Oatmeal.

We pack up and almost in unison we all look for a more private place to take care of habitual business. No playbook on how to accomplish the shitty but necessary task. Toilet paper is a lightweight, easy to pack, comfort that ranks only behind food on the list of have to haves.

We boot up one at a time.

Last minute instructions come from Donnie on what to expect. With Shorty gone, Donnie is our de facto and logical trailblazer.

I take the lead. I'm the first set of eyes on what's to be overcome with Donnie (the alpha) bringing up the rear.

It's one switchback after another. We do this for hours. Inches at a time. Like a boxer, Guadalupe offers up a constant and unwavering set of irritating jabs to the kisser in the form of exposed sun and heat. The red bandana tied around my head keeps the stinging, salty sweat out of my eyes. The switchbacks carry on. Each curve and bend a subscription to a new angle or vista view but also an annoying notice that this is our course. We climb at a snail's pace.

The incline increases. Donnie shows us how to place a 5-to-10-pound rock on the front-ends of our chairs. The move keeps all wheels on the ground. Bigtime helpful. Without the extra weight our chairs want to wheelie, making staying in your chair a rodeo ride.

The grade of the path steepens. The water bars remain a constant. We are forced to exit our chairs a good fifteen times. Bobby Leyes and I leave our chairs, scoot backwards, and pull a nylon cord with our teeth. The cord is tied to our chairs.

Another climber casually walks by us sipping his water. It's awkward. He wishes us well. Most of them do. I don't hate him. I don't want to be him. I just want to go up this mountain. I'm sure I'll see him in a couple hours, finishing his day hike, on his way home to the wife and a couple beers.

Donnie's in the rear instructing the three of us. As it gets steeper, he advises where to attack and where to use caution.

G.I. Joe Moss, the irreplaceable double amputee, is our human turbo booster. He jumps in and out of his chair effortlessly and helps us over abrupt sections and water bars. I don't care to imagine what the climb would be like without Joe.

The film crew and support staff offer no help. None is expected or wanted.

It dawns on me. The moment stuns me into reality. I can no longer hear the coming and goings of base camp. Progress.

The hot day begins to cool. The western horizon taking the sun towards night. Without a reservation, Guadalupe offers up a room with a view. The Rock Ritz.

Rope to back of my jaw and scoot/pull entire weight of Quadra over steep rugged incline was the only way. Vietnam Vet double amputee, Joe Moss, watches to see if support is needed.

She does have a heart.

We find a horizontal, shaded area, just enough away from the trail to not be in the path of hikers descending down. The level ground isn't familiar but is welcomed. The ground pads allow us to stretch, rest, and decompress.

Conversations are friendly and hopeful. We're on the verge of physical and mental exhaustion but sharing words matters. It's easy to silo up, conserve energy, and isolate my thoughts. Instead, we laugh about our day. A "Dusty ole Road" indeed. We mock Shorty's Texas drawl. I recognize I am with friends. Good friends. New friends. It's unspoken but fully understood. We have each other's backs.

The initial plan is to reach the summit by the earliest, tomorrow, early evening. Not going to happen. We mock Shorty again.

"Will only take two-and-a-half, maybe three days," we all remember him saying.

We chuckle sarcastically at our absent leader. We remind ourselves he's the reason we're in this mess.

With our sleeping bags and pads laid in a semi-circle, the conversation simmers. Bobby notices (through the feel test) that he's rubbed his skin somewhat raw on his backside. This isn't good. I feel his angst. We wear foam cushions beneath our pants but sweat and friction take a toll.

The dozen plus times out of our chairs, navigating up loose rocks, lift-reset, lift reset, exhale, clear the tree limb obstacle, pull my chair up the trail, teeth or grip doesn't matter, just get my chair to a flat enough space, lift, use the bigger (more solid) rock to launch, head down/ass up, nose-to-the-toes, don't you dare miss, before landing back in the chair.

I push a good seven feet. Things get steep. Again. Back out of the chair. Again. I have to lift. Again. I cannot drag. My ass is on the line in every way.

Guadalupe demands our best

I do my own version of the skin test.

All good.

Daybreak. More oatmeal. New and improved ways to pinch a loaf, visit brown town and drop the kids off, lay ahead.

Donnie is next level. He hangs precariously from a tree limb, just off a sheer cliff to drop his deuce. We look on in shock. We look away for audacity's sake. I peek back in astonishment. It's like a BigFoot sighting. Joe and Bobby grab my attention with a snicker and an exaggerated open palm, eyes to the sky look. Like an echo in a cave, we harmoniously agree, "That boy is crazy."

The morning banter decreases. Words begin to take on weight. Guadalupe's attempt to diminish pace and drive.

I'm focused on my britches. I leave them out atop my sleeping bag. The cooler night and accompanying dew have my pants damp. Irritating. I shake the things almost dry.

We're out of our chairs throughout the day. Bobby keeps using the term "relentless." Sun baked dirt, loose rocks, and the consistent narrowness of the trail tests our capacity to remain logical and shrewd.

Donnie continuously grunts his way over water bar after water bar. Bringing up the rear has him working more solo than the rest of us. I begin referring to Guadalupe as "sum bitch" with each unsuccessful tire spinning, gravel spitting, stuck, go-nowhere-push-up-this-beast. Joe continues his focused, workmanlike, trudging, helpful grind. Guadalupe is the minor leagues to the creepy crawler, deadly jungles of Indochina and the dastard deeds of the Viet Cong. His understated confidence is at times lost on us whilst at others is the reason we push on.

Seeing folks climbing and then descending is not cool anymore. It's demoralizing. Their journey is measured in hours. We're on our third day.

Despite the cool evening temperatures, the midday heat stifles.

Bobby begins to wear down. The mental chore and worry of a raw ass are overwhelming. Within the first week of injury, all spinal cord patients are given a diatribe of chilling facts, photos, videos, and one-on-ones concerning butt sores. The nightmare reality is the things can kill you. Not the way to go. We must do everything possible to maintain our butt health.

It's that time.

How do we get Bobby off the mountain? We discuss. Demoralizing.

On a steep and rocky overlook of the desert floor we come to a game time decision. The support crew is going to help Bobby down Guadalupe. I think about what we've navigated up. I'm moved to tears. Bobby wells up too. We all give him bear hugs of support and love. A vital chunk of our mountain soul is lost. Another Guadalupe gut punch. A bitch slap across the jaw.

Bobby and the crew exit down.

A squeaky, fit, cute blonde ambles past us. She stops. Works her way back to us.

Don't say it. Please stay quiet, I think.

"I just want to say."

Don't do it. Just shut your hole.

"I read about you guys in the paper," she says. "And I just want to say—and I hope you don't mind me saying—just how inspirational y'all are."

She did it. Couldn't help herself.

The three of us. Having lost half our tribe, and the latest less than an hour ago, can't get rid of Barbie fast enough.

Her group continues on. Our three-plus days of grime is embedded beyond clothes, into our temperament and disposition.

"Good luck, getting to the top," I say. In other words. Leave now. She adds a final dagger. "I'll see y'all on the way down."

We carry on as three. We're a tad quicker but move with less joy. I'm fighting an overriding, pulsating, and continued toxic thought. *Get me off this damn mountain.* Instead, I transfer onto the dirt, scoot on my ass, and pull my chair along with my teeth.

After a couple hours of this, we see our summit/destination for the first time since base camp. We welcome the changeup. Exhilaration. The plan is to get up and beyond the upcoming switchback and get a closer look at her. Adrenaline and motivation give us all a flush/reset mindset. We're excited for a change.

Little do we know we're looking at a false summit. We think we're closing in on the pinnacle or high point of the mountain, only to realize the real summit is even higher up.

Another wave of unwanted emotion. We are now physically and emotionally gassed.

We're in need of a spiritual lift. Something to take our minds off climbing. Enter Park Rangers Jon and Paula Jarvis. They're in the minority and supportive of the climb from the beginning. Both have been up and down the mountain checking on us.

"Each day I'd hike up to see them," says Paula Jarvis. "I saw their emotional bonds deepening as the heat and the difficulty of the treacherous terrain sapped them and took a toll on their bodies."

Like a winged angel, Paula opens her pack and hands over a handful of homemade muffins and an iced down, six-pack of cold beer. Our eyes lock in on her like wolves upon prey. She reaches into her pack and hands each of us an ice cold Coors beer. Without a doubt, the best beer I've ever had (and I'm a Budweiser guy). We all have another until the six-pack is no more. The barley and hops add a needed level of normalcy to our outrageous situation. We devour the muffins.

"Perhaps beer wasn't the greatest idea before they made camp that night— but it was well appreciated and certainly didn't seem to impair them," recalls Paula.

After the respite of food and grog, Jon Jarvis brings up a subject on all our minds. How are we getting off this Dusty ole Road?

There's an Army base in El Paso that Jon and the Park Service have contacted. Our golden ticket is again Joe Moss. His *Purple Heart* earned during Vietnam gets dropped into the conversation. Jarvis says there's a good chance we can get airlifted off Guadalupe by helicopter.

After beers, cookies, and encouraging news, we carry onward and upward.

The sun lowers.

Day four begins with a bother. I have skin issues. My ass isn't raw or overly concerning, but the skin is irritated from the numerous times I've been in scoot-mode. I don't like it. I'm too invested. I'm getting to the top. Screw you, Guadalupe.

We boot up. Again. Upward.

The terrain is noticeably steeper and narrower. It's also scarier. I'm hugging the mountain as inch-by-inch we progress up. Joe is out of his chair almost exclusively. I don't have the same option. Long legs and a dodgy tailbone need the stability and protection of staying upright in my chair.

Donnie is trekking in his chair at the rear of our procession. His chair gets pulled and rocked laterally by Guadalupe's demon side. Donnie, and his chair, begin a slow slide toward the pitch below. His sleeping bag bungeed to his chair pops and somersaults down a hundred-feet below. I imagine the bag careening downwards like one of us falling out of control.

A sharp wind blows. It's Guadalupe laughing out loud.

A bit later in the day. The section of the mountain is slow and intense. The trail is just wide enough for my chair. I lose balance and lean into the mountain. I'm over backwards instead. Thud. I taste dirt. I'm fearful. Frightened. Clinging. I come to a stop. Thankful. Pebbles and small rocks continue their gravitational pull down. I've only fallen a few feet. Pull yourself up. Remember to breathe.

Safe. I'm quick to humor. It's the whole laugh-or-cry approach.

"Just a Dusty ole Road," I say to the eyeful group with sharp sarcasm.

As we finally circumnavigate the most recent harshest/steepest death-ride of Guadalupe, two things become clear.

Descending down this thing is not an option. Cannot be done safely. Too difficult. Too dangerous. There's talk over lunch of a horseback ride down. My ass doesn't like that idea. Realization. Even getting down is a climb.

Then we notice an increasing number of small planes and helicopters circling above. Jon Jarvis is with us today. We see and hear him on the radio. He's annoyed. The press is circling overhead expecting our arrival at the summit. These knuckleheads are all flying in Guadalupe's no fly zone. Jon doesn't mince words. He uses an accomplished and practiced vocabulary of swearing. His urgency is crystal clear.

The planes and helicopters remind us we should be at the summit. We are not.

It's also the hottest day of the journey. The temperature is in the nineties. The winds have subsided. We could use a breeze. No dice. Guadalupe is up to something.

We look like extras from *Lawrence of Arabia*. We cover our heads with towels, bandanas, and hats to keep the sun from frying what's left of our membranes and stretched logic.

In the distance we see weather moving in. Dark, dank, and angry looking conditions. *Wizard of Oz*, "there's no place like home" type circumstances that have us immediately thinking of cover. We've been warned of Guadalupe's severe thunder and lightning storms.

Well, shit howdy, here it comes.

Crack. A bolt of lightning takes the wind from my lungs. Jon Jarvis reiterates, "Guadalupe Mountain National Park rates second among all National Parks in most air-to-ground lightning strikes."

What was calm is now chaotic and dangerous. We pull our rain gear out from the built-in storage beneath our chairs.

Winds increase at an alarming frequency. Another bolt of lightning snaps with the intensity to move teeth.

We maintain calm but also urgently need out of these aluminum chairs or one (if not all) of us are human, Roman candles.

The temperature dips below seventy-degrees. Minutes earlier the heat stifles. Another alarming factor in the survival equation.

We nervously climb looking for shelter. Up the trail is a rock overhang. Blessed cover. With few words we execute. Teamwork, fellowship, brotherhood, and muscle have us huddled under a rocky precipice. Mother nature's efficiency for the night.

If Sandy only knew. I've had zero contact with her and Justin. He's two-years old now. I've come to rely on Shorty for back-and-forth updates. Talk about potential lost-in-translation scenarios. I miss my family more with each passing night. These thoughts I need to manage. It makes the climb maddening, frustrating.

We're out and away from our chairs. Safe living quarters. Boom. Crack. Crash. Bang. The rain, thunder, and lightning create a cocktail of fear, shock, and wonder. We're all closer to God but not in a good way. We're in his wrath.

The moon rises.

Camp is set.

The storm blows through. Its impact is long-lasting.

Our conversation deepens.

Donnie brings it all to the surface.

"If we pull a muscle...

If we fall out of our chairs...

If one of our chairs falls off the cliff...

We help each other get to the top…
We're not losing anyone else…
We're all going to make it to the top."
The best bedtime story ever.

I awake to take a midnight relief. I see Joe, with his small flashlight in crevices and beneath rocks. His fear of snakes has him up and uptight. Joe sees less danger climbing Guadalupe than the perils of what lays in her life-forms and spooky breaches.

"It's okay, brother," I say. "Ain't no snake coming between us and the peak."

He has a look not seen before. I leave him to it. He's appreciative of my concern but unmoved. Sleep is my greatest reward. Each siesta the grand prize beyond a day of rocks, dirt, and the next unknown Guadalupe travesty.

I imagine Joe's only rest is when exhaustion overrides fear.

Guadalupe has her own specific hold on my friend Joe.

Is today the day?

Jon and Paula Jarvis read us the most recent newspaper filings. Our story is growing in interest.

The media jumps on the news that I have skin/ass issues. My stubbornness and ego are Grand Canyon wide and Colorado River deep. I get it. Newspapers need drama. Reporters are looking for angles. I'm a guy climbing where others take elevators. My backside could be in better shape. The constant transfers from one rock to another pays a price. The padding simmers any dire consequences but doesn't alleviate what's irritating.

I'll heal when I get home. I'll do whatever it takes to heal this first layer of skin. Guadalupe's price of admission.

Some national media outlets use the term "crippled" when describing us. Another, calls us "powerplegics." You can guess which one we take on as our moniker.

Day five. Please no more false summits.

Jon, and lead scout Pete Sevy, warn that today will be our greatest challenge. The most rugged and steepest incline—with sheer drop-offs—Guadalupe has on offer. The trail narrows. We negotiate with extreme caution. I'm in the lead.

We come to a bridge connected to the face of the mountain. This side of the bridge offers a rare downhill segment. The section is gradual but the narrowness of the trail pinches. The mountainside drop-off is consequential.

I climb to an approachable spot for the descent. I calculate my pathway.

Donnie pushes beyond me for the first time in our expedition. He surveys, and his crazy ass just takes off and lets it rip. Wheels on the ground, his hands come off the push rims enough to pick up momentum. He's putting it all on the line. He dances with gravity across the bridge, speeds past the more troublesome section just beyond the bridge, takes a hard left-hand turn around the bend; a final burst and he arrives at the flats. He lets out a primal—death defying—scream of celebration.

It's my turn. I go at a pace of respect. There's a railing on the bridge I can cling to if things get gnarly. Down I go. Don't need the railing. Beyond the bridge is where the danger lies. I move cautiously. Calculated. I brake heavily at times and power push at others. I make my way to Donnie and the more level terrain. Sweet relief. I turn to Donnie and share a brief moment of triumph. We turn to watch Joe address the dicey section of the mountain.

Joe's more comfortable out of his chair and pulls it along right beside him an inch at a time. It's a precarious approach but one that works for him. It's transformative watching Joe. He's our rock, our aforementioned helping hands through the unforgiving uphill, more difficult portions of the climb. I think Joe can do all of Guadalupe out of his chair. For a stud, double amp' like him, the chair is more his pack mule than a vehicle to get from A to B.

After the downhill, the climb abruptly steepens. The angle of the slope increases all the way to 35-40 degrees. Serious grade.

It's going to take our best efforts but the peak is doable by day's end. We climb. Rocks become boulders and the inclines are unrelenting. Joe maintains his steadfast and resolute status. He's our brakes when needed (which is often) and a boost over things when we're stuck. Joe literally jumps out of his chair and pushes us in certain sections. His help is welcomed. We get to a point where all I have to say is "Joe" and he's there knowing what I need.

I'm a scout. The first in line to best choose the correct path. Five days on Guadalupe and I'm not a rookie climber anymore. The summit looms. No false ones today. It's the real deal. The pinnacle. An energy, I thought long gone, awakens. I point to and then lead the way.

Donnie is the tactician, the professor of the climb. His muscle mass to body ratio allows him to climb over rocks (in and out of his chair). He instructs us past, through, and beyond the inconceivable. As crazy as he is on the mountain, he knows exactly what he's doing.

The trail ends. It's all rock hopping now. Boulders are as big as Volkswagens. We pull our trusty Quadra Mountain Mama chairs with us. The Quadra rides are family and we're not leaving them behind.

Park Ranger Jon Jarvis informs us earlier in the day we will be getting helicoptered off Guadalupe. Jon and his wife Paula have become advocates, protectors, and friends.

"I called Fort Bliss in El Paso and let the Army know that we had a Vietnam Vet on the summit needing a ride down," says Jarvis. "There was no hesitation from the Army."

Many years later, Jon Jarvis is appointed the Director of the National Park Service from 2009 through 2017.

The summer sun begins to fade. We're almost there.

Jon lets us know the helicopters will be unable to pick us up tonight. The evening's high winds make the task too dangerous. A night sleeping on rocks. Guadalupe certainly has her ways.

We carry on.

The final block on the second tier of John Wooden's Pyramid of Success is Intentness. The great coach knows that without Intentness we can't become all we want to be. Coach John Wooden writes, "An intent person will stay the course and go the distance. He or she will concentrate on objectives with determination, stamina, and resolve. Intentness is the quality that won't permit us to quit or give up, even when our goal is going to take a while to accomplish."

At the top of Guadalupe is a pyramid shaped monument. In 1958, the steel pyramid was erected on the Guadalupe peak, Texas' highest point at 8,751 feet. The marker honors the Butterfield Overland Mail Trail route used in stage coach travel well over a hundred years ago.

The three of us agree to reach the summit and pyramid at the same time. We leave our chairs a few feet below and drag our worn-out bodies the rest of the way. At 7:20 p.m., July 16th, 1982, we arrive atop Guadalupe. Together. Euphoric.

We grasp, touch, hold-on-to, and kiss each other and the moment. There are crystal clear times in one's life. This is one of those. I take in the 200-mile view of the vibrant, summer Texas landscape. The world feels small and massive at the same time. I take it all in with a glance.

We hear Shorty and his Texas drawl, yelling and screaming along with our other brothers from base camp. The bulky walkie talkie comes through clear. We take turns giving individual quotes over the radio and in front of the video crew.

Putting words to overwhelming feelings is quite an ask.

Just like taking on Guadalupe, we give it a go.

We are asked to give our impressions to the camera crew atop Guadalupe.

Donnie Rogers, "It took me five days to climb the highest mountain in Texas. So, for the rest of my life, I can do anything I want."

Joe Moss, "It's been about 13 years since I've worked with a group of guys and did something as a team, and I can't explain the feeling. I wish everyone could do this."

Myself, "If you've ever done something that's unimaginable. This is twice that." I stammer over the word "unimaginable," which I still hear about today from Donnie.

Wait a second. A champagne bottle appears. Donnie latches onto it and shakes it like a Polaroid picture. He holds it above his head in triumph. Pop. Champagne shoots into the Texas sky.

"Dang, is there any left?"

Donnie takes a healthy swig before handing it over. Joe, and then I, do damage to what remains.

We sit in front of the pyramid. Time is ours. Joe sits in the middle. He has the champagne in his right hand, resting on his amputated stump. His smile speaks of accomplishment and joy. Donnie has his left arm around him. He's wearing a *Willie and Family, On the Road Again* t-shirt. Donnie's shoulder length hair is pulled back and tied off. His bushy mustache is crusty. He sits on a cushion and chuckles into the horizon. His arms are much tanner than his hands from wearing gloves the past five days. We're all filthy, but my yellow Casa Colina tank top and yellowish UCLA hat are the grimiest. I'm wearing elbow pads, gloves, and a grin that just won't stop. I'm more laid out atop the rocks, relieving pressure from what needs healing. I look forward. Proud. This fellowship will last. Jon Jarvis comes over. He's Park Ranger personified with a name badge, park badge just above his heart, and an army-green Ranger baseball hat. His smile is deep. I wonder how much his ass was on the line with us and this climb. It's about to be a tale of folklore not to be repeated. Jon is on one knee with his right arm around Joe. We are connected.

We pose for the photograph like gods of the mountain.

The explicit and camera-ready celebrations subside. We begin to survey our overnight stay in the garden of rocks. The crew and Rangers all leave us to ourselves our final night on Guadalupe. The western skies offer a kaleidoscope of colors, tones, and expanded emotions. An appropriate masterpiece for time and place.

A starlit night follows. We're enveloped in a blanket of stars. We're cowboys atop the trail, resting our tired limbs but there's a striking difference. An anticipation. Tomorrow we will be flatlanders. The prospect of a toilet, bed, and beers. It feels like Christmas Eve and tomorrow is the big day.

We have our final mountain talk. We're reflective, humbled, and insightful. We speak of the beginning. We are underestimated and not welcome to even try initially. We knew, even within our crew, the doubts of making it to the top. We agree that every corner of a switchback, every rock, every water bar, each loss of fellow climbers creates an inner emotion that has to be dealt with. This adds strength and character to the group. We got down to three but we're still working as six. In our minds all six make it to the top.

The banter only stops because we're all exhausted from the most gruelling undertaking of our lifetimes. We'd talk through the night if only we could.

My last image, before nodding off, is of Joe and his small flashlight, looking for snakes in our bed of rocks.

I dream of helicopters.

Sunrise has us anxious and awake. We're on the lookout. We gaze out as far as possible. Our birds of steel and sanctuary are nowhere on the horizon. We know they're coming. It just can't happen fast enough.

Before we see them, we hear a rat-it-tat-tat-tat. Not one, but three helicopters are circling overhead and around the peak. The olive drab, military helicopters with the red cross insignia across its nose look like the beginning of the popular *M*A*S*H* television show.

The winds have eased from last night, but there's still a hum to the morning breeze.

The first copter circles. The wind's mph increases slightly. It tries to set down atop the rocks. It's not the flattest space to land. The bird aborts and pulls off and away.

Guadalupe exposes all.

In the words of helicopter pilot, Chief Warrant Officer Dennis Patterson, "In my 10-years of flying to landing zones around the country; the experience on Guadalupe Peak was my worst and most challenging because of high winds and sloped, rocky terrain."

Our disappointment is obvious. We're wide-eyed and shocked. The degree of which we want off this mountain, and particularly these rocks, cannot be underestimated.

The second copter moves into the approaching air space. He hovers and puts it down on the rocks. The bird is half-cockeyed and on a tilt. A couple servicemen hustle off. Our support crew assists with a two-man carry onto the helicopter. Each of us are party to the great escape plan. There's an urgency in loading our chairs. The copter blades continue their twirling action adding to the rush and awe of the moment.

I find out later that the three pilots are there to back-up one another. They all want to be the '*One*' to get us off Guadalupe. Competition. I like it.

We're hooting and hollering. The captain lifts and nose-dives the bird of steel straight down into an essential banked turn. Scarier drop than any rollercoaster imagined. What takes six days and five nights to climb, takes less than five minutes to land in the base camp parking lot.

I eye the Guadalupe peak from our escape vehicle. We all do. She demands it.

Without remorse, I give her the bird.

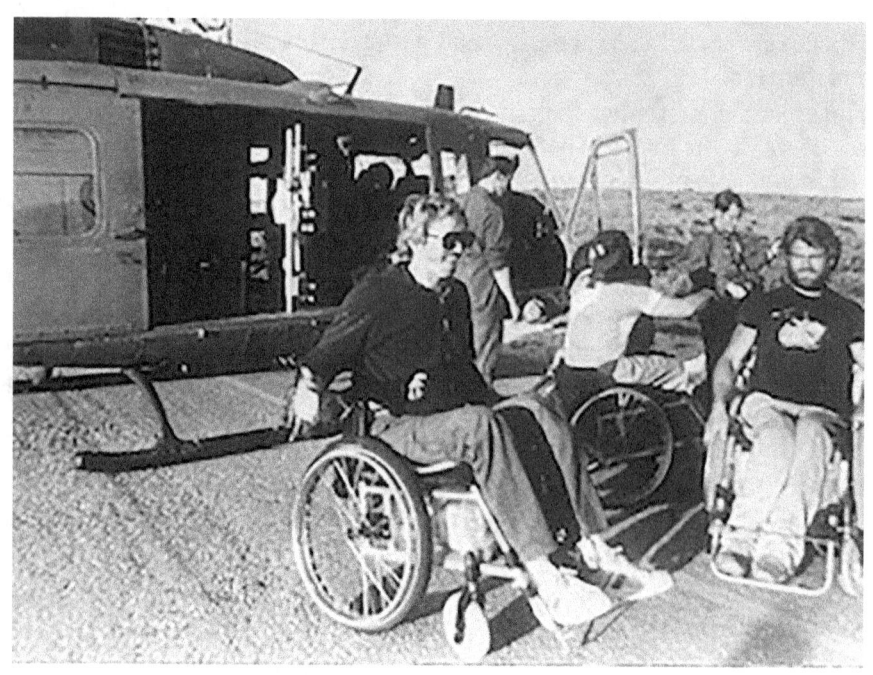

Our base camp erupts with cheers and raised fists as we duck beneath the blades of the helicopters, and disembark.

Where is Shorty? He dreamt and conceived it all. I want to be the first to wrap my arms around him. I kiss him on the cheek and bear-hug him for over a minute. History brings perspective. Historical times take a dream. I understand this fully in this instant of time. Shorty Powers is the man of the moment. A moment that lasts a lifetime, in more ways than one.

I find Bobby Leyes and John Galland and squeeze them with all I'm worth. I want them both to feel me, as I certainly felt them every inch of the Guadalupe climb.

We wave to our pilots and crew. Our best version of an escape plan minimizes into the horizon. Servicemen in helicopters flying back to base. I'd like to be there after they land their birds, back at the Officers Club, describing what the hell they just did and witnessed. I can only imagine.

I make my first call to Sandy in a week. My greatest fan. Her sacrifice—this mountain separation is only the beginning of decades of the same. Her voice sounds so good. I want home.

Our little jaunt up Guadalupe has us in the news and on front pages of newspapers around the country. The most notable is a story and photo of us on the front page of the *Los Angeles Times*. I hope this proof helps with my prolonged absence from work at Casa Colina.

All of Texas and New Mexico knows about us. Evening news reports and daily newspaper filings have created a compelling human-interest story. The age old—can these guys really make it—tale.

There's an itinerary. The closest town to Guadalupe is the familiar Carlsbad, New Mexico. We have a press conference to attend and an appearance at a rodeo to round out the day. In true Shorty fashion. First things first.

Our convoy of vehicles stop at a small and quaint General Store. It's time for some eight-in-the-morning beers. The aging couple open their store for us. The refrigerator has one door and serves only Coors beer. We drink with a gusto reserved for afternoons or evenings. Joe, Donnie, and I are still caked in a week's worth of dirt and Guadalupe grime. I stand on my braces intentionally, relieving the climb's damage to my backside. The rustic room of the General Store is hardly big enough to contain our crew. There's a buzz and chatter (led by Shorty of course) that is full of life and stories of the climb. I am, like Donnie and Joe, simply exhausted and dog-tired.

The beer buzz has me worn-out. I'm weary but overjoyed.

Forty-five minutes after exiting the General Store we check into our comped hotel. I've never been a week without a shower. The white of the tub turns brown. It isn't till nearly a half hour later the tub is somewhat white again. I revel in smelling like cheap, hotel soap.

I set the alarm for the afternoon press conference. The Civic Center is next door to our hotel.

Donnie is in the bath having a prolonged soak. A stranger comes into his room.

"Are you Don Rogers?"

"Yes."

"The President of the United States wants to speak with you."

Donnie sprints to the press conference. Shorty, Joe, and Donnie all take turns chatting with President Reagan as well as New Mexico Governor Bruce King. Ronald Regan calls us American heroes. He also sends us a personalised White House telegram.

In short, I'm tardy for the President's call. By the time I enter the room the President has just hung up. We finish the news conference and adjourn for continued beers.

I take some good-natured ribbing for stiffing the President of the United States. Such is a day in the life of a heavy-eyed, Guadalupe-conquering, ass protecting man dearly wanting a day with his wife and son.

The beers flow. Next on the itinerary is the evening's rodeo. A Saturday night full of cowboys and cowgirls celebrating their culture. Horses, bulls, expensive belt buckles, and beer are the required tools of a Carlsbad rodeo crowd.

The six of us load up onto a horse-drawn wagon. We're all in our Quadra climbing chairs. The wagon circles the infield of the rodeo. People are on their feet giving us a standing ovation. They're not stopping anytime soon. These are good-hearted folks keeping up with our climb and invested in our group reaching the top. It's spectacular. We're all so happy. Being part of civilization has its rewards. The ovation continues across the entire 360-degrees of the outdoor arena.

I put my arm around Shorty. He's in his element. He's wearing cowboy boots and making hand gestures to pretty cowgirls.

He takes time away from the adoration.

"Damn, Kiley. We did it."

"I want to say thanks. This is all you."

"Ah, shit. Ain't nothing." Shorty takes a beat. "Let me ask you. Was there ever a time you thought you might not make it?"

"Never, man. Just a Dusty ole Road."

DEAR DAVID:

I AM DELIGHTED TO JOIN CONGRESSMAN DAVID DREIER
AND SO MANY OTHERS IN HONORING YOU AT THE GALA
"TRIBUTE TO COURAGE" DINNER IN LOS ANGELES.

EVERY AMERICAN WHO KNOWS YOUR STORY IS INSPIRED
BY IT. YOUR HEROIC CONQUEST OF DISABILITY HAS HELPED
TO BLAZE A PATH OF HOPE FOR ALL DISABLED PERSONS. YOU,
JOE MOSS, AND DONNY RODGERS ARE TRUE NATIONAL
HEROES -- LIVING EXAMPLES OF THE TRIUMPH OF THE HUMAN
SPIRIT OVER PHYSICAL ADVERSITY.

YOUR EFFORTS AS DIRECTOR OF THE CASA COLINA
WHEELCHAIR SPORTS PROGRAM ARE IN KEEPING WITH THAT
SPIRIT, BRINGING GREATER ATTENTION TO THE PROBLEMS AND
THE POTENTIAL OF DISABLED PEOPLE.

NANCY JOINS ME IN CONGRATULATING YOU AND IN
SENDING BEST WISHES FOR CONTINUED SUCCESS. GOD BLESS YOU.

    RONALD REAGAN

1605 EST

1630 EST

Personal telegram of recognition
from President Ronald Reagan.

Joy and content to
be down below.

MY BROWN-EYED GIRL

The smile of a daughter is the purpose of every father.

— Unknown

She has my nose and her mother's expansive eyes.

It's November 1983 and three-plus years since the birth of Justin. We openly want a daughter. A sister for Justin. Justin takes on the nickname, Juice. His unabashed, wild, and free nature become a constant at the many basketball tournaments and tennis matches.

Our first pregnancy defies medical odds and predictions. In my eyes, I'm fulfilling what I've seen and known as a husband, father, and provider. I cannot fully explain how—and why—I've always cherished the genuineness of family.

We're concerned. Doubt enters in. Is my spinal cord injury adjusting my dreams? Again?

Life can be a strange old dog. Sex, initially a chilling mystery post injury, is a desirable connection that has me returning to sender. Things are good. We keep doing what comes naturally in the hopes we might have a second child.

In 1983, pregnancy tests are not as easy as peeing on a stick. A doctor tells Sandy that she is indeed pregnant. I remember the day, newly injured and the doc telling me kids aren't an option. Here we are now. Making plans for another. The surprise, wrapped around the anticipation of it all, outweighs any need to know the sex of our next.

We don't want to know the sex of our next offering but we know we'd love a girl. I admire the adoring spark, within a southern ease, that Sandy and her mother, Madonna, share.

Sandy is sure it's a girl and never wavers from the inside knowledge and belief only a mother has. Sandy's brother-in-law, Jay, is visiting from Tennessee. As I enter the house Jay springs through the hallway.

"Sandy's water has broken," he says. "Time to get to the hospital."

I do my best but inside I'm reduced to an anxious mess. Jay and I are bouncing around the house like actors in a bad sitcom. Sandy is stoic, reminding us what not to forget. I'm panicked, nearing blackout. Sandy's brother-in-law brings no levity to the situation. He knows he has to stay home and watch his nephew, only adding to his anxiety. He's an endearing mess.

We head to Pomona Valley Hospital, just down the street from my job at Casa Colina.

199

Ten little toes and fingers wrapped in a pink blanket. I'm thrilled but also anxious in holding her. I take a breath. I visualize the inevitable moment. We eye one another. She's in my arms. Her eyes widen. We both know. I'm her father and she is my daughter. A depth not known before, the one reserved for daddies and their baby girls, engulfs. Danielle Marie Kiley enters into a world, never to be the same on August 27th, 1984.

It's a different merry-go-round ride with Danielle. Where our first, Justin, welcomes all with open arms, Danielle (Dani) is wary. Dani uses her eyes like others use words. As an infant, she knows how to give the stink-eye to those she doesn't know or trust.

On the flip-side—from day one and to this day—her brown-eyed stare thaws the heart of her old man.

She's the risk taker of the family. First day on the slopes she skis like a hood ornament. Let it rip. Straight line to the bottom. As an 11-year-old, at a sleepover, Dani and her friends sneak out of the house. A jailbreak. She jumps the fence and breaks her foot. She doesn't want to fess-up with mom and dad. A day passes and she's in tears. Sandy picks her up from the overnight jailbreak. Danielle doesn't want trouble. She tells her mom her foot hurts and might be broken. It is. She is indeed from my bone and marrow.

Little do I know that someday I will be giving her away to another. I fight through the tears and conflict. This inevitable act stretches my emotions longer and wider than I imagine possible. I still see her as a little entertainer singing into her hairbrush.

I'm a grandfather now. Four strong, young grandkids. My granddaughter Lily is easy to spoil. She's surrounded by two brothers and her cousin. It doesn't matter that she's our only granddaughter. She rules like Queen Elizabeth and loves beyond measure. I will protect her for all my years. I will always wipe away those alligator tears that wrap my heart around her little self. When I'm done roughhousing with the boys, I always make time for her. One on one.

Danielle is on the other side of the room. She's in her mother's arms. Her oval eyes take it all in. Sandy and I exchange a glimpse lasting forever. I am blessed. We are blessed.

My brown-eyed girl.

Danielle and Justin, blessings.

Our risk-taker.

PART SIX

Winning isn't for everyone.

— Kobe Bryant

THIRD SERVINGS

Battles are lost in the same spirit in which they are won.

— Walt Whitman

Going into halftime we're up four, but there's cause for concern. Curtis picks up his third foul ten-minutes into the game. Jim Worth and Albert Campos are connecting but shooting a low percentage. I sub in my childhood neighbor, friend from my youth, and first year standout, Jimbo Miller for Curtis.

It's destiny that Jim and I are paired together once again and that wheelchair basketball is the conduit. I hear Jimbo loses his foot in a forklift accident. We connect. It isn't long before the kid, five houses down from ours, is my teammate and future Hall of Fame recipient.

Jimbo is solid but raw. He has little experience at this level. It's easy to see the many dividends Jimbo will pay—but we need Curtis Bell to counter Detroit's Daryl 'Tree' Waller. Tree is long, strong, and slick around the basket. Waller is surrounded by future Hall of Famers Gary Odorowski, Mo Phillips, Denver Branum, Joe Sutika, Wyman Davis, and aforementioned Bud Rumple. I have 15 of our 26 first half points. Not a good recipe for continued success.

In 1982, within the NWBA basketball scene, things are trending in the right direction. Almost all the players have transitioned to lighter aluminum chairs. Contests are faster, more athletic, and the anodized frames have added a needed splash of color to the pageantry of the game.

Sports 'N Spokes chronicles disability sport with a fevered cleverness not seen since.

Cliff Crase, Editor and Columnist for *Sports and Spokes,* predicted the 1982 Final Four: "Starting with the mighty Midwest Sectional. If the Chicago Sidewinders show up, I'll just die! For the past few years, the gods have indicated that Chicago just didn't have it, using excuses like age and losing their top star who is one of the finest five players in the US. The Kansas Chairman was recommended, and durn my hide if Coach Karr of the Sidewinders didn't pull some yahoo strategy out of his bag of tricks and dump all comers to be declared champs of the Midwest."

Crase and his wife Nancy, along with maestro PVA/NWBA photographer Curt Beamer, drive the monthly magazine into a must-read and viable advertising option and outlet. In the 1982 issue covering the National Wheelchair Basketball Tourney, I am on the magazine's cover and its back page advertisement for Abbey Medical. Beneath my image and shooting the ball, it reads, "You'll cut like a cat, fast break like an All-Star; and don't think it won't show up in the box scores." This is the first basketball ad of its kind.

Deep inside the magazine, Crase offers up the NWBA Bottom 10 with the Memphis PVA Delta Dribblers taking top honors, followed by the forgettable Heart of Illinois Hobbleknockers.

Albert Campos and Jim Worth continue to run their two-man action. Jim is able to get the ball inside to Albert only to have Tree help off Curtis and either block or disrupt his shot. When the defense sags, Jim goes to his trusty mid-range game. The shots aren't falling as the Worth/Campos combo shoots a combined 3 for 16. The Westland Sparks of Detroit take the lead five minutes into the second half. I hit a 12-footer and we're back up by a point. Curtis does a good job not collecting his fourth foul but he has to sacrifice his defensive zeal doing so. Waller and Denver Branum gain confidence in the post and begin to take charge.

Legendary Long Beach Flying Wheels' Bill Johnson puts it this way, "When Bell committed his third foul with ten minutes left in the first half, from that point on he seemed to be out of the game. Kiley kept yelling at him, 'Don't reach.' Waller kept Bell out of position in the second half. Campos and Worth missed critical shots. Too much responsibility was placed on Kiley."

Mo Phillips and Denver Branum get hot late in the game. They score 12 of the team's last 14 points and win going away 54-47.

The Sparks team is one of the greatest teams the NWBA has ever seen. I admit that but deep down, I feel we're better. Today and always.

Los Angeles Lakers Head Coach, Pat Riley, terms the phrase "three-peat." The quest of winning three championships in a row. The instant I hear these words, I know I want in on this selective club. Up to this point in my life, some of the great teams in sport to win three championships in a row are:

Boston Celtics, 1965-1969 (as a Lakers fan it is hard to write this one down)

UCLA Bruins, seven consecutive NCAA championships, 1967-1973

The Oakland Athletics, 1972-1974

Long Beach Flying Wheels, five consecutive championships, 1960-1964

The likes of Bill Russell, Bob Cousy, John Wooden, Lew Alcindor (Kareem Abdul Jabbar), Catfish Hunter, and Reggie Jackson and wheelchair baller Bill Johnson are the greats setting the highest of bars within the 3-peat dynamic. Can Curtis and I join this revered line-up of achievers and greatness? As the years pass, I watch Michael Jordan and Scottie Pippen of the Chicago Bulls 3-peat twice. Kobe and Shaq accomplish the feat with my beloved Lakers. The Dallas Wheelchair Mavericks are three-time, 3-peat champions between the years 1996 through 2017.

The tournament in Minneapolis, Minnesota is our shot at the 3-peat. We fail. I fail. We will begin again. Detroit's Westland Sparks are a great team. They have now won seven overall championships. My team, the Casa Colina Condors, only have two at this juncture but we're going to win more—a lot more. The Long Beach Flying Wheels have five championships. We're in the elbow-only-room, middle of the pack, uphill portion of a basketball marathon.

How do we break free from the pack and find our stride?

Coach John Wooden, speaking on Initiative, "Cultivate the ability to make decisions and think alone. Do not be afraid of failure, but learn from it."

Cliff Crase reflected on the 1982 NWBT, stating, "Dave Kiley, player–coach of the Casa Colina Condors did the ol' hat trick at the 34th NWBT awards banquet. Dave, the finest guard in the NWBA, won the Captain Ure Sportsmanship Award, was selected as the Most Valuable Player of the tourney, and was voted onto the All-Tournament First Team. Not a bad couple days on the hardwood. Dave has emerged as a leader in wheelchair sports: coaching, organizing, and teaching training tactics as well as being one of America's finest wheelchair athletes."

My second time winning a tournament MVP whilst losing the championship game. The first time with the Capital Cagers.

I felt empty then.

I feel empty now.

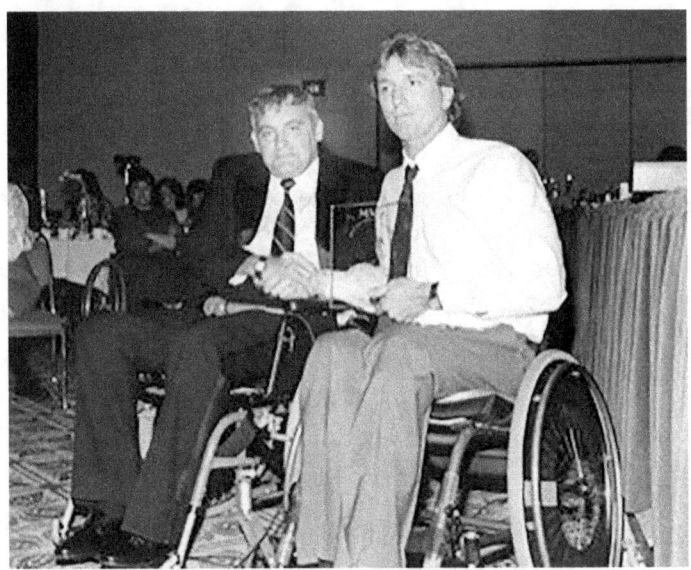

Cliff Crase, of Sport 'N Spokes *and NWBA Hall of Fame, presents me with my second MVP of Final Four National Championships.*

Losing sucks. It's that simple. I don't do well praising others. I swallow humble pie with a repentance full of self-blame and nagging images. *If only I made that baseline 14-footer.* Sure, I'm falling over, about to feel the hardwood (again), but if I could have knocked that shot down, it could have been a rallying point for the team. The closer I am towards perfect, the closer the team bonds to a collective. It's only the collective that truly achieves.

If.

If.

If.

Sports produce winners and losers. It's the constant that will never change, face and accept. For me, time is the only way to heal losses. Only a non-player says, "Wait till next year." I want to do it over. I want to do it now.

The waiting is indeed the hardest part.

The words meaning to encourage are often the worst of them all. I overhear a friend of a family member say, "It's only a game. He gets so worked up." No time for people like that or what they think.

Early in the '82 season, we lose to the LA Stars in our yearly trek to San Diego's preseason tournament. It's our only loss that year before losing to the Sparks in the championship game. In 1983, we dominate the San Diego event. Making sure the LA Stars see our fangs and feel our resolve.

Throughout the '83 season the Condors handle business. Jimbo Miller is rounding into a legendary big man. He is learning from the best in Curtis Bell and Albert Campos. Jimbo's emergence gives us increased options. We're able to counter opponents' runs with increased size or press up with a smaller, speedy line-up.

The newest challenge is how to stay humble and hungry? How do we not settle and become complacent? The overriding plan is to win and keep on winning, instead of waiting to reverse a painstaking loss in the national championship game. The focus and mindset work. Thirty games into the season we are undefeated.

We're hosting the final four tournament. Sleeping in our own beds. Eating our chosen foods. Being around those that we love and love us.

Detroit's Westland Sparks are in the tournament and on the opposite end of the draw. The chance of meeting them in the championship game is very real.

Spring 1983 in Southern California is a high-point for disability sport. Lightweight, colorful chairs are now the norm instead of the exception. It's not uncommon to see wheelchair players in evening community tennis classes. Awareness is spiking, and even though the reaction is over-the-top with fluff piece, feature stories, and corny news pieces, the normalcy of Joe wheelchair guy or Wendy wheelchair gal in the day-to-day mix of things is accepted within the grace of a black and white population covertly wanting a kaleidoscope of cultural colors.

The Showtime Lakers are the hottest ticket in town. Young Magic on the break dishing to Michael Cooper and newcomer rookie, James Worthy. I have season seats for all the Magic era games. Four seats and all my buddies want in.

Lakers' owner Jerry Buss heightens the entertainment value of his product with a fastbreak—star power—style of play. The addition of high-volume celebrities and the noteworthy addition of the electric Laker Girls are contributing factors. I love the production value and theatre display of the Lakers during this time. Winning helps. The Laker Girls play into my "sizzle" mindset with athleticism, beauty, and a shock-and-awe flair for the moment.

This isn't lost on me. I help put a public relations plan into action. The plan is to play the Final Four tournament in a facility that can handle the size of a decent crowd whilst also allowing us a favorable home court advantage. A partnership is arranged with Cal Poly Pomona University and their Kellogg Gym.

The next step is to mimic the Lakers' big game approach. Pack the stands with a home crowd that inflates runs and influences calls whilst also deflating the opposition's will and ability to comfortably communicate. We use many of the same fund-raising connections to get all these valuable friends—and all their friends—out to the semi-final and championship game.

We speak directly to the Lakers. Coach Pat Riley and cult hero Kurt Rambis agree to attend the championship game. Even better, the Lakers Girls will be performing at halftime. The group is a Southern California lightning rod for wannabe dancers and is a cultural change, serving sport as an entrée into the entertainment world.

Teammate Ron Scanlon, an 8th degree black belt and master in kung fu san soo, does a jaw dropping halftime demonstration with his black belt, able-bodied partner. The crowd cannot believe their eyes.

Kung Fu Master Ron Scanlon.

Lastly, the championship game is televised live on KTLA, channel 5 in the Los Angeles market. An unqualified first.

With everything in place, the only thought is to seek and destroy our opponents. The championship game will be televised, the Lakers Girls will be performing—no option but to win. The pressure motivates. Winning is the only way the story can play out. No exceptions.

The team is amped. The crowd is bigger and louder than the NWBA has ever seen.

We beat Nashville's Music City handily in the semi-final. My connection with Curtis Bell begins to take on an esoteric—I know where he's going before he gets there—unstoppable dimension. Curtis racks up points. I pile on assists. Al Campos and Jim Miller strangle Nashville in the post and dominate the boards.

Next.

Detroit's Westland Sparks lay ahead in the final. Poetic justice.

Cal Poly's Kellogg Gym is packed. I remember shaking Coach Riley's hand but that's about it. Redemption lies within 94 feet of length and the 50 feet of width of a regulation basketball court. With no shot clock in the game yet, the Sparks use patience and the clock as a strategy. To me they're saying they can't keep up: lots of ball swings, threats of an inside/post attack only to swing it back out and start again their passive dribbles. Thank goodness for the impending shot clock.

Curtis, Miller, and Albert play big and deny Darryl "Tree" Waller the efficiency he enjoyed a year previous. I keep Mo Phillips in check and we hold the Sparks to a mere 42 points for the game. The seven-time champions never find their rhythm and flow.

The Casa Colina Condors defeat the Sparks, 50-42.

Tree Waller from Detroit Sparks, surrounded.

Throughout the game, I feel the crowd in waves. When places get full, the sensation of the roar of the crowd gets beneath your seat and into your wheels. It's strange, daunting, and magical at the same time.

I also feel the pride of leading the organizing committee to fill the venue. The sight takes my breath away and the memory is one of early historical legend.

Undefeated season. Payback against Detroit. National Champions with our home crowd watching and cheering. Check. Check. Check.

"Team spirit is the ultimate expression of interdependence. Just as team spirit embraces an element of enthusiasm, it also houses a component of cooperation. But where cooperation makes others better, team spirit makes the group better," explains Coach John Wooden.

Great teams have trust. Trust is a byproduct of the truth. The truth is complicated.

Athletes have a vision; a version of themselves built through dreams, hard work, support systems, and pride. If any of these components fracture or get dinged through competition, coaching, or lack of performance, the chances of fallout and drama increase dramatically. This can be toxic and spread like cancer through a team in the form of backbiting, gossip, division, and the outcast of certain members.

Condors win championship in a packed house…undefeated season.

The better a team can handle trust, and work as close to the truth as possible, the greater a team's spirit. It's because of an evolving team spirit that groups have the earned ability to overcome adversity. Teams unable to deal in truths will not be long-lasting. The blame game will cycle and spin until it's time to get off. It's a fine line that needs continuous tending to.

In 1984, the Casa Colina Condors know the real battles are against one another. In Southern California our opponents maintain high-performance levels, but they're not evolving. The best players in the southland (and beyond) want to be a Condor, but good luck cracking the starting line-up or getting high-leverage minutes.

Southern California touts over twenty teams in two conferences. Many are in close proximity to one another. Some transition away from the Condors whilst others seek us out and ask to join. We welcome this list of unsung heroes as they're some of the best Southern California has to offer.

Winning is our best recruitment tool.

Throughout our run we also have some of the best women joining the Condors in: Rene Keres, Jamie Danskin (HOF), and Tiana Tozer.

As a player-coach, the plan is simple. Make team scrimmages and practices more of an event than our conference games. Tuesday and Thursday nights in the Pomona Valley, the toughest, most fierce, best brand of basketball is happening amongst no fanfare and without referees.

Ralph Waldo Emerson Junior High School on Lincoln Street in Pomona is where the battles take place for nearly a decade and a half.

The drive into the parking lot.

The process of unloading chairs.

The red bricks of the single story, small school.

The smell of the gym.

The aroma of adolescent sweat and burgeoning desires.

Cotton candy.

The creaky, wooden stage at half-court.

The suicides.

Sprint turn.

Sprint turn.

Try not to puke.

Scrimmages defying what's expected.

Expect the unexpected.

Grow.

Full house conference games.

A hundred fifty plus in the crowd.

Feels five times that.

My history.

Our history.

We run a three-big line-up with Curtis Bell, Jim Miller, and Albert Campos that pummels average teams and breaks the will of the few that think they can compete with us. My job is to get the ball up and over the defenders and into the shooting pockets of either Jimbo or Curtis.

The great Bill Russell once said, "For me to be great, I needed to give space for others to be great. Then the team is great." Bill Russell wins eleven NBA championships. Five more than Michael Jordan or Kareem Abdul Jabbar.

Our scrimmages are throw-downs. It's rarely first-team versus second-team. The teams are even. Games to 15 or 21. Call your own fouls. A recipe for edgy, highly contested, alpha filled, king of the hill, shit-talking scenarios. The fouls are hard and the responses exaggerated. We keep arguing over the score. No one can stand the taste and sting of losing.

The emergence of Jim Miller and his ability and desire to score in the post, adds a volatile (I'm going to push right through you) scorer. I love it. It's like stacking the deck with an extra set of aces.

Jim Worth feels the squeeze. His game time minutes are adjusted to accommodate Miller's rise. Worth has veteran, big game experience and remains vital. Mike Duran and Paul Haugen are high scoring, class 3, standouts but don't have the size or experience of Albert, Jimbo, and Curtis. My backup and quality class 2, Ron Scanlon can start throughout the league. He is somewhat cursed to be playing behind me but accepts his role and plays with a fierceness that I admire. Bob Murdock and Richard Jensen vie for the class 1 minutes, with Murdock the starter and Jensen logging valuable crunch time minutes. Then there's class 3, Barry Thomas. Barry is the enforcer on the team. He sets people straight. With a couple front teeth missing, his scowls and pointed threats can come off as unhinged and scary. As one of my Recreation Therapy patients, I know he's more bark than bite but there's been more than once that Barry Thomas has had my back—been my personal enforcer. With Kung Fu Ronnie and Barry, only fools would choose to mess with us.

Fouls called or not called, testosterone filled insecurities, verbal jabs, lack of performance, watching a peer perform at a high level, having to hear about it, getting the score wrong, and the funky smell of the junior high gym are all a short fuse to what's highly combustible.

Newcomers to the Condors, feeling the need to prove themselves, are often marks for the most alpha-laden on the team. Near brawls ensue. No one wants to back down. Everyone has something to prove.

Rumours hit the streets; the Condors have infighting and aren't getting along. Opponents fuel the slander. Untrue. We have our own unique heartbeat. Practices can turn into street fights. Sure. It's always someone's night. He's hotter than a firecracker, hitting shots, filling passing lanes with easy finishes, and defensive steals. It's his night and it's rubbing the rest raw.

It's just another training session in a season littered with internal on-court battles. There's a better than average chance the conference game this upcoming weekend won't come close to what just went down tonight in our cracker box gym.

It's a brick by brick, layered perfection. All trusts are well earned.

That night we do what we always do after practice, grab beers at the local liquor store. It's just past nine at night on Garey Avenue in Pomona. The parking lot behind the liquor store is dark and the scene a bit sketchy. Beers are popped. Highlights of the scrimmage are debated. With each sip our volume increases. We talk, laugh, bond, and bust on one another like brothers do. It's not uncommon for the cops to check in on us.

"You guys know where you're at, right?"

"Yes, sir," we answer.

"How's the team?"

"Undefeated," Curtis answers.

"Get home safe. Don't make it a late one."

"Yes, sir."

The routine lasts. Season after season we debrief the night's session over beers. There's also countless get togethers at my place for backyard barbecues or pool parties at Richard Jensen's with wives, kids, and girlfriends. A select few of us go on deep sea fishing trips and to Lakers games.

In games, with the scoreboard the almighty truth, we're a pack of lions hunting prey.

It's easy when you do it right.

We do it right.

We enter the 1984 Final Four undefeated. We have a willingness and are eager to push the boundaries of performance. We're superlative and extraordinary. I know this because our rivals can't shut up about us. They talk a lot of crap. They disparage our methods. They're envious of our results.

Let them say what they want.

We say, "Scoreboard."

We say, "Next."

The Music City Lightning take down Detroit's Westland Sparks in the semi-final of the Final Four tournament. Little does anyone know their 1982 championship would be their last. The Sparks, with seven championships, are a great team and program. They are a vibrant, historical touchpoint in the NWBA.

We enter the 1984 Kansas City Final Four tournament undefeated and with history on our minds. We know if we win, we are within one championship of the Long Beach Flying Wheels. Bill Johnson's ugly remarks when I was with the Sacramento Cagers still motivates.

I am driven to win the tournament, to capture our fourth national championship, but I'm also driven to capture the MVP of the big game. I've won two whilst losing the game. I keep this ego-driven, small brain incentive below the surface but the thought of trudging up the stage to be the best loser in the room disgusts and adds a resilient coating of *not-this-time*. Curtis and I go on to share the MVP award for over a decade. Curtis earned the MVP of the championship game last season.

It's Condors/Lightning for the title.

The Nashville team is high octane. Roger Davis shoots from deep and can get piping hot. Ron 'Bird' Alsup and Rod Short are table-setters that finish and knock down mid-range looks with regularity. Their big Willie Buchanan has the capacity to dominate games in the post. Our twin towers of Bell and Miller will have their hands full.

I'm hot from the start. I have wheel (speed) and chair skills on Music City. I own the transition game, resulting in wide open spaces for my mid-range bank shots and shot-fake drives to the rim. Between the free throw lines, they cannot keep up with me. Leading up to halftime, Curtis, Miller, and Murdoch have solid performances. I do damage passing and shooting the ball and have the Lightning contemplating strategies and priorities

Albert Campos, stifling shadow defense on Roger Davis, has the sharp shooter calling for picks and rubs to get free. This plays into Albert's strength. His ability to read the help, along with his superior chair skills and length, keeps Davis frustrated and out of the scorer's book. The boys dominate the boards.

There is cause for concern.

I pick up my third foul in the first half. I'm not coming out—player–coach benefits.

There's a whistle with 8:47 left in the game. It's on me. Fourth foul. I banish myself to the bench for a blow. I substitute myself back in quickly. The rational move is to sit me until 3 to 5 minutes to go. Another foul and I'm disqualified from the game. The irrational move is to keep me in the game. To trust my instinct and savvy. I stay in the game and do not foul again.

To their credit the Lightning refuse to relent. They battle.

It's my day. I continue my barrage of perimeter buckets off-the-glass and driving spin layups. I'm 14 years old again, working over my brothers and boys from the neighborhood in the sunset driveway games. How many times did I count down from three? Two. One. Let it fly. Nothing but the bottom. I rehearse the moment so often it feels natural. Ordained. It's not fate. It's a manifestation of vision, effort, and belief. My chair is a blur. It feels like it's turning for me. I'm the fastest on the court but I am slow of mind, not letting the restrictions of thought or anything resembling failure in. I hear only the voices of teammates. I shoot again. The release of the shot, wrist pronation, exaggerated follow-through and eyes on the target. This one is off the backboard. A seventeen-foot, forty-five-degree, bank-shot. Just like Coach Wooden taught and Pistol Pete executed. It's perfect.

I sling a behind-the-back pass to Bell for an easy score. I feel Music City's energy has diminished. I'm a boxer stalking/hovering before the knockout.

An alley-oop to Jimbo Miller. Then another to Curtis.

I find the scoreboard.

I'm pulled back into the breath of life. Our bench counting down from ten. I hear the crowd again. See the referees hustling off the court. The buzzer sounds.

It's over.

I yell like a hyena beneath a full moon. Curtis finds me. He understands more than anyone. He's a champion. I hug him tight, like a brother of this moment, not fully understood but never forgotten.

I win the championship game MVP.

My first as a winner.

My third overall.

We've now won 65 games in a row.

Kool and the Gang's "Celebration" plays throughout.
A forever Condor
winning
soul song.
I want more…
…more championships
…more MVP's.

I want to win a hundred games in a row.

Jimbo/Curtis doing the heavy lifting again while Al Campos approves the celebration. Friends for life and all 4 in the NWBA Hall of Fame. RIP Jimbo.

SERVE SOMEBODY

I have to serve this game I love so deeply. It's unquestioned. It's an intrinsic pull, finding ever-increasing life in helping along the magic shapes of accomplishment. Whether at the highest levels of play or the introduction to dribble, pass, and shot, the rush of being an ingredient in the recipe of athletic learning is one I'm drawn to for over six decades.

Sometimes it's the simplicity of a six-year-old feeling the ridges of the ball, bouncing it, and eventually finding a consistent, sturdy dribble: eyes up, left and right hand equally skilled with the ball, before finding the open teammate with a robust, accurate chest pass. The process can take a week, months, or years depending on skill levels, disability, and commitment. The observation and taking part in the development is affirming and long-lasting.

Other times, it's seven to eight-and-half courts, urban music thumping, 3-on-3, high-level, tournament action with ballers doing work. My name is associated with the event. I'm on the mic, working the room amongst the frenetic sounds of men and women competing to either score or defend until there's an ultimate tourney champion.

Regardless if it's John Chambers and I scrapping together a sports camp in the late 70s at Sacramento State or the twentieth year into a self-titled, rite of passage, 3-on-3 tournament, the buzz is the same. The game is growing. Skill levels are increasing. What was learned previously is executed today. Imperfections only add to the grind of getting it right the next time or the time after that. Before basketball finds its glory in arenas and expansive sports halls, it's the ball of the streets and cracker box gyms that offer the greatest canvas for the aspiring.

To be a witness isn't for everyone. The days are too long. The food is often too fast. The time away from family is far too long. To be a witness also transcends. It's the subtle, outside hand, hook pass we've worked on for weeks with only incremental successes. Today it clicks. The grasp of the skill allows us to move to the next improvement. After she successfully completes the pass, we share a glance that reminds me why.

Why I drive the miles?
Why I'll do the same for the next.
Why I need to be sensitive to her after raising my voice?
Why I miss my own son's game and daughter's competitions.
Why I serve.

Shorty Powers is an innovator, a ground breaker. Amongst all the jokes, laughs, high times, and rush of creating opportunities for his beloved subculture, I learn how to serve by watching him and his wife Nance.

The Guadalupe climb changes what I imagine is possible. I'm an eyewitness to the art of relationship-building and sponsorship agreements. No matter the absolute commitment, without quality sponsorships an event, camp, or competition isn't all it can be.

Shorty and Nance know this in spades. At their Turning Point Extravaganzas, the initial activities include: water skiing, lake pontoon and kayak fishing, jet skiing, archery, air rifles, and handcycling to name a few. The disability sport population takes to the yearly event in droves. A proud, native Texan, his sponsor relations run deep. It isn't long before his Turning Point events are offering big time raffle prizes to all its participants: ATV 4 Wheelers, a Chrysler PT Cruiser, exotic trips, and more. I witness (and take part in) the excitement within the day of the drawing. It's contagious.

Turning Point is responsible for the first adaptive bass fishing tournament decades ago: lightning-fast bass boats, large cash awards for placing and biggest fish caught, a fish fry/crawfish boil and evening ceremonies that last well into the wee hours.

I like being a passenger on the Turning Point express. It's so well run. There are so many activities to enjoy each and every year. It's hard for me to stay off Caddo Lake and fish the hours away. This is my place. A seemingly fathomless body of water, full of unseen creatures demanding my skill and patience to find and extract. The hours pass like minutes. A time of fellowship. A time to find an out of view section of the lake and simply *be*.

Shorty with a big bass.
Opened the outdoors to all.

It's around 2002 and Shorty wants to add a basketball component to things. He wants me to host a tournament within the structure of his megaevent. I'm not into it. What about my fishing time? I do this to get away from basketball. I don't want the responsibility. Shorty persists. I show no real excitement. *Please my friend, back off this idea.*

He, of course, does not.

I relent. I begin to think creatively how to make this happen.

The notion of 3-on-3 comes to me. Smaller numbers. Play in the half court. Multiple games happening at once. What if I pick the teams from individual player registrations? An even competition with greats of the game next to up-and-comers or serviceable lower division players. Athletes can travel as individuals, not as a team. Easier. Women battling with men. I'm intrigued. I call Shorty with the idea. He's uninterested in the particulars. He trusts me to get it right.

I have to sell Dallas, Texas, in the summer. It's sticky hot. On the plus side, Texas is geographically central, and Dallas has a hot bed of local talent. I get on the horn with the best of the best. My line to them is, '*If you love ball* (and I know they all do), *you gotta love playing in a summertime 3-on-3 event.* Out of the gate, I have the game's best: Pat Anderson, Andrea Woodson-Smith, Bobbie Nickleberry, Jermell Pennie, Jeff Glasbrenner, a teenage Matt Scott, and Southern California transplant, Willie Hernandez.

The first year of the event, I ask everyone to bring a light and dark jersey to compete in. Laughable from where I sit twenty-plus years later. I'm taken by the attractiveness of the 3-on-3 format. The tournament is a hit with the players and also within the structure of the Turning Point Extravaganza. We play at the local recreation centers on Fridays, and the semifinals and finals at the Turning Point's venue, the Bachman Recreation Center, on Saturday. It's a hot box of a gym with a rubber floor. I realize in year one, the Bachman Rec Center serves us just fine as some serious, quality basketball continues to be played there throughout the years.

The early-year memories are epic. The one I see like yesterday is Pat Anderson hitting a roll-off, fade away 30-footer to win the event. No emotion. Just Pat being Pat.

The events and memories build.

One year, Shorty presents Sandy and I with the presidential suite of the host hotel. At first, we're in awe and appreciative. That night we discover Shorty's host hotel is also a swingers destination spot. We imagine all the lively deeds in the many corners and landing areas next to where we lay our heads. To this day we laugh out loud at the hilarity of it all.

Shorty adds a Texas hold 'em poker tournament fundraiser. Basketballer players (for whatever reason) imagine themselves as big time poker aficionados. The entries continue to grow in the 3-on-3 portion of the Turning Point weekend. Shorty gives away huge prizes for the Texas hold 'em evening.

I tap into my Quickie relationship and introduce new ball chairs for the winners whilst also beginning to hand out small levels of prize money.

The event carries on for years as the David Kiley Invitational 3-on-3. I'd have never thought that the initial task by Michael Shorty Powers, to run a basketball event for Turning Point, would turn into a worldwide brand and the best tournament of its kind in the world…renamed DK3.

I meet Little James (LJ) Yates as a 7-year-old. These days he's a grown man.

A teammate of mine sets up a meeting with his family. I meet mom and dad. We talk about basketball. LJ has three older sisters and a younger brother, all athletes and all ballers. LJ is a spectator to his siblings' practices and athletic events.

LJ is partially sighted and technically blind. He has a severe contraction in his right arm and is using a power chair.

I bring my basketball chair to our initial meeting. There's a basketball hoop in the family's backyard. I knock down shot after shot, throw up a few from as deep as their backyard allows. I knock those down, before excessively spinning an assortment of layups off the backboard. LJ is wide-eyed and has an overt, assured grin. He's excited. The spark before the flame.

I have him jump in my ball chair. There's a bit of trepidation as my chair is high tech with a shorter wheelbase and might have the newbie baller spinning out of control. He does some cautious laps around the court. His confidence and potential grow with each passing minute. The spark is now a fire in LJ's eyes and assertive body language. Shoulders back and head held high, I eye LJ, knowing that we are onto something here.

Upon my return to the Yates family of ballers, I bring a chair more suitable for LJ's needs. The kid has limited potential with his lack of vision and the fact he's one arm dominant. It's going to be an uphill climb, but more importantly it's another living/breathing example of what the human spirit is capable of. Stay in the disability sport game long enough and you'll find what's unimaginable one day is standard practice the next. I keep showing up. I notice the increased interest and participation of LJ's sisters and brother.

It's time for LJ to begin shooting the ball. His dad, a quality baller himself, stays in touch. LJ's laps around the backyard court are ever-increasing. He is counting the numbers and relaying them back to me.

Throughout this time, everyone refers to LJ as Little James. I do also. This needs to change into a basketball nickname. I begin calling him LJ. It sticks. Our bond deepens.

My next visit to the Yates' backyard, LJ and I begin working on his shooting mechanics. It isn't long before he makes his first shot. The celebration is more subtle than imagined, but the impression on both of us is powerful. I see in his eyes, through thick bifocals, the familiar and focused look of a shot maker on an impressionable journey.

LJ wants a jersey. I arrange to get him one from our Charlotte program, Abilities Unlimited. He's beside himself with joy, and the simple act of wearing a jersey puts him on a more level playing field with the others in his house. His ability to make shots increases with each of our sessions. I'm drawn to the kid as he displays a loyalty to his mushrooming craft that I not only relate to but admire.

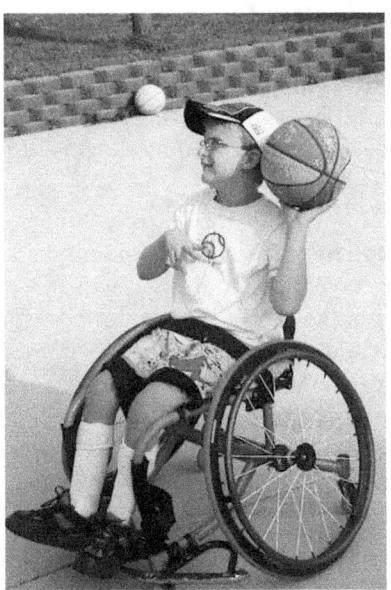

LJ, "The Miracle."

Friendship is on the foundational block of Wooden's Pyramid of Success. Coach John Wooden explains friendship as "com[ing] from mutual esteem and devotion. Friendship is doing for others while they are doing for us. It's called ministry when all of the doing goes one direction. Friendship goes both ways. Friendship is like a good marriage—it's based on common concern. Friends help each other; they don't use each other."

LJ's parents get him to a *prep* practice. Prep league is for younger kids. They shoot on an eight-and-a-half-foot basket instead of the standard 10-foot goal. LJ is now on a team like his brother and sisters. He's the newest Charlotte Rollin' Bobcat. In a team sense this is as good as it's going to get for LJ. The reality is LJ will never be able to keep up defensively. His right arm limitations disallow the needed hand-speed and power-pushing to keep up at higher levels of play.

LJ dedicates himself to making shots. He's a gym rat beyond compare. He takes to meeting me at our local YMCA. His vision doesn't allow him to see me upon entering the sports hall, but like a bloodhound, he sniffs me out and enters into my strenuous shooting routines. I can't wear him out. I get word from other YMCA members and staff that LJ is in the facility all the time, getting up shots for hours at a time. As he grows and adds strength, LJ begins bombing from distance. He does these one-arm, left-handed, center field heaves that are accurate and consistently on-point. He's a vision to behold with thick-lensed glasses and his bespoke shooting technique. He's taken to wearing a headband and compression sleeve on his shooting arm.

I'm witnessing a modern miracle.

LJ cannot see but the ball has eyes.

On his prep squad he takes most of the team's shots and is our opponent's number one priority to stop. He can use his right arm just enough to propel his chair the 94 feet of the court. LJ gets the most out of what's humanly possible from his right side.

Over the years LJ becomes a 3-point specialist. The eight-and-a-half-foot goal days are behind him. LJ is shooting on regulation goals and from deep. How he sees the hoop I'll never understand. To use his cell phone, he practically pushes his phone right next to his face. He's crushing 3's. One after another.

Swish.

Swish.

And swish.

He takes to knocking down half-court shots with the same zest he takes to the arc of layups, free throws, mid-ranges, and threes. A Gen Z creation, LJ wants recordings on either his or my cell phone. I have multiple videos of him successfully making half-court shots as well as a three-quarter-court shot.

Insane.

For the next eleven years LJ is my roadie. I pick him up to practice and take him home. If basketball is involved, LJ is riding shotgun in my black, Ford F150 pickup truck.

We're headed down Interstate 77 in Charlotte, North Carolina. Like always, LJ has a basketball in his hand. It's like a security blanket. He can spin the ball on every digit of his good hand. Impressive. I'm driving, and LJ is busy spinning it as we travel south in Charlotte rush hour traffic. I see him reaching toward me with the ball, it's spinning on his index finger and just like that, the ball gets sucked out my open sunroof. I look in my rearview mirror to see the ball bouncing into oncoming traffic. An 18-wheeler crushes it. LJ looks at me with an alarm and surprise not seen before or since. He takes a beat.

"Coach, we gotta go back and get it."

"You think either one of us is going out onto that busy Interstate?"

"But coach, my ball."

"I saw your ball get crushed by an 18-wheeler."

LJ is on the verge of tears.

This is a story we tell throughout the years. It's yet to not get a heartfelt, belly laugh.

Basketball is LJ's core sport and love. He also participates in many more. The Turning Point adaptive adventures LJ takes on are: a weekly go at our rock-climbing center, sailing, striper fishing in Georgia, and water skiing.

These days I see far less of LJ. Where does the time go? LJ and I connect for the odd sporting event or on his birthday. As an adult, he lives in a supervised apartment in Burlington, North Carolina. LJ is as gregarious and extroverted as ever. This will never change.

Life certainly changes.

These days, LJ gets few visitors. His family doesn't make the time. This saddens me. The basketball continuum is not there for a visually impaired, non-driving, defensive liability, trick shot, long range bomber. Like many before him, his high school years are the glory days.

Sandy and I drive the hour-and-a-half to Burlington to have a birthday lunch with LJ. He's in his twenties now and pings my phone with messages, posts, and videos like it's his job. I make sure to respond back. A vital part of me wants him to know I'm here.

Sometimes in the life we've created, it's all we have.

Sometimes in the service of others, we're really servicing ourselves.

It's a conscious decision to stay connected to basketball long after my elite playing days are over. The David Kiley Invitational 3 on 3 event begins to push towards its twenty-year mark.

It's also a lot of yearly, exhaustive work.

Beside the annual event in Dallas, the tournament is organized and played in Charlotte, Rocky Mount, North Carolina, and Venice Beach, California. There are conversations and conference calls of hosting in European countries like

France and Great Britain. Japan shows the most interest of any nation. Japanese ballers make the trek to Dallas for various DK3s.

I have a yearly, front-row seat of not only the greats of the game but also its next generation. It keeps me on the front line of the sport. It feels good, and right, to have my name associated with such a robust fellowship. Ask any baller, the game is far more than baskets, scoreboards, and rivalries. It's a community that looks out for one another, understands the intensity of the work, and takes on the ever-present percentages of failure. The failures bond us. Successes allow us to climb the victory ladder, but it's the blunders we share, openly and honestly, that are relatable and allow us to understand and take on each other's stories.

Sponsors grow. Organization sharpens. We tighten the bolts on the bracketology process over the years. Things run on time. I'm blessed to have Hall of Fame-quality Tournament Directors in Frank Burns, Pat McCoy, and Doug Garner. Garner even offers up his University of Texas, Arlington, venue. I gladly accept.

A phone conversation with Willie Hernandez, owner of Per4Max Wheelchairs, sparks a creative decision. Inspired by Ice Cube's Big3 popular basketball league, Willie suggests changing the name from the lengthy David

Kiley 3 on 3 Invitational to DK3. I partner with Ish Tanyeri and Dromos Marketing Agency in 2018. DK3 is now a brand.

The conversation I have with Willie and the partnership with Dromos Marketing are the two biggest and best decisions I make for the future of my event.

We're ready to take on something big, a grand gesture saluting our subculture.

I've always loved the movie *White Men Can't Jump*. Wesley Snipes and Woody Harrelson play basketball hustlers trying to outdo one another on the courts of Venice Beach. A Los Angeles coastal community, Venice Beach is where art and crime converge. It's an iconic spectacle with its muscle beach, vibrant rollerbladers, world class skateboarders, south swell surfers, celebrity sightings, and ever-growing homeless population.

DK3 and Dromos Marketing partner to help fulfil a dream I've always had: to host an event on the outdoor courts of Venice Beach.

Ish and I work on the event for over a year. First, we decide this version of

DK3 is for Veterans only. The Wounded Warrior population is spiking with increased terrorism throughout the world. What a great way to celebrate these women and men protecting our freedoms. DK3 offers a valuable distraction from all the baggage these men and women carry from the wounds of war and service. I'm overjoyed to host this family of veterans. We become friends for life and DK3 is the connection.

The hoops we jump through are numerous and complicated: forms, letters, insurance, ground transportation, meals, and permits are triple-checked until all are secured. We also need cash money. Palms aren't necessarily greased, but I make sure to carry a knot of hundreds during the many negotiations. The bill for marketing materials intensifies. The setup of the courts changes as sponsors haggle with us for placement. Some want their product next to the spectators whilst others want theirs by the food or entrance to the courts. It's nonstop. Thank goodness for the many volunteers. This army of good souls is the biggest reason we're able to pull off such a feat with the visual backdrop of images, banners, spectator seating, music, beverages, and food.

A vivacious and dramatic relationship is formed with Nick Ansom, the founder of Veniceball. A Venice local, Ansom, creates the Venice Basketball League and works within the Venice Boys & Girls Club programming basketball.

We go to Nick with our latest concern—security. To tear down and set up again is too Herculean an effort from one day to the next. The expensive and less human answer is to hire gun toting, highly-paid (by the hour) professional security. The chance for high drama is enough to keep us up throughout the night. Nick provides an unimaginable option. Pay the local homeless to look after things.

In his words, "These courts are their home. You give them a hundred bucks and they will protect all your setup like it's their own."

I look at Ish with big, cartoon eyes, before answering back, "Let's do this."

Nick Ansom's streetball legacy is elite. He travels the globe establishing outdoor basketball courts for communities that need them the most. His Venice Beach connection is an interesting one indeed. His family moved from France to Los Angeles when he was thirteen. Nick roams the boardwalk of Venice, post-Dogtown years, but gangs and crime are prevalent. Ansom pays no heed and instead takes to the breezy, coastal courts of his first love—basketball. He learns his English on the courts of Venice and credits his time there as the needed ingredients to the man he is today. Long, lean, tan, and blonde, Nick looks like the Venice Beach Court Whisperer he is.

Saturday morning, I look up and there is the incomparable Frank Burns. He's pitching in wherever he can. His decision to show up from Chicago unannounced and out of nowhere, takes my breath away. He gets the meaning of this place, with these people and this profound time. Frank reminds me of beginnings, accomplishments, and the journey ahead. Throughout the weekend we're both in tournament mode but my time with my old friend takes on an even greater meaning as without him and the professional opportunities he's created for me, I'm unsure if an event like this is possible. Seeing Frank is to laugh out loud repeatedly. His take on life is to work hard, never take yourself too seriously, and see the humor before all else in things. Sadly, this is the last time I'll see Frank before his untimely passing.

I'm taken by the opening ceremonies with the required color guard and star bangled banner. This customary procedure takes on full-body, chill-bump status when surrounded by a crew that has given so much. We gather arm and arm for the blessing of the event, led by me. This is a DK3 standard.

Saturday's play is breathtaking. So many legends (both street and professional) have taken to these courts and today a new legend owns the day. Military veterans, not in uniform but bonded together, having it out in open competition.

Chairs banging footplate to push-rim, shots firing up with a callused, taped hand in their face, specific and world class defensive communication—"get flat/ get flat, identify shooter, trail the roll, find her shooting hand."

There is next level shit talking banter. There is no mincing of words. There is much to be learned from the Veterans' direct and succinct messaging. I think of all the butt-hurt feelings I've seen and dealt with. There's a specific rawness and effectiveness in the way these soldiers communicate with one another.

Then there's the ever-present athlete/Veteran picking themselves off the pavement after a fall, checking for blood whilst also checking on one another. The comradery is palpable. Infectious.

Six simultaneous courts full of action.

Sponsors happy with their investment.

A background of waves washing in before heading out.

Hundred-foot-tall palm trees bowing with the wind.

The legendary boardwalk bursting with foot traffic.

Street life abound with vendors, food, and the art of the deal.

The scene is rocking thanks to the vibing spins of DJ/Kelci Newlin. The DJ is sponsored through the efforts of Courtney Ryan and Molly Bloom.

There's a liberal, billowing haze of marijuana from the boardwalk shops. Breathe in deep enough and the chance of a contact high is an ever-increasing possibility.

A Bakersfield group, the Pickle Pellet Heads, is feeding the masses with their smoked Boston Butts and Brisket. The Pickle Pellet Heads are a charitable group of recovering alcoholics keen to do good by smoking a variety of meats. Kevin Ryan (Courtney Ryan's father) brings the group to the event. Then his niece, Phoebe Ryan, sings like a songbird through the PA as participants, volunteers, and staff eat like kings and queens. The mountain of leftovers is given to the large homeless community surrounding Venice Beach.

I take everything in. Every aspect of the DK3 Venice Beach tournament is about someone serving someone else.

Sunday morning all is good. Our set-up is intact. After I exhale, I reach into my wad of Benjamin Franklins and begin paying off the team of homeless security guards. Nick Ansom has it right. These guys looked after our things like they were their own.

It's "survive and advance" day. Yesterday's outcomes seed the teams for today. Win and move on. Lose and you're a spectator.

We're down to the semifinals. The growing crowd is settling in for an afternoon of 'money' basketball.

Venice Beach rears its edge of humanity, irrational head. A drug induced, dreadlocked, homeless streaker dances across our semifinal matches. Both games come to a halt. Whatever he's on must have a large quantity of happiness, as dreadlock guy cannot stop smiling whilst simultaneously dancing and avoiding his detractors. Some of the Vets don't think a naked/dreadlock guy is amusing or adds a level of comic relief. Amputees begin to chase naked/dreadlock guy down. Wheel Heads try cornering him. Many look on in snickering shock. It's comical but with poor timing. The beautiful blue, Venice Beach center court is a spectacle of the absurd where just moments ago it represented the best of woman/mankind.

My youngest brother PJ crosschecks a naked/dreadlock guy into a sponsor's booth as my mother looks on. Just another tale of her boys in action. The sponsor is new. I see shock and awe in their faces as their booth gets demolished.

He's subdued. The Vets circle and hover above the naked/dreadlock guy but cooler heads prevail. The cops show. They know the guy and are familiar with his antics.

Play resumes. '*That's Venice,*' I say to myself over and over and then into the microphone to a splattering of laughter.

Streaked in Venice Beach Vets event. Brother Tom, a lifetime of support and love.

Champions are crowned with a big, oversized, two-grand check. My great friends at Per4Max donate the prize money. My old teammate, Albert Campos, along with Chris Pettway and Matt Grashen are the victors of the Venice Beach DK3.

It takes a long time to realize, but I get it fully now, surrounded by the likes of Frank Burns, the Pickle Pellet Heads, Ish, the Ryans (Kevin and I are kindred spirits), Per4Max, my brother PJ, the severity of the homeless, the dozens of volunteers freely giving their time, my mother, and a 60-plus field of warrior Veterans battling it out—winners are made on the court and champions are made off it.

She is eleven when I become aware of her.

After the tragic deaths of Gigi and Kobe Bryant, I decide to create a Mambacita Scholarship in honor of the two. The scholarship gives financial support to younger female athletes wanting to attend Junior Wheelchair Basketball Camps. I couldn't be happier to help support dreams similar to the ones Kobe and his daughter Gigi shared.

Adrina Castro, or Itty Bitty as she is referred to more than her given name, applies for a scholarship. The task requires an essay. Itty Bitty's desire to get better pops off the page. I'm taken by her drive and respect for the game. We become Facebook and Instagram followers. The young lioness is all over social media posting her workouts and basketball arc with pure joy. From the jump, I know this kid loves the game and is at an elite level of relentless presence on social media.

Itty Bitty wins one of our first scholarships with her essay.

I am consistently taken in with the capacity and will of the human spirit. The spirit takes on the odds. It has the ability to persevere and overcome. It's with the guidance of the human spirit that athletes drive to reach the ultimate performances. If you truly have a love affair with the game (like I do), you're in a place to see others thankfulness for the same. You're able to see the posers from the soulful. Itty Bitty is the real deal. She is working to be great. I like what I see. Adrina Castro is more than a social media buzz. Her game is her statement. Her nonverbal, body language speaks, 'I'm coming for y'all. Get ready. It's close to my time and there's nothing you can do about it."

This is where disability sport shines. Advanced technologies with lighter frames and wheels are still in its infancy. It's less than 50 years ago that the Quadra crew began busting down the door of what's possible. These days Aaron Fotheringham is landing double backflips off a Super Ramp in his Box Wheelchair. Death defying. I cannot imagine what the future has to offer in adaptive sport.

At twelve years of age Adrina Castro is selected Junior Athlete of the Year by *Sports 'N Spokes* magazine.

At thirteen, she begins inquiring about competing in DK3. Itty Bitty knows and plays into the fact that women are competing in DK3 as part of our mission statement. She wants in and asks for entry into our next event. My job is to ensure that every athlete is ready to compete with the best players in the world. I tell Itty Bitty and many others, "Not quite yet. Keep doing the work and get back with us."

Adrina Castro is now fifteen years old. She has grown in all aspects of her game and physical stature. I'm coaching the Charlotte Rollin' Hornets women's team. Our second game is against Arizona. The Arizona team features three Paralympians: Courtney Ryan, Josie Aslakson, and Jen Poist. Our strategy is to double team Ryan as last year she lit us up. Itty Bitty takes full advantage and knocks down open look after open look. We contain Courtney Ryan but this time it's Itty Bitty that lights us up. Her performance takes me by surprise. Impressive.

It's time to pick participants for the 20th annual DK3.

I'm seventy-years old, given my life to basketball and disability sport, have created a brand, and am grateful for life beyond comparison. I am also tired. I need unlimited time with my grandkids. I am not missing tee-ball games, dance recitals, family picnics, or Sunday/fun days anymore. I let the important few know this will be my last DK3 rodeo.

Itty Bitty comes knocking again. She wants in the DK3 competition. I see her name and check the box: 'approved.'

Working within the Ed Owen, Recreation Therapist model of doing for others and doing what's right, the art of coaching kids is inevitable. Grassroots programming/coaching starts with an idea—a premonition that things are doable, even if you don't really know how. Having the spirit and understanding of Ed allows me to never give up on an idea, a person, or a concept. The Junior Division of the NWBA names an award after the Great One. Ed Owen, Junior Division, Coach of the Year. I win the award. I reminisce about our times. I look forward to telling of our relationship to all that will listen. The great things he did for me. Sadly, COVID-19 cancelled that year's championship tournament and accompanying awards ceremony. Ed and I share a quiet lifetime of memories together instead.

Coaching youth adaptive sports is at times the best, funniest, and most life-affirming experience there is on planet earth. Coaching adaptive sports also demands a depth of purpose. Coaching kids in adaptive sports is an exhaustive love affair with the generations beyond ours. It's doing whatever it takes.

The more kids I find, the more solution-oriented I become. The easy finds are basketballs, practice facilities, jerseys, limited sponsorships, entry into NWBA league competition, and volunteer help.

The biggest rub is transportation.

Understandably, there's plenty of kids in need, plenty of broken homes with single parent families and numerous siblings. These households don't have the resources to fund a sports chair much less the needed time to shuttle their kid the two-plus hours to weekly training sessions.

A flame has been lit with these upstart athletes. They want to be a member of this thing that they've only witnessed. They see their school athletic teams and brothers/sisters performing but never get a chance to wear a jersey themselves. The first shot they make, the spark is fanned and the kid, void of real activity, wants in.

Kids like this find me. I do not find them.

I am pulled to these youth in need with their specific challenges. The poor student with behavior problems seems to follow many into the adaptive sports experience. Even more reason to be all in. I've always known that without sport, minus the competition and not dealing with winning and losing, I am less than half the person I'm meant to be. These youngsters need the same canvas to paint their story. Some have unlimited potential. Others are in desperate need of belonging to a team or a like-minded group.

I serve both faithfully.

After-season celebration and campout at my home.

Geography is a massive obstacle. The junior athletes are out there but the issue is they're spread out there across hundreds of square miles and throughout dozens of school districts. My job is to corral them in the creation and execution of a team. Able bodied peers gladly meet at the school gym, local YMCA, community center, or Boys and Girls Club for practices or games. All of these facilities are in their given area. Not so with adaptive sports. It's a bit like herding cats. Some will get lucky as practices are scheduled minutes away from their residence whilst others need to travel two or three plus hours to participate.

"I don't have a ride," I hear over and over again. "Can I get a ride from someone?"

That someone is a coach. That someone is me.

Some families move heaven and earth to get their child to practices, scrimmages, and games. Others use me as their personal Uber driver to cart their child to training and across state lines for competitions.

I absorb this. It's the cost of answering the call of, "Hey, Coach."

As coaches we have choices we must come to terms with. The layers of coaching youth within disability sport are many; do we have the budget and ability to compete nationally? Are we more an experiential team with everyone playing and minutes distributed more evenly? As the team eventually grows do we have the resources to create a Junior Varsity team? How hard do I push as college scholarships are readily available for young women and men? Most importantly, how do I consistently get the team together to organized practices so all of the above is a consideration?

Some families take advantage of what's a genuine act of kindness and possibility for their child. Others don't have the time, resources, or even a driver's license.

Kids cannot fall between the cracks and get lost because of the "Achilles Heel" of not having transportation. I chose to be that coach. For two decades, I add a couple hours to and from practice picking up young ballers. Practice days are grinds. Sitting in traffic is a soulless task. The questioning, invisible parrot on my shoulder asks, *'Why. Why?'* I peek into the rearview mirror and eye three young athletes: one napping and two talking smack in anticipation of practice. Riding shotgun sits LJ (his customary spot) spinning a basketball on his pinky finger. The subtle magic are these moments.

It's been a good weekend, full of promise, growth, and a couple wins. We've downed the required fast food and are less than four hours from the first drop off. I should be home in five hours. I get an initial whiff. *'Please. No.'* Of the three junior athletes in my truck (my beloved baby), two are pointing fingers and holding their noses.

"It's him. It's him," they say half mocking and fully grateful it's not them.

It's no doubt, the one sitting in the rear passenger door has crapped his pants. I do my best not to gag. The other two are more brutal, "It's always brown town with you. Arghhhh."

I command silence. All four windows are lowered. I tap the cruise control to increase speed three times.

"Diarrhea?" I ask.

He shakes his head no.

I feel for the kid. His parents never get a handle on his Spina-Bifida and personal care. This needs to be his defining moment. He must invest in a successful bowel program and be disciplined with it or he will not be able to travel with the team. When we get to his house, I reiterate to him the importance of this moment. The Junior Rolling Hornets have expectations—lots of them. Education and personal care are at the top of the list. We're training kids for life, not just to make baskets.

I first meet Jacob Tyree and his father at the Charlotte Airport. Jacob is slight, fit, and athletic looking in his everyday chair. I give him the pitch. Young Jacob is keen, but he lives in Roanoke, Virginia. A three-hour drive from Charlotte, North Carolina. I wait for Mr. Tyree to nix Jacob's excitement (and mine) with the obvious. It's a six-hour, round trip, once a week pilgrimage to attend a two-and-a-half-hour practice.

No way.

Instead, Mr. Tyree extends his hand and asks for the address of our practice facility. The Tyrees attend practice for years. Jacob is a constant that coaches count on to not only build programs but to spike performance. Jacob goes on to attend the University of Illinois. He plays collegiate basketball and is an integral part of this legendary program.

After graduation, Jacob Tyree initially takes a job as an IT technician for Roanoke County Public Schools. A sportsman and advocate for disability sport, Jacob uses his platform to help educate the student body on Paralympic sports and its athletes. Jacob currently works with Move United as a Training Coordinator. Move United serves the entirety of the United States offering disability sport opportunities.

Parents make the sacrifice. Their child becomes a man. That man pays his taxes and contributes to a society in need of such examples. What's six-hours in a car compared to that? If only Jacob Tyree is the norm. He is not. His family is not. They are the exception.

There are times I feel taken advantage of. Not always, but enough to be wary of promises. Talk is cheap.

If not for myself, and plenty of other coaches giving freely of their time and vehicles, kids couldn't participate in the greatest, most poetic athletic endeavor going. For some it changes their life. It opens the door to education and a world far larger than neighborhood politics. For others it's a memory of what could have been. I bank those memories. They appear from nowhere and when least expected.

Connections through sport can last a lifetime or perhaps just a moment, but I know if I don't give kids rides to practice and games, there's a chance for a consequence that cannot be predicted. It can mean the difference between a great life, a hard life, or no life.

Camps are essential. Personal, team, and national team arcs are dependent on skill development, collective responsibility, and high-level competition.

I'm taken in by the concept of camps in the early 80s with the Paralyzed Veterans Association (PVA) and NWBA summer camps. Both are once a year and cover the fundamentals of the game. Another, more worldly, aspect of camps is the collection of like-minded baller/warriors. During breaks or meals, ideas are shared on pushing techniques, shooting details, chair designs, practice drills, nutritional supplements, cross training, strength and conditioning, passing angles, and the ever-expanding navigation and possibilities of life in a chair.

In the early days of the PVA camp the instructors are mostly able-bodied. There are barely any wheelchair instructors like me. I'm taken aback by the yelling and berating they use when instructing.   This is nonsense. Things will need to change.

Frank Burns and the University of Wisconsin-Whitewater, holds the first ever overnight camp. Frank's simple, yet also groundbreaking concept of using collegiate dormitories to house disabled athletes, kick-starts numerous collegiate summer camps. These camps thrive in numbers, coaching levels, and upstart, world class talent. I'm an instructor at Frank's initial camp and instinctively see and feel the confluence and stir of something big.

In the early eighties, the National Foundation of Wheelchair Tennis (NFWT), led by Brad Parks, hosts its initial Wheelchair Sports Camp for youth. He asks if I can be the camp's director? Held at Saddleback College in Mission Viejo, the camp focuses on tennis but also swimming, archery, basketball, track & field, and nutrition. The NFWT camp is unique. It's comparable to an able-bodied YMCA camp. It's also a camp led and instructed by disabled athletes.

I take to the leadership role of Brad's camp easily as I have been hosting my own camps through our Casa Colina junior programming: basketball, tennis, and track and field are the core sports. Many of our Casa kids attend the Saddleback camp. Young standouts like Jason Van Beek, Ricky Carter, Eric Swanson, and Tony Lara begin their athletic journeys at Casa.

Jason Van Beek goes on to win four collegiate championships at the University of Texas, Arlington, and nine NWBA championships with the Dallas Wheelchair Mavericks.

Tony Lara (RIP) falls in love with tennis. He plays competitively in the open division and goes on to become a United States Tennis Association (USTA) tennis instructor. Tony continues his passion-driven love of the game and creates, "One More Push" to help others access tennis camps, clinics, and exhibitions.

Southern California with its fair weather, accessibility, and increasing population in the 1980s is the epicenter for boys and girls with disabilities to access exposure to quality programs, organizations, and adult athlete mentors.

In 1985, Abilities First Sports Camp in Chico, California, begins offering a yearly sports camp. The Northern California based camp grows to offer water skiing, canoeing, and an outdoor adventure component to the traditional ball sports. Abilities First is a Sacramento Valley mainstay and continues to offer quality programming to this day.

It's the early 90s. I have an idea. I want to use well known players as instructors. Instead of coaching the fundamentals of basketball, I decide to concentrate on offense. Welcome to the "David Kiley Shooting Camps" presented by Quickie Wheelchairs.

The greatest way to expand your individual skill sets is to create weapons. The ability to shoot the basketball needs to be at the top of every baller's to-do list. Knocking down perimeter, mid-range, an assortment of layups, and free throw shots makes the game easier. If there are five confident shooters all pulling from the same side of the rope, a team can call less structured plays and instead play a "read and react" style that flows in the rhythm of the game. The advancement of rules and the implementation of the three-point-shot adds a layer to our game that is akin to the slam dunk in the NBA. You want to feel some wild energy from a wheelchair basketball game, watch a couple titans like Trooper Johnson and myself trading 3's, late in a competitive game.

The shooting camps happen in three cities across the summer. I want the environment to be more intimate and cap the number of participants at thirty. The shooting camps are a hit mainly due to the big names associated with it. Top level scorers with known reputations. Players prefer offense over defense. Coaches prefer defense. This is a player's camp.

My instructors are Ron "Bird" Alsup, Steve Berger, and Trooper Johnson. Quality shooters. Tough as nails competitors. I then bring in (who else) Jimbo Miller and Curtis Bell to handle the nuances of coaching bigs in the post. All coaches are Quickie athletes. A marketing plan in action.

Quickie is critical. A budget is created for instructor's flights, accommodations, reversible jerseys, and stipends. We also bring along some in-kind sponsors to help with meals, swag, and niceties. The Quickie marketing department promotes the "David Kiley Shooting Camps" with professional ads in *Sports 'N Spokes* magazine. Marilyn Hamilton, a forward thinker, is quick to move the needle forward in support of unique camps and programs. The "Randy Snow Tennis Camps" soon follow my shooting camps. I am honored to be an instructor at his tennis camps.

The first shooters camp is held in Las Vegas. Living in Vegas, making all this possible, is an old friend, John Chambers. I immediately ask John to be my Camp Director. John secures the University of Nevada Las Vegas (UNLV) as our venue. First class facility. John Chambers, a noted storyteller, with the ability to rub elbows with the biggest and brightest, then tells me iconic UNLV coach Jerry Tarkanian, or "Tark the Shark," will be making some appearances throughout the camp. A year prior, UNLV captures the NCAA collegiate crown beating Duke by 30 points, whilst scoring 103 points, in the championship game. True to his word, Coach Tarkanian gives the group more than one rousing talk about the ability and value in shooting the basketball.

There's John and me in the 1978 Sacramento summer heat, on a shoestring budget with a wing and a prayer, hosting the first disability youth sports camp of any kind—and now this? Vegas? UNLV? When you talk about the history of adaptive sports and specifically wheelchair basketball, John Chamber's name needs to be revered. A true trailblazer.

Vegas is the city that inspires the growth of other shooting camps in Kansas City, Boston, Pittsburgh, and Charlotte.

Fond shooting camp memories include the last day layup contest. Rules are simple. Miss and you're out. Make and you keep moving through the layup line. Last person left wins. Coaches are making side bets, athletes are trying their best to figure the focus versus easiness of making layups; and, to add a layer of spice to the proceedings, I announce the winner of the layup contest will win a made-to-order David Kiley signature All-Court Basketball chair from Quickie.

The favorites never win. It's usually the humble, I know this is my only way to get a new ball chair—let me get up an extra hundred shots before lunch—less familiar but hungry soul baller, looking for more.

In the spring of 2004, Turning Point and Shorty Powers break barriers and boundaries with an Outdoors Mentor Camp. Over the course of a long weekend Shorty and his outdoor experts match up newly injured with the likes of Donnie Rogers, Randy Snow, John Galland, and this guy. The motto for the weekend is, "Life Beyond the Sidewalk."

I recruit Mitch Domina from Kansas for the Turning Point event. As a teenager, Mitch sustains a spinal cord injury crashing his motorcycle. A sponsored, rising motocross star, Mitch fails to land a training session back flip. Life-changing paraplegia.

Meeting Mitch and his parents takes on an even greater meaning as I am in the hospital myself undergoing major surgery to alleviate chronic nerve pain in my left leg. Whilst awaiting surgery at Denver's Craig Hospital, old friend and Recreation Therapist Joe Gomez asks if I'll run a basketball clinic for his patients. I agree and meet Mitch. I immediately sense Mitch and his parents' stressful uncertainty facing their new challenges.

Mitch has limited movement and rotation as he's wearing a body jacket to stabilize his spine. I remember the days. A bond is formed. Mitch participates nonetheless. I can see he appreciates the pace, style, and effectiveness of which I move my chair. Later in my stay at Craig Hospital, Mitch and I attend a Denver Broncos/Oakland Raiders football game through the Rec Therapy department.

Mitch has a good time. The lightbulbs of a changing—and still worthwhile life—begin to take shape for Mitch.

My nerve pain surgery is a success. Sleep is a blessed rest again. The daily shooting pains through my left leg subside. These times also keep me connected to Mitch Domina. He attends a water ski clinic I run through the Lake Norman YMCA. He takes to snow skiing. We compare notes.

I tell Mitch about Shorty Powers, Turning Point, and Lake Caddo. He's in.

Lake Caddo is its own world. Pontoon boat tours on the historic, sleepy lake speak of lily pads, cypress trees, Spanish moss, the unique trumpet sounds of barred owls and the ever-present metronome of bull frogs keeping perfect time. The occasional gator sighting reminds that beauty does indeed come with a beast.

I remember my first days on the lake: learning to enter and exit with precise transfers, paddling through cypress trees and moss to open, clear water meadows before eventually bass fishing from the kayak. These moments change perspectives. These moments are life changing

The things that Shorty and his boys show me, I am now able to pass on to Mitch. I see in him the shared experience of taking on what's intimidating and daunting.

The pupil is now the teacher.

Mitch follows my lead.

We reach the desired clearing.

A breeze speaks.

We breathe in.

Anxiety levitates and freedom is there for the taking.

Mitch Domina recalls, "The activities started with a boat ride, which I think was the first time I had been on a boat since my injury. I was kind of surprised by the veteran guys who had no problems getting on and off, switching seats on the boat, and going to the bathroom when they needed to. This let me know, hey, that's all totally possible and no reason I can't enjoy time on the lake with friends when I get back home. Next, we all hopped in two-person kayaks. I was partnered up with DK. The lake was covered in lily pads and cypress trees that hung down and touched the water. It was quite a sight. We took off paddling. I definitely felt I needed to carry my weight when it came to paddling. But DK would stop from time to time and cast a fishing pole, and when he did, he would obviously stop paddling. I thought, "Well, I need to paddle harder!" Little did I know I was scaring all the fish away and DK never caught a thing. We got back and relaxed a bit. One of DK's friends Randy Snow showed up on a modified three-wheeled motorcycle that was adapted for a para to ride. Me being from a motorcycle background, I was amazed at this and quite interested. This was the first time I had seen such a thing. DK and some others wanted to go [to] the local store for refreshments. I thought ok, which car are we taking? Nope. They just began to push their chairs down the street for what felt like miles. I did my best to keep up and not look like I was struggling. Later that evening we all went out on some big fan, air boats to skim across the swampy waters. I definitely had never been on one of those either. It was dark out, and watched as they spotted frogs with flashlights, looking for the glow of their eyes and then caught them. Later I found out this is called "gigging." The next day, the caught frogs were cooked up along with some catfish. I didn't have it in me to try the frog legs, but the catfish was really good."

After a number of years struggling to find his calling and true self, Mitch parlays one experience to the next. He is the first in his family to graduate from college and the first person in a wheelchair to graduate with a Mechanical Engineering Degree at Kansas State University. He currently works designing and creating large factories for Fortune 500 companies. For kicks Mitch designs and builds one-off cars with his dad. He envisions himself developing next-level mobility aids for the elderly and disabled.

I'm not betting against him.

I've never taken to the nickname "King." A Goofy crown, opulent jewels and a stash of golden bars are a visual I can't shake. The nickname was given to me decades ago. I don't remember by whom, when, or where, but still the moniker follows me.

My social media presence is built through Dromos Marketing and, more succinctly, Ish Tanyeri. I enjoy scrolling relevant posts. The memories, laughter, and revelations can be profound, but building a brand and creating a platform are best left for a professional like Ish. With her guidance, we launch *The Wheel Print Podcast with DK*, take on professionalizing the NWBA's Hall of Fame, and brand DK3 with a flair, sizzle, and competency that attracts.

My last DK3. It's promoted under the title, "Buzzer Beater. The King's Farwell." Ish's efforts are in full effect. The good folks at the University of Texas, Arlington are the vital backdrop to all that's to come. There's a reception at the host hotel after play on Saturday evening. Tickets are purchased by players, families, and guests. The scene feels big. I have a couple tricks up my sleeve, but the evening's festivities are out of my control. My wife, Sandy, and Ish are the show's puppet masters.

I eye my Hall of Fame jacket hanging in the corner. The baby blue blazer is a creation of triumph, setbacks, and willingness to persevere beyond those setbacks. I am about to conclude a seven-decade, Mad Hatter ride with the game of basketball and the characters that play it. From the neighborhood games in the driveway to the finals matchup tomorrow, it's about to be over. I decide then and there, '*No crying. I will keep it together.*' Dark blue jeans with the baby blue blazer. Excitement and nerves rising.

Elevators are a conduit inviting perspective. Twenty years endorsing 3 v 3 basketball. The Commonwealth Games add the 3 v 3 brand to their most recent competition. The International Wheelchair Basketball Federation has plans for 3 v 3 basketball in the 2028 Paralympic Games in Los Angeles. How did we get here?

The elevator door opens to a ground floor buzzing with commotion. I'm snapped back into the reality of the now, and away from hazy, nostalgic, and faraway notions. I am present.

Lee Montgomery, Hall of Fame combatant and comrade, is the evening's emcee. Lee has a quick wit and is sure to find the funny in exchanges. Willie Hernandez and Doug Garner take turns behind the mic. Their words are gracious and speak to a history all in the room can share. Nonetheless the attention has me squirming. Then comes video speakers: Megan Blunk, Steve Serio, Trevon Jenifer, and Ryan Neiswender. All Paralympians and elite players. Tokinori Tanaka from Japan comes on captioned in English. Tokinori leads the 3 v 3 movement in his homeland.

I can't sit still. The accolades and credit praising down begin to overwhelm. As if that's not enough, my son Justin and daughter Danielle both appear on video. I see their faces. They're parents now. The realization affirms. I'm feeling love and emotion from all angles.

It's my turn to surprise folks. I have this vision of dancers prior to the semis and finals. A Lakers Girls thing. I give my DJ, Pennie, a call and ask his advice. Pennie has worked with a dance crew. They're good and price-friendly. He adds a spicy caveat, "DK, they're big bodied women. The Curvey Queenz."

I search for them online. I eliminate any preconceptions. They're perfect. We sign them up for the reception. The Queenz take the stage. I follow. I have my flat bill ball cap behind the lectern as the Queenz music starts. They place a giant pimp chain around my neck and gold-rimmed shades on my face. I put on the flat bill and adjust it to the side. I act like a fool in the routine. The room reacts with volume and approving cheers at the comedy of a 70-year-old acting like a teenage hip-hopper. It's perfect.

I stay on stage and my mom appears in the next video. I lose the air in my lungs. A couple deep breaths and I'm back. I move to the mic and address the room:

"I share with all in the room that you've probably never seen me play. If you have, you saw an older version of DK, the player. Most of my heyday came before VHS, much less cell phones. You have a front row seat to witness, witness how I serve the game and serve you the athlete. I have a few accomplishments but what truly matters to God, and myself, is how I serve and the attempts to make the world a little bit better. Excelling in sport in one thing. Helping others is another. I know God is pleased. We all have the responsibility to serve somebody."

My brothers Tom and Steve make their way to the stage. They amuse the crowd with childhood stories and brotherly memories. Steve and Tom are good brothers willing to support my athletic dreams but are also there to volunteer and assure my events are run more smoothly. A massive thank you for that.

The final act is the first ever mic appearance by my Queen. She tells her story. The mother of our children, love of my life, and grandma to four has all the ears in the room. She is beautiful, as is her thoughtful story of us. She delivers a speech without nerves. A selfless lioness always in the shadows of my every bright light moment. Not tonight. Tonight, the spotlight is hers. The Queen reigns.

The inevitable question unspoken is the inevitability of DK3. Will it continue? If so, who's to lead the charge?

I announce, I'm joyfully passing the torch to Matt Scott. In 2004, I give Matt the nickname Neo (meaning "the one") from the movie *The Matrix*. Little did I know then that nearly twenty years later how true the nickname is. Matt is the right man for the job. A two-time Paralympic gold medalist with various corporate relationships. Matt is seasoned enough to carry the load yet also connected to the youth of the game as a shining example. His media skills are next level. He's done commercials for Nike and Visa. His Instagram account has tens of thousands of followers highlighting his fashion sense, sporting/celebrity relationships, mad workout routines, and his continued love for the game of basketball.

Matt and I do a fireside chat onstage about the future of the event. He graciously agrees to keep the brand DK3 moving forward. He can name it the MattScott3 as far as I'm concerned but instead, he chooses to keep my name involved even after I retire. I'm awestruck. Players and volunteers pledge their continued support moving forward. It's a defining moment. Matt brings joy to everything he does. A quality human being.

The end of the evening nears. The nerves finally subside. I have never felt so much love, support, and appreciation. A joyous ending (without tears). I am content to move on.

Tonight, it's "Good to be King."

I find my Queen. It's getting late. Tomorrow is a long, final day of competition.

I have one last box to tick.

There he is. I thank him for bringing his guitar and serenading the crowd. His playing brings a levity to the proceedings. Everyone knows Pat Anderson is as good a Wheel Head basketball player that's ever hit the court, but to watch him strum chord progressions is to watch another—humbler—side of his greatness. Pat records with his wife, singer/songwriter Anna, under the name Lay Awake.

Pat and I do the handshake, bro hug. Less than three days ago, he was competing for Canada in the World Championships in Abu Dhabi. Tonight, he's in Arlington, Texas, helping celebrate 20 years of DK3. Words aren't enough to describe how much this means to me.

I bring him in close. This conversation needs to remain between us. "Pat, just go out and win this thing." I frame it as a favor from one generational player to another. "You won the very first one 20-years ago. What a great story it would be. More importantly, you can change the world of your two teammates."

Pats smirks. Message sent and received.

Itty Bitty (Adrina Castro) is teamed with Houston's Selvin Velasquez and Pat Anderson. Selvin, a good friend, is a solid, fundamental player that understands the subtleties needed to win basketball games. Pat can score from anywhere and possesses lightning quick hands. One second, he's stealing the ball from you like it's your lunch money; the next, he's ball-faking and dribble-driving past you for an easy look. Sag off him too much and he'll hit a deep 3-pointer.

The wildcard is Adrina. Will she be able to handle the pressure? Will she be able to knock down the inevitable open, mid-range looks? Squads will have to double-team Pat. He's every team's defensive priority. At 15 years of age, it's a calculated play that the pressure of the moment will get bigger than the capabilities and capacities of DK3 first-timer, Itty Bitty. How will she respond?

It's knock out day. Only winners move on. Get to the semifinals and you're in the money rounds. We've been able to jack up the prize money purse, but I've kept it under wraps. A farewell surprise.

The Selvin/Bitty/Pat team gets off to a strong start. After day one, they record five wins with only a single loss. This gives the trio a strong seeding as they advance towards the semifinal. Adrina is stout on defense with good chair positioning (keeping herself between her opponent and the basket), an overriding willingness to scrum for loose balls, and she comes up with important defensive rebounds at critical parts of the game. Itty Bitty is tough.

"It's only because of my Mamba mentality that I'm able to put in the work to play with and against some incredible players," writes Adrina Castro. "It motivates me to work hard. That's how I apply the Mamba mentality." The Kobe Bryant mindset (a girl dad to three) rings crystal clear.

A defining moment. Itty Bitty has the ball but is pinned against the sideline. The defender, a USA gold medalist, double amputee seizes the moment. Adrina brings the ball to her outside hand. The move allows her space away from the charging bull wanting the ball. The ball is now in her non-dominant side. She's stuck for a moment. She has nowhere to pass the ball. The bull leans into Itty Bitty. He knows the ball is on her weaker side. He denies her strong side. His back wheels are off the ground eliminating her space to operate. The tattoos surrounding his biceps are on full display as he reaches up, taking away her vision. Itty Bitty dribbles the ball low and quick. She creates an extra inch, maybe two, of space. She ball-fakes a hook pass to Pat—too obvious—before finding a moving Selvin with an over-the-top lob for an easy basket. The bull, somewhat disappointed but more so admiring of the execution, smirks before offering a fist bump to Adrina. The fifteen-year-old keeps her game face on and returns the fist bump with one of her own.

Team Selvin/Bitty/Pat reach the semifinals. The money rounds. They take down the only undefeated team and odds-on favorite. In the semifinal, Pat is bringing out the best of his teammates. He trusts both of them to take shots, deal with the ball, and make in-game decisions. Both respond confidently and deliver with a resounding victory.

The court is surrounded with spectators and athletes for the finals. DJ Slow Yo Roll (Jermell Pennie and Johnny Rip) complete the powerful vibe with a chorus of thumping urban beats and rhythms. I'm on the mic adding commentary, insights, and observations. I'm quick to take various mental snapshots.

In the finals Bitty is swarmed by her much larger, entirely male opponents. Their strategy is to get her to cough up the ball with aggressive reaches and intimidation. Not to happen. Her ball skills are fundamental and sound. This allows her to find the needed windows to distribute the ball to Pat and Selvin. Anytime Pat Anderson is on the floor his superior ball skills force teams to help off other players. The times they help off Bitty, Pat delivers the ball into her awaiting hands and she calmly knocks down the mid-range shot with her exaggerated left hand follow through.

Game over.

Pat, Selvin, and Bitty are DK3 champions. All three deliver at high pressure moments.

The winning team comes up to receive their awards and champions' check. We've purposely not disclosed the amount. The mock check is flipped over by the new future of DK3, Matt Scott. The check is for a whopping $15k. Each player receives five grand.

The winners of the 20th DK3 and $15K, along with Matt Scott, 'The future.'
From left to right: Me, Pat Anderson, Adrina (Itty Bitty) Castro, Selvin Velasquez,
and Matt Scott.

Pat Anderson, another feather in a cap overflowing with championships, medals, and personal triumphs. A true class act.

Selvin Velasquez, an intelligent, strong, and smart lover-of-the-game. He knows when to play his role and when to make the moment his.

I instinctively go back to thirteen-year-old Adrina Castro, or Itty Bitty, pestering me (like only a thirteen-year-old can) for entrance in DK3. It dawns on me she's been preparing for this moment the entire time. At fifteen, she's a champion, depositing substantial memories and monies.

She represents what I like to call 'The Soul of the Game.'

JOAN BAEZ

Someone had to change the world. I was the one for the job.

— Joan Baez

When you win 98 games in a row you're breathing in rarefied air.

In important ways, the more you win the tougher it gets. Hunger, ambition, and a focused seriousness are bound to take a hit. Conference games don't demand our best efforts. We tap into our extensive bench to finish off the numerous blowout games. In-season tournaments like Kentucky's Bluegrass Invitational demand our best and we deliver. We take on the best the country has to offer and win the prestigious tournament. International teams start making calls to book games. The national teams of Mexico, Japan, Germany, Australia, and Italy all schedule games with us throughout our run.

The world wants in on what we have brewing with basketball. The constant is winning. How are they doing it? What can I gain from being around it? Is there a secret? A formula?

Within the Inland Empire, we are it. Another round on the house for the Casa team. Our watering holes provide us with celebrity status. We are offered not only libations but also ego altering times of praise and acclaim. Various members of the Condors are consistently featured in print and television news stories. I see myself and my family pasted on a larger-than-life billboard for Chino Valley Bank on my morning commute into work.

The good times keep rolling. Friends of the program offer up tickets to concerts and sporting events. Our winning streak is a continual point of reference. I'm at an LA Kings game. The ice hockey team is star-studded with Wayne Gretzky introducing Tinsel Town to his immense talents. I have great seats right behind the glass. How I access them eludes me, but during

The Great One—Gretzky.

245

this time there are no limits; if it's on offer, I figure a way to access all things. The game is a humdinger. A cross between athletic allure and street violence. I'm mere inches away from the action. I receive an invite to meet Gretzky and others, like all-star Luc Robitaille, in the locker room after the game. It's a different universe surrounded by stars. I reach my hand out to shake hands with Gretzky. He welcomes the exchange and tells me he's heard of the Condors and our winning streak. He reaches behind him, hands me one of his hockey sticks, and signs it. A sporting treasure I proudly display today.

The Condors are asked to do exhibitions throughout Southern California. We have routines, jokes, trick shots, and a one-upmanship with one another that entertains. We're full of no-look or behind-the-back passes (my favorite), reverse spin layups, fifty-foot hook passes, a couple half-court shots, and (with minimal exhibition-style defense) basket after basket with the ball never touching the floor.

We have a cocky, surefire confidence with the ability to back it up. The majority of the group is in their athletic prime. Our time is now. We know it. We feel it. To wear the baby blue and gold Condor jersey means you are one of the best there is.

Arrogance is bound to creep into the equation. We see ourselves as better than others and a visible brashness begins to take action.

The variance and degree of difference between arrogance and cocky is slim enough for one to appear as the other. It's deceiving. Both sides of the coin are lined with golden intentions. The arrogance side of the coinage is more susceptible to overlooking details and undervaluing opponents.

We begin believing in our ego more than the truth of the game. The truths are simple:

1. Be on time
2. Be prepared for all eventualities
3. Be of clear mind and focus

Arrogance is not seeing the sucker-punch coming.

Documentarian filmmaker Ken Burns says it best, "It is the great arrogance of the present to forget the intelligence of the past."

Sectionals. Eugene, Oregon, 1985.

One more victory and we punch our ticket to the Final Four, the potential at the elusive 3-peat and an unthinkable 100-game win streak. Casa Colina Hospital Administrator/CEO, Dale Eazell, and my department head, Lenore Hersch, are travelling with the team. Both want to take in the history of it all.

Folk singing superstar, Joan Baez, is staying in our hotel. Like the overconfident, wannabe gunslingers that we are, we invite Ms. Baez to Saturday's semi-final game. We're on a proverbial and literal roll. Joan Baez, singer of social justice and protester of the Vietnam War, future Rock and Roll/ Hall of Fame recipient agrees to watch us play. She's accompanied by her manager.

We handle business and it's 98 in a row. One more victory and we're off to another Final Four. Another geographical stage to display our talents. Another belting of the chorus, "Celebration time. Come on."

Ms. Baez sets up our entire contingent with tickets for her show that night. The drinks begin to flow. This is where the leader in me, the coach, tempers the mood by abstaining and setting an example for the rest to follow. The player in me, the brother in the tribe, is about the ever-growing slice-of-life that has nothing to do with the objective, the reason we're in Eugene, Oregon, in the first place.

I order another.

Following the concert, we head back to the hotel bar to meet up with Joan and her crew. We party deep into the night. The crew are quick with a joke and deep into their stories of the road. We lap it up like starstruck, just-off-the-bus, hucksters. The boys are taking turns dancing and yucking it up with Ms. Baez. The alcohol adds a funky vibrato and rhythmic sway to what previously was stoic and workmanlike. We're losing our edge. CEO Dale Eazell is buying drinks throughout. It's a great time filled with no respect for what's long-lasting. With each sip and every tick of the clock, we lessen our chances to obtain our goals: a NWBA championship, the prestigious 3-Peat and 100-game win streak.

I'm oblivious to my leadership role.

We play midday Sunday. By this time, Joan Baez and her crew have exited the hotel. They're on to their next town and show. They're on to their next good time. We're left with poor rest, vigorous hangovers, and a confident hankering to get win number ninety-nine.

It's gametime. The Alberta Northern Lights from Edmonton, Canada, is a dangerous club but doesn't match up with our combination of big men and myself. We've played the Lights many times. They're strong in spurts but have yet to match our overall team consistency. Their strength is their team speed with Reg McClellan (player/coach), Ron Minor, and Randy Wyness all above average at moving their chairs. Roy Sherman is their lone big man. He's good but doesn't compare to the legend of Curtis Bell or the instinctual impulses of Jimbo Miller.

Our play is mediocre. Suddenly we're the team full of inconsistencies and sloppy, lifeless play. McClellan leads with his voice and pivotal decision-making. Sherman is holding his own in the post. We are a team spinning its wheels. Where we usually string together multiple runs of easy points and determined stops. We struggle to find a flow. Good intentioned shots aren't falling. The spark, or magic, of the Condor collective, is instead a grind to stay even with these guys.

Another shot off the front iron.

We give up an easy two.

Ball watching.
Swing the ball. Allow Curtis to work the weak side.
Why didn't we swing the ball?
Up hard on Reg.
No. Don't sag.
It's wet. Basket McClellan.
Big possession. We're down one.
I see you driving the lane.
Keep your head on a swivel.
Look up.
The ball bounds off his shoulder.
An easy two the other way.
Our will refuses to lose.
The game goes into overtime.
We continue to chase.
This isn't us.
We take. We dominate. We control.
This is outlandish.
The Lights lead by two with three seconds to play.
We run an inbound play from half-court.
I focus and communicate overtly to Jimbo.
The ref hands me the ball.
I instead throw the half-court hook pass to Curtis.
Away from the decoy of Jimbo.
Curtis Bell makes big shots.
Always has,
Always will.
He makes another.
We should have
them but we are not
ourselves. We're out of
gas. We forget to respect
the game. The Alberta
Northern Lights have
just taken down Goliath.
It takes two overtimes,
multiple hangovers,
and a great effort by the
Alberta Northern Lights.
It's over.

98-game win streak...no more.

Big game, second overtimes are when your best is absolutely needed. It should be the time of peace of mind, serenity, poise, and confidence. We instead chose the black-of-night path and living in the moment. A slippery, toxic descent into normalcy.

Winning 98 games in a row is a feat I'm proud of. I've heard it spoken about thousands of times amongst the team, at my many speaking engagements, award ceremonies, basketball clinics, or sooner or later the subject comes up when chatting with modern day ballers. I'm a coach of a team that wins 98 games in a row. An impressive sounding feat.

As soon as I leave the floor that Sunday afternoon in Eugene, Oregon, I bury it. I dig deep and bury it in a vault so far beneath the surface, it lives amongst the tales of folklore and Hall of Fame speeches forever.

The boys take ownership and speak openly about the previous night's tale of woe. The shared remorse reminds me how much I love these guys. Collectively we all share in the responsibility of the loss.

Then I write this thing. It forces me to examine myself through a lens of truth; to bring to the surface what's beneath the mess of untruths, deceits, and a story I've told myself so long, it takes on the warmth and honor of the truth.

I've always chalked this one up as a program loss. Even an administrative loss. A massive team loss.

It's none of those things.

It's on me.

I face now that I am the leader and coach of this amazing group, chasing history in the form of winning basketball games. I needed to act accordingly. I did not. Where did the leader in me go?

That Sunday, chasing win number 99 in a row, chasing a 3-peat, chasing history, we are the hungover club team hoping to win besides ourselves. We might as well have lit up a pack of Camels at halftime.

I've needed to say this for decades. '*I let you down boys. I am sorry.*'

It hurts when what's buried rises.

"*To become our best, good judgement and common sense are essential. No matter the task—whether physical or mental—if our emotions take over, we're not going to execute near our personal level of competency, because judgement and common sense will be impaired. When our emotions dominate our actions, we make mistakes.*"

– *Coach John Wooden on Self-Control. Second tier on the Pyramid of Success.*

SPORTS ILLUSTRATED

I'm SI worthy.

— DK

It's the building of the dream. Before the glow of winning and the all-consuming effort of doing it again; previous to the despair and salty, life-changing awareness of losing—there's the dream.

The carrier of the dream is *Sports Illustrated* magazine. Its photographs of Sandy Koufax, Maury Wills, Johnny Unitas, Roman Gabriel, Jerry West, and Elgin Baylor line the walls of my bedroom as a kid. I get lost in the articles whilst making sure to keep an eye on the photo of Elgin's mid-range jump shot. The colors hypnotise. The purple and gold of Jerry West's Lakers jersey goes up against the vivid white and green of Bill Russell and the Celtics. Dodgers blue versus the dirty black, grey, and orange of Willie Mays and the Giants.

On our block, the Seymours subscribe to and receive *Sports Illustrated* every Friday through the mail. Our household sees no need for such frivolities. I purchase the magazine, when my adolescent finances allow, at the local 7-Eleven. If not, I camp out in the Seymours living room until the magazine becomes free and then pounce upon its pages. I'm a jackal for everything it has on offer.

In the 60s, 70s, and 80s, *Sports Illustrated* captured the greatest images in all of sport. Its iconic cover of the 1980 USA Olympic team defeating the formally unbeatable Soviet Union, tells the story minus a headline. Where a header should be is instead an American flag. Beneath the flag are fans and athletes in a joyous celebration. What starts as a hockey game turns into something far greater. *Sports Illustrated* captures the eternal moment like no other.

In 1987, I attract the attention of the magazine and its glossy, larger-than-life pages. They want to feature "Southern California Lifestyles" in one of their editions.

No disability sport athlete has ever graced its pages. Sad but true.

I have a scheduled track workout at Cal Poly, Pomona. The magazine calls and tells me their photographer will meet there. I'm not nervous but I am conscious that days like this have limitless potential.

Sandy is at work. I have both the kids. Justin and Danielle busy themselves on the football field-size range of grass inside the track. They've seen Dad do his sport thing. The yawn factor is high. I watch them chase each other, kick a ball at one another, before succumbing to the wonders of picking grass and running with butterflies.

The photographer gets the shots. It takes close to an hour. He tells me that *Sports Illustrated* ought to be paying me for my time. Never occurs to me. He offers to take some pictures of the kids and me. Perfect. Sandy will love this. He fires off some shots of dad and his cubs. We exchange numbers and I shake his hand for the opportunity. I store my track chair away before grabbing Justin's hand on one side and Danielle's on the other as we make our way to the car. I have no idea the photographer is still taking pics of us from a distance.

The magic of this precise moment transcends. *Sports Illustrated* scraps the idea of its "Southern California Lifestyles" and instead chose to include the photo of Justin, Danielle, and myself holding hands and heading home. The photograph is taken from behind and speaks to a long and finished day.

It all happens quickly and minus much communication. Its annual, end of the year collection tells the story through photographs of what transpired during the year's sporting seasons.

It's out. I head down to my local 7-Eleven. I grab every issue on the rack and plop the pile down on the counter. The clerk looks at me with a cheesy smile. I can't help it. I blurt out, "I'm in here. I'm really in *Sports Illustrated.*"

I show him the photo without being asked. I'm filled with so much pride I'm unable to register his response. Myself and the kids are in the centerfold, double-page portion of the historic magazine. It's an overwhelming, wow moment. We're tucked between Reggie Jackson swinging for the fences and the Cubs' Andre Dawson ducking a fastball just above his nose. The drama of the

photographs speaks to why the magazine is so beloved.

Then there's us. A slice-of-life pic far superior than the assignment of myself, a track, and trying to go faster. My initial and deepest Wheel Head fears (the ability to father children) are not just realized but now on worldwide display for all to see. The missing ingredient in the photo is Sandy. She's the reason why. Another humble example of her.

The photograph grows legs. A Casa Colina board member does an oil painting of the photo. Casa then makes a thousand, numbered lithographs. It's named, "Strength of Love." It can be seen hanging in hospitals and business offices around the

Strength of Love.

world. One hangs over our fireplace to this day.

Sports Illustrated readers react to the photo. It touches a nerve.

Stuart C. Tentoni of Hartland, Wisconsin, writes to the magazine, "The photograph of Dave Kiley's children giving him a lift home was the most emotionally touching picture in the history of your magazine. If only the rest of society could see wheelchair athletes the way Kiley's children see him. Speaking of Kiley and his children, how about letting us see a picture that shows them from the front?"

Sports Illustrated replies to Stuart, "Here you are. That's Justin 7, on the left and Danielle 3, on the right." –ED

Who knew that being my true self is the lightning rod and reason I make the issue with so many greats. Images of Mike Tyson, Martina Navratilova, Magic, Dr J, Sugar Ray Leonard, Larry Bird, Jackie Joyner-Kersee, and Carl Lewis vs Ben Johnson are definite page-stoppers. These are the pics fans need

to see. *Sports Illustrated* defines itself photographing the fathomless layers of sport. A sun-soaked Dennis Connor, high seas over both shoulders, dripping saltwater whilst captaining his crew to the *America's Cup*. Russians playing baseball. The St. Louis Cardinals' mascot finishing off his McDonalds and reading the sports page.

Michael Jordan adorns the cover—ready to throw another one down—beneath the title, *'87 Images to remember from the Year in Sports.*

The tenderness and striking image of a man tending after his children is nothing new. It's almost cliché. Common. Still, the photo resonates.

It's not a dream at all.

IN THE DISCUSSION

You're either on the bus or off the bus.

— Ken Kesey

Looking back there's no doubt. The 1992 "Dream Team" is the best, most dominant basketball team in Olympic history. Better yet, the USA Olympic team is the best collection of ballers in the history of the sport. Michael, Magic, Bird, Charles, and the boys didn't have a game closer than 32 points in the tournament. Case closed.

Seoul, Korea. 1988. The Paralympic Games finally intersect with the Olympic Games. For the first time the Paralympic Games follow the Olympics. Disability sport athletes use the same village and venues as their Olympic counterparts. Groundbreaking.

In 1976, the games are held in Toronto. The Olympic games are in Montreal. Same country but separate in every way. No fans to speak of.

Moscow hosts the Olympic Games in 1980. Sixty-five nations (including the USA) boycott the event in protest of the Soviet Union's invasion of Afghanistan. Athletes don't pay near the same price as soldiers fighting, and potentially dying in the name of war, but when sport and politics collide it's a travesty. To train for four years and not have a stage to perform is depressing.

The 1980 Paralympics are held in Arnhem, Holland. It's a funky, tick-box event that lacks any of the professionalism associated with today's games. The venue reminds me of the many junior high gyms I either practice or play in. Amputees are not allowed to play in the games for some indescribable reason. No Curtis Bell. Because of finances (or the lack of them), the team is made up of players that also have the potential to medal in track and field. This formula of team building is not conducive for success. It's the polar opposite. There's a lack of any fundraising by our governing bodies. This must change.

The Dutch are strong contenders. They have a raucous, flag-waving, orange-clad crowd, and home court advantage. It's the semifinals. The game with them is close. The officiating is horrible. I receive a technical foul for throwing a backboard pass to a teammate. What? Obviously, the refs have never seen this legal pass and blow their whistles instead. The orange throng eats it up and increases their volume.

A couple days prior, I am in the infirmary with excruciating leg pain. It's a phantom-type pain similar to the kind amputees suffer. The local medical team refuse to give me anything. Twenty-four hours later, they finally relent and give me a small injection of something that breaks the cycle of agony. The next night, I'm hardly myself. I lead the team in scoring but feel like I'm playing in a haze.

The Dutch squad and their fans are victorious. We come back to win the bronze the following day but it's bittersweet. I leave the 1980 games knowing that the NWBA and the National Wheelchair Association (NWAA) did a lackluster job—at best—in raising the money needed to field the best team possible. It's a defining time.

The 1984 Summer Olympic Games are in Los Angeles. Perfect. A confluence of space, time, and location can shine a needed spotlight on disability sport. First flashing red light. The organizing committee is working out of New York. Hmm. How does this work? Still, there's chatter that Los Angeles will be hosting the first-ever, true Paralympic Games.

The news hits like the first time my twelve-year-old self got the wind knocked out of me. Royal gut punch. Can't find any air. An effort to host the Paralympic Games in Los Angeles is scrapped; tanks and fails.

In another makeshift effort to tick a box, our games are moved to Stoke Mandeville Hospital in England. A lovely village town in Aylesbury and a quick rail ride into London, Stoke Mandeville is commonly referred to as the birthplace of the Paralympic movement. I appreciate the history lesson but it's not 1948 anymore. Our games are not evolving. In fact, we're reaching back into time.

This feels like a crime. I'm asked to fundraise again. My able-bodied Olympic compatriots do not have to raise money to compete. Performance is their currency. Why are we different?

I send a letter to the NWBA and NWAA. If I have to raise even a nickel, I'm skipping the '84 games in protest. Crickets. I hear nothing. I ask Curtis Bell to support my stance. He initially balks but comes along for the greater good. I know how difficult this is for him. The Stoke Mandeville Games are the first to allow amputees. This is a seismic shift in the landscape of our sport and I'm asking him to sit it out. We do it together.

To prove to the governing bodies that our protest is worthy, I go ahead and raise money for the team. I have a robust relationship with a local, Inland Empire, bingo entity. Their skill is raising money and they're damn good at it. I go on to use this model as a revenue stream for Casa Colina programming. I put Jim Miller in charge. Bingo indeed. The boss of it all comes to me. She needs a non-profit to give twenty-five-thousand dollars to. Her bingo organization has already given to Casa and is looking for a new and worthy recipient. I know just the cause.

I present the USA Wheelchair Basketball team with a check for twenty-five grand.

The act speaks for itself, and yes, I want the NWBA to know without malice—It's not that hard to do the right thing.

The team is grateful for the financial support. It's needed. Without Curtis and me, the US loses to Sweden in the semifinals and to the Dutch in the bronze medal game. Both losses are by a slim two points. This is a difficult time. Eight years previous, Ed Owen and I drove from Southern California to Toronto, Canada, to compete. My naivety tells me this is the path. Whatever it takes to play at the highest level. A mere eight years later, I'm married with kids and deep into a professional path. Perspectives change. Priorities adjust. Today, I'm sitting out the Paralympic medal round games in protest. I'm in my basketball prime but not performing on the biggest stage. I'm an island without a country.

After our *'We're not taking it anymore'* stand, things slowly begin to change. There's a larger focus in finding the money. The days of Paralympic athletes using bake sales and car washes as viable modes of fundraising declines. I'd like to think that Curtis Bell and I play a supporting role in this essential and long overdue awakening.

Team USA is stationed in the tunnel. The Opening ceremony awaits. These are things we're made to do. Pomp and circumstance. It's a yawn-fest. No one ever attends. Today should be no different.

The 1988 Paralympics in Seoul, Korea, is the first time the Paralympic Games are an extension of the Olympic games. We share venues, a bustling village, and event staff. The Paralympic Games follow the Olympics by three weeks. This is still the working formula between the two worldwide showcases. The Seoul Olympic Organizing Committee (SLOOC) formulates a support plan which allows the sharing of the Seoul Olympic workforce, facilities, and key personnel. The SLOOC gives a subsidy of close to thirteen million dollars to the Paralympic Games of 1988.

It's our turn to enter into the arena. As I get closer to the entrance of the tunnel, I can see movement in the far end of the stands over a football field away. This is a first. I push towards the opening and light of the tunnel. I hear the roar of appreciation as the United States enters. The hair on my arms stands vertical. I enter. The stadium is full. Over seventy thousand strong. The applause hits like a wave at our backs. It's literally moving us. I eye my teammates, my brothers. Like me, they're taking it in as best they can.

We've arrived at a moment. A time in our subculture that will be told and spun countless times. The day disability sport legitimizes itself to the masses. The day we are accepted by the Olympic movement.

There are also no boycotts or politics from quarrelling nations. A hundred and sixty countries put aside their capitalist or communist notions and instead chose to celebrate sport. Competition is the deciding factor.

The games begin to cement what I already know. We are really good. Perhaps, even great.

Our pool play games are won by 37, 14, and 57 points over Sweden, Great Britain, and Brazil. The stands are full. The thrill of performing intensifies.

Within all of my visualization techniques and tactics there's always a backdrop of patrons. At the 1988 Seoul Paralympic Games what I've always seen in my brain is finally before me. I feel no nerves. I'm free to do what I've always known I'm on this planet to do. I perform.

In the quarterfinals we beat a strong Israeli team by 25.

In the semifinals we take down Germany by 36.

The finals are high drama: USA vs the Dutch. Our nemesis plays well but are never in the game. We win by eleven, 74-63.

Curtis Bell, Ed Owen, Darryl "Tree" Waller, Albert Campos, Gary Wooding, David Efferson, Joe Manni, Rod Williams, Mike Schlappi, Rick St. John, Arnardo Valdez, and me. Led by Head Coach Frank Burns and assisted by Paul Jackson, we are too big, too fast, and far too much experience for anyone to handle.

Ever.

The dastardly duo.

This is the greatest USA basketball team to date. It is the Paralympic "Dream Team." Nine of the twelve USA players are in the NWBA Hall of Fame, as are both coaches. The group has a collective 49 NWBA championships. Darryl Waller leads the tribe with a whopping 12 championships. Curtis Bell tallies eleven.

It's also a touchtone time for our game. Following the 1988 games, disability sport athletes garner an acceptability that isn't there previous to Seoul. We come through in the moment but we also help forge a path that worldwide, elite athletes ride upon today.

I'm sure the 2016 and 2020 gold medal winning men's team has something to say. Perhaps they would like to counter my bold claim.

Love it. Let the discussions begin.

CURTIS

Individually we are a drop. Together, we are an ocean.

— Ryunosuke Satoro

We're both the hunter and never the prey.
It's our pack to lead.
No one else has the needed nasty.
One minute, I see in him a reflection of myself.
The next, a man I can never be.
Our tensions are numerous.
Physical.
Threatening.
We both want what is meant for one.
Recognition.
Acknowledgement.
MVPs.
In wanting to be the one we became two.
A duo for the ages.

My first memories of Curtis Bell are in Champaign-Urbana, Illinois. Earliest days of my career with Ed Owen and the boys. We're undefeated. No way we're going to lose. There's a certainty to our championship desires. I take exception to how cocky this guy is. He plays for the Indianapolis Mustangs. I watch him with a motivation reserved for only a few. We meet in the finals. We're undefeated no more.

This is Curtis Bell's second championship and a missed opportunity to claim my first during my rookie season. The wheels of our relationship begin to take route.

A more recent memory. I remember it like yesterday. It's the year 2000 and the USA Paralympic Basketball team is training for the upcoming Sydney games. Curtis and I are both 47 years old. We're the last of an old guard from the "best ever" 1988 squad. The coaching staff puts together a 2-on-2 tournament. Curtis and I are paired together as a team against the younger likes of Trooper Johnson, Will Waller, Jeff Glassbrenner, Paul Schulte, and Chuck Gill. We beat all comers and find it relatively easy to use our experience to punish the next generation. We talk smack at a gold medal level.

CB wants it—but not this time.

Curtis recalls that day,

"We went through the entire team. It was easy. And we still didn't get a chance to start," a proud Curtis recalls fondly during a recent fishing trip.

Team USA goes on to win a bronze medal on a last second 35-foot 3-pointer by Paul Schulte, defeating Great Britain, 57-54. Curtis and I play sparingly.

My connection with Curtis truly begins in the summer of 1980 before our first season together with the Casa Colina Condors. We use the Southern California landscape and a multitude of pick-up games as our initial common thread.

"The summers were great. We'd play from nine to noon at the Long Beach VA. Have lunch. Then play pick-up games outside at Mile Square Park," recalls Curtis. "We'd then have a backyard barbeque at Bobby Murdock's house and jump in his pool."

These times are vivid. We begin to cautiously and unwittingly reveal ourselves to one another. A more human, less competitive side of ourselves becomes more available.

Curtis patiently teaches me how to bass fish. I lose a ton of his baits, unable to tell the difference between a bass bite and a log or stick. I'm yanking on my rod only to see another five-dollar lure disappear. This happens way too often but Curtis, ever calm and reassuring, teaches me to remain still and let the bass tell me when to set the hook. I find a peace and exhilaration to fishing that lasts.

We go on to fish all over the Unites States together. Both freshwater and out to sea. We drop fishing stories on one another to this day. We talk a couple times a week on the phone. It's always the same: fishing and basketball. Expanding stories and aging embellishments.

Whilst I'm in Sacramento, Curtis plays for the Raiders and within the tutelage of Ed Owen. He spins a story I know too well: Ed will not play Curtis until he improves his pick and roll knowledge and technique.

"I never set a pick in my life," remembers Curtis decades later. "I didn't have to. He benched me." There's an extended beat. It's Ed speaking to us both in the breeze. "In the end, Ed Owen made me better." I nod my head in agreement.

We continue to reel them in. I can see the kid in Curtis every time he holds up another bass. His smile beams. He puts the catch on ice. There will be an evening feast. He casts. His line flies and then drops where he intends.

The smile simmers. He's determined to land some more before the sun sets.

I hook one on the line. It feels big. It's my turn to show him how it's done.

Curtis Bell and I are a combo built to spoil your day and do damage. Any competitor's will to get it done against us is squashed. I run the floor, deal with the ball, and make sure we play with the proper pace. Curtis owns the paint, plays big, and finishes with a regularity that demands the defense to prioritize him. His one-on-one moves around the basket are subtle and effective. Curtis talks hand positioning endlessly. Where's the defender's hands? What part of the wheel are they grabbing? Too far back, Curtis explodes forward. He doesn't have to wait for me to deliver the ball. Easy bucket. Hands too far forward, he spins and presents his outside hand. As he spins my pass is already in the air. The ball lands seamlessly. More buckets.

We know what the other is doing before it happens. A certain look from Curtis confirms what I'm thinking. I now know when to release it, where to put it, and I'm certain of the result. In the most competitive moments of games Curtis and I are at our best. He has a way of coming up with rebounds and entry passes at the most crucial of times. I swear, he can squeeze his butt cheeks together and raise up a couple/three inches. Curtis is the only person I've seen with the ability to rise to the level of the ball in flight. I take great pleasure in scoring, but my real jam is assisting teammates with a great pass, dish, or dime. Having Curtis on the receiving end of things allows me the freedom to sizzle no look, behind the back, and backboard deliveries. I just know he will come up with the ball and finish with style.

My inner Pistol Pete unleashes itself. It has to. Curtis Bell is as cocksure a human being as there is. He wants every pass to come his way. I remember throwing a game-winning pass to Jim Miller. Curtis is the perfect decoy. He's the expectant option.

Curtis comes to me after the game, "You should throw that pass to me every time."

I'm celebrating with the team. We didn't play our best but when the situation demanded we executed a well devised scheme and won the game. Jimbo is playing an increasing role. His end-game bucket solidifies this.

The following week of practice tensions are high. The shit talking starts in layups. As strange as it sounds this is what makes the Condors extraordinary. Curtis and I are consistently the battling alphas. I'm the coach. I pick the teams for scrimmage. Curtis struggles with this. In his eyes he's the most qualified to be the coach. I disagree wholeheartedly. I don't like the job, but I'm the one for the job. I know Curtis isn't accepting of my role and decision-making as coach. This rubs me a certain way. The wrong way. I put Curtis on the opposite team. He's teamed with Albert Campos. I'm teamed with Jimbo. Scrimmage is spicy. The fouls are hard. There's collateral damage. Our angst for one another manifests itself onto our teammates. They're picking themselves off the floor as we both want to prove to the other our defensive superiority. We both commit too many fouls although neither admits it. Jimbo and Albert get into the act. Not ones to shy away from conflict, they seize the opportunity. Albert steals the ball from Jimbo. Jimbo calls a foul. Here we go. Albert fires the basketball at Jimbo's head. He catches it and smirks as if to say, *'That's all ya got?'* The scrimmage continues. Tension. I hit one from deep in transition. I say something to Curtis. Probably something of his inability to fire and hit from that range. Next trip down the floor he hits a slick mid-range, forty-five-degree angle bank shot. Impressive, but I'm not about to let him know. "That evens the score," he barks for all to hear. He's doing this on purpose. He knows my team is up two. We're a basket away from winning the game. We trade barbs about the score. Cooler heads reason my team is up one. It's still game point. I pass fake towards Jimbo and drive the lane. Curtis awaits. Perfect. I take it right at him with the ball. He's on me like a glove. I eye a window to release the ball. With my left side I spin one up off the backboard. He reacts with his upper torso in an attempt to block the shot. Our chairs collide. The ball spins off the rim. Curtis rebounds and throws a pinpoint outlet pass. I call a foul. He hits me with his chair. All hell breaks loose. Obscenities. Accusations. A few choice hand gestures. The team stops. They've seen it before. I hear a ball bouncing in the background. Then another. Curtis pushes to the sideline and gathers his things. He quickly puts on his prosthetic and begins walking out the gym pushing his chair. I'm not having it.

"If you leave, don't come back," I say.

The balls stop bouncing. Heavy stillness.

The remaining minutes of practice are uncomfortable but not unsettling.

There's a recent memory of Albert Campos and Curtis measuring each other for a bout of fisticuffs during another spirited scrimmage. Curtis hops atop the stage of the junior high gym and tells Albert if they "go" things will never be the same and he's not going to fight him. He also throws in a crack about an "unfair fight" which revs Albert's motor to the brink.

Curtis enters back into the gym. The team reacts with love. They're not surprised he's back with them. I give him my hand. He accepts. We shake.

Winning covers our scars. It doesn't mean the team doesn't have problems or issues. These issues push us to be better together, no matter how uncomfortable things get.

I push everyone to their limits. The biggest concern should be my silence. If I'm not barking at you, challenging you to find a better version of yourself, then I've moved on. I'm looking for someone else to fill a role you either don't have the aptitude, or talent, to fulfil.

This is the brutality of elite sport.

"The fire of practice turns into a bond that no one is going to break," remembers Curtis in a recent chat. "No one. There's a fight almost every other practice but I know when it's gametime somebody is about to get their butt kicked."

We love each other like brothers and we fight like brothers.

Most people don't like to deal in absolute truths. Curtis and I deal in almost nothing but absolute truths. Basketball games are decided by a scoreboard. When we fish, we use a scale and weigh who has the biggest catch and greatest amount.

Like my brothers, it's always a competition with Curtis. We begin to compete for an award that only one of us can receive. This dynamic pushes us to a higher level of performance in the biggest games and championship moments. Between us, we win 11 NWBA MVPs.

- Curtis wins the MVP award in 1975, '80, '81, '83, and '92.
- I win the MVP in 1978, '82, '84, '86, '88, and '90.

The alpha in me pounds my chest and screams, *"I have six and Curtis only has five."*

Here's a Most Valuable Player story Curtis remembers fondly to this day, "My first World Championships were in Nova Scotia, Canada in 1983. I was happy to pass the ball and share the wealth. The US won. At the end of the event there was an MVP award given. Dave wins it. I didn't know they gave an MVP. In 1986 the World Championships were in Melbourne, Australia. We dominate. Dave, Randy Snow, and I were really kicking butt. We went undefeated and won gold easily. I was on a mission for the MVP and won it going away."

In one breath this kind of cockiness pushes me to a place of anger. In another, this is exactly the kind of guy I want to partner with in winning championships and gold medals. Curtis proudly verbalizes what I can never imagine saying out loud. In the dark reaches of my inner competitive sphere, I want it all. The winning, adoration, worship, and praise are rebounding dreamy images only surfacing when in a meditative and visualized alone place. I allow myself to see it. I do not allow myself to say it. Mary Lou Kiley raised me so.

A Melbourne sizzle-memory forever etched in my membrane involves Curtis. We're playing the Dutch in the final. They double-team me near the half-court line and are squeezing me towards the sideline. Curtis gives me a head nod. His eyes tell me all I need to know. I spin away from the double team and just before I'm about to enter into the backcourt for a violation and turnover, I whip a behind-the-back screamer of a pass to Curtis. The ball is up high. Too high perhaps? I'm starting to think so. Curtis reaches up with everything he has.

Gathers it in and scores with a stylish finish. This is the telepathic relationship we share.

I'm reminded of the play over the years. It's a tale of folklore for those in attendance. A classic cocktail hour tale.

From the instant I meet Curtis Bell, I know he's a force. He's a guy that moves the needle. He pushes me to the brink, physically and psychologically, but the challenge of Curtis improves my strength of character. Our times fishing balances the relationship. On the court there's constant banter. On the lake the wind speaks and the trees listen. We're passengers.

In 1989 Curtis' wife Julie falls ill. She begins to suffer from focal seizures. She's also pregnant. The focal seizures have her thinking she's somewhere else other than where she actually is.

"I didn't know how to handle it," laments Curtis. "I didn't want her to lose the baby. I needed to take care of her. I mean, she was my wife."

Curtis sits out the 1990 season. Julie relocates back to Indianapolis to be with her parents. Curtis is by her side. Julie and Curtis welcome their son, William, into the world despite the odds.

Our friendship strengthens. Minus the need to be the biggest, most aggressive competitive alpha, we bond like normal friends. We talk on the phone. We find ways to meet up and fish. The fishing expeditions are numerous and cover the many corners of North America over the years/decades.

The Casa Colina Condors win the 1990 NWBA National Championship. I finish with 17 points and 13 assists in the championship game. Campos and Miller shoot a combined 14 for 15. Our defense stifles. We defeat the Arkansas Rollin' Razorbacks going away.

"The most glaring quality was Casa's defense," remarks Frank Burns who was in attendance. "Without Bell, they wanted to shut down Arkansas' inside game. That's the mission. They succeeded."

It's Casa Colina's seventh championship, tying us with the great Detroit Sparks teams. We also move two championships beyond the Long Beach Flying Wheels in the record books. I am the tournament's most valuable player.

On the surface I am stoic and take the MVP award in stride. Another day in my life. I share the moment with my teammates. They make the award possible. All the road trips. The gruelling training sessions. The path to the finals presses your psyche. The win or go home mentality is a stress test not intended for the meek.

The team celebrates. It feels great. It feels weird. My first NWBA championship without my fishing buddy.

"The guys won in 1990 without me," recalls Curtis. "So hard. So jealous."

Curtis and I both get the call. It's the NWBA Hall of Fame committee and we're both going to be inducted. It's the beginning of spring in the year 2000. The NWBA finals are in Chicago.

Julie passes in December of '96. It hits Curtis hard. I'm not sure if he's ever recovered. I reach out to him. We cast lines from boats, piers, and docks. The stories flow. We laugh amongst the stillness. We're more mature. It matters less who catches the prize fish. It matters more that we're in the same space searching for a bite. We still find space to one-up one another. It's in our blood and bones.

It dawns on me, Curtis Bell is one of my best, lifelong friends. I watched him deal with the passing of Julie in December of '96. He remarries to Mary Jo and loses her in 2021. My friend has been through so much heartache. A father of three and grandfather of four, Curtis finds a strength of character reserved for family men.

We both find the Hall of Fame proceedings underwhelming. First off, we're both still playing and far from finished. The protocols for selection seem arbitrary. We both expect more. Note to self: The Hall of Fame needs a ceremony to remember. Higher standards.

Frank Burns introduces me with a familiar wit and midwestern humor. Frank is larger than life in these moments and demands everyone's attention. My old friend rises to the occasion. I let loose with more than one belly laugh through the proceedings.

Sports 'N Spokes' Cliff Crase introduces Curtis. It's less personal and more about his astounding numbers.

Curtis and I are a dominant duo, but let's be clear, without the likes of Albert Campos, Jim Miller, Mike Schlappi, and all our other teammates there is no "duo" conversation. Without "team," without dependence on the guy next to you it doesn't work. Our greatness, in our time, is due to the strength of the team. Curtis and I are routinely the two best players on the floor—but not every night. Jimbo or Albert often rise to the defining, winning moments of games. Albert Campos is as good a defensive player that's ever played. Jimbo's outlet to a streaking teammate is the best I've ever seen. Casa Colina doesn't win without great role players. I have so much love and respect for all those who put on a Condor jersey…*well most anyways.*

 Together the Kiley/Bell tandem are able to achieve what no other championship tandem in the history of American adaptive sports. Here are some undeniable truths:

- Amassed a 98-game winning streak over a two-and-half-year period.
- Won 19 NWBA Final Four Championships collectively.
- Won 11 NWBA Final Four MVPs collectively.
- Won 5 World Championships collectively.
- Won 7 paralympic Gold Medals collectively.

Russell/Cousey.
Magic/Kareem.
Jordan/Pippen.
Kobe/Shaq.
Kiley/Bell.

We deserve a spot right next to these legends.
If not a notch above.

"Julie wants me to play. It's tough stopping. But she wants me to play in '92." Curtis returns from a self-induced retirement looking after his beloved wife.

"I know with Casa there's nothing to do but show up. I do. We carry on," says Bell.

In the early nineties, I hand the coaching responsibilities to the mercurial John Chambers. A Deadhead (follower of the band Grateful Dead), John is a coach that garners everyone's respect. We relate to him, have competed with or against him, and I appreciate he's making the line-up calls—not me.

The other added ingredient within our recipe of success is the emergence of Jim Miller as our go-to post presence. With Curtis absent, Jimbo takes advantage of the additional scoring opportunities and cements himself as a proven and dependable twenty-plus-points-a-game scorer.

The bond with Jimbo runs deep. He grew up in the same Costa Mesa neighborhood as I did. In fact, he lived a mere four houses down from us. We played youth, able-bodied basketball together as well as yearly Thanksgiving driveway games. I lose track of Jimbo until a large oil drum falls from a forklift he's operating and takes off half his foot. These days we're embedded teammates doing damage across the league. You can't dream this stuff up. Life is stranger than fiction.

John Chambers is the right leader to bring Curtis back into fold. He knows when to praise. He knows when to challenge. The twin towers of Bell and Miller are back.

Too big, as is his game.

The 1992 NWBA Final Four Tournament is in Albuquerque, New Mexico. The favorites are the Arkansas Rollin' Razorbacks. They won the championship in '91 and have emerging studs in Tim Kazee, James Coughlin, and Darren Schenebeck. Unfortunately for them, they fall apart in the second half of the semifinals against the Ottawa Royals. Leading by 21 at halftime, the Razorbacks crumble and lose to an inspired Ottawa squad 69-60.

We handle business in the other semi, beating the upstart Dallas Mavericks by 15.

Before us lies the promised land. An eighth championship quantifies us as the greatest team to date. Case closed.

Midway through the first half we go on a patented 21-5 run. We're up 45-31 at half. I lead the team in scoring with 14 points. My job in the second half is to get the ball to Jimbo and Curtis. They finish with 27 and 23 points. We win going away 84-61, playing one of the most complete games in Casa Colina history. *Sports 'N Spokes* magazine has us hitting 65% of our shots and knocking down 13 of 15 free-throws. Our breakneck, man-to-man defense—led again by Albert Campos—holds Ottawa to 38% shooting.

"Jim Miller and Curtis Bell dominated the boards," says Frank Burns. "Casa's defense led to Ottawa taking poor shots."

"We had a mission to win the title. We had more experience at the Final Four. Our guys played awesome defense," says Head Coach, John Chambers.

We are the best. Our eighth championship overtakes the Detroit Sparks and their seven.

Forced away from the game for a couple years, Curtis goes on to win his fifth NWBA Tournament MVP. I know how much this means to him. I'm content. With all my friend has had to deal with, his MVP performance is astounding.

A month or so after our championship run, *Sports 'N Spokes* magazine arrives in the post. I'm taken by a shot from legendary, Hall of Fame photographer, Curt Beamer.

The action shot has Curtis shooting over Ottawa's Reg McClellan. Dominant in length and brawn, it's easy to look at Curtis' photo and see a bigger guy shooting over someone smaller. I see Curtis' posture: long, powerful, and perfectly balanced. I see the ball, directly above his eyes and far above the outstretched reach of the defender. The moment before the extension of the shot, the ball sits perfectly on the fingertips of his dominant hand. His left hand, the guide hand, gently balancing flawless form.

The photograph is proof of a man working his craft at the highest of levels.

In a second look of the photo, all I see is his eyes. An overt, determined need to be better than anyone else. I know this look as I am this look. This like-mindedness is an undeniable pull. It's stronger than any of our quarrels, philosophies and inevitable disagreements.

Curtis' eyes are two darts focused on one single-minded objective—winning.

At this moment he is the force. He is everything.

PART SEVEN

When you come to a fork in the road. Take it.

— Yogi Berra

STEEP & DEEP

To win, you have to risk loss.

– Jean-Claude Killy

It's late March. We're at the end of another run. Albuquerque, New Mexico, is the backdrop. The Casa Colina Condors are crowned champions for the eighth time. We win it all. I'm ecstatic.

The normal play is an unabashed celebration with lovable teammates, leading to repeated choruses of Kool and the Gang's "Celebration." It never gets old.

Instead, I shower quickly, slap high-fives with teammates, and find the side-door to the parking lot. I hop aboard a Rocket Ship headed to the French Alps and an entirely different dream.

I'm with my coach, Michael Byxbe. I've been with him since the beginning of this odyssey. He is so good at what he does, I find learning from him—a voyage devoid of ego or waste. He challenges me and then explains before showing me how.

Our lengthy flight not only crosses two continents and the Atlantic Ocean, but the travel has me caught between winning a season-long, playoff-driven, incremental basketball climb, to a hundredth-of-a-second difference between victory and defeat. I sleep in the oxygenated air of getting it done and the anticipation of starting anew.

Michael is driving at night through the alps. The verticality of all the peaks, covered in snow is obvious even through the darkness. The sheer drop-offs are constant. A vehicle is headed towards us. They're headed down the mountain. We inch closer to one another. I hold my breath. My heart rate increases as does the elevation.

The next morning, I wake and venture outside. I look up to the jutting, steep peaks that defy anyone's ability to accurately describe. Another deep breath. Collect thoughts. Focus on the path of elite training.

It dawns on me. The 1992 Winter Paralympics in Albertville or Tignes, France.

I head towards the village of Tignes near the Italian border and part of Escape Killy skiing. Three-time French gold-medal-winning Jean-Claude Killy grew up in these parts. Engulfed by the French Alps, I understand the power behind the beauty of Jean Claude's magic in the 1968 Winter Olympics in Grenoble, France. His three gold medals in alpine skiing set the mark for all others to dream and attempt to follow.

I am next in line.

After a day to acclimate, Team USA (still feels good to write that) takes to the alps. We eye where the races are staged and on what runs.

The downhill start shack is visible at the top of the mountain. It's the steepest descent I've ever witnessed. Everything about the Alps is unique, picturesque, and formidable. I practice my visualization and breathing in every spare moment I find. The butterflies are already working. Perfect. I'm alive more with each passing moment.

The snow is light and so dry it fills our vision with snow diamonds or crystals softly floating around the team. I've never seen a snow dance like this before. We're all overwhelmed by the pure beauty of the clear, blue sky against the absolute white of a mountain and all she can conjure up.

We eat on the picturesque deck. We can't stop looking up to the chutes. They're closer to vertical than I imagined. We spot a skier in one of the chutes. Only the hardcore experts dare go there.

The beauty and the beast.

A small flurry of snow diamonds land on my shoulder.

It's God asking, "How do you like me now?"

Lake Tahoe is magic. A freshwater lake, high in the Sierra Nevada mountain range, Lake Tahoe shares its deep waters with the states of California and Nevada. As a student at Sacramento State, I find the time to trek up Highway 50 and experience its unspoken wonders. To take in Lake Tahoe is to stop, stare, ponder, and repeat.

It's the mid-eighties. I plan a Casa Colina Hospital outpatient trip for nearly half a dozen spinal cord injury enthusiasts. The plan is to take lessons, learn to snow ski, and ride a chair lift. I have zero experience with adaptive skiing and unlike other outpatient excursions, I'm a rookie like everybody else. The more subtle goal for the trip is for these newly injured to learn how to travel by airplane, navigate the hotel room experience, whilst doing an activity they can share with family and friends. Recreation Therapy at its finest.

Alpine Meadows Adaptive Ski School is where the seed is planted. The first ski I used wasn't a ski at all. It's a sled, designed by Peter Axelson, named the Arroya.

In the 60s, Norway's Bidar Johnson adapted the Pulk sled to enjoy the winter sports of his homeland. He uses two shortened poles to propel himself. Bidar refuses to let his traumatic injury slow him down. Previously the Pulk was used for hauling supplies, family possessions, and small children across its frozen Norwegian landscape.

Axelson engineers a more advanced version of the Pulk (the Arroya) and thus begins my need for downhill speed. Peter Axelson will become a good friend, ski buddy, and major influence in the progression of mono-skiing.

The flight home to Southern California is full of smiles, exhaustion, and tales of overcoming fear and apprehension. I take joy in knowing that these moments are life-changing. They're also the foundation, leading towards the stepping-stone arc of getting good at something that is athletic but also a journey of the soul.

I return over and over. I'm attracted to potentially excelling at something I loved doing as a kid. Returning to the scene of the crime adds an understated charge. San Dimas (my home) sits at the base of the San Gabriel Mountains. I find myself, basking in the warmth of the sun, looking at the San Gabriels, imagining myself on its slopes—killing it.

The vision becomes reality. I meet some extraordinary coaches in Michael Byxbe and Katherine Hayes. We take to one another. Michael is a friend of Quickie's Marilyn Hamilton. She's a friend of mine as well. I begin seeing him more and more at wheelchair tennis tournaments. Marilyn is a top skier/tennis player. The connection with Byxbe is seamless and strong. He pushes and stretches my limits. The kayak-looking sit-ski with shorthand picks and stainless runners underneath has me going to the top of mountains under Byxbe's watchful eye. The top of the mountain chairlift rides, with the Arroya sled beneath me, sends chills. The process of getting on and off is scary enough. Then to ride up the mountain, with half the sled hanging beyond the seat of the chair-lift's bench, still puckers me up good.

I'm doing it. I ski (or slide down) steep runs. The hill is at times inches from my face. Verticality, speed, and the absolute need to turn the Arroya away from the impending tree line has everything I have on edge. Michael Byxbe is not about groomed runs. More and more he has me into everything not groomed. Byxbe then has me into some powder. The fresh fallen, ungroomed snow is extreme and exhilarating. I'm awestruck and scared in the same breath. I not only survive. I excel. I begin to entertain competitive thoughts.

Tahoe, before I let it run in an Arroya sit ski…crazy.

First, I need my independence.

I am tethered by Byxbe. I get it but I hate it. When it's steep, there's a greater chance of the Arroya sliding out of control and into some deadly scenarios. Michael and I both know the tether line needs to change. I want—I need to cut the cord. During this time all adaptive skiers are tethered to an able-bodied skier. I'm not the only one itching to be free.

The Europeans are experimenting with Ski Bobs. The Ski Bobs are mounted on two small skis. In place of today's streamlined minimal seating are larger fiberglass or Kevlar shells atop a leaf spring. Archaic but groundbreaking when you're searching for a truer skiing experience. I purchase, through Casa Colina's Sport Program, a version of the Ski Bob. It's called a GFL Technik out of Germany. Invented by Hans Olpp and Henie Braun, their final patent is approved in December of 1986.

The GFL shows up. Fellow Rec Therapist and forever-friend Jeff Kalin and I take the mono-ski out of the box and set it up. I'm intrigued by the outriggers. I will use the forearm crutch-like ski poles, attached to small skis, as a pivotal way to turn. Only one thing left to do and that's test drive the thing.

That night, Jeff and I take this banana boat of a single ski up to Mountain High Ski Resort for an evening ski. The Wrightwood area skiing playground is an hour-and-a-half drive from Casa Colina. Night skiing is a challenge with harder packed snow and icy conditions but we are stoked to try the new setup. We communicate with the lift operators. They stop the lift and help Jeff lift the GFL and myself onto the chairlift. I ski off the lift easier than imagined. Small wins.

I'm stable on the single ski beneath me. Once I'm over the terrifying realization that I'm at the top of a mountain, with a ski I've never used before (and that I've never turned before)—all is well.

I make the quantum leap from the Arroya, which sits flat on the snow, to a single ski with leaf springs to serve as a suspension. I find my independence by putting myself in a turn-or-die situation. I'd never advise learning like this but it sure works for me.

Jeff Kalin and I team up on many future ski adventures, but I'll always be extraordinarily appreciative of our relationship and the night we ventured into the unknown.

Skiing for real.

That's the chase.

I begin to race in regional and national competitions. It doesn't take long before I'm outgrowing the GFL ski. Peter Axelson is the fastest Wheel Head on the mountain. A Stanford engineer, he builds a new version of the mono-ski. It sits atop a motorcycle mono-shock. The design, with its new age suspension, gives Peter an explosive competitive advantage.

I can't keep up. This must change.

I pick up the phone and call Axelson. I seek his permission to copy his design. He respects that I've come to him. He allows me to examine his setup. There's also a shot of Axelson tearing it up on the cover of *Sports 'N Spokes*. The photo becomes our template. I know enough about design to connect the dots and begin the process.

Local prosthetist, orthotist, and business owner, Jan Krezmenski, is my go-to fabricator. Michael Byxbe, my friend, instructor, and coach joins the crew. Byxbe keeps reminding us, "The lighter the better."

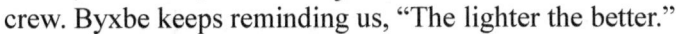

Anytime we want to beef things up with heavier hardware, Michael routinely barks back, "If you're not breaking equipment you're not skiing hard enough. Keep it light."

Jan and I spend many late nights building our custom mono-ski. We call it the J+K for obvious reasons. There are adaptive skis commercially emerging in the United States through Sunrise Medical and Dan Fallon's Fallonski. There is no temptation to jump on either ski. Sunrise Medical's Shadow Ski is a byproduct of Quickie, and the fit has potential, but the Axelson design is superior. Can we improve on what's already the best?

Jan cuts and welds the aluminum. I forge local relationships with motorcycle shock absorber companies like White Brothers and Fox Shocks. These are top of the line suspension companies used by the best motocross riders in the country. J+K is a small, custom business on the rise.

We invest in our seating system like no other. We need to be unique in the name of performance. The standard is a generic bucket seat. The skier's only custom option is width and length. We begin making casts of people's butts and hips. The form fitting, custom seat fits the adaptive skier like a ski boot fits an able-bodied skier. This changes the game. It's the norm, not the exception, for adaptive athletes to have one butt cheek bigger than the other, or for one hip to be more atrophied than the opposite one. The custom seats are what folks want and need. We're happy to share but our simple genius comes with a cost. Wherever across the United States you might live, you have to get to Jan's shop to have the casts made. This involves flight, hotel, and product. Commitment. Expensive.

We build a loading device to raise the J+K onto the chairlift and release it for ski away exit. There's a greater independence and better working relationship with adaptive skiers and the mountain's staff. Lift lines keep moving. A connectivity between all skiers on the mountain strengthens. Respect is given and received.

Orders begin to flow into J+K. The seating concept, suspension, and loading device don't just put us in the game, it puts us at the top of the game. We find out the hard way that one-at-a-time, custom design is a back-breaking business model. I understand what Jeff Minnebraker and the Quadra crew dealt with being the first out the gate. Exhilaration and exhaustion within each idea, build, and commitment to deliver.

My skiing takes off. I now have the equipment and skill level to not just keep up, it's time to overtake. Katherine Hayes is my race coach. We take advantage of my lifelong visualization tactics whilst adding a fast and finish race mindset. Podiums are the convergence of speed and consistency. Throughout my time on various mountains across the globe, I am able to keep my DNFs (did not finish) to a minimum.

Michael Byxbe has me into double black diamond runs with gnarly descents and chutes. High pucker factor indeed. We enjoy skiing in the trees. The snow is deep and untouched. Michael skis above me. He understands we're into the heavier side of things and wants to be *'there'* if needed and not below me if he needs to hike back up. The guy has my back. My confidence grows with every second on my ski.

There's strength in numbers. Fellow skiers and quality human beings, Chauncey Taylor and Steven Anderson (expert skiers) start travelling and skiing with Byxbe and myself regularly. The two are friends of Michael's and great fun to ski with. They become my friends. Marilyn Hamilton is also part of the crew. She's a boundless skier and trailblazing friend. We're all pushing the limits of J+K and my mono-skiing.

It's the best of times. I need to race, and the desire to win is intense; but these times, skiing powder so deep, I need a snorkel, with these guys is unsurpassed. The shared stoke of skiing above the clouds, downhill carves, and the chase of finding ungroomed powder, connects us in a powerful—we're into a secret no one else knows—kind of way.

J+K Ski first custom seating system with mono shock. Marilyn Hamilton, Jan Krezmenski, Jeff, and 'No-No' Kalin.

I love powder and the halfpipe.

Michael and I continue to train. He coaches. I follow his instructions. A valuable lesson is Byxbe's "Falling Leaf" technique. The skill works on the steepest of descents. I rock slowly forward and aft from the ski tip and then to the tail. The "Falling Leaf" helps grow confidence when the pitch of the hill is closer to vertical. It's much like a leaf falling from its tree in a gentle breeze and rocks back and forth as it makes its way to the ground. It's a move I commit to before pointing it downhill and linking turns. This proves a lifesaving skill I use often and teach others. Michael then teaches the trick-art of doing 360s. I get good at it quickly. I enjoy linking consecutive 360s in succession. The move leaves able-bodied skiers gawking. I do the move all the time and love the boundaries it pushes.

I revel in being out of my chair, in my ski, mastering my outriggers and sharing my skills with the general population. I'm not operating within the confines of my disability and its more limited perceptions. Snow skiing puts me in the world. I use adaptive equipment but the objective is the same: ski with style and be one of the best on the mountain.

Byxbe has me skiing with regular ski poles instead of outriggers. Yikes. Outriggers are short, chopped forearm crutches with a ski tip attached. The adjustment forces me to use my body considerably more to turn.

I take on intermediate runs with success. Next, we're into gates and a course. Skiing gates with ski poles is a task. Successfully finishing the course is reason enough for celebration. The ceiling is lower when using poles instead of outriggers but the practice strengthens my core and broadens my skiing. I'm the first ever to do it. It forces me to use my upper body and truly carve turns instead of leaning onto the outriggers, into the snow and scrubbing speed. I'm willing to try anything. I love every aspect and every second of the shared experience.

A real blessing of my newfound love is the convergence of my lifelong love, my family. Sandy takes adult lessons. Justin and Danielle take youth and 'Ski-Wee' lessons. It isn't long before the four of us are all on the slopes together. Skiing the intermediate runs, Sandy is graceful and light on her skis. She's beautiful in those tight ski pants. Justin (Mr. Technical) is focused, looking to perfect his stylish turns. Danielle (the hood ornament) skis wide open and is an absolute risk taker. I do my best to slow her down. The crowning moment is a snapshot of the four of us at Alpine Meadows. We're all on the same chairlift ascending a beautiful mountain on a perfect day. I want the moment to last forever. It's a gift I cannot truly express. Looking to my right sits Justin, Danielle, and Sandy. We are a family riding the quad-chair together, taking in the incredible sights.

This is my skiing nirvana.

In 1989, I earn a spot on the US Disabled Ski Team. Initially my time with the team is a proving ground. Races are happening at Park City, Winter Park, Vail, Durango, and other unbelievable resorts. It's all exciting and new to me. The snow lifestyle is intoxicating. Before camps and training, I get up earlier than the rest to take a fitness push in snow conditions. My knobby tires spitting aside snow in an intense workout. I eye the moon setting and the sun rising in the San Juans.

I'm a beast and improve myself any way I can.

Richard St. Dennis, Rick Ruscio, Peter Axelson, Mike McDougal, and Bill Bowness are racers that challenge me. Jim Martinson is the cream of the crop and I make unseating him my mission. This doesn't happen fast enough. We get to where we're taking turns beating one another. Jim attacks every turn and his approach backfires from time to time with falls and skiing off course. When it all comes together, he's a blur and stunning to watch.

My consistency is growing. The coaches take notice. They also notice I handle big air well in jumps and when racing. I pride myself launching air in a tuck and gently landing into a carved, high-speed turn.

We're training in Durango, Colorado. The coaches ask me to test a jump. They want to know if it's doable for a mono-ski. They asked me. Hell, yes. I land the jump in front of the entire team. It's a defining moment in the arc of my skiing. Serious confidence swells within this crash test dummy opportunity. I am so proud to be trusted and then asked by the coaches—over anyone else—to prove my skill and comfort with big air jumps. The opportunity allows me to showcase my comfort with high-speed launches and landings.

I'm beating the old guard on a regular basis. My climb up the ski team's totem pole surprises some but not me. I can see my path and where it's leading. Podiums.

It's time to make a statement. The 1990 National Championships in Winter Park, Colorado, is the stage. The question isn't if I medal? The question is how many? Instead, I tear my labrum in my shoulder, just out of the starting gate in the downhill. Painful. Debilitating.

Instead of seeing this time as the setback it is, I tell my 37-year-old-self to follow doctor's orders, rehab beyond what the therapists mandate, and recover quicker than anyone expects.

I'm back on the slopes in early 1991. In fact, I ski over 200 days throughout the year and across the globe. I'm either free skiing, training in USA race camps, or entered into various competitions. During this time, I'm also playing basketball with the Condors. This manic, somewhat psycho uber need to excel has put me in the best shape of my life. My mindset and body are more the shape of a 19-year-old. My middle-age responsibilities to supporting my family are unwavering.

I am a partner with NeoLife Around the World. A global health and wellness company, they hire me as a professional speaker. Once I work past the nerves of stage fright, I take to the job seamlessly. I've always been good at spinning a tale, telling a story. The money is great and the travel is top notch. Sandy and I fly business class and stay in five-star hotels across Europe, Jamaica, Africa, and the United States. Justin travels with me to Italy. Danielle treks with me for two weeks to Stockholm, Budapest, and Johannesburg. NeoLife even sets up a safari trip for Danielle and me in the African bush. These are once in a lifetime adventures.

I appreciate the chance to motivate and inspire others through the spoken word, but speeches are not my jam. I refuse to deliver a canned speech and simply hit repeat. I must take in life's wild ride and incorporate this in my messaging. I have to keep it fresh. I get tired of hearing myself speak and after a while begin to withdraw. It's tiring listening to others spew their same rehearsed, tired stories and sell their hundred-page books of inspiration. Not my style. Feels like a con. Not me. The feedback is excellent. I'm a good speaker but the fit isn't long-lasting.

I have an idea that will rapidly increase the probabilities of winning multiple medals in the Paralympic Winter Games in Albertville, France. What if I live for six straight weeks in Lake Tahoe? The various resorts and slopes are a perfect training ground. The 1960 Winter Olympics were held in Tahoe's Squaw Valley. Friend and fellow mono-skier, Bruce Cornell, has a place at the top of Lake Tahoe Donner. His offer to stay with him stands. I run this by Sandy to gauge her support or reservations. I understand how one-sided an ask this is. Ever graceful and one of a kind, she gets my inner desire to be the best in the world. It's a conversation full of emotion. Separation from family hangs heavy. I look in the mirror and see a father, husband, and the burden of world class athleticism. In time, Sandy gives me her reluctant blessing. Her sacrifices, so I may do my competitive thing, are full of love.

Next, will Casa Colina and my bosses be on board with my dream of winning Winter Paralympic gold? I need them to cover my salary for a month-and-a-half. Elite training in a resort setting is pricey. I must cover expenses for the family: mortgage, food, and the inevitable curve balls of life. Casa steps up. They always look at sport as part of my job and commitment to the ever-growing disability sport movement. There are linked marketing benefits that we can use for the hospital and sports program brand. I'm given the green light from the Casa Colina brass. This relationship is tremendous and responsible for a major part of my athletic successes.

I ask NeoLife if they'd be willing to offer financial support for my Tahoe training. They respond with a resounding, 'Yes.' The NeoLife relationship isn't a lengthy one, but my appreciation for them is. I have everything in place. The money needed is there. The real price to pay is leaving my family and relying on Sandy to look after the kids. We make plans to visit one another on weekends in Tahoe and San Dimas.

I ski and train most every day. I'm lifting weights multiple days a week. Shovelling snow is a recurring and mighty task. I take to cross country Nordic skiing. Candace Cable is my conduit. Cross country skiing is truly demanding and serves my need to live in beast mode.

I'm the first one on the mountain. I'm the first person on the chairlift. My goal is to lay "fresh tracks" for all to see. This is my daily routine. On race days I want my competitors to see me booted up with carved snow dangling from my previous run. My game face is on. The overt statement is, '*I want it more than you.*'

A typical day at Alpine Meadows has me on the snow at 7:30 a.m. I ski hard until 11:30 or 12 p.m. As the masses, looking to work off last night's festivities, hit the slopes, I am packing up. The repetitive action strengthens my resolve. It's me against everyone.

Michael Byxbe has me working on starts. We do this over and over. We're searching for that tenth-of-a-second competitive advantage. We find a run with steepness and pitch. I have my outriggers in the 'up' position. I rise and explode into start mode. As I come out of the start gate, I lift the back end of my ski up and push out of the start shack with all I have. The outrigger handles have a quick release to flip the ski-tips down. Focus, timing, and power. We work on this valuable skill set for a solid hour. Byxbe then has me climb—with my outriggers—to the top of Alpine Meadows. I eventually get to the top of the other side. It's a brutal feat to pole yourself up, one foot at a time, in a mono-ski. The reward is the free ski down the other side.

I take to the grind of snow ski training. It's more a search for the soul compared to basketball, tennis, or track. Skiers and surfers fall from the same sprinkle of God's grace. Mountain and beach people are happy, and in a good mood, with smiles on their faces. Daily chairlift rides are a constant reminder that life is grand. Each ride up reminds me, we're all passengers of a creation beyond our imagination. I'm on a soulful sojourn, and most importantly—I know it.

I'm working to improve within four different disciplines: the Slalom, Giant Slalom, and the speed events of the Super Giant Slalom (Super G) and Downhill. I carry different skis for each. Byxbe lets me get away with nothing.

"Gotta carry your own gear," he repeatedly barks.

This takes a well thought-out plan. Mono-ski body, skis, riggers, and a bag of gear are all secured to my snow chair. During a heavy snow day, the task of getting my kit from the parking lot to the lodge is the toughest workout of the day. Again, I am in the best shape of my life. The ability to be independent from the parking lot to the hill is a confidence-builder beyond comparison.

When I'm not skiing or recovering, I am waxing or sharpening the edges of my various skis. There are no shortcuts here. Elite performance demands getting the best out of your gear. I'm fortunate to have an expert like Michael tuning my skis but all other equipment preparedness is on me.

Once a week the mountain allows eight-to-ten US Ski Team members on the hill for speed training. Just past sunrise we have the mountain all to ourselves. The anticipation is a buzz. I drive my Chevy Suburban from Tahoe Donner to Alpine Meadows. A pristine drive through the valley, with the vastness of Lake Tahoe ever-present, has me geeked. Metallica blares through quality speakers.

I'm ready to go fast.

The mountain is ours, with freshly groomed and packed runs. The sun rises to the east. The calming chairlift ride reminds me why I'm here. I eye the Sierra Nevada mountain range as if I'm a bird above it all. It's time to go. I'm screaming down the Super G course with no one in sight. Next, I'm on the downhill run. I'm going too fast to see anything but the course. Jim Martinson is not in this gaggle of skiers. He is on his own snow at Crystal Mountain in Washington State

Down, I go.

Tuck position.

Speeds nearing 60 miles per hour.

Helmet head bobbing like *Top Gun*.

He is my focus.

Sharp edges carving packed snow.

A final long left turn.

A finishing aerodynamic tuck.

He's behind me.

The world is in front.

I'm dripping with confidence and begin to win and finish races consistently. It isn't that long ago I was tethered to a sled. These days I ski whatever mountain I find myself on with the individuality and freedom that spikes my joy. As a US Ski Team member, I ski any resort in the country for free. Life is good.

Jim Martinson is my rival. A bilateral lower limb amputee injured in the Vietnam War, Jim is a warrior competitor. In 1981 he wins the prestigious Boston Marathon. Mammoth accomplishment. He engineers and develops the Shadow mono-ski before ultimately being inducted into the Ski and Snowboard Hall of Fame. Stud.

Classifications are made with the idea that racers have the same or similar function. Martinson and I compete in the same class and against one another. Classification in disability sport is tricky at best. Sometimes you're the hammer. Sometimes you're the nail. Jim has the perfect makeup: no legs, only the wind beneath him, full function of his core and all his weight over his ski and shock absorber. No excuses.

Jim and I are friends but it's getting awkward. There's a tense friendliness off the hill. When we see one another, there's a calm before the storm temperature to our exchanges. On the hill, he gets my game face. I refuse to warm to the enemy in any arena of play. Jim is '*it*' right now. This drives me like nothing else.

I understand I must beat him. It's important and strategic to leave everything else in the rearview mirror. He's the one being chased. Jim Martinson has been top dog for a while now. I'm the competitive pest, nipping at his heels.

'Downhill Gold' prior to Paralympics, Jim Martinson on my left—silver.

I learn the value of finishing races. It's what the coaches are looking for. They need fast, dependable, and reliable finishers. I am quickly becoming that guy.

Just prior to leaving for France and the 1992 Winter Paralympic Games, the coaches bring me in for a meeting. They've chosen me to race in all four events in Albertville. I am honored. I feel relief not pressure. The work and commitment to craft pays off.

Jim Martinson is chosen to ski in two events.

I expect to win gold on all four courses and feel exceptionally froggy and geared to succeed in the slalom and downhill events. These are my proven events with repeated championship results.

My previous, former-life motocross experience helps me understand the suspension of my gas-powered Fox Shock beneath my seat. The fast, quick rebound responses needed for slalom course successes feel in sync with the tight turns needed for slalom gates. For the downhill—the ultimate test of speed—I need the suspension much quieter, with less travel of the shock, during top speeds. The greater distance between gates demands a greater glide.

The vastness and severe pitch of the French Alps in Albertville, demands critical shock absorber adjustments beneath my seat. I feel confident I have the right settings for each race.

The Paralympic flame is lit. Here we go.

Day one. Slalom. I'm amped. There's a brief moment of levity. In the pre-race announcement of start times my name is pronounced Killy, *not* Kiley. *Sounds like I'm a distant American cousin to the great, triple-gold medal winning Frenchman, Jean-Claude Killy. I like the connection and the way it sounds over the loud speakers. Dave Killy it is.*

Jacques Blanc of Switzerland is my most formidable competitor. Jim Martinson is the wildcard. He's fast and a dangerous competitor but struggles to put back-to-back runs together. My only thought is gold. Jaques Blanc has his own plans. He links two runs together and his combined times beat mine. I ski fast without any mishaps. Jaques Blanc simply runs faster. I'm a silver medalist in my first Winter Olympics event. Damn.

To make a podium in my first Winter Paralympic event is a worthy feat. The silver in Slalom adds to Team USA's medal count. The coach's decision to have me race all events looks tactical and on-point. Then I have to listen to the Swiss anthem. The American flag beneath the Swiss. Bittersweet.

I recalibrate for the Giant Slalom the next day.

After the first run the course is reset. In the Giant Slalom there are many blind turns. Prior to each run, racers are allowed to inspect the course. This is a critical component to confidence and success. I must memorize the blind turns and even choose landmarks to judge where I need to be in a succession of setups. I might choose a tree as a landmark after turn three or a peak after turn five. Without these vital memorizations, I can come over the top of a blind spot and miss my gate entirely. Game over. I have the course memorized after three inspections (or slips). When you slip a course, you don't turn with your edges to keep the course pristine and minus any ruts.

See the course not the gates. Use your edges to turn, not to slow down. I'm prepared.

I'm at the start gates. I close my eyes and use my hands to help visualize each turn. I'm confident out the gates. The hour-at-a-time starting explosion sessions with Byxbe add a layer of poise.

My first run is nearly flawless. I'm in the lead. Jaques Blanc is in second.

Second run. I'm comfortable and fast on the upper portion of the course. Carving a turn, I hit a patch of ice. My edge in the back slips out. The bucket at my hip hits the snow. No time to think. I pop back up with all my weight and might. I right myself on my ski. I'm in shock and go straight into shred mode. The bottom half of the run has me in the zone. Things are slow and wild in the same instant. I hear nothing. I see everything with a glance. I'm a blur at the finish line.

My first run positioning makes me the last skier on the mountain. A quick, post-race carve has me positioned to eye the electronic timer and scoreboard. The number one flashes after my name with a time of 2.41.38. The number two is beside Jacques Blanc with a time of 2.42.75.

My first Winter Paralympic Gold. I can't help but think of my near disaster and overcoming it. Poetic justice.

I take my place atop the podium for the medal ceremony.

The National Anthem rings true.

Any days off from competition is an overt invitation to free ski and explore. A day off in the French Alps is an opportunity to step away from rivalries, clear the mechanisms, the clutter of analysis, and simply be another guy skiing down a fabulous resort mountain.

It sounds strange but you have to allow yourself the space to live a good life. I'm an expert skier. This means the world to me. I think of Sandy, Justin, and Danielle. I can never repay you all for the love you've given and allowed. This time in my life is the balance needed from the intense path of basketball and contributing to the group or team. I wouldn't be here, in the Alps, a Paralympic Gold and Silver medal already tucked away in a drawer next to my bed, without the valued and specific help of coaches, fellow skiers, and support staff. I know this in spades, but I also fully realize ski racing is the art of one. It's the solo mission of skier, hill, and time. This is where I thrive. This is where I am the most alive. To find this rare air, it's important to ski for the rush and stoke.

I am one, but also just another happy, smiling face in the crowd.

Byxbe and I take to the mountain. Our skiing is unrushed and full of style and freeform. We ease into the lodge for a quick lunch. We eye a table with a couple teammates and standup amputee skiers, Greg Manino and Jim Lagerstrom. We join them. The conversation quickly turns to a cornice jump the two have just come from. A cornice is where you're unable to see over the top of the drop. It also means serious dropping, air time.

This grabs my attention. Greg and Jim (a couple amazing skiers) raise their eyebrows as if to say, 'You doing this?' The invitation validates my expert skills off groomed runs.

Michael and I gear up and head up the slopes behind our one-legged guides. Up the chairlift we eye the Alps steep peaks. My heart is ready to jump from my chest. Byxbe has my camcorder and is keen to film whatever happens. I see the cornice. I've never jumped off anything like this. My teammates assure me I can do it. "The landing is nothing but powder," they say. "No rocks."

This is a 'Yikes' moment. A frequent term shared between Byxbe and myself when encountering things of magnitude.

After a rough and treacherous approach to the cornice, we're there. I joke with Michael of the ski edges we'll need to sharpen after poling over a sheet of rocks.

I ask the boys one last time, "No obstacles. Right?"

"Yes," they say confidently.

It's two-way trust. They believe in my ability. They've watched me grow.

The longer you wait at the top of a cornice the bigger the mental challenge becomes. Previous escapades with Byxbe prepare me for this moment. I position and line up my ski. I vault off with a huge push off my outriggers. My nose dives. I lean my head and body back to compensate, much like a rodeo cowboy does when a horse is attempting to rid him from her back. Forty feet of drop and air-time later, I plunge into so much powder all I can see is white. The landing comes quicker than imagined. I have to ski out of this. My reputation hangs in the balance. Success. Video proof. I meet Byxbe at his perch. He continues to film Greg and Jim on the cornice. Perfection. Expert skiers doing their thing. We trade high-fives. My joy, pride, and confidence are booming. I can only think of one thing to say, "Let's do it again."

We do.

It's race day.

There's a mantra hung on my wall at home, 'My mind must convince my body that speed is what counts; not survival.'

I drop in for the start of the Super Giant Slalom (Super G). I'm a jet pilot flying at minimal elevations. My mono-ski sits low to the snow. I feel every grain of speed beneath me. I get to my tuck position at every opportunity; outriggers stretched in front of me, off the snow and as speed-friendly as possible. I use my hips to make subtle turns and avoid scrubbing away any speed.

I'm burning the course. One with the ski. It's a feeling you only understand when you're fast and representing your country simultaneously. The previous day and the cornice increased my self-belief. My self-chat is nothing but positive and powerful. Ski racing is so mental.

I hear my coaches say, "Sometimes you have to slow down in order to go fast."

This is so true at the top of any speed course event. The ability to stay calm early allows me to hammer down the middle and bottom half of the course.

I hear Byxbe. His constant, simple slogan of inspiration, "Go 90 or go home."

The finish line appears. It feels like I just started. This is a good thing. I dominate the field of the Super G and easily win the USA another Gold medal. Jaques Blanc finishes a distant second.

Any celebrations are short lived when you're a four-event skier.

The next day is Downhill day. The Downhill is the feature event of any competition. Fastest man or woman alive.

I see myself in each turn. I'm chasing tenths-of-seconds with each setup. I see myself maintaining speed when the course allows and seamlessly getting to my 'tuck' position when it's 'go time.'

The competition switches to teammate Jim Martinson. I have his number in the slalom. He's motivated. How can he not be? We have battled for two years chasing victory. He's built for speed, and skis with more gusto than all others. I have nothing but respect for the Vietnam Veteran. He served our country. He lost both his legs above the knee.

Today, he's representing his country in an entirely different way.

Comradery and admiration are now secondary to the task at hand.

I memorize the course. I slip the course four times.

I explode out of the start gate with a thunder and lightning attack. It's as steep a groomed run descent as I've ever experienced. I get into my tucks. I'm early and clean. I feel speed like never before. I'm not thinking. I'm acting and reacting to what I feel.

I have no idea how fast I'm going. I only know I've never gone faster. Good downhillers don't fall. The results are too treacherous—too life-changing. The rush of speed counterbalances everything else. Like everything addicting, I want to do it again.

What takes a lifetime to accomplish is over in the blink of an eye.

I look up at the theatre-type screen; spectators watching the happenings and results. The number 1 flashes next to my name with a time of 1.23.76. I reached a top speed of 63 miles per hour. I'm dragstrip fast. No one can beat me today.

Two more racers attack the course. I sit back and watch on the big screen. They're nowhere close to my winning time.

It's Martinson's turn on the course. The big screen everyone is watching becomes small and resonates in high definition. My focus is laser. I tune everything out.

Jim is all over the course early. He's reckless. He's far better on the lower portions. He crosses the finish line.

My confidence soars. Stumpy's (Jim's nickname for obvious reasons) sloppy work at the top of the mountain will ultimately cost him.

There's a number 1 next to his name, with a time of 1.22.93.

My heart sinks.

My breath leaves my lungs.

Jim races on the edge and looks wild, but today it's the perfect way to be the fastest man in the world. Jim and I are great friends. We speak about our ski days each time we get together. The Downhill inevitably comes up. Jim smirks. I shake my head.

Jim goes on to ski in the wildly popular X Games in 2009 at 63 years of age. If I have to lose in Albertville, Jim Martinson is the right guy to go down to. A Hall of Fame skier.

The USA wins the medal count for the 1992 Winter Paralympics with a total of 40. Germany is a distant second with 22.

I come home with 4 medals: 2 gold and 2 silver. My coaches place trust in me and I deliver for my country.

I call it the time of my life.

Geared up for slalom in the 1992 Paralympic Games.

LOST

Never confuse a single defeat with a final defeat
— F. Scott Fitzgerald

Too many times plans aren't worth the effort of thought or the paper they're written on.

My plan is to retire from basketball after the 1992 Barcelona Paralympic Games. My successes in the Winter Games just a few months prior align with my innermost vision to exit from elite sport as the best ever. The idea of capturing gold at both the winter and summer games, in the same calendar year, drives the competitive beast that is me. I'm nearing the age of forty. I'm in the best shape of my existence. I'm putting the world on notice.

The journey for Barcelona gold starts in 1990, Bruges, Belgium of all places. The canals of Bruges link the city to the sea. Bruges is scenic, wealthy, and known as the lace capital of the world.

In 1990, Bruges hosts the World Championships. I appreciate the World Championships even more than the Paralympic Games because it's all basketball. No distractions. Bruges, Belgium, hosted the World Championship in 1975. We lose a nail biter to Israel. A memory like this reminds and stings to this day.

I'm in the truck, on the way to meet the grandkids and sitting at a red light. A quick twitch snaps my neck to the left. It's the '75 Championships and a missed top-of-the-key, open shot. The green light snaps me back into the now. The guy behind me hits his horn. If he only knew.

After '75 the USA dominates, winning the World Championships repeatedly.

In 1990, we're missing Curtis Bell. He is looking after his wife. Even without Curtis the team is strong. Gold is the expectation. Coach Harry Vines leads the way. The Arkansas coach has us prepared. We make our way through pool play. In the quarterfinal, I come up lame with a sore and swollen wrist. Harry and Trainer Kathy Curtis tell me the semifinals are out of the question. I have to sit the game out. This is not the plan. My visual preparation does not include cheerleading the boys in the medal round of a World Championship.

We win the semifinal. Coach Vines knows we can win without me all along. The final awaits. As expected, the French team comes through the opposite side of the draw. They've never beaten us but have two formidable stars: the duo of Michel Gradelle and Eric Benault. Gradelle is a fast point-guard type with range and quality finishes at high speeds. Benault is a massive lefty with above

291

average finishing skills in the post. I have two days off. Treatment is scheduled. My wrist is far from a hundred percent. To compound the injury, we're playing on a tartan or rubber type floor. The floor is slow and drags compared to the glide of a hardwood floor. My injury is related to pushing on this substandard surface.

It's a battle with the French. Back and forth the entire game. We're leading until the final seconds. Benault, the big lefty, hits an inside post look to put the French up a point. There's a timeout on the floor. Coach Vines calls a play. Albert Campos sets a high cross-pick for me. The offside stay wide, remain threats, and keep their defenders busy. This leaves the middle open. I drive hard with the ball off Albert's cross-pick. We've done this hundreds of times before as seasoned teammates. Campos holds the pick until I pass by. The middle of the floor is open. Benault sags. Not a problem. I'll throw one of my no-look passes to Albert for the score and win. This feels like practice. We've done it so many times together. Here we go. Time to win the game. I underestimate Benault's reach. He gets a piece of my pass. The ball deflects to a Frenchman. Game over. I never miss a pass like that with the game on the line.

The team is devastated.

I'm inconsolable.

We return home with a silver medal. Sucks. There's an immediate doctor's appointment for the wrist. I have torn ligaments.

Turn the ball over then surgery. Gulp. Humbling.

The World Championship loss in Bruges haunts me for the next two years. I set my sights on Barcelona and the Paralympics to get revenge on the world.

Two years is a long time to wait for a chance to win our way back to where we belong. My passion for snow skiing during these times helps defuse the lasting memory of losing. I find myself staring at the ceiling in search of solace and sleep. I'm unable to completely let go of those final seconds in Bruges.

I tap again into my single-mindedness of effort and exertion. I will not be outworked.

My left wrist doesn't recover as expected. I lose range of motion and there's talk of fusing it in a locked position. I filibuster such silliness. Not the first time I need to adjust my physical forms in reaction to injury. No big deal.

Trooper Johnson establishes himself as a strong national team member. I like the guy. We're cut from the same fabric: ornery and unafraid of any defining moments. We get down to basics and spend time training on the outdoor courts of Capistrano Beach in sunny, Southern California. With the Pacific Ocean and its high tides inching closer and closer to our training court, we do work. Our one-on-one games are barbaric. Physical games, on the verge of a street fight, are regular consumption for the coastal elite walking their purebreds or soaking in the sun. We get heated with one another but we also love it. Finally, there's someone else deranged enough to train like a barbarian. We talk about the Dream Team and their complete domination of the basketball world, just weeks earlier at the Barcelona Olympics. We'll be on the same court, use the same locker rooms, and share the same training venues that Michael, Magic, Charles, and the boys drew their lopsided and historical victories from.

In Trooper, I know he's riding shotgun with me in every way as we look to take down all the sporting world has to offer. He dares to dream. I see the dream.

We head to France for a friendly tune-up game. The same French team that exceeded expectations and beat us by a point in the World Championships. We're travelling separate from Team USA to get the game in. It makes sense. France is in the same time zone as Spain, and the acclimation process eases with competition, and then a short flight into Barcelona and the '92 Paralympic Games.

Head Coach Harry Vines is a big personality. He's quick witted, boisterous, and likes to use the term "Goober" when describing mistakes and the man behind it. He also despises the French. I'm not sure if it's a World War 2 thing or a specific baguette, beret-induced memory, but Coach Vines is not a fan. Harry informs me the French organizer tells him, "This is a show. The USA is not going to win."

A friendly game indeed.

As soon as we tip off, we get a whiff of the French home cooking. I'm called for a travelling (three pushes) violation whilst dribbling the ball. Smoke is coming out of Harry's ears. The travelling call is comical. I intentionally drop the ball off my push rim. The ball bounds to the far end of the gym. The rotund French referee is forced to amble after it.

With 1:30 left in the game we're up. A bogus 3-second violation is called— one of three outlandish calls within sixty seconds. The game is rigged like I've never seen. We lose the game and can't wait to get out of the country.

The USA team for Barcelona is formidable. We have a Casa Colina crew of Curtis Bell, Jimbo Miller, Mike Schlappi, and me. Harry has his own Arkansas squad of Tim Kazee, James Coughlin, Derrin Schenebeck, and Gary Woodring. Add Trooper Johnson, Reggie Colton, David Efferson, and Arnardo Valdez to complete the strongest team in Spain.

It's time. Our first game is against the host country, Spain. The country loves basketball and is passionate about supporting its squads. The Paralympic Games opener is bound to be electric.

We load the bus in anticipation of the first game of the tournament. I've been visualizing this moment and the opening tip for months. I see myself, over and again, receiving the ball off the tip. I roll into a 3-point shot. The defense is unexpecting. I see and feel the ball in detail with backspin, arc, and follow-through. I hold the gooseneck pose and see the ball travel through time. It's perfect. I see this over and over and over.

The bus ride is the best of my basketball life. We approach the venue. There are thousands of folks milling about looking to gain access to the game. Fans are crazed—yelling, screaming, and waving their hands at us. The Spanish fans aren't ugly about it, but their collective passion is unmatched.

The game is a sellout. Our bus travels down a path beneath the venue into a private entrance. Is this what it feels like to be a rock star?

My teammates are all smiles. There's a childlike wonder. We enter through the VIP section and into our changing room. We hear the chatter of fans and the bass driven thump of jock jam tunes. Everything is building towards a crescendo where anticipation meets the reality of performance.

In one moment, it's important to soak every second of this in. We may never pass this way again. In the next, it's imperative to remain steadfast and assured.

I'm the captain and lead my teammates into basketball nirvana. The maxed-out Spanish crowd looks to will their team to increased performance levels with volume and devotion. It's incredibly loud. My chest is reverberating more and more as the noise factor increases.

I focus on my vision during warmups and shooting drills. There's a distinct inner quiet amongst the commotion. Here we go.

Curtis Bell is in the center circle for the tip and beginning of play. I'm in a mind and place to realize the moment. The reality of now is before me. Sure enough, Curtis tips it to me. My man. The Spanish defenders sag and relax for half a moment below the 3-point-line. Complete focus is a tall task. Their lapse is my window. I've played this movie in my mind repeatedly. I'm the star, director, and producer.

I roll into my 3-point bomb. I hear nothing. See everything. Splash. Wet. Nothing but net. I turn my vision into the manifestation of actuality and truth.

The game is closer in the early stages more than we like. The home crowd supplies the juice the Spanish players feed upon. They play with a fight and energy that impresses but, in the end, we are too deep and too good. We pull away late, winning the game 71-62.

The game is a dream fulfilled. I didn't understand until tonight, the power and confirmation of a game staged the right way. Any achievement or success is dependent on the details. Up until now the nuances of elite disability sport are seen as a bridge too far.

What we do is electric. We know this but our bullhorns only reach so far. At our core we are performers. We should not be the stage hands or part of a production team. Yet, we are. Tonight, the professionals are in charge. On and off the court.

I know I validate sports. These pages speak to that.

Tonight, sport validates me.

MONKEYSHINES

Some people outgrow childish shenanigans.
Some of us master them.

– DK

Trooper and I are roommates. We want it this way. Our tribal times training at the beach have us both wanting to not break the circle. The Paralympic Village is right on the water. The view from our room looks into its vastness.

Coach Vines is next door. The living quarters are modern but tight. There's a small gap at each room's window. This allows you to hear or even chat with your neighbor across the way. Having Trooper as a roommate equals shenanigans. One morning I chose to sleep in. You'd be surprised how much down time there is at the Olympic or Paralympic Games. Trooper takes issue with my choice to catch a few more winks. He's bantering about something. I want to sleep. I roll over and lay face down in an attempt to ignore him. Not a good idea. He picks up my chair and flings it on top of me. I can't believe this guy. Infuriated. Flustered. Angry. I instinctively rise to action. Trooper is snapping photos. This simmers the situation. I'm awake for the day. Funny guy.

The tournament's pool play is a formality. Our closest game is the opener against Spain. We're winning but we're also searching for our rhythm and chemistry. Coach Vines is respected and someone we'd all lay down for, but it's difficult for me to find a consistent flow with his platooning of the Casa and Arkansas teammates. We keep winning. That's all that matters.

After a quarterfinal victory over a tenacious Australia squad, we await the result between Canada and France. Of course, it's the French with a single point victory. The semifinals are set: USA vs France and the Netherlands vs Germany.

Perfect.

The night prior to the semifinal game I cannot sleep. It's not the competitive—I'm so hyped I can't rest—kind of thing. It's the ill-timed chronic, leg, spinal cord injury, pain thing that compounds and debilitates.

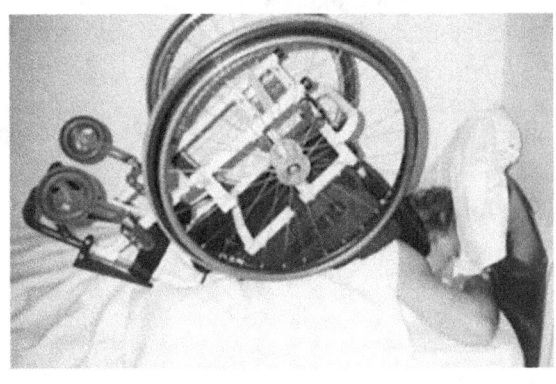

I'm writhing in pain. I do my best to suffer in silence but Coach Vines hears me from his room and our shared window. We meet in the dark of night. The team sleeps peacefully. He offers me a Darvocet. Coach takes pain medication for his gout. I'm tempted in every way to take anything to numb the pain of a thousand invisible men stabbing me repeatedly. There's a bigger picture. We play France the next day. *Thanks, but no thanks.* I decline the offer of his Darvocet. I agree to take possession of a Darvocet in case I'm in pain later.

We crush France 71-47. Sleep doesn't matter. This one is special. Gone is the stink of the 1990 World Championships and losing in the final moments. Gone is the ambush just prior to Barcelona with their rigged game and heavy dose of home cooking. Nothing motivates me more than big losses. The team flips the storyline. I cannot be happier.

After the semifinal, myself, Trooper, Tim Kazee, and Mike Schlappi are watching the Dutch play. We suspect we'll see them in the finals.

My wife, Sandy, brings me a batch of her homemade, oatmeal raisin cookies. My favorite. I'm glad to share my loot with the boys to a certain extent. The idea of her cookies tucked like a buried treasure in my corner of the room brings a smile. Trooper snatches the bag off my lap and starts to reach inside. My counter is to pull the bag away from him. Trooper, with his big mitt of a hand, slams me in the chest with an open palm. The slap to the chest takes my breath away. Without premeditation, I react with force and punch my friend, training partner, and fellow warrior straight in the face. I've just dotted the eye of my roommate. A reminder he's forced to wear the rest of the games.

We're both taken aback. This is not the time or place to elevate things.

Shocked and embarrassed, the only thing I can think to do is exit. I leave my teammates bug-eyed and speechless. Once beyond the venue, I sprint towards the beach and a skateboard park near the Mediterranean Sea.

What have I done?

Overwhelming shame.

Numbing remorse.

A jerk reaction.

I have no excuse.

Feeling ever alone, I eye the skateboarders. Their tricks are complicated. They fail more than they succeed. They stay at it until there are successes.

I face Harry and Trooper and apologize profusely. I face the team. They look at it more as comedy than conflict. Everyone is accepting and looking to move on.

The Dutch have just finished trouncing the Germans by 29 points. We'll be playing them in the gold medal game.

After the French semifinal we have a day off. I've just had one sleepless night and fear another one will send me reeling. So much of what I do is beyond the physical. Focus and visualization are key ingredients and difference makers in my performance.

Perhaps exhaustion, through sleep deprivation and the regret of punching my roommate in the face, will allow for some blessed shut-eye.

It does not.

The evening leg pains rears its ugly head again. I take the Darvocet. Darvocet is not listed on the banned list. Coach Vines has checked. It doesn't help at all. It's a low-grade medication that's only a touch stronger than aspirin. The leg pains sear through me. My left leg feels like it's meat on the grill. The nights are always the worst. The timing could not be worse.

These are the same leg pains that kept me out of the semifinals of the 1980 Paralympics in Arnhem, Holland. Not again. Never.

These are the same leg pains that I eventually deal with through surgery. The risky, twelve-hour procedure at Craig Hospital is life-changing and allows me to sleep through the night ever since.

I will play in the gold medal game.

We will win.

It's the gold medal match. The Dutch are led by Gertjan van der Linden and Koen Jansens. Two competitors that will do whatever it takes. The game lacks any kind of flow. We're rotating lineups routinely. It's hard to know when and where I fit in the rhythm of the game. I've hardly slept in three nights. In the fourth quarter, we finally get on one of our runs. We create some separation. The Dutch make a late run to get within 3-points. There's a tense moment or two, but the game is never in question.

Battle of Alphas. Going against Gertjan van der Linden.

297

We win one of the lowest scoring finals I've ever been involved with. I score a paltry five points. I could care less. The USA wins the gold medal, 39-36.

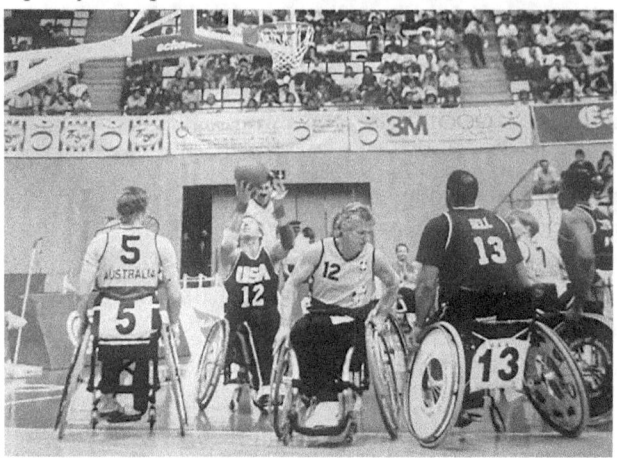

Reverse bucket against Aussies.

The bench rushes from the sidelines. There's a volcano of players and chairs atop one another. It's exactly like it should be when you're the best team in the world. I'm the captain of said best team in the world. Trooper and I hug. We both know. Everybody knows. We're at the top of the totem pole looking down at all of those wishing they could feel what we're feeling right now. I see Coach Vines. We hug with unabashed enthusiasm. We are Paralympic champions. We do it in front of a sold-out house. I find Sandy with my eyes. We connect. She gets me. I feel Curtis' big mitts on my shoulders. We're champions again. We did this just a few months back at the Final Four. I turn and hug him for all I'm worth. Then Jimbo and Schlappi. There's water on my head. No idea who the culprit is. I begin to gather myself. Straighten up. See things through a parallel plane again. The Dutch. They've had to sit and watch. Been there. Distressing. I find their coach first and then the team. I make my way to Gert. I offer my hand. The worthy opponent. Our grasp is sincere. We look each other in the eye. I stay calm. Respectful. I'm a tumbler of emotions. It's been two long years. I turn back to Team USA. Knowing where and why, I scream from my gut. My fists are clenched.

Golden moments. Jimbo-CB.

298

My eyes are lasered to the highest point of the arena. Another teammate grabs me and squeezes. I eye the boys. They look how I feel. We don't want the moment to end. The etiquettes of our game bring us back. Workers begin scurrying to arrange the medal ceremony. I think of my year. Winter Paralympic gold and now Summer Paralympic gold. This is exactly how it is supposed to be. The work to get here is so misunderstood by the rank and file.

Champions of the world. Little did I know it would turn into a fight of a lifetime.

Amongst the medal ceremony and continued celebrations, I am pulled for a random drug test. I am one of two USA players selected. The other is Mike Schlappi. Been here before. No worries. Minutes later we're reunited with the team.

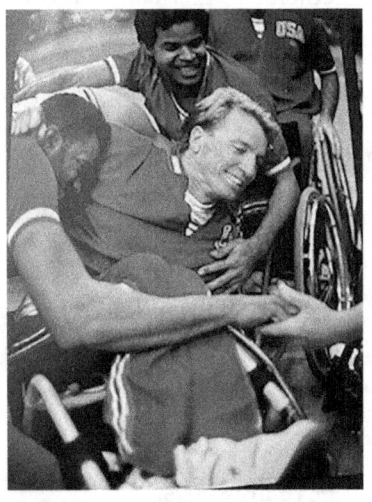

After the closing ceremonies, we board the airplane for home. I share some laughs with running partner, Randy Snow. He wins double gold in tennis—singles and doubles. Brad Parks is his doubles partner. Good friends enjoying tremendous success.

The Paralympic basketball tournament takes every day of the event to complete. It is an absolute test of mind, body, spirit, and soul. There's only one way to rise above complete exhaustion. Win the prize. Wear the gold medal. We do just that. It feels beyond my wildest expectations.

Word gets to the airlines that we're the gold medal bunch and we're moved to first class. We drink and party. The combination of our natural and alcohol-induced high resonates throughout. Once in the air, we're sitting atop arm rests, spinning tales of an undefeated tournament. We talk of our admiration and

299

basketball knowledge of the Spanish fans. Then we talk about home. Sharing our memorable journey with the ones we love. To see and share our experience with wives, girlfriends, family, kids, and friends; the valuable becoming more extraordinary with each passing minute and mile leading us closer to home.

About three hours into the flight, I see the co-pilot leaving the cockpit. He's coming our way. He engages with Angelo Nicosia or Fudge, our Assistant Coach. Fudge points at me. The pilot heads my way. Is this a joke?

Who gets a call from the cockpit?

It's Mike Mushett, USA assistant chef de mission on the line. The chef de mission oversees the logistics of the team during international competitions. He tells me I've tested positive for a banned substance and that there's talk of stripping the team of its gold medal.

"How can this be? Must be a mistake."

Mushett informs me they'll be opening the B sample soon to ensure their initial findings. Mike then says—I'll never forget this—"It doesn't look good."

In one instant, I'm a big-time winner. The captain of the ship. An all-time champion on the celebrated road to retirement. I love when a plan comes together. Another hand slaps my back. Without words I feel the adulation.

The next instant…

I'm a cheater.

A lowbrow scum.

It's difficult to find air for my lungs.

My heart pounds.

It wants to escape.

Dizzying.

Words singe my ears.

"They're talking of stripping USA of the gold medal."

"It doesn't look good."

I hear nothing else.

Words loop through me with cancer efficiency.

I eye my shoes.

They don't talk.

They don't question.

They wear the miles.

I force myself to raise my eyes.

Everyone looks younger.

Winning brings out the child within.

I'm back to my shoes.

Above all else

Avoid eye contact.

This is unknown territory. A nightmare playing out in real time. I motion to Fudge and ask him to get Harry. I'm unable to speak clearly. Words are mumbled incoherently. I motion towards Harry. Fudge connects the pieces of the puzzle.

Harry, and his square shouldered Arkansas frame, looms over me. I couldn't feel smaller.

"I didn't pass the drug test. Darvocet. Only hope is the B sample. When we land in New York, we'll know. If the B sample is negative, we're good."

I'm in tears. My shoulders are close to convulsions. Maybe they are. I don't know. The B sample is a 99 to 1 shot. I feel like I'm blindfolded and my fate hinges on making a full court shot.

Coach Vines loses his color. He sits down and gathers himself before heading back to his seat.

New York City is a couple hours away. The team will disembark. Each member, heading their own direction towards a desired and welcoming home town. I'm a man on loser island. I have no hometown or direction towards it. I'm sinking fast.

We hit New York. Mushett confirms the positive B sample on the telephone. He informs me the B sample tests positive for a small trace of Dextro-proxphene. Darvocet is a derivative of Dextro-proxphene. This is why Darvocet is not on the banned list. This is why Harry offers me his pill of relief.

What should I do?

Never more unsure of myself or my next move.

Fear and remorse engulf.

Am I responsible for the loss of my teammates' gold medal?

Take mine.

Not theirs.

Fury.

Rage.

Fear.

Gloom.

Isolation.

I find Trooper. I let him know. I have to. I avoid the rest of the boys.

I'm unable to avoid everyone. All the Casa boys are on the same flight to Los Angeles. I think I tell Curtis. I don't know. I'm slipping into a depressive darkness.

It happens fast.

The bottom awaits.

Home doesn't comfort me. Nothing does. It feels like I'm losing everything. My family suffers the most. I am inconsolable and broken-hearted. I am embarrassed and unable to face anyone. Work is supportive but I know I am putting my career to the test. All I can think to do is isolate myself. I stare at the walls like my life depends on it.

Before I can muster the strength to fight what turns into a three-year-plus battle, I wallow. I don't know how to navigate this one. I don't have the resolve to do much besides wake, hardly eat, and sleep. The people in my life I love the most, are the same ones I've disgraced.

After less than a week in Southern California, I get a call. It's Gert of the Dutch team. His call is a precursor of just how crazy things are about to become. There's a heaviness to the international conversation. He blurts it out.

"Is it true?" he asks. "Did you take cocaine before our gold medal match?"

I stay calm but inside I am on fire.

"Of course not," I answer. "Don't believe everything you hear."

I explain to Gert exactly what happened. In no way is the Darvocet taken to enhance my performance. I remind him I score a measly five points in the gold medal game. I inform Gert, I hadn't slept properly for three nights leading up to the final because of my leg pains. I let him know there is no intent.

I thank Gert for the call. Gert is a friend and respected rival. I ask him how he heard I tested positive. He's noncommittal but says there's a rumor spreading throughout his team.

I hang up the phone incensed. I'm snapped out of my doldrums. At this moment, I know I will fight this with everything I have. This cannot go down like this. I think of my teammates constantly. Brothers who deserve far better.

I'd do anything to not take the ineffective red, spiral-looking painkiller that night. I continue through the evening with a burning in my legs.

Pain relief indeed.

Twelve years prior, at the 1980 World Championships in Arnhem, Holland, I missed our semi-final game with severe leg pains. I'm admitted to the infirmary. The medical team does everything it can to slow down my nerve root pain. This includes various drugs. I compete in the final, floating in an induced fog. We lose the game. There's nothing about dealing with my leg pain that is performance enhancing.

On the other hand, I took the damn thing. An undeniable fact. I own that. I have to. Unaware of the cataclysmic fall from grace derived from that fateful 2:30 a.m. decision, I realize now, I must press on. I am not a cheat. I don't take shortcuts. Why? Because they don't work.

Appealing the result of the drug test is worthless.

Neither Harry nor I know Darvocet is a derivative of the banned Dextro-propoxyphene but the choice is made. We're paying the price. Another insult to injury, the United States Paralympic team is shown a film on its flight to Barcelona on the dos and don'ts of any potential drug testing in the games. The basketball boys are not on the flight. We miss the film as we're in France competing.

The key is to appeal the procedure.

Does the International Coordinating Committee of World Sports Organizations for the Disabled (ICC) keep my test result confidential? Do they allow me the opportunity and right to be present at the opening of my B sample? Does the ICC have proper personnel and coverage attending the gold medal match between USA and the Netherlands? The last event of the 1992 Paralympics. Does the ICC allow me a fair and proper due process?

I'm ready for the bureaucracy and multi-layered, multi-national agendas of the power players that govern our sporting landscape. Letterheads, titles, faxes, meeting minutes, and insincere endorsements of opposing viewpoints will be the upcoming norm.

American writer Mark Twain once said, "Few things are more irritating than when someone who is wrong is also very effective in making his point."

This is my immediate future.

I'm certain of this. If my rival, friend, and opponent (Gert) is leaked information on my failed drug test, I am about to fight a battle tilted heavily against me.

After our win, I'm randomly selected to be drug tested. I'm asked, "Have you taken anything in the last 36 to 40 hours?"

I answer, "No."

I'm thinking about celebrating with the boys. It's where I need to be. I piss in the cup like I've always done. My ever-improving aim hurries the process. I have no inkling or thought of the Darvocet. My mind is somewhere else completely. I, in fact, swallowed the Darvocet a little over 40 hours ago. Doesn't register. Maybe it's because the pill offers no relief whatsoever, or more likely, it's the fact my teammates are whooping it up without me, but the thought to mention the Darvocet does not figure into my celebratory mindset.

I leave the sterility of the drug test staging as quickly as possible. Everything I love is beyond these walls. What I cherish is out there. Sadly, this will play against me.

THE FIGHT

When you feel like quitting, remember why you started.

— Unknown

On **September 13ᵗʰ, 1992,** my world transforms.

I am now a man on a mission to save his teammates' medals whilst desperately trying to save my name and reputation. I am about to take on a litany of miscues, oversights, breaches of confidentiality, and personal animosities in the name of making a profound, albeit unfair, statement against me and the gold medal winning, USA Wheelchair Basketball Team of the 1992 Barcelona Paralympics.

On **September 15ᵗʰ, 1992,** the B sample of my drug test is opened. The test is positive for trace amounts of Dextro-propoxyphene. I am not given the opportunity to be present for the opening of the B sample.

The International Olympic Charter Against Doping in Sport Handbook: Procedures during testing and analysis, states:

Section 4.2.4   The athlete or his/her N.G.B. (National Governing Body) has the right to explain his or her case and can insist that the second sample (sample B) is analysed within 21 days. If the athlete admits his/her offence, disciplinary procedures may be taken on the basis of the A-sample.

Section 4.2.5   The athlete has the right to be present or be represented during the analysis of the B sample.

I'm not given any option to explain my side of things or be present for the opening of the B sample. These are two fundamental rights clearly explained in the IOC doping handbook. In 1992 there is no Paralympic Anti-Doping Handbook. There is no International Paralympic Committee or IPC. It's not until after the 1992 Barcelona Paralympic Games that the IPC is officially empowered and put in place. The ICC is disbanded in favor of the IPC after Barcelona. This muddies the waters considerably.

I'm caught in the perfect storm of political regime change. It's clear to me the exiting powers at the ICC want me off their docket as quickly as possible whilst the impending powers at the IPC want to move forward with an agenda that ensures a mess like mine never takes place again.

These days the IPC doles out a 116-page Anti-Doping Code Handbook for Paralympic athletes. United States Paralympic athletes are all required to work with the United States Anti-Doping Agency (USADA). The USADA is responsible for educating all Olympic and Paralympic athletes. Today, athletes are required to let USADA know of their whereabouts so they can be randomly tested. Today's athletes are informed.

In 1992 we are shown a short movie on an airplane we aren't even travelling on.

On **September 17th, 1992,** a report is written from the ICC Medical Commission Doping Committee and the desk of Canadian Michael Riding, MD.

Through my years of trying to protect my teammates' gold medals and clear my name, I save all correspondence, faxes, memos, and minutes of meetings pertaining to my case.

In his report, he states:

"The difficulty with sleeping was caused by nerve root pain exacerbated by a playing injury...Insofar as the drug was taken to treat a sports injury, the outcome of the game may have been affected."

This couldn't be farther from the truth. Yes, I have a swollen left foot. Mostly, my big toe, if I remember right, but in no way did the Darvocet have anything to do with that injury. I am unable to feel my feet. Nothing is *'exacerbated'* at all by an injury. I play dozens of games throughout my career with banged up feet. My leg pains alone are why I take—what my coach and I think—is an agreed-upon painkiller.

Riding continues, *"One of the primary reasons for the doping control is the protection of a competitor's health and thus overall, this is a serious situation, in that this drug was taken without reference to the team medical staff."*

This, I own. We made a poor decision in the middle of the night to alleviate immense pain, and I'm willing to accept a just sanction or penalty. In no way, though, should the team lose their medals and gold medal standing. Again, this did not enhance my performance in any way.

I resent the fact I'm not allowed to tell my part of the story in Barcelona as per my right in Section 4.2.4. of the aforementioned IOC handbook.

I come to find out that the majority of the ICC brass leave the Barcelona Games prior to the basketball finals. Riding is an isolated ICC delegate left on duty whilst his fellow delegates are either resting or on flights.

Riding summarizes, *"We recommend:*

1) That the USA Team forfeit the match.

2) That Dave Kiley forfeits any medal.

3) That David Kiley be suspended from all competition for six months by the IWBF."

Due process be damned.

On **September 20th, 1992,** a memo is written from Sir Philip Craven to ICC President, Senor Guillermo Cabezas. Craven is the IWBF president and ICC Technical Delegate to the Barcelona Paralympic Basketball Tournaments.

Craven's memo states:

"Since I learnt of Kiley's positive test by rumor from my wife when she returned from Barcelona in the afternoon of 16th September, I have investigated the facts surrounding this case and must state that I am most concerned about the manner in which the disclosure was made to the world's press on 15th September. After which time it took three days for a formal communication to be made to either yourself or myself. There was a total breakdown in security and in the ability to communicate amongst the persons left in Barcelona once the announcement had been made by Michael Riding."

Craven continues, *"Though persons within COOB'92 (Committee Organization of Barcelona) did not communicate with either yourself or myself an individual within the COOB'92 organisation did find the time of 16th September to fax a Dutch player a copy of an internal, handwritten memorandum form announcing in Catalan (a Spanish language) the positive doping test of David Kiley."*

I feel like a man unjustly arrested and then not read my protected Miranda rights. To this day, rereading these memos and faxes heightens my anxiety and tests my resolve that a decision was made once they saw my name and what country I'm from. Is this true? I will never truly know but I know how it feels. It feels unjust, hurried, and lacking any checks and balances. Drug testing for Paralympic sport is in its infant stages. What better way to plant your flag? What better way to mask policy mistakes than to take down a top scalp like mine. A winter and summer, gold medal champion.

Sir Philip Craven, a Brit from no-nonsense Northern England, is my most powerful and greatest ally. At the 1973 Wheelchair Basketball World Championships, Craven was a strong player on Great Britain's Gold Medal-winning team. Sir Philip competes in five Paralympic Games for his country between the years 1972 and 1988.

Craven is a one-man treasure-trove of accomplishments and leadership roles. In 2005, he is knighted by Queen Elizabeth for his services in Paralympic Sport. He serves as President of the International Paralympic Committee from 2001 to 2017. He's a Board Member for the Organizing Committee for the 2012 London Olympic and Paralympic Games.

Sir Philip Craven serves as Foundation Board member for the World Anti-Doping Agency (WADA). During his time with WADA, and as President of the IPC, he bans the Russian Paralympic Team saying Russia has "catastrophically failed its para-athletes, and their medals-over-morals mentality disgusts me." Russian Paralympic athletes do not compete in the 2016 Rio Paralympics. This draws considerable ire from Russia's president, Vladimir Putin.

In his memo to ICC President Cabezas, he concludes:

"I am convinced that the outcome of the competition was in no way affected by this temporary lapse of mind on the part of David Kiley when all he wished for was to have a decent night's sleep. I, therefore, strongly recommend to yourself and the ICC Executive Committee to <u>not</u> disqualify the

*USA team and confirm them as Men's Paralympic Champions, but to sanction
the two individuals who performed irresponsibly relative to the ICC Doping
Regulations."*

After my conversation with Gert and his absurd claim of cocaine use, I am
convinced I need to fight this with all I have. It feels like I'm scaling Guadalupe
Peak again except instead of verticality, loose rocks, and narrow trails to
combat, I'm climbing over bureaucrats, back-room secrets, and untested/infancy
policies. Either way, I trudge forward an inch at a time.

I practically ignore Sandy and the kids. Justin is 14 and Danielle is 10.
They need me. I should be loving them with all I'm worth. Instead, I hide my
tears and send another fax to teammates, Coach Vines, the NWBA, the ICC, or
the IPC. I'm reeling, playing out one possibility after another. My mind runs
through so many scenarios. I'm losing a handle on reality.

Quickie leaves me off its poster of Barcelona, gold medal winners. This
breaks me. Kills me. My chair sponsor thinks I'm a cheater. More hidden tears.
Then anger. The need to battle.

September 24th, 1992: nine days after my B sample is opened, whilst
travelling home from Barcelona, minus any option to be present for the B
sample opening, ICC Secretary General, Joan Scruton sends a letter to half-a-
dozen presidents of organizations associated with the Paralympic Games. She
writes:

*"The ICC must now make an urgent decision with regard to withdrawal and
reallocation of the Paralympic Medals and recommendations for sanctions...
according to the ICC handbook regulations."*

My teammates and I are being steamrolled. There is no due process.
Worse yet, the ICC does not have the prudence to have a process in place.
Unimaginable.

September 26th, 1992, Philip Craven sends a memo to acting ICC President
Jack Weinstein. In it he writes:

*"The rules state that the athlete has the right to be present at the
meeting where the positive test is announced to the athlete and the national
team manager/chef de mission. The ICC had no laid down guidelines for
the Chairman of its Doping Committee to follow with regard to how an
announcement should be handled if a positive test was suspected after the last
event of the Paralympic Games.*

*This situation was exacerbated when no ICC Executive members remained in
Barcelona at the time that Michael Riding chose to make his announcement. In
my opinion the announcement was hurried and Michael Riding felt isolated and
had to take Executive decisions without consultation with the ICC President.*

*Even more importantly he made a fundamental error in disclosing to Mike
Mushett the proposed sanctions that his committee would be recommending.
This was totally out of order as the proposed sanctions should have been kept
strictly confidential within the ICC until ratification or amendment had been
made.*

The effect of announcing the sanctions was two-fold:

The world of wheelchair basketball and the world's press became aware of the probable sanctions six days before the ICC President received Michael Riding's report.

Dr. Riding in announcing the sanctions and stating that there was no right of appeal gave the impression to the US Team that the decision was a 'fait accompli' (leaving someone with no option but to accept it) and that a defense, where the true facts would be known, would serve no purpose.

I, therefore, put it to you that only owing to Michael Riding's actions are we now in a situation where you can say that the facts and the need to implement the ICC rules are two completely separate matters.

The facts should have been fully investigated prior to a positive announcement being made."

It's ever-apparent to me the ICC (soon to be the IPC) lack the sophistication and proven protocols to successfully and fairly implement a transparent anti-doping program. My positive test is announced far too early in the process. The ICC is its own judge and jury. Life-altering decisions are made within phone calls, faxes, memos, and private conversations. The rules are scant to say the least. It's not until after my failed drug test that a standard appeals process is put in place along with a Therapeutic Use Exemption for medications.

Therapeutic Use Exemption (TUE) allows athletes with medical conditions or illnesses to confidentially take medications that may be on the World Anti-Doping Agency (WADA) banned list.

WADA states, *"Before taking any medication, an athlete must check the status of the medication on the list or with their Anti-Doping Organization (ADO). If the substance is prohibited, the athlete will need to apply for a TUE.*

The purpose of the International Standard for Therapeutic Use Exemptions (ISTUE) is to ensure that the process of granting TUEs is harmonized across sports and countries."

There are checklists, forms, and physician guidelines to abide by, but it's good to see common sense dictate the health and well-being of the greatest athletes in the world.

This is the most dramatic and meaningful outcome of the 1992 Paralympic doping debacle. This event in history is the reason the landscape of anti-doping and its list of banned substances take into account the overall health—not only of Paralympic athletes but all athletes—with a Therapeutic Use Exemption.

Wheelchair basketball begins as a method of rehabilitation after soldiers return home from World War II. Trailblazers across the globe begin shifting the narrative in the 60s and 70s through performance and increased organization of the sport through national governing bodies. The 1988 Paralympic Games in Seoul, South Korea, legitimize disability sport—and wheelchair basketball—as the Paralympic Games mirror the Olympics with shared athlete villages and sporting venues. There's limited drug testing. I cannot remember myself or any of my teammates being tested in Seoul.

In Barcelona, testing is accelerated but without consideration of disability, pain-treatment issues, or a formal appeal process for the inevitable back-and-forth needed to arbitrate a just ruling. Mistakes are made. This is a natural outcome when taking on such a massive and widespread undertaking.

Problem is, no one wants to own up to any blunders or slip-ups.

There is certainly a lack of cherished common sense.

Gertjan van der Linden, of the Dutch team, remembers three decades after our gold medal clash, "The day after the final, we already heard rumors that the USA had used doping. I know Dave never consciously used doping, and in disabled sports, we often used pain relievers that we needed for the pain we experience."

Gert goes on, "I told everyone that I won silver and received gold. Additionally, I shared the story of how this came to be. It's a rule, and we can all have our opinions about it, but for our sport, it was a dark chapter."

On **October 13th, 1992,** a letter is written from the desk of ICC Secretary General Joan Scruton to IWBF President Philip Craven. She responds to Craven's request for clarification on the appeal process. Scruton writes:

"I know of no appeal procedure against the ICC Handbook rulings. With regard to consideration of any sanction relating to the future, as you know the matter has been referred to the IPC, who will control future Paralympic Games."

The following is directly from the current, IPC Anti-Doping Handbook:

8.1.2 The Independent Tribunal will be Operationally Independent, and will conduct its hearings fairly and impartially and **without interference from the IPC or any third party**, in accordance with the Procedural Rules and in full compliance with the World Anti-Doping Code and the International Standard for Results Management.

8.1.3 Hearings held in connection with a Games shall be scheduled and completed within a reasonable time. They may be conducted by an expedited process where permitted by the Independent Tribunal.

Things, thank God, have changed. Hard and true rules are in place. There's the decency of checks and balances, an accepted appeals process is in place, and the agendas of power brokers are far closer to being eliminated. Raw deals are exceptions and not the norm.

The gut punch of Barcelona and the gold medal match will never subside. Making history is not for the meek.

On **December 3rd, 1992,** a letter is written from the desk of Paul DePace, Chef de Mission of the U.S. Disabled Sports team, to Joan Scruton, Secretary General of the ICC, and Philip Craven, President of the IWBF. The letter is titled, "APPEAL—DAVID KILEY DOPING INFRINGEMENT." DePace writes:

"Dave Kiley and the U.S. Men's basketball Team were denied their fundamental rights as Paralympic athletes to due process and equal protection by not being afforded an opportunity or venue to present testimony (particularly, testimony of Mr. Kiley) and all relevant explanations to the ICC or other appropriate bodies prior to the imposition of penalties against both Mr. Kiley and the U.S. Team. Furthermore, the processes to be followed and adhered to in connection with a Paralympic Games doping infringement (particularly following the conclusion thereof) were (and remain) unclear and confusing, and such lack of clarity and confusion have produced an unfair, uninformed and inappropriate result; Expert professional medical opinions and pharmacological information contradict the claim that the medication was performance-enhancing and reflect that the medication taken by Mr. Kiley had no impact whatsoever on the Gold Medal match.

The USDST respectfully requests a hearing before the ICC in connection with this appeal.

As a final concern, it is our understanding that the ICC is scheduled to disband within six months of the Paralympic Games. We further understand that there exist no provisions for the transfer of jurisdiction on issues related to the final dispensation of medals related to the 1992 Paralympic Games."

The defunct ICC and burgeoning IPC conduct a meeting on **March 24th and 25th, 1993,** on the island of Cyprus. The meeting is held on request of the United States Disabled Sports Team (USDST). I have to be there. I must be heard. Gold medals are at stake. I'm consumed by what I've done. I'm consumed by what's being done to me and my teammates. One second, I'm beating myself up. The constant question of, *why?* Why couldn't I have ridden that night out? Why does the consumption of one, non-performance enhancing tablet, have me booking a flight to the middle east—on my own dime? The next instant, I am infuriated by the administrators and bureaucrats that want to wash their hands of my fight to keep what we've earned.

It's a dirty game that devours the next three-plus years of my life.

Enter, Dr. Bob Steadward.

Steadward is the initial IPC President. A Canadian from Saskatchewan, Steadward serves as IPC President until 2001. He is then, oddly enough, followed by Sir Philip Craven who serves as IPC President until 2017. The two have varying degrees of opinion, and it's safe to say, rarely see, eye-to-eye.

The flight to Cyprus is long and arduous. I play through hundreds of scenarios. Visualization strategies, used since childhood, escape me. The proverbial light, that drives the journey, is dark and black as night. Unafraid to fight the power, I lack the relentless visual picture of success. In sport, I lean heavily on seeing where I need to improve, what I'll do to get there, and the awaiting glorious result. Am I out of my realm or are the cards that stacked up against me?

Before the plane touches down in Cyprus, two deep-seated thoughts rebound through my input-overloaded mindset. A conversation with a lawyer in Los Angeles. He looks at me for a beat, looks at his shoes and then says, "Your chances are slim to none in this matter without any precedence to help guide your argument."

My second, deep/dark thought, *Don't fall asleep. Next stop for this airplane is Teheran.* I've since come to learn, through sport, that Iran is full of gracious/caring people.

It's a short night in the hotel. Exhaustion, jetlag, and emotional anxiety are the perfect cocktail for the insomniac in me. I practice my speech in front of the mirror, on the veranda, and staring at the ceiling. I make eye contact with invisible listeners and imagine an audience so swayed and moved they visibly alter their thinking process.

It's my turn. I know I must keep a lid on my anger. Earlier in the process, Steadward makes clear to all in our contingent that today's proceedings are in no way an appeal but instead a hearing.

A real doubt of doom lands. Their minds are made up. This is not about fairness or due process. This is about politics and risk management. This is about future agendas and policies. This is a coverup of mistakes made in process, athletes rights, and breaches of confidentiality.

I carry on, "You seem to not want to hear it but I will say it anyway. Zero intent. If you are intent on making an example, then use me. My teammates do not deserve to have their medals taken."

This is where I scan the room and look to connect with one person. Is there one person within the upstart International Paralympic Committee willing to look me in the eye and take on what I am saying?

I read the room: flat, expressionless, lifeless faces more interested in what's for lunch than the plight of my teammates or myself. I have nothing to lose. Here goes, "None of you have ever won a gold medal. I'm unsure of your sporting background at all."

I take a second. The comment has no effect. Steadward is scribbling notes.

"But I know for sure you don't know what it's like to win a gold medal and have it taken away."

After I say my piece, I, and the small USA delegation, are asked to leave the proceedings. IWBF President Philip Craven is next on the docket. One thing for sure, nothing about the Cyprus meeting is transparent and authentic.

Craven speaks to the disproportionate punishment to the offense committed. It's too severe. It's made within an array of personal and policy miscues that disallow a fair and proper due process. Craven is then asked to leave the meeting.

I find this move toxic. I get having the Americans out of the room. We're invested. We have much to win and lose. Why Philip? Should he not be in the room—even if he disagrees and is the lone opposing voice? Should the President of the IWBF not be able to see the proceedings, operation, and decision-making protocols of the IPC? These are the initial steps in a decades-long relationship that should be tendered through trust and honesty.

On the plane ride home, Philip and his lovely wife, Jocelyne, are across the aisle from me. He's with his partner. His trusted ear and rebound of warmth. Where's Sandy? What does she really think of all this? I know less with each passing day. I adjust my thinking. It didn't go well here. No one asked me a single question in the four-cornered room of decisions.

In Philip and Jocelyne, I feel empathy and see the brutality of truth. A truth without trust or honor isn't a truth, but instead a travesty of power. Philip knows, far greater than I, that my fate is indeed *fait accompli.*

I am unable to see this. I am a fighter. Give me a puncher's chance. My teammates' gold medals depend on my influencing the fair-mindedness of partisan overseers. I have entered into their world. I am a Stranger in a Strange Land.

I feel doom.

Surrounded and encompassed.

Cyprus is a bust.

I look over at the Cravens.

Tears flow down my cheeks.

I return home to Southern California. I am able to garner the minutes of the ICC/IPC meeting. I am only in the room for a portion on the second day of the proceedings.

It begins simply enough:

"The President stated that it was important the matter be discussed as fully as possible before asking the US Disabled Sports Team to present their case. The Coach of the basketball team, who was very much involved, had been asked to be present; as this was not possible, a deposition had been signed by him."

Next paragraph in the minutes of the Cyprus meeting, *"Bob Steadward expressed concern about allowing such an appeal against sanctions imposed by the ICC for a doping offence; this could set a dangerous precedent for the IPC. The Committee should ratify the decision of the President pro-tem at the time."*

It was moved by Jens Bromann, seconded by Bob Steadward

that this Committee ratify the decision taken in Barcelona.

The words on the page stick to memory upon the first read. The day previous, with myself entering into and pleading my case, this group, a committee representing integrity and fairness in elite disability sport, has already ratified "the decision taken in Barcelona."

I am a stooge before a kangaroo court. Steadward, in his role as IPC President will make sure—time and again—the charade of a fair and level playing field but really the ground is tilted. My teammates and I don't stand a chance. Cyprus and the thousands of miles travelled, at a staggering cost, are the beginning of a Steadward-led, cavalcade of egregious acts and statements of self-interest and acts unbecoming to his position and title.

After presenting my case, and after IWBF President Philip Craven is asked to leave the room, the meeting carries on, "This meeting formally accepts the decision of the ICC Doping Committee that Dave Kiley tested positive for the banned substance.

CARRIED UNANIMOUSLY

AGREED ACTION TO BE TAKEN:

The USDST be asked to return the gold medals. With regard to reallocation of the medals, a letter be sent to the 3 countries concerned—The Netherlands, Germany, and France.

"I have no proof," says Craven. "But I am sure their decision was ratified before arriving in Cyprus."

Unbelievable.

I am cooked. I just don't know it yet.

The next three years are a professional and personal struggle like no other. My sanctuary of home and family is crumbling. My forever strength, built through a shared experience of love and trust, feels more foreign than I've ever known. I can't seem to get out of my own way. Am I my father? His oldest son, self-absorbed in misery and destructive acts. Folks seem to enjoy labelling me a cheater. The same Wheel Head brothers and sisters I've represented internationally for decades are writing into *Sports 'N Spokes* magazine raking me over the coals. My most brazen rivals call me a cheater to my face. I isolate myself. I stare at picket fences. I count how many bricks it takes to build a wall. I make bad decisions. I love Sandy and the kids completely. Still, I build walls instead of bridges.

My coach in Barcelona, Harry Vines, is living within his own inferno of loathing and doubt. Harry has since passed away, but in talking with his wife Cheryl Vines, she remembers the years after Barcelona as "the toughest years of our marriage."

Harry, never a favorite son of the NWBA leadership, receives a four-year ban from international competition. The gutless move from our national governing body isn't a surprise. Harry never minces words and the NWBA's Commissioner, Stan Labanowich, is often at the receiving end of Harry's truths and barbed opinions throughout their years of delegate meetings. Labanowich is running buddies with the IPC brass. The harsh penalty against Coach Vines is the NWBA's way of proving to its IPC bedfellows that they'd rather support the leadership of the IPC than its own.

It's no surprise when I am banned from international competition for two years by the NWBA. My penance to be paid. More ammunition for those wanting to kick me whilst I'm down. I maintain a steely exterior. I show an outward strength. Those wanting to watch me crumble before their eyes, with often cryptic, sometimes pointed remarks, are met with resilience, grit, and a personal stamina that gives no quarter.

I continue to find my blessings on the court. The thousands of hours between her lines offer a busy calm amongst the madness and toil of keeping our gold medals. During this time, Harry (resigned to the fact he will never coach internationally again) and his Razorbacks take their frustrations out on all comers. They play angry when they hit the floor and leave little doubt. With a strong cast, all in their prime, the Arkansas Rollin' Razorbacks and Head Coach Harry Vines capture two NWBA championships during this run.

The pettiness doesn't subside. The NWBA fails to invite Harry to coach at its PVA/NWBA summer camps. The Paralyzed Veterans Association camps are a seasonal mainstay. The exclusion of Harry Vines, a future NWBA Hall of Fame member, is distasteful and repugnant.

Cheryl Vines has vivid memories of Harry taking a call from Curtis Bell's wife, Julie. She lays into him good and, with increased volume, demands, "How can you and Dave let this happen to Curtis and the team?"

It all feels upside down. I'm not the only one teetering on the brink.

FAX MACHINES

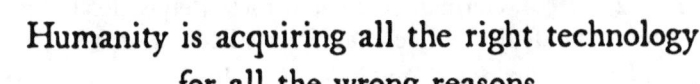

Humanity is acquiring all the right technology
for all the wrong reasons.

— R. Buckminster Fuller

I begin to live through the lifeline of fax machines. Rendered to become obsolete once the internet and emails splash on the scene, the annoying screech of an incoming fax keeps hope alive. The next fax is a reminder of just how dire the situation is.

Early **January 1994** begins the request to give back our gold medals. From the desk of Joan Scruton on **ICC** letterhead to Chef de mission Daul DePace:

"I refer to your letter to me on the 25th of August 1993, further to the ICC request for the gold medals in the possession of the US Basketball to be returned in order that they could be reallocated to the Dutch Basketball team who were declared the winning team following the disqualification of the US team for doping infringement."

On **January 12th, 1994**, Stan Labanowich writes to IPC President Robert Steadward:

"The NWBA has had no success in retrieving the medals from the players involved in the 1992 national team. The Executive Committee had earlier directed that they be delivered to this Office by November 1, 1993. To date, none have been received.

I feel we have done everything possible to gain retrieval of the medals. Please let me know what the IPC's stance is on this issue so that we may understand and pursue the matter further."

The last paragraph is the first evidence that our Commissioner, Stan Labanowich, is playing a dicey political game of staying in good standing with the IPC whilst still finding a positive outcome for his United States basketball squad. There are multiple references in these memos of shared phone conversations between Steadward and Labanowich. There is a saying in a program I am closely associated with these days, *"You're only as sick as your secrets."* I greatly suspect Stan and Bob share a couple.

January 24th, 1994, Robert Steadward to Stan Labanowich on the return of the gold medals

"There are many decisions that the IPC Executive could make, one of which could be suspension of the USA basketball team from participating in the 1996

Paralympics in Atlanta, a decision which in my mind would be disastrous.

I cannot understand why the players refuse to return the medals. They are meaningless to them and the situation only creates an embarrassment between the USA and the other teams involved."

What Steadward refers to as *meaningless* is instead priceless.

On **February 2nd, 1994,** German delegate Mr. Hartleb writes to the International Stoke Mandeville Wheelchair Sports Federation (ISMWSF):

"Coming back to our fax dated September 14th, 1992 and November 5th, 1993. We kindly ask what has happened concerning the substitution of the medals of the basketball teams taking part in Paralympics, 1992 in Barcelona.

Our team has been waiting more than a year to receive the silver medals."

With the bygone ICC and Steadward serving as their own judge and jury per the ICC rules of the Barcelona games, the next strategy is to go before the Court of Arbitration for Sports (CAS). The third-party entity, created in 1984, arbitrates disputed decisions for the Olympic Games.

From the CAS website, "The CAS has the task of resolving legal disputes in the field of sport through arbitration. It does this [by] pronouncing arbitral awards that have the same enforceability as judgements of ordinary courts.

It can also help parties solve their disputes on an amicable basis through mediation, **when the procedure is allowed.**"

Written on iconic USA Basketball letterhead on **February 7th, 1994,** from Warren Brown/USA Basketball to Marvin Lapicola, Chair Committee Wheelchair Basketball, BCC: David Kiley:

"USOC (United States Olympic Committee) legal counsel, has forwarded the attached information concerning CAS. Please contact me to advise whether the NWBA will apply to CAS for consideration of this dispute.

The USOC would consider lending its support to the NWBA's petition in this manner."

February 22nd, 1994, in a letter from Philip Craven to Stan Labanowich:

"The IWBF has always wanted a just outcome. However, as the German Federation has formally approached the IWBF stating that enough time has passed and that the medals must be reallocated, note must be taken of the best interests of all our member nations.

Therefore, I have to lay down the following conditions:

It is the responsibility of the NWBA to lodge the appeal with the IOC Court of Arbitration for Sport in Lausanne, Switzerland.

Should the NWBA secure the support of USA Basketball and/or USOC written proof of this support is required by 31st March 1994.

Written proof by the 21st March is required from the IOC Court of Arbitration for Sport that this type of appeal can be heard by them and that they would hear the appeal with or without representation of the ICC/IPC.

That a firm date is established for the appeal and is made known in writing to the IWBF.

All twelve gold medals are returned to the IWBF Secretariat Office by the 21st March 1994, so that dependent on the previous four conditions in this letter being met by the NWBA, they will remain in the IWBF bank vault until the outcome of the final appeal is known.

The result of the appeal from Lausanne would be final with no further possibility for comment on later.

I hope you view this letter as a document which represents the best interests of both the USA and the other countries of the IWBF involved in this long-standing medal issue."

Labanowich responds to Craven on **February 25th, 1994:**

"We hope to have all twelve gold medals by that date. You must understand, though, that the promises made to the players in our effort to retrieve them was that we would maintain the medals in the NWBA bank vault in Lexington, KY, where they would remain until the matter has been settled."

From Philip Craven to Labanowich on **February 25th, 1994:**

"I fully understand your comments regarding the promise you made to the players as to where the gold medals would be deposited until the matter is settled.

However, in making my decision that the medals should be deposited in the IWBF bank vault, I had to take into account the views of the other nations that could be affected by the final outcome of the issue."

On **March 17th, 1994,** from Warren Brown/USA Basketball to NWBA Commissioner, Stan Labanowich. Warren Brown is arguably the most powerful basketball personality in the world, He writes:

"It seems apparent from this information that David Kiley and the United States Men's Basketball Team were not afforded, in fact denied, commonly established and universally accepted fundamental rights to be heard, further, that although on the banned list the medication taken by Mr. Kiley as a practical matter apparently played no role in enhancing or even positively affecting his performance in the gold medal game, further, that the penalties were arbitrary, capricious and inconsistent, and imposed by the ICC without following its own established procedures; finally, that the penalties imposed were too severe in light of the circumstances, which if properly heard initially undoubtedly would have mitigated the result you now must appeal."

From the desk of Stan Labanowich to Robert Steadward on **March 18th 1994:**

"This letter is submitted to formally request that the IPC enter an arbitration agreement with the USDST and the NWBA pursuant to which the IPC will agree to have the resolution of the matter arbitrated before and resolved by the CAS in Lausanne, Switzerland."

On **March 25th, 1994,** from Ronald Rowan/General Counsel USOC to Stan Labanowich:

"This is to inform you that the United States Olympic Committee supports arbitration before CAS to resolve the dispute regarding the status of the USDST gold medal award."

On **March 25th, 1994,** from Labanowich to Craven:

"We have been assigned case number CAS94-102, and have been asked to submit, in addition to the materials already submitted, relevant documents related to the case. We have begun that process and will have all information in the hands of CAS before the end of the week."

On **March 25th, 1994,** IPC Secretary General Andre Raes writes to Mrs. Jan Wilson/USOC Disabled Sports Services:

"The issue, being put on the agenda of the latest IPC Executive Committee Meeting in Lillehammer March 1994, has been discussed and the following decision has been taken: 'All members of the USA Wheelchair Basketball team, participating in the Barcelona Summer Paralympics, are excluded from all IPC Official Competitions, including the 1996 Summer Paralympics in Atlanta and further Paralympics until the medals have been returned to the IPC secretariat.'"

This is the first explosive shot across the proverbial bow. It's a shockwave to any player looking to have another shot at gold. The threat is steadfast, bold, and resolute in its transparency. Is this a change of direction in the IPC's course of action? I wonder.

On **March 28th, 1994,** Robert Steadward/IPC President writes to Stan Labanowich:

"From our last telephone conversation on or about March 23, 1994, you indicated that you have collected all of the gold medals from the USA basketball team that they received in Barcelona at the 1992 Summer Paralympic Games. I would appreciate it very much if you could return those medals to Andre Raes at the IPC Secretariat so they can be redistributed to the Netherlands.

"At this time, I am not prepared to commit the IPC to an arbitration agreement. Our rules and the rules of the former ICC are very specific regarding positive tests in doping. There is no appeal on a positive test and sanctions are imposed according to our regulations, policies and by-laws. As well, the ICC was responsible for the 1992 Summer Paralympic Games and not the IPC. The IPC is responsible only for executing any doping sanctions. The ICC also permitted a hearing from the USA basketball player in question as well as the USA team doctor and chef de mission of the Barcelona Games. The original decision of the ICC was upheld. Therefore, we believe that the case is closed."

The International Olympic Charter against Doping in Sport (Annex 7, Guidelines for sanctions and penalties) states in part:

"It is possible for a competitor to take a preparation without knowing that it contains one or several substances of a banned class, since in many countries the composition of some pharmaceutical preparations may not be listed on the label. Thus, a certain flexibility is necessary regarding the decisions that a governing body may wish to take when a laboratory reports on a banned substance of this type."

Meet South African, Leon Labushagne. Labushagne wins a gold medal in the discus-throw in the 1992 Barcelona Paralympic Games. He goes on to win gold again at the 1996 Atlanta Paralympic Games.

Leon tests positive for three banned substances in Barcelona, none of which are performance enhancing.

Poor guy, the ICC are going to rake him over the coals good. Three banned substances. He might get a lifetime ban.

The doping committee's **September 10th, 1992,** proposal to the ICC states:

"After long discussions and considering that doping control is for the protection of athletes, and to ensure fair competition, we consider it unfair to punish the innocent athlete for the blatant incompetence of the South African Federation.

Therefore, we formally censure the South African Federation for its failure to observe the ICC doping rules. The athlete, Mr. Labushagne was withdrawn from further competition but will be allowed to keep his medal."

Again, from the minutes of the ICC Executive Committee on **September 10th, 1992:**

"Asked why the decision was taken for the athlete to keep his medal and yet was banned from further participation in the Games when it was not his fault.

Dr. Riding said it was a matter of legality. Once the athlete knew these drugs were banned, he withdrew from competition. Once the situation was clear the appropriate action happened. There was no performance enhancement and to withdraw the medal would not be fair. It may not be a logical decision but we certainly thought it was fair."

Is it fair to take a team's gold medals within the same non-performance enhancing ruling? There is obviously flexibility for Leon but none for myself or teammates.

My positive test is more benign than Labushagne's in that my test only shows trace findings of the banned substance. The finding of this valuable information solidifies what I know to be true. There is now precedence to file in a brief and send to the Court of Arbitration for Sport (CAS).

We can compare the ICC's **September 10th, 1992,** minutes of Michael Riding to Riding's written report submitted to the ICC on **September 17, 1992**. In reference to my failed drug test, Riding states:

"There is no point in performing doping tests if we are to disregard the results. Although quantitatively there is not a high concentration of propoxyphene metabolites in the urine, qualitatively, the drug is undoubtedly present and it is on the banned list. It is therefore, in every way, a positive test.

The medal-withdrawal must be done by the ICC President. Therefore, we propose to submit our recommendations to IWBF for ratification prior to submission to the ICC."

What's good for one is certainly not good for the other, especially if the other is Dave Kiley and the United States Wheelchair Basketball gold medal-winning team.

Sir Philip Craven, the guy that creates the IWBF and serves on the board of the World Anti-Doping Agency, recently put it this way, "David Kiley is one of the greatest five basketball players of all time. The sport speaks its mind. If they disagree, they'll tell you. With the IWBF, the sport declared itself independent. This was not an anti-doping offence. They have Dave because of their rules and lack of process, but they're not against DK. They're against wheelchair basketball."

Late in 1994, there's a front-page story in the *Los Angeles Times,* with the headline, "Athlete's Quest for Lost Gold." The story, by Elliott Almond, begins:

"David Kiley awoke in pain.

Stabbing, gripping, tormenting pain.

What he did next changed his life as the world's greatest wheelchair basketball player."

Pre-internet, the Sunday, December 4th, 1994, edition of the *LA Times* has a daily circulation of 1,104,651 and a Sunday circulation of 1,502,120. The *Sunday Final, Column One* feature piece sits opposite the headline, "Serbs Break Vow, Won't Free Captives."

Elliott's story is over 65 column inches and serves as an in depth look into the chances of reclaiming our gold medals.

Elliott introduces a key player in the saga of retrieving what is ours—Anardo Valdez.

"For disabled athletes like Kiley, the issue has added complications because their physical conditions might require medications that the able-bodied could function without.

'We're still handicapped. We need our own set of rules,' said Anardo Valdez, Kiley's teammate on the 1992 U.S. Paralympic basketball team.

Perhaps the most poignant symbols of the battle are the gold medals— being held by the International Wheelchair Basketball Federation in Sheffield, England, until the dispute is settled.

Initially, the American players had refused to turn over the medals because they were so angry—at first with Kiley and their coach, then at the system. They had done nothing wrong, so why were they being punished? they asked.

Only after international officials threatened to bar members of the team from the 1996 Paralympics in Atlanta were the gold medals returned.

All except one.

Valdez, a former Marine from New York who played for two decades, refused.

'I don't think the medal should leave America,' Valdez said. 'We won it.'

He was banned for life by the National Wheelchair Basketball Association."

The following is a press release, written by Gerard Moreno, on Anardo Valdez's stance on keeping his medal and not returning it to the NWBA. Anardo's press release becomes public a month after the *LA Times* publishes its feature news story on me:

Banned For Life

At the 1992 Paralympic Games in Barcelona, Spain, the United States Wheelchair Basketball team won the Gold Medal by defeating the Netherlands 39-36. After the victory the U.S. was stripped of its Gold Medals because one athlete, Dave Kiley tested positive for a banned substance. The ruling was made by the now defunct International Coordination Committee of World Sports Organizations for the Disabled. With no means to appeal a decision.

The team initially refused to return the medals until an appeal was heard, but after threats for international officials to bar the U.S. team from the 1996 Paralympics in Atlanta, 10 of the 11 medals were returned.

Anardo Valdez, now stands alone in defiance of the ruling to give back the Gold Medal by the International Paralympic Committee (IPC) which replaced the ICC. The punishment given to Valdez was banishment from the NWBA for life.

Anardo Valdez, before making his decision, investigated the rulings and processes involved without taking sides. Kiley is an incomplete paraplegic and feels excruciating pain back and legs. Coach Harry Vines worked closely with the team and was genuinely concerned about Kiley's suffering and gave him the painkiller. The drug itself, Darvocet, is not listed in the banned substance handbook, but is a derivative of one that is. U.S. officials failed to adequately inform the wheelchair basketball team of the substance regulations. This is an error by the officials and a valid reason to protest, concluded Valdez.

The test was improperly conducted. Kiley was not present to analyze the test and the results were not confidential, but announced to the world. This does not follow the standard protocol of international sports. Another mistake, thought Valdez, and again a valid reason to protest.

Phil Craven, President of the International Wheelchair Basketball Federation admitted, even he, was unclear on the drug-testing regulations. A memorandum written by Craven supported the U.S. team's protest. This memo was not supported by our own NWBA representatives at first, but after elections and appointments to the IWBF took place, their views changed and support for the U.S. surfaced. This was very strange, thought Valdez—even stranger was the absence of certain U.S. representatives at the first hearing in March of 1993 in Cyprus. Was it political posturing, conflicting affiliations, rivalry or all of the above? One can only speculate. Only the representatives involved know the real story. Valdez believes there is an underlying truth. The bottom line was the decision to uphold the ruling was made before our grievances were heard and vowed support for our team was not there. Another mistake or intentional negligence? There are too many odd coincidences to be overlooked.

At this point, Valdez's feelings of betrayal by our own representatives were established along with a lack of faith that due process will never be served and a just resolution found.

Through the perseverance of Kiley, U.S. Olympic Committee and the IOC, International Olympic Committee, the IPC Executive Committee has agreed to appear before the Court of Arbitration for Sport in Lausanne, Switzerland. The court, created by the IOC, is expected to hear the case in 1995.

"A different set of drug rules needs to be adopted for the disabled because we are physically different," says Valdez. There has been no precedent to the punishment given to the U.S. team, even in the able-bodied sports world. The Atlanta Games will be held in 1996 but without Valdez. For him this controversial issue has ended, his Gold Medal won by the United States team is secured. For Kiley and the rest of the U.S. team the long fight continues.

A photograph in the *LA Times* vividly shows and explains what administrators, commissioners, and officials will never truly comprehend when it comes to sport. It's the medal ceremony. We are awaiting to receive what is golden. Twelve United States ballers, hand-in-hand with both arms raised to the ceiling. Behind us, the full house Barcelona crowd stands and applauds. We have accomplished what we dared to dream. It is the mountain top of sporting accomplishments.

The *Times* story by Elliot Almond continues:

" 'The fact that my teammates lost their gold medals is totally unacceptable,' Kiley said, adding that he is prepared to give up his medal for the sake of the others.

It appears that he is finally making headway. The IPC executive committee agreed last month to appear before the Court of Arbitration for Sport in Lausanne, Switzerland. The court created by the International Olympic Committee, is expected to hear the case early next year.

The International Olympic Committee, perhaps the world's most influential amateur sports organization, persuaded the IPC to agree to arbitration after IOC President Juan Antonio Samaranch was petitioned by the U.S. Olympic Committee on Kiley's behalf.

For disabled athletics to gain a foothold in the established sporting world, they need IOC support—and money. They gave Samaranch leverage to force the IPC to resolve Kiley's case.

Yet, resistance lingers.

'I'm really surprised (the Americans) made a decision to continue to pursue a situation that had already been duly adjudicated,' Robert Steadward said. 'We've forgotten about it and gone on to more important matters.'"

The above Steadward quote shows me just how disconnected he is from the Paralympic mentality. If I had his mindset, I would have none of the eight gold medals I earned. I willingly want to give up my gold medal. Steadward underestimates my resolve in getting my innocent teammates back theirs.

Elliot's story, in the *Los Angeles Times*, is a fair and balanced exercise of quality journalism. In it, he captures my rawness and situational angst whilst also giving the viewpoint of my opposition:

"An ill-tempered competitor likened to tennis great John McEnroe, Kiley often incensed officials by not mincing words. More than a year ago he called officials 'a bunch of able-bodied demigods who don't have a closeness to the sport.'

Kiley amassed thick files of paperwork on his case that he has sent to all of his '92 teammates. Next year Kiley plans to run for commissioner of the U.S. National Wheelchair Basketball Assn. against Stan Labanowich, the commissioner who suspended him but who is also trying to help win an appeal. Kiley realized that the only way to change the system was to become involved in the process.

The community has supported Kiley's efforts to have a fair appeal after becoming aware of the discrepancies. The Netherlands, Germany and France, the teams that finished second through fourth in Barcelona, last summer urged the IPC to give the United States due process. They want a resolution so the medals, now held in a safe-deposit box in the Sheffield bank, finally can be distributed.

Some officials are concerned that any standards short of those imposed by the International Olympic Committee would create a credibility problem for the disabled athletes striving to be recognized as equals.

'We can't fall into that naïve trap,' Steadward said. 'Years ago, people with disabilities used to be on all sorts of drugs for all sorts of reasons. We found as our sport grew more from a rehabilitation mentality to a sporting environment... there was less need to take a lot of drugs.'

Whereas Kiley and his supporters want a list of banned drugs that differs from the roster used by the able-bodied, they want the same standards of punishment and protocol.

During last summer's World Cup soccer championships in the United States, Kiley watched with interest as the sport's most famous player, Diego Maradona, was withdrawn by Argentina after testing positive for stimulants. Argentina was allowed to continue playing, however.

Maradona, who was once suspended for using cocaine, received a 15-month ban.

'My own country gave me a two-year suspension and gave my coach a four-year suspension,' Kiley said. 'You can't just take any guilt and hand down a punishment of the highest level of which there is no precedent in the able-bodied or disabled (sport).'

That punishment has caused Kiley two-and-a-half years of pain, but until the medals are returned it will not end.

'The heaviest price is the nightmare of it all,' Kiley said.

The nightmare of awaking in pain".

"Therefore, we believe the case is closed."

The closing line from IPC's Steadward, in answering our appeal before the Court of Arbitration for Sport hangs heavy. Without the IPC agreeing to go before CAS, our case will sink into the abyss. Quickly forgotten by all except myself, my eleven teammates, and our coaches.

On **April 28th, 1994**, the President of the NWBA, Stan Labanowich, writes to Robert Steadward of the IPC:

"As I explained to you over the telephone, and in previous conversations in person in May, 1993 in Jasper, Alberta, and in September in Berlin, Germany, it was our (the United States Disabled Sports Team) wish to see the matter resolved of impartial arbitration and in the IOC's Court of Arbitration for Sport (CAS) in particular.

Because of the inaction on the part of the IPC, it has brought IWBF President Phil Craven to require that the NWBA provide proof of having arranged for the case to be heard before the CAS and to deposit the medals to his office by March 31, 1994. Duly delivered, those medals are now in safekeeping in the IWBF Secretariat in England awaiting redistribution.

We feel this entire matter merits final resolution. To that end, and despite your statement "…we believe that the case is closed," we invite the IPC to enter arbitration with the USDST/NWBA before the CAS."

On **May 6th, 1994**, Philip Craven writes to the National Wheelchair Basketball Associations of France, Germany, the Netherlands, and the USA. The title of his memorandum is **"Up-date on the Dave Kiley Drug Issue and the USA's pursuance of a true Appeal Procedure."** Craven's highlights include:

"Section V of the ICC Handbook—the ICC had less than 1 page on Doping Control Regulations for the 1992 Barcelona Paralympic Games. The "International Olympic Charter Against Doping in Sport," from which the ICC took its few regulations, is a document containing 126 pages…

When I read a clandestine copy of these minutes in May 1993, I could not believe what I was reading. The minutes were supplied to me by a back door route as Joan Scruton refused to let me have a sight of a copy as I was not a member of the ICC Executive Committee even though I had been present at the meeting.

The CAS has given a case number to the U.S.'s appeal but at the moment the IPC will not commit itself to an arbitration agreement. This the IPC states in the letter of 28th March, 1994, from Bob Steadward to Stan Labanowich.

If it is ruled by an independent court that the medals should be reallocated then this will be done. If the U.S. appeal is upheld then the gold medals will be given back to the United States."

On **May 11th, 1994,** Philip Craven receives a letter from IPC 's Andres Raes. Raes states:

"We were informed that the gold medals from the USA basketball team which they received in Barcelona at the 1992 Summer Paralympic Games were recently returned to the IWBF.

IPC has received complaints from the German Federation regarding the failure of medals exchange from bronze to silver.

IPC, as successor of the ICC, would appreciate receiving the gold medals so they can redistribute to the Netherlands.

IWBF President Philip Craven then writes to IPC Secretary General Andre Raes on **May 27th, 1994.** Craven states:

"Further to our recent telephone conversation, I can confirm that the gold medals that were awarded to the USA in Barcelona are now in the possession of the IWBF.

It is patently obvious on reading the minutes of the ICC Meeting in Cyprus that the USA was not afforded the appeal that they requested.

The IPC should now agree to binding arbitration by the IOC (International Olympic Committee) sponsored CAS in Lausanne, Switzerland. The IPC President, Bob Steadward, has to date refused this right. Maybe you could be influential in changing his mind."

On **July 28th, 1994,** a proposal is agreed upon by France, Germany, the Netherlands, and the United States. The proposal looks to "resolve the outstanding issue of the final designation of the Paralympic medals in the men's wheelchair basketball event Barcelona 1992."

The proposal is signed by Maurice Schoenacker/France, Ulf Mehrens/ Germany, Rob de Koning/Netherlands, and Stan Labonowich/USA. The proposal states:

"That the President and CEO of the International Wheelchair Basketball Federation (IWBF) be instructed to write to the President of the International Paralympic Association asking him to include the request of the IWBF for the IPC to become co-signatories to an agreement TO Arbitrate before the International Olympic Committee's (IOC) Court of Arbitration for Sport (CAS) concerning the final designation of the Paralympic medals 1992 in wheelchair basketball on the agenda of the next IPC Executive Committee for their meeting in Paris in November this year.

That if by 1ˢᵗ December 1994, no positive response is received, the IWBF Executive Committee will be empowered to establish a Tribunal of respected individuals to resolve the issue within four months."

September 14ᵗʰ, 1994, a letter is written from Andre Raes, IPC Secretary General to Gilbert Felli, IOC Sports Director. Raes states:

"Following to your letter of August 23ʳᵈ, 1994, regarding the position of the IPC on the subject of the disputed USA Basketball team suspension at the Barcelona Paralympic Games, and after discussion with Dr. Robert Steadward I can confirm IPC's agreement to arbitrate before the International Olympic Committee's Court of Arbitration for Sport, on the condition that no expenses for IPC are involved."

On **December 8ᵗʰ, 1994**, I write a letter on Casa Colina letterhead to my Barcelona teammates. In it, I state:

"It's been relayed by Marv to me that the IPC wants possession of the medals during this process. In addition, the bastards want us to pay for their expenses.

I have faith in Phil Craven that he will not let go of our medals. Marv said that Phil's position is that this process will occur with or without the IPC.

On another note, I hope you realize the position Anardo Valdez is in with a life ban from B-ball. It's not right and is just another nightmare outgrowth of a system that went haywire a long time ago. I'm giving him my support."

TUNNELS AND LIGHTS

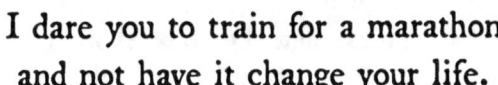

I dare you to train for a marathon
and not have it change your life.

— Susan Sidoriak

As a strategy, the IPC, led by Bob Steadward, can appear to be agreeable. With only a calendar year before the International Paralympic Committee oversees its first winter and summer games ever, a certain level of cooperation appears to be on offer.

On **February 23rd, 1995,** Steadward writes to NWBA Commissioner Stan Labanowich:

"In principle, the IPC is in favour of cooperating with the NWBA and participating in the IOC Court of Arbitration for Sport (CAS). We are also prepared to accept the decision as final."

He then deftly drops a bomb, misdirecting us from our true aim and objective.

"However, our cooperation is contingent on your agreement to one additional condition, which is stipulated in number 3 of the Arbitration Agreement.

If this is acceptable to the NWBA, please sign and return. If, however, you do not comply with number 3 of the Agreement, then there can be no hearing."

The third arbitration in the agreement states:

"Prior to the IPC agreeing to participate in the aforementioned tribunal, The NWBA shall ensure that the gold medals awarded to the United States men's wheelchair basketball team at the 1992 Barcelona Paralympic Games be returned to the IPC Secretariat."

Just over a week later, Labanowich responds to IPC President Robert Steadward. On **March 1st, 1995,** he states:

"Insofar as the medals are being held in escrow by the IWBF, the NWBA is powerless to comply with your late condition. The IWBF serves as a neutral party to this dispute and is well suited to maintain possession of the medals until a decision is reached, whereupon the IWBF promise is to distribute the medals accordingly. Even at this date, for the IPC to insist on possession of the medals as a condition of appeal is prejudicial to the interests of both parties since it serves no purpose in regard to the appeal.

In order to move the process along without further delay, I propose that the IWBF pass the medals on to CAS to be held by that body and to be redistributed once a decision has been reached. If you are in accord with this proposal, I believe we can persuade the IWBF to agree to transfer the medals to the CAS."

Labanowich then neatly cc's:

Phil Craven, IWBF (International Wheelchair Basketball Federation)

Ron Rowan, USOC (United States Olympic Committee)

Warren Brown, USA Basketball

Paul DePace, USDST (United States Disabled Sports Team)

Gilbert Felli, IOC (International Olympic Committee)

Correspondences between the chummy Steadward and Labanowich begin to take on teeth and bite. Bob and Stan dig into their separate trenches whilst shooting arrows across the bow.

On **March 9th, 1995** Steadward replies to Labanowich on his Mind, Body, Spirit—International Paralympic Committee letterhead:

"The IPC is not in any way trying to be difficult, Stan.

The IPC does not believe that non-compliance is prejudicial to our interests. To us it demonstrates a lack of respect and cooperation by the NWBA towards the IPC.

We are not here to negotiate, Stan. We are fully prepared to cooperate by participating in the Court of Arbitration and will respect and submit to the ruling of the Court as long as our <u>previous </u>requests for medals return are observed prior to court hearing."

On **March 15th, 1995,** Labanowich rifles back a lengthy retort to Steadward. On page two, Labanowich states:

"This brings me to the point of my previous correspondence and that is that since the medals are currently in the possession of the IWBF, it should be acceptable to the IPC to have CAS protect them until a decision has been reached, given that the IWBF is willing to transfer them. Whichever organization emerges from arbitration with a decision in its favor can be confident that the medals will be allocated fairly and promptly to the appropriate nations.

Quite frankly, it is likely that the world sporting community, the world press and financial sponsors of disabled sports will consider it unfair for the IPC to insist on physical possession of the medals as a pre-condition of arbitration. The IPC, as an organization, should concern itself with justice and athletes' rights, rather than the assertion of its power. The NWBA asks only for an impartial hearing to settle a long-standing dispute involving its athletes which the IPC has obviously been reluctant to engage in. (In fact, IPC expressed a tentative willingness to submit the matter to the CAS only after the IWBF and its members, including all four Barcelona semifinalists nationally, called for submission to the CAS).

If the IPC is unwilling to sign the Arbitration Agreement which I have enclosed, the NWBA shall have no other recourse but to petition the IWBF to follow through with its promise to settle the dispute as prescribed in the decision taken during the IWBF World Congress of July 18, 1994 'to establish their own tribunal to resolve the issue.'"

Labanowich CCs the same powers of sport as previously. Except this time, he adds the members of the 1992 U.S. Paralympic Team to his list of recipients. He then amends the disputed "number 3" in the Arbitration Agreement to read:

"The appeal before the CAS will begin when the first-place medals awarded to the United States men's wheelchair basketball team at the Barcelona Paralympics, and currently in the possession of the IWBF, are tendered by the IWBF to the Secretary General of the CAS, to be allocated by the Secretary General in a manner consistent with the final CAS appeal."

On **March 21st, 1995,** the Arbitration Agreement is signed by both Robert Steadward, IPC President, and Stan Labanowich, Commissioner NWBA.

As we get closer to the finishing line, it's time for both sides to lawyer up. We are working with Wildman, Harrold, Allen & Dixon, a law firm out of Chicago, Illinois. Douglas Carlson is our lawyer of record and will be representing us.

On **April 28th, 1995,** Carlson receives a memo from the Court of Arbitration for Sport and the desk of Jean-Philippe Rochat. Rochat states:

"This is to acknowledge, on behalf of the CAS, receipt of your letter dated April 3, 1995. I have taken knowledge of the Arbitration Agreement and I confirm to you that the CAS accepts to hold the first-place medals awarded to the U.S. men's wheelchair basketball team at the Barcelona Paralympics and currently in the possession of the International Wheelchair Basketball Federation. Those medals will be held for the duration of the arbitration proceedings.

I understand that within fourteen days from the date of receipt of the medals, you will submit the statement of appeal which will duly bring the case for the CAS."

It feels like we are finally working from a solid base. Everything is funnelling through the Court of Arbitration for Sport. Labanowich has put all our cards on the table. His threat of petitioning the IWBF if the IPC backs away from the CAS appears to be working. The IPC and Steadward will ultimately be forced to allow a fair and due (third party) process to take place. I'm grateful to all the semifinal teams taking this action. It's the right thing to do.

I do notice the IPC—and Steadward in particular—signature is absent from the document signed by all the semifinalist teams.

On **May 10, 1995,** Coach Harry Vines writes to James Peters of the Paralyzed Veterans of America (PVA). Coach Vines states:

*"We need to raise $7,000 to assist Commissioner Dave Kiley (*I am elected Commissioner of the NWBA over Stan Labanowich—more on that later)*, attorney and other personnel with travel and other expenses. This is a final appeal which will resolve this issue once and for all and we are confident the appeal will go in our favor."*

On **June 6th, 1995,** I write to my Barcelona teammates and coaches on Casa Colina letterhead:

"As the seasons roll by, the battle goes on for our gold medal. Enclosed please find the draft of our brief, to be filed with the CAS by Thursday, June 8th.

This document is very impressive, and I believe it will serve our needs—to reclaim the gold medal for what is rightfully ours. Upon receipt of this brief the CAS will set a date for arbitration and we shall finally conclude this long and very painful process.

The U.S. contingent will consist of our attorney, Doug Carlson, Phil Craven, Marv Lapicola and Stan Labanowich. I am confident that this group will be successful and the ordeal will be brought to an end.

To date, Harry and I have raised $4,000 to fund our defense; another $4,000-5,000 is needed: $3,000 to access CAS; $5,000 for airfare, lodging and meals.

I am asking each of you to consider pledging or helping me to raise the balance. Anything you can do would really help."

Our legal representation of *Wildman, Harrold, Allen & Dixon* and more specifically Doug Carlson are working pro bono. Patriotic Americans offering their services at no charge.

On **July 11th, 1995**, Robert Steadward writes to the CAS Secretary General, Jean-Philippe Rochat:

"Has the Court of Arbitration received the first-place medals from the IWBF, in accordance with our Arbitration Agreement with the NWBA, and if so, how many medals were received in total?"

Jean-Philippe Rochat responds to Steadward on **July 12th, 1995**:

"Referring to your telecopy dated July 11, 1995, I acknowledge receipt on May 16, 1995 of ten first-place medals."

Steadward responds to the CAS and Rochat on **July 21st, 1995**:

"In your letter on July 12th, I noticed that you have received (10) first-place medals. According to our Arbitration Agreement of March 21st, with the NWBA, it was agreed that all (12) medals awarded to the U.S. team players in Barcelona, were to be returned. Prior to our participating in the Court of Arbitration for Sport, we will require both a full explanation from the NWBA's legal counsel as to why the medals were not returned, and return of the two outstanding medals.

At the present time, on behalf of the IPC, I am seeking legal counsel in the preparation of a brief statement of defence."

Steadward and the IPC are again posturing and positioning themselves for yet another underhanded position and decision tilted their direction. I can smell it. I know how this guy works.

From the desk of Douglas Carlson, Attorney at Law to Dr. Robert Steadward concerning two missing gold medals on **July 28th, 1995**:

"The USA team was awarded twelve first place medals at the Barcelona Paralympics. In 1994, pursuant to a directive from the IWBF, the NWBA attempted to retrieve all of the medals from members of the USA team. In March, 1994, USA team member Curtis Bell forwarded his medal to the NWBA by Federal Express. The NWBA received from Mr. Bell an empty Federal

Express envelope which appeared to have been cut open and resealed in transit. Efforts by Federal Express to find the medal proved futile, and in August, 1994, the NWBA sanctioned Mr. Valdez for this refusal by suspending him indefinitely from playing on any NWBA member team. The NWBA forwarded ten first place medals to the IWBF, and the CAS currently holds these ten medals, subject to the AGREEMENT arbitrate.

If the NWBA is not allocated the first-place medals by the CAS appeal decision, the NWBA offers to pay the cost of creating two duplicate first-place medals.

Reasonable options presented for reasonable people. You'd think.

A copy of this letter is being sent to Mr. Rochat of the CAS."

On **September 7ᵗʰ, 1995,** Douglas Carlson writes to Jack Agrios. Agrios is Respondent Counsel for the International Paralympic Committee. Carlson writes:

"At its March, 1994, meeting the IPC banned from competition at the Atlanta Paralympics all USA wheelchair basketball players, coaches and officials who participated in the Barcelona Paralympics. The apparent reason for this was the failure of the NWBA to tender the Barcelona gold medals to the IPC, as opposed to the IWBF.

As a gesture of good faith, I am sending to the CAS a check in the amount of $2,000 (U.S.) to be used to replace the two missing gold medals if the CAS should rule against the NWBA.

Trials for membership on the USA wheelchair basketball team for the Atlanta Paralympics will begin October 1, 1995 and will continue for one week. Seven members of the 1992 USA Barcelona team have been invited to the trials. All of these men returned their 1992 Barcelona gold medals.

IPC has never specifically rescinded the March, 1994 ban....."

On **September 7ᵗʰ, 1995,** Douglas Carlson also corresponds with Jean-Philippe Rochat of CAS. Carlson writes:

"Enclosed please find a check in the amount of $2,000 (U.S.) payable to CAS."

From the desk of Jack Agrios, Barrister and Solicitor for the IPC to Secretary General of CAS. On **September 18, 1995**, Agrios writes:

"We note the proposal of the sum of $2,000 U.S. in satisfaction of the outstanding two gold medals that were to have been returned. It is apparent this is an indication of good faith under the difficult circumstances that have occurred."

Douglas Carlson and Robert Steadward are cc'd on the correspondence.

On the same day, **September 18ᵗʰ, 1995,** Agrios writes to our legal representation Douglas Carlson:

"We wish to advise that we have reviewed the contents thereof with Dr. Steadward who advises that this matter is on the agenda for the next meeting of the General Assembly in Tokyo in November and we have been advised that

there will be a recommendation for the reinstatement of the United States Team. We trust that this addresses the concerns you have raised."

I am upbeat but also suspicious and concerned. I have a reserved confidence and growing encouragement that the team will retain their Barcelona Games gold medals. I can see losing my gold medal and am prepared for such an outcome.

Coach Harry Vines' and my suspension from international competition for four and two years respectively is exorbitant and inflated. The byproduct of administrators needing heads on a stake.

Through it all, past the one-two Canadian sucker-punches of Riding and Steadward, I've come out the other side of things. It's taken practically a full, 4-year Paralympic cycle to fully reacquaint myself with my career and sense of *who I am* moving forward.

My family is again my priority. I need to be involved with my wife and kids. Not from a sense of responsibility but on a human, father, and husband level. When Sandy marries me, she marries basketball; but she didn't marry this. This world of schemes and the backfoot odyssey of predicting what's next. Sandy is my rock. Then. Today. My time with Danielle and Justin bring me peace and joy through this time of professional and personal torment.

Family is irreplaceable.

"The most important thing in the world is family and love," – John Wooden.

On **November 27th, 1995,** I write to the 1992 Barcelona Team:

"I have received word that the date for our arbitration is set for February 9th. This situation has been prolonged for nearly four years, and we should have closure in approximately ten weeks.

Keep everything you own crossed, and hopefully the '92 team will be reinstated as the official Gold Medal winners."

LONG AND WINDING ROAD

> "The wild and windy night
> That the rain washed away...
> Don't keep me waiting here
> Lead me to your door"
> — Paul McCartney & John Lennon

I've waited over thirty years to tell this story.
I bury the experience and memory.
Fighting nearly four years to keep what's ours takes a toll.

In our brief submitted to the Court of Arbitration for Sport:

National Wheelchair Basketball Association,
independently and on behalf of the United
States Disabled Sports Teams,

Appellant,

v.

International Paralympic Committee,
independently and as a successor to the
International Coordinating Committee of
World Sports Organisations for the Disabled,

Respondent.

The National Wheelchair Basketball Association moves the Court to amend the request for relief to state as follows:

"The National Wheelchair Basketball Association requests that the disqualification decision be reversed, and, in the alternative, either (a) that the USA Wheelchair Basketball Team retain the 1992 Barcelona Paralympics Championship, and that the USA team members retain the 1992 Barcelona Paralympics Championship, and that, with the exception of Mr. David Kiley, the USA team members retain their gold medals."

When you go subterranean, what's concealed inches every passing day into memory lapse.

Have I forgotten this day of decision?

It's unclear. I must simply carry on.

"Dextro-propoxyphene is not a performance enhancing drug; if anything, it is performance inhibiting, as it makes you drowsy. Neither Mr. Vines nor Mr. Kiley knew that Darvocet had a component on the banned list."

I am taxed and dog-tired with every mention of 'Dextro.'

I die a little more every time I see 'propoxyphene' in print.

I am more than a manufactured tablet and induced term.

"Under the ICC rules in effect at the 1992 Barcelona Paralympics, withdrawal of a medal from an <u>individual</u> found guilty of doping was discretionary, and it was contingent upon receipt of a proposal to withdraw the medal from the ICC doping committee. ICC Rule 1.1.6 stated:

'A medal may be withdrawn from a competitor found guilty of doping by order of the ICC on a proposal by the relevant ICC Doping Committee.'

'The ICC Doping Committee did not propose that the USA team forfeit <u>any</u> medal. It did, however, propose that Mr. Kiley forfeit <u>any</u> medal.'"

Self-absorbed, able-bodied, power-lovers routinely praising each other.

Helping those not capable of governing their own.

Who is the Jackie Robinson or Billie Jean King of our tribe?

"The ICC Doping Committee rendered its proposal to The ICC Executive Committee on September 17, 1992, and the ICC rendered its decision on September 29, 1992. At no time between the ICC Doping Committee meeting of September 15, 1992, and the ICC decision of September 29, 1992, was Mr. Kiley invited by the ICC to be heard before it. This was unfair to Mr. Kiley, and it was particularly unfair to the USA team.

"Disqualification of the entire USA team is unwarranted and unfair. It is particularly unfair and unwarranted when compared to the lack of sanction imposed [on] similarly situated athlete[s] at the same Paralympics."

So much time in the blender of half-truths, policy maneuvering and blowhard bluster.

Lawyer terms like good faith, difficult circumstances, oral submission and Yours very truly.

Too much depends on integrity; trust and truth of words on a page.

"Like Leon Labushagne, Mr. Kiley did not know that the drug he ingested was on the banned list. Like Mr. Labushagne, there was no performance enhancement.

A trace finding so insignificant that, relative to a restricted drug, the ICC doping laboratory was instructed not even to inform Dr. Riding of a trace finding."

You oversee sport.

I compete within its immensity.

The difference is profound.

"The disqualification of the USA team and the withdrawal of the gold medals did not constitute 'fair and equal' treatment of the USA team. The decision must be reversed."

I've waited over thirty years to tell this tale.

I just now remember why.

There is no such thing as '*Good Faith.*'

On the first page of their brief, the International Paralympic Committee, Dr. Bob Steadward and counsel set the trap.

Beneath the **Jurisdiction** heading:

"ICC rules did not provide for an appeal process of its decision; however, by an Arbitration Agreement, dated March 21, 1995, the IPC and the NWBA agreed to this appeal. Paragraph 3 of the Arbitration Agreement provides:

The appeal before the CAS will begin when the first-place medals awarded to the United States Men's Wheelchair Basketball Team at the Barcelona Paralympics and currently in the possession of the International Wheelchair Basketball Federation (IWBF) are tendered by the IWBF to the Secretary General of the CAS, to be allocated by the Secretary General in a manner consistent with the final CAS appeal decision.

There were twelve gold medals awarded to the USA Wheelchair Basketball Team. Only ten gold medals have been returned. The Arbitration Agreement does not specify a time limit for return of the gold medals; however, it is submitted that it can be implied that the gold medals must be returned within a reasonable time after entering into the Arbitration Agreement. In any event, the provisions of the Arbitration Agreement have not been met, and as such, it is submitted that there is no jurisdiction to proceed with the appeal."

The Court of Arbitration for Sport only works "when the procedure is allowed."

The IPC, only weeks away from overseeing the Winter Paralympics makes a weighty decision to basically bypass the proven judgements and amicable mediation of the CAS.

The final paragraph from their legal brief reads:

"The only result that can flow from this mandatory direction is forfeiture of the championship and withdrawal of the gold medals. In light of the foregoing, it is submitted that the appeal should be dismissed."

There is no hearing before the Court of Arbitration for Sport. There is no hearing ever—of any kind— for the undefeated 1992 gold medal winning United States Paralympic Men's Basketball Team.

We lose our gold medals.

Sir Philip Craven puts it this way, "Sports can only be based on fair play. There's no fair play in any part of this process."

Leading up to the 1996 Summer Olympics in Atlanta, Georgia, World Champion swimmer Samantha Riley tests positive for Dextro-propoxyphene at the World Short Course Championships in Rio de Janeiro, Brazil.

Riley, an Australian of Aboriginal descent, wins gold in the 100- and 200-meter breaststroke at the Rio World Championships. Swimming's international governing body, Federation International de Natation—a French term (FINA) carefully considers what—if any—penalties to impose on Riley.

There are no rash or hurried decisions imposed.

Samantha Riley publicly states, "I am absolutely devastated. I support FINA a hundred-percent in their fight against drugs and I realize it is getting harder to catch the cheats—but I am not a cheat."

In dealing with a headache, Riley's coach, Scott Volkers, admits to giving Riley a headache tablet that is prescribed for his wife. He did not check with Australian team doctors.

Sounds eerily familiar.

"I made probably the biggest mistake of my career," laments Volkers.

Riley's legal counsel, Peter Basten, goes before an executive meeting with FINA for two hours in Berlin, Germany, pleading Riley's case.

FINA announces a "strong warning" to Samantha Riley after her failed drug test. Riley will keep her World Championship gold medals and will be competing in the 1996 Atlanta Olympic Games. FINA could have banned Riley for two years. They do not. Instead, FINA has this response, Dextro-propoxyphene "has no potential to enhance her performance or give her an unfair advantage."

"I am very satisfied," says Prince Alexandre de Merode, the chairman of the International Olympic Committee Medical Commission. "I think they made a decision that is fair and just. I think it was an intelligent interpretation of the rules. This decision gives credibility to the anti-doping fight."

Minus unprofessional, twitchy, and isolated leaks like those of Michael Riding and his ICC Doping sub-committee, the timeline from Samantha Riley's positive test to a favorable and just outcome takes three-and-a-half months.

Minus the oily maneuvering of Dr. Robert Steadward and his upstart, IPC cohorts more intent on flexing power and covering up a prior administration's mistakes, then digging down and unearthing a just decision through the appropriate courts, a just and logical result is never allowed to prevail.

Since the creation of the WADA on **November 10th, 1999,** Darvocet and Dextro-propoxyphene have been taken off the banned list.

It's determined the drug is not performance-enhancing.

THE OVERTHROW

If I'm terrified, then I know I'm doing something right.

— Michael Stipe

In sport, to change is to replace.

Coaches are often dismissed midseason in search of a spark or philosophical swing that translates to better performance. Lineups are shifted, adjusted, and customized to compete better. Trades are executed and athletes uprooted so teams can add a needed and strategized piece to the puzzle of competing at higher levels.

The process is brutal. Too many times good people, working as close to their capacity as humanly possible, are let go because of age, philosophies, performance, or personality conflicts. The stink of being replaced lingers. It enters into your dreams. It's the darkness of sport, sucker-punching perceptions of self. It's far worse than missing a big shot or calling the wrong play. If there is a next time, it's somewhere else and with different colors flying. There's added wrinkles across your already worn eye-line, misplaced animosities, and a revenge factor no one wants to admit to.

Get through it and you're golden; a bit tarnished maybe but golden nonetheless. Overcoming replacement inspires a fortitude of character and newfound charisma of change. It's the way of the world. Every success story seems to begin with an unfathomable rock bottom.

Other times change is inevitable. It's the byproduct of timing and a long overdue foreseeable shift. Too long-in-the-tooth or overly comfortable all the shots often lead to an idleness and slippage that sinks a quality product to average or subpar.

On **December 4ᵗʰ, 1994**, *Los Angeles Times* writer Elliott Almond spells out my intentions for change, "*Next year Kiley plans to run for commissioner of the National Wheelchair Basketball Association against Stan Labanowich, the commissioner who suspended him but who is also trying to help him win an appeal. Kiley realized that the only way to change the system was to become involved in the process.*

He had planned to retire after Barcelona, but the loss of the medal has fuelled his competitive drive."

Almond's story announces my intentions. A message is sent to the NWBA and its members that there will be opposition to Labanowich. Stan has been in post seventeen years and runs unopposed throughout.

Dick Bryant, Hall of Fame inductee (2008) as a player, former Commissioner, and President of the NWBA, has this to say about my attempt to beat out Labanowich for the Commissioner's job, *"It was time for a change. The Commissioner (Labanowich) had become an island of power. Though a board of directors was in place, Stan felt he did not have to answer to the board. Members/players had grown tired of our organization being stuck without changes or improvements for over a decade. I felt David Kiley was the one who could overthrow Labanowich and many supporting members felt the same way. The change has the opportunity to give the NWBA the jump-start it truly needs."*

I have to check with the job. If I'm able to pull this off, Casa Colina will be the national office of the NWBA. Feels like a big ask but it's not my first. In one of his final acts of support for me and disability sport, Dale Eazell, CEO, grants me his approval. Mr. Green Light. The bossman never turns me down. I'm grateful but I am also overwhelmed with the possibilities. If I win the upcoming election, I've just taken on another full-time job.

What am I thinking? After everything I've lived through? More career angst? More time committed to something other than family?

Change is needed but I am not an administrator. I'm a jock. A crew of delegates approach me. They certainly desire a change of direction. They want me to oversee and run their National Governing Body (NGB). The delegates urge, persuade, and prod me to run against Labanowich. None stronger than Dick Bryant. I tell myself, I am not the one but I cannot say 'no.' I fear failure. I have no playbook. I am not coached-up to oversee wheelchair basketball across North America.

The loudest drum I continuously bang concerns USA national teams. Teams representing the United States of America must be funded. This needs to happen nationally and internationally, anywhere across the globe. I've had to fundraise my entire international career. No more. Our countries' best athletes will be supported in every way. The previous regime has done a woeful job backing its national teams with travel expenses, sponsorships, nutritional health, and performance incentives.

In the spring of '95, word has sifted through the masses. I'm taking on the leadership that's been in place the past seventeen years. The old guard is incensed. The side of change is elated and encouraging. I am on the phone or retrieving a fax almost every day.

Things are moving fast. Perhaps too fast but I am *all in.* In 1996, the annual meeting is held at the Final Four Championships. Team and community delegates raise legislation, motions, and amendments to be voted on. The election of officers follows. It's not uncommon for things to get heated.

Usually held in a large hotel ballroom, NWBA delegate meetings are a mix of Jimmy Hoffa-led union chaos amongst a massive disability rights gathering. Frank Burns once turned to me during a certain delegate meeting, "The room looks like a train wreck convention." Hilarity amongst disorder oddly makes perfect sense.

The Labanowich contingent want a live debate. They're banking that a hardened and primed Labanowich, with his IPC, IWBF, and NWBA seasoning can make me look like an inexperienced hack of a candidate. Not a bad strategy.

My team sees through the attempt. They refuse to allow me to fall into this trap. Labanowich and his cronies want me to stumble amongst the temperature of a live debate. It's proposed that Labanowich and I ask each other questions as well as the taking questions from delegates on the floor. I lean heavily on Dick Bryant and a team of advocates seeking change within the commissioner's office. I'm advised to accept the terms of the debate. Terrifying.

I have just over a month to prepare. We set a strategy. It's plain and simple.

One-word answers whenever possible.

"No."

"Yes."

Use as few words as possible.

"I believe I can."

"No. I will not fail."

"I can get the job done."

The plan is to not ask any questions. After time someone (from my team) will call for a motion to vote. I can handle and execute the plan. Yet, my inner voice is telling me I am crazy for agreeing to be a part of this scheme.

I remember the past four years and find my resolve again.

The commissioner's office oversees and operates our entire sport of over 180 teams. Women's, men's, junior's and USA national teams lean into the commissioner's office for guidance and leadership. Mundane but necessary essentials to our sport Include:

Communication through a monthly newsletter,

Game reports and scoring leaders across all play,

Team rankings,

Searching and finding hosts for regional and sectional playoffs,

Final Four venues,

Delegate meeting space and agenda,

Host hotels with the foresight of hundreds of wheelchair users loose on their verandas and bars,

And the vital imperative of our elite, national team athletes receiving elite-like treatment from its own governing body.

I ponder if the National Wheelchair Basketball Association governs the largest national body in the world. I know it's beginning to feel that way. Labanowich runs the NWBA office out of the University of Kentucky. He fills his worker roster with students and interns to carry out day-to-day operations. Volunteers working in unison with a volunteer commissioner position.

Let's get this straight. Stan Labanowich is a good man. He's a Hall of Fame inductee. He serves as wheelchair basketball administrator for nearly two-decades. I'm not sure how or why he loses the pulse of our sport but its members have spoken and they want change. It's important to remember— and even more important that I remember—our sport is bigger than any of us individually.

The debate day arrives. I'm beyond nervous. I'm edgy and short with people in my circle. I go over scenarios until words spew from my hole and sound unrehearsed. Guess I'm prepared.

I sit behind the microphone near the back of the large hotel banquet room. The debate questions come with barbed intentions. Will I hang myself? This is the overriding question posed by my opponent and weathered following. One after another, I do as I'm coached. The plan plays out perfectly. My rivals are left flummoxed with my uber-short and succinct answers. One by one they take their seats and shake their bowed heads in frustration. The room is divided. A nervous energy dominates amongst the delegates. There's plenty of Labanowich supporters including the NWBA board itself. I feel the laser glares and stink-eye from the Labanowich regime. An individual from my team makes a motion to conduct a vote. The game plan is in full effect.

I'm petrified about winning the election.

I'm dismayed by the status quo.

I win the election. Not a landslide but convincingly enough.

I am the new Commissioner of the NWBA.

I remind myself to squash any prevailing doubt.

It's not lost on me that for the past few years I've been *Fighting the Power* and now I am the power. There's sufficient chatter that my commissioner's run and eventual overthrow of the post is a revenge-filled campaign motivated by receiving a two-year suspension from Labanowich for my failed Barcelona drug test. There is a scant scent and hint of truth to this superseding assumption. There comes a time in things where you need to be at the head of the table, not the beaten and browbeaten voice of a defeated peanut gallery.

Taking on the responsibilities of the NWBA's commissioner's desk, and then its presidency, is a maturer version of service that follows throughout my years. I'm tired of throwing ineffective pebbles against the armoured chest of power. Be part of the powerbroker circle. Listen with patience. Pick and choose when to speak with vibrato.

Don't change.

Evolve.

I understand more that disability is a minority. I'm content within the context and differences between black, brown, woman, gay, and mindful differences between myself and the world at large. What I'm realizing more, and in certain instances for the first time, is the conscious or subconscious prejudices and assumptions of working alongside a Wheel Head administrator and commissioner. For too long Wheel Heads didn't do the job of governing themselves. Here I am, still actively playing basketball, working full time in disability recreation and sport, whilst running and winning an election for Commissioner of the NWBA.

It doesn't take long in post for me to realize and understand fully that our subculture of disability sport spends freely and can be an attractive product to Madison Avenue public relations firms. Our minority of strength through adversity translates to a public that more than likely has a Wheel Head as a friend or family member.

The time to strike is now.

If your dreams don't scare you, they're not big enough.

As Commissioner of the NWBA, I dare to dream big. My Casa Colina office doubles as headquarters for the NWBA. My open-door policy rotates ideas back and forth with teammates, delegates, and with international faxes from across the globe. It's a hectic and stirring time.

The office walls serve as a disability sport think tank. No idea is too ludicrous.

My vision is to change most everything. Not because of ego or the need to change for the sake of change but simply because it's time. Chair manufacturers are big, competitive, worldwide businesses. Sponsorships are commonplace. More extreme sports like water skiing, snow skiing, and mountain climbing are recreational outlets for the common man/woman within disability sport.

The 1996 Atlanta Paralympic Games announces Wheel Head Mark Wellman as its Opening Ceremony Torchbearer. Wellman makes worldwide news scaling Yosemite's National Park's El Capitan. The first ascent of the renowned cliff by a paraplegic.

The NWBA can no longer afford to stay within its 1983 model of success. It's 1995. We can't lead until we've caught up with the groundbreaking beat of our time.

- Our logo sucks. It looks like an old lady's handicapped parking placard. I create a contest within the NWBA: send in design options. The winner receives a new basketball chair. The response is tremendous. My Barcelona teammate and rivalrous buddy, Trooper Johnson, models the NBA logo of Jerry West and uses his own silhouette for a fetching and powerful image.

The addition of red, white, and blue americana coloring plays perfect in form and intent. The NWBA logo—like the NBA's Jerry West driven logo—is used and seen repeatedly to this day.

- The NWBA has a typed and stapled newsletter that's been completed and sent for years to team representatives only. Minus the invention of websites in 1995, a glossy and bound magazine is the preferred look. Our new magazine, *Bank Shots* goes out to every member within the NWBA. I partner with the Paralyzed Veterans Association (PVA), Zia chapter out of Albuquerque, New Mexico to print and mail to our members. The Zia PVA relationship is a sturdy one. They cover the expense of printing and postage whilst receiving praise and adulation from our massive member base. *Bank Shots* is to our members what *Tennis Magazine* is to tennis enthusiasts. The pages contain rankings, profiles, coaching tips, stories of the game's past, action photos, and sponsor advertisements. The advertisements create a new and vital revenue stream for the NWBA.

- We begin earning valuable dollars right away in support of our National Team members. No more bake sales, car washes, or hitting up the rich aunt for international travel and incidentals. I hook up with an aggressive telemarketing firm. Ours is an easy sell. In the mid-nineties, telemarketing is a growth business with positive interactions and results. The swindlers have yet to get into the game and our story is one that patriotic Americans across the country want to invest in.

- To date, all teams play in one league against one another in conferences across the country. This creates a disparity against the haves and have nots. It's not an even playing field. My office implements divisional play with the help of the same folks that got me elected. It begins with Division 1 and Division 2. We identify the best high-level teams and create a smaller but much more competitive division. Every game is a battle that spotlights our best to our league but also our sponsors. The majority of the NWBA competes in Division 2. This motivates D2 teams to get better, potentially win their division, and move up to D1 to play with the best men and women the game has to offer. We take on the 'relegation' structure of Europe. The harsh reality of moving up or down a division through positive or negative results in the final, year-end standings isn't suited for the timid. My gut response is to say, *Work harder and get better*, but the commissioner in me listens compassionately and makes an informed and thoughtful ruling(s).

- In 1996, I fly to New York City and present a proposal to the NBA and the David Stern Community Relations Department. Stern is the Commissioner of the National Basketball Association (NBA). My proposal intends to establish the first ever NBA/NWBA All Star game during the weekend's popular Jam Session. The opportunity is a first. An enormous opportunity to bridge the NBA and the NWBA as partners on the highest profile basketball weekends. I come away with a deal. The NBA is in. It makes sense. Wheelchair basketball will be a part of All-Star weekend. We rally our NWBA teams to select our best to compete in New York City for the All-Star game. The game, held at the Jacob Javits Convention Center, pits the west against the east. Three-point shots are flying, points are scored in bunches and the NWBA's best rise to the occasion. In attendance is Commissioner Stern as well as New York Knickerbocker great, Patrick Ewing. The west wins a nailbiter. Trooper Johnson (the logo) wins a timely MVP for the game. The NWBA's street cred begins to garner a rhythm that lasts. The All-Star weekend is a grand and continued stage in which our game shines with athleticism and muscled polish.

1st NBA-NWBA All-Star in NY in my commissioner role. Coach Paul Jackson receives championship trophy from Patrick Ewing and the NBA.

My pivotal time as commissioner and then president of the NWBA lasts five years. I like to think changes, like the ones above, put the NWBA on more equal footing with NGB's across the sporting landscape. Not disability sport but sport itself.

So many friends, players, coaches, teams, and other organizations throughout sport help inform the newfound truths and opinions. I think, I know. The real truth of the matter is that without help and an ever-increasing desire to listen to good advice, my time as an administrator might have been one of ego and blunders.

Instead, the NWBA becomes financially viable and its members are the desired change. We are a minority but we are a collective minority working towards the good of our game.

It feels good to trust again.

PART EIGHT

The presence of a problem
is the absence of an idea.

— Timothy Nugent

HEADS CAROLINA

══

TAILS CALIFORNIA

Baby, what do you say we just get lost.
Leave this one-horse town like two rebels without a cause.

— Jo Dee Messina

There's an ocean of California water beneath the bridge of our California lives.

I'm restless. Not competing and training for either the Winter or Summer Paralympic Games in 1996 allows me the unimagined but needed space to reflect. I've been at it for over twenty years. An astounding time in sport. An immensely wild, worldwide ride chasing victories and all its fascinations and allures. Barcelona still slumbers in the faraway corners where darkness resides. The Barcelona emotions are always simmering but with each passing day, I'm doing what men of my generation do. Pushing feelings of unmerciful pain down far enough that for today they're forgotten. Put enough days together, and well…good enough for now.

Southern California takes perception and an increasing rationalization of how, why, and how many.

How do we afford what we see?

Why do we feel like such a singular amongst so many?

How many times are we willing to sit in traffic, again?

The answer is usually climate, Pacific Ocean, and accessibility. The powerful trifecta equates to the *California Dream* but at what cost? Would simpler not be better? Do we need it all or would just a slice be better?

There's a shift in my core. My career is in sports. My blessing is family.

There's a job interview in North Carolina. A new adaptive and wheelchair sports program is on offer. Beginning again. Building from scratch. Sounds intriguing. I'm offered an interview and quickly accept.

The Charlotte Institute of Rehabilitation is after the same model I built at Casa Colina. I like what I see, hear, and feel about the place. The money is more than right. North Carolina has lush walking trails, change of seasons, rocking chair, waterfalls, and wind on water transparency that calms every last nerve.

It's a feeling within.

I get the job.

I give notice to Casa.

No regrets.

Gratitude and appreciation.

Sandy is excited to be closer to her family in Nashville, Tennessee. I share her enthusiasm. Geographic change is a wonder and breath of unlimited newness. Each turn of the wheel something never seen before. A first of many multi-colored, layered and personally progressive firsts.

I find a place on Lake Norman in Mooresville. Neighbors aren't piled atop one another like SoCal living. There are no dividing fences to keep yards private, preventing neighbors from getting to know one another. Space. Space to be.

Prior to moving into our leased home on the lake, Sandy and the kids tour the Charlotte area. We all take in the sights. Justin is fifteen years old and Danielle is eleven. As a collective we are prepared and ready—as can be—for the 2,500 miles difference between the west coast and Carolina countryside. We're not living in Mayberry but the differences are beyond subtle.

It's June and the kids' first night in the new place. The sun sets across Lake Norman. I can get used to this. A deepening burnt orange of the sun fades. It starts with a few before the onslaught of the many.

"What's that?" asks Danielle.

"Those are Cicadas," I answer

Cicadas are these bug-eyed critters that reside in the south. Together they create a massive, overriding chorus of high-pitched screeching. It sounds like there are millions of them plotting an attack on all of mankind. Once you've taken on the summer sounds of the Cicadas, it's actually a peaceful reminder you're away from the city, stoplights, and sirens. There is a transition period, though.

The next morning there is a knock on the door. It's the neighbor boy. He looks to be about 10 years old. Danielle opens the door. Ben (the neighbor kid), with his thick, redneck-in-training accent asks, "Wanna go fishing?"

"No," barks Danielle adamantly.

Ben asks again.

"No." Danielle turns towards the kitchen and leaves Ben at the door.

We meet Ben and tell him to come later. I'll go fishing with him.

"I hate this place. I want to go back to California."

Danielle storms to her room like only an 11-year-old girl can. We laugh but at the same time the question is asked. How will the kids do in this new environment?

The move proves to be nothing but a blessing. Danielle and Justin take to Carolina just fine. Justin has a bit harder go of it. He's in high school and peer groups are in place. Juice navigates it all over time. He plays on the basketball and tennis teams. A chip off the ole block.

I begin bass fishing at Lake Norman in a kayak. Within a few years I purchase an entry level bass boat. I find my sanctuary. Bass fishing is a new competitive outlet for me. As is my nature, I want to be the best. I begin travelling and touring with the Paralyzed Veterans Associations Bass Tour. In my third year, I finish second in angler of the year. I miss first place by a single fish. In another PVA tournament at Rend Lake, Illinois, I miss winning a

My Ranger Bass Boat.

dreamy bass boat by mere ounces to finish second. I lean on ole buddy Shorty Powers to add me to his Turning Points, 'Team Challenge.' The group is a

collective of the best adaptive fishermen in the country. We're fully sponsored with rods, reels, trolling motors, bait, tackle, and apparel. Awesomeness personified. In 2005, I buy my dream bass boat—A Ranger Comanche, a two-hundred-horsepower beauty that I own to this day. The beast's garage kept its entire life. I love to fish; I mean love.

Sandy finds a lot for sale not far from our lakeside lease. The wooded lot is surrounded by nature and is on an eight-acre pond. We buy it and begin building our dream home next to my newest and most favorite fishing pond. Sandy has the vision. She throws herself into the dream project with all she has. My one ask is a basketball court in the backyard above the waterline. She does the rest.

Life just keeps getting better.

Early in our North Carolina summertime, I get a call from Andy Houghton. Andy replaces me at Casa after my departure. He wants me to help lead a trip to war-torn Bosnia. Andy is the leader of the trip and its endless details. He asks me to put the basketball team together. He's calling it the 'Wheels of Hope' tour.

I say, "Yes," without exactly knowing why.

HOPE

> Only the dead have seen the end of war.
>
> — Plato

Power versus Peace.

Living as one—a multinational objective built through exchanges, attentive listening, compromise, and noble understanding. The path of togetherness—as difficult as it may be—far outweighs the despair, death, and destruction that awaits when greed, supremacy, and status of grandeur infect a burgeoning faction out to 'get theirs.'

Of course, I'd heard of what was happening in Bosnia but it's easier to flip to the sports page or tap the remote to basketball, golf, or any of the growing live sporting events that cable television is commanding in the mid-90s. These indulgences are the American way.

Michael Jordan playing right field in the minor leagues receives just as much, if not more airplay, than half a million lives lost in Rwanda or a conflict in a land that used to be Yugoslavia.

When I get the call, I cannot say "no."

The tour, put together through the laborious, boots-on-the-ground efforts of Leland Montell (Country Director for International Medical Corps), Andy Houghton (who assembles the USA all-star team), and funding secured by Carolyn Bechtel (Leland's sister)—come together with rapid fire. They want me as the face and name of things. I quickly agree.

As always, Sandy and the kids sacrifice for my worldly ways. To live the indulgences of an international sports figure only works because of their sacrifice. I've said "yes" to so much. I become a go-to source as a professional, but believe me,

Carolyn and Drew brought all together.

none of it's easy on my family. Also, phone contact in Bosnia is a nightmare. The challenge creates a deeper sensation of missing home.

The trip needs to be organized, funded, and launched in just two months. A deluge of a winter awaits and a somewhat peaceful détente is currently in place. We need ballers that can alter plans on-the-quick.

Senator Bob Dole, a decorated WWII veteran, kicks in an initial $10k. Others follow in support, including the (Ted) Turner Foundation. We reach our goal of $60k quicker than imagined. Colours-N-Motion and Quickie Wheelchairs are firing on all cylinders and churning out custom, sport wheelchairs to a worldwide clientele. Their involvement and in-kind giveaways to the "Wheels of Hope" tour is seamless and generous.

The aggressively scheduled tour through war-torn, bullet-ridden Bosnia and Herzegovina, Serbia, and Croatia are a mission of peace through sport. We're promoting wheelchair basketball with the humanitarian goal of bringing attention to the war's disabled veterans. In addition, we'll spotlight an awareness and importance to the rebuilding of these countries' access for their increasing disabled population. Our emphasis will center on the positive aspect of organized wheelchair sports in communities looking to heal.

The Bosnian War is sinister. Thousands upon thousands, perhaps millions, maybe even multiple millions of land mines litter the region; laming, dismembering, and killing not only soldiers but far too often children simply chasing a football towards its goal.

A byproduct of our mission is to bring awareness to land mine safety in a region that still has far too many live mines.

It's not easy picking sides in the break up of what used-to-be scenic Yugoslavia. The Muslim Bosniaks, Orthodox Serbs, and Catholic Croats lay claim to what they say is rightfully theirs. It's convoluted and confusing whilst full of war crimes and gut-wrenching misdeeds. A deep, dark, rabbit hole one can easily get lost in.

To be an athlete, lending his name to the act of doing good, is far easier than the convictions and hardened belief systems that are willing to destroy and kill. The trip proves to be a fever-dream of emotions.

Sport teaches us that it's the differences that make the product and team more complete. The adjustments and the arcing understanding of who's next to you takes valuable and tendered time. The learning comes in increments but once there's trust and a shared experience the percentages of doing what's extraordinary increase dramatically.

Sport is not war. There are many analogies of the battle or fight that are spoken of in coach-speak and shared on television through talking-head pundits. Talk is cheap. There is only one way to obtain a deserved and honest opinion: get there, do the work, humble yourself, and pray for the strength to comprehend what the human spirit is capable of—at its mightiest and its worst.

Barnstorming excursions are as good as the folks involved. The chain of athletes and characters that venture into the battle-weary land of misery and hope is a recipe of strength, humor, and fascination.

There are seven athletes, a referee, a translator/driver, a Combined Joint Military Task Force (the Greeks), a NATO (North Atlantic Treaty Organization) led Stabilisation Force (SFOR) and myself.

I'm the arranged and proposed voice of things. Press conferences, interviews, and city ceremonies are commonplace but it's the will of our mass that's the backbone to all moving parts. It doesn't take long to understand that for the next few-odd days, any debts are to one another and to the victims of this land.

The following is the fascinating group involved. Each is asked to remember their times there.

Susie Grimes—A Northern California, Bay Area personality. Susie is impactful in advancing the women's game in the NWBA. A smooth lefty, she finishes strong and doesn't back down to any man in the low-post. Susie Grimes digs deep into her feelings and mindset. Like the rest of us, she has to. Processing the trip and its many varied components is an emotional roller-coaster.

From Susie Grimes:

I watch a farmer hoe his field, planting food for his family. The field is marked with the familiar yellow tape, indicating it has active land mines. His house is in rubbles, and piles of bricks lay next to the crumbling walls waiting to be rebuilt. The wintertime snow lays on the ground. We pass through another village. It's devastating. I don't understand the graffiti markings on houses, until our interpreter explains they're declarations—a way to identify a families' ethnic group as Serbian, Croatian, or Muslim.

I saw how the newly formed country of Bosnia was struggling with the psychological trauma caused by shelling, bombing, starvation, and atrocities committed against neighbors. Our tour came during a time of recovery, rebuilding, and the urgency to form a cohesive national identity.

It is difficult to process my emotions during my time in Bosnia and to simultaneously perform on the basketball court under physically stressful conditions. It's hard acclimatizing to playing in gyms without heat during the cold, winter temperatures. This causes muscle fatigue and cramping. As teammates we give each other strength and support. Our mission requires me to summon an inner resolve.

The unifying power of sport is never so obvious and potent to me. I see how the exhibitions bring people together and, at least for that moment, supplanted the horrific division among Bosnians. It teaches me the depth of my inner-strength and reinforces my belief in the possibility of positive social change. My perspective on what is important in life is reformed, and I develop a greater sense of gratitude, which is now a foundation of my world view.

I take the lessons I learn in Bosnia to heart.

Many years later, I reflect on the tour experiences as a source of re-inspiration, humility when I need it. The experience adds a tenacity to endure through life's most challenging moments.

Tiana Tozer—Likable and easy to be around. Tiana and I are cut from the same cloth. Deeply competitive, there's an easiness and comfort in our exchanges but beneath awaits a keen edge towards competition and worth.

From Tiana Tozer:

Marin, one of the trip organizers and translator, tells me the Bosnians are confident of victory as we have women on our team. For me, one of the unforeseen, and biggest accomplishments of the trip is the challenge to female stereotypes. The Bosnians watched as the guys treated us as equals. I think it surprised them that two women started on our USA team over two men but we were the better players.

The 'Wheels of Hope' tour was right after the '96 Atlanta Paralympic Games. The USA women's team was favored to win gold. We ended up with the bronze.

Bosnia's physical destruction mirrored my mind. I was as broken as the buildings and countryside surrounding me. I was trying to bring help and healing to a people devastated by hatred, as I fought against the loathing that threatened to envelop my own life. What I came to realize is that my gold medal game was played in a small, unheated gym in Bosnia. The Bosnian people treated me like a champion. It was the Paralympic experience I would never have.

It didn't matter to them that I was broken. I think they loved me more because I was.

For that, I will always love them.

Like them, and their country, I'm a survivor. The tour was a healing experience for me. In the midst of all the destruction and devastation, I was able to start healing from my Paralympic experience.

Andy Houghton—Andy and I are connected as he fills my position as Director of Wheelchair Sports and Adventures Program. I built the Casa program with blood, sweat, and tears. Drew is a great choice to carry on the legacy of Casa Colina. He's been to Bosnia prior to the 'Wheels of Hope' and is connected with Faruk Sabanovic. Faruk becomes disabled, taking a bullet from a sniper. The two work together before actualizing wheelchair basketball as the vehicle to bring a more normalized, day-to-day awareness to Bosnia and its increasing disabled population. Once the tour gets rolling, Andy takes more of a back seat but his role cannot be underscored. He's a massive reason it all happened.

Joe Babakanian (Babs)—Babs is a chatty, friendly soul and gives everyone the benefit of the doubt. More a tennis player than a baller, what he lacks on-court, he determinedly compensated for with effort and communication. Babs is quick to say yes to the trip. The two of us are Southern California pals. He is our comic relief when we need it, and during intense, emotional situations, he has an ability to ground those around him. An aspiring rapper/musician, Babs sings the national anthem before one of our games and does a great job. We all lean on his energy and positivity.

From Babs:

I remember the warmth and love the people of Bosnia shared with us. In the middle of winter, after years of war, they opened their homes and hearts to us all and allowed us to be a vital part of their country's healings.

When I think back to those days in Bosnia, I'm reminded of the relentless drive and fight the people of Bosnia have. I needed to apply that mentality to myself, and grab life and make the most of my own disability. I had a newfound energy when I returned home. To give is to get. For me, it was a turning point.

Mark Shepherd—A Paralympic baller and shooter/scorer. Strong-willed and with a story to tell, Shep is good at keeping things light even though I know beneath the banter is a compassion deeply affected from what he saw.

From Shep:

To understand the damage that war inflicts, one only needs to drive around. Our group can't go half a kilometer without seeing the destruction wrought on the country and people of Bosnia. Bombed out buildings and homes; businesses burned to the ground, dark and desolate. Farmlands, still full of mines, remained unusable. At the time we were in Bosnia, there were still over three million mines undiscovered. It was a brutal aftermath to behold. In the macro sense, it was a sad commentary to what war does to a people and a country. A vision, I will never forget.

The Bosnians had prepared for our arrival. Everywhere we went, their representatives rolled out the red carpet. What they gave to us in the way of support and friendship was utterly amazing. Seeing the countryside, they had little to give. Despite it all, their generosity was incredible.

A young man named, Faruk Sabanovic, welcomed us. Faruk became disabled after getting shot, by a sniper, through his backpack while going to school. His injury left him paralyzed. He had a personal investment in the success of our trip.

Faruk's goal was to develop the Bosnia-Herzegovina Paralympic Committee. To get started, he needed to expose disabled sports in his country. Therefore, he sought us out. We were grateful and humbled to be a part of it. Faruk went on to launch his goal, and do other great things. He is now a filmmaker in Bosnia-Herzegovina.

Everywhere we played was packed. Everyone we met was welcoming. I've been all over the world to play sports. Believe me when I tell you, it was the trip of a lifetime.

Craig Shewmake—A fellow southern California compadre, Craig and I battle against and then with one another on Casa Colina Condors teams. Craig is an easy fit in this effort as he can defend, finish, and has deep range. His heart is a transparent thread throughout the squad.

From Craig:

During our trip to Sarajevo orphanage, I notice this one young boy about 8 to 10 years of age checking me out. I talk to him and his friend briefly, as we go about the tour of the facility. It's a memorable visit and hearing some of the horror stories of how these kids lost everything in their world is humbling, sobering and indicative of the cruelty we impose on each other. I say my goodbyes and encourage everyone to attend our game the following day.

Later in the day I'm shopping at one of the local outdoor markets and I notice the boy with a couple of friends wandering around. He comes over, says "hello." I notice he's wearing a pair of old tattered, leather, dress-up shoes. Figuring, this is the perfect spot to do something nice for this kid, who has been through so much, I buy him a pair of tennis shoes and a wind breaker type jacket. He doesn't want to accept the gift but I insist. We go about our ways.

We arrive and play our game the following day. Great game. Great event. I look to see if the kids from the orphanage are watching. I don't see the boy anywhere. After a few minutes I notice him in the background being kind of shy. His friend taps me on the shoulder and tells me how embarrassed and ashamed he is. I'm shocked. What's wrong? How can this be? Did we do something bad in the game? Was he mad that we beat his beloved local team? No, nothing of the sort. He had gone back to the orphanage after our little shopping encounter, and the other boys stole his new shoes and jacket. He doesn't want me to know and be upset.

Now let's think about that for a second. This young man, orphaned by a brutal war and coming to watch a USA wheelchair basketball team play in his hometown, almost doesn't show up because he feels embarrassed that my feelings might be hurt because others had taken a gift I'd given him. A gift of SHOES!

Carolyn Bechtel—Leland Montell's sister, Carolyn Bechtel is the mover/shaker that a trip like the 'Wheels of Hope Tour' demands. She brings along her *other* brother, Alan Durekel to assist where needed. Alan proved invaluable but that's such a Carolyn move, an under-the-radar tweak for the good and ease of all involved.

Carolyn believes in the tour enough to donate substantially.

Ideas are just fireside, camp stories, minus the spending jack for hotels, vehicles, insurance, food, and security. Carolyn has the relationships and knows the protocols. Because of her we have food, shelter, and a level of safety. Because of her, we can exhale, in a land that too often leaves you breathless and wondering, "Why, God? Why?"

From Carolyn:

This team is the truest of American ambassadors: bringing good will, hope, inspiration, peace, and sportsmanship.

Leland Montell—With a carefree and easy-going presence, Leland brings a calm to situations where others panic or throw in the towel. I've never understood the proposal-writer/grant-writer's life. What's to envy in their long, arduous hours in front of screens? Successes are achieved only through the behind-the-scenes, cooperative, and foundational work of professionals like Leland Montell.

From Leland:

I wrote up a proposal and began shopping it around. I approached the U.S. Embassy, the U.N., the Embassy of the Netherlands, my own organization (the International Medical Corps), and others. All agreed it's a great idea, but no one would fund it. Frustrated, I asked Carolyn for help. She's supportive and even came to Bosnia to meet Faruk and learn more.

There were times when I feared we wouldn't be able to pull it together. One day, as I was suffering a bout of pessimism, a guy comes in the office from a U.S. aid organization called Hands Raised Together. I gave him a briefing on humanitarian assistance in Bosnia, and at some point, during the meeting mentioned our proposal. To my surprise, he returns the following day and gives five grand in cash for the tour. That's the spiritual boost I dearly needed at that time.

Andy and Carolyn brought things together in the United States, while my team worked to organize the tour in Bosnia/Croatia. Over my career in humanitarian assistance, the week spent on tour with the team ranks amongst my most inspiring.

Alan Dunckel—Talking to Alan is a lesson in humility. Maybe it's because he's from California, but I found myself gravitating towards him more and more. The guy keeps a smile across his face whilst endlessly helping load and unload gear. Disability sport inspires. I'm proud of my wheel prints in the pursuit of a greater landscape for all athletes, but it's guys like Alan—hustling and assisting, wherever needed, that truly lighten the load.

Marin Tomas—In many ways, Marin is the trip's conscious. A Croatian, he knows firsthand the culprits and their laundry list of dirty deeds. In practical terms, he's our interpreter and lead driver. It would have been easy for him to pit us against the Yugoslavian/Serbs. His country takes the hits, and Marin knows intimately the effects of exploding shrapnel. Somehow, he keeps it light and sprinkles in a timely twinkling of levity when spinning stories of war and casualties. An interpreter far beyond languages and dialects.

Faruk Sabanovic—Extraordinary expeditions need a lightning-rod. Faruk Sabanovic personified why we put our lives on hold. His passion and intensity are constant, when all around tired minds begin to drift to familiar beds and the blue-parking lifestyle normalized back home. Faruk's omnipresence exemplifies his strength of character, his depth. Nothing here is normal to us Yanks. The moment a sniper's bullet finds his spine, Faruk becomes the advocate in a country—despite all its crimes, still longing for sport and competition. He makes it so.

David Gerletti—A Los Angeles native with decades of national and international officiating experience. He gives every game an extra layer of legitimacy. David is a quality official and an easy-going, great guy. David, at times, gets a piece of my temper, and in turn calls more than one technical foul against me throughout my playing career. Away from competition, we share laughs and profound conversations. I came to understand what a thoughtful and quality human he is.

From David:

There's a lot of history here (Bosnia/Herzegovina). It's a maze of different concepts, religions and ideologies. They have to figure out, on their own, how to get along.

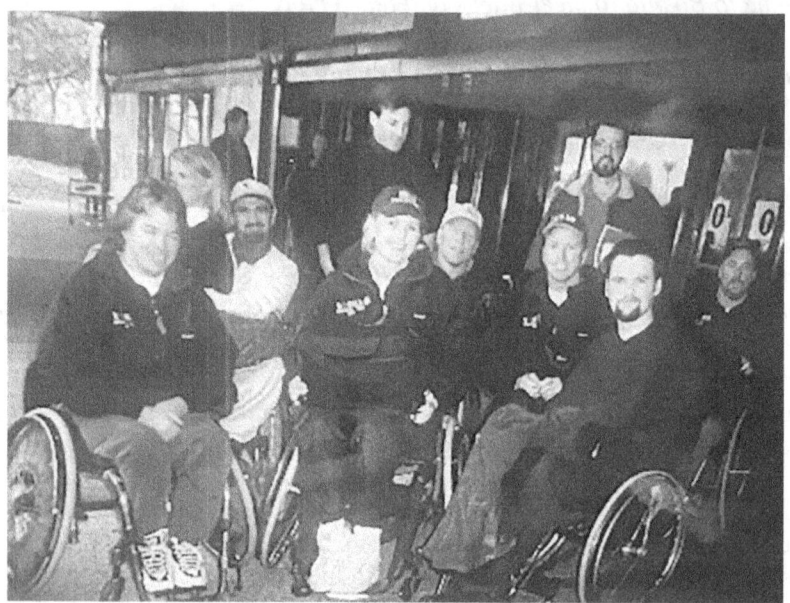

Wheels of Hope Basketball team and crew.

The following is a daily journal I kept during the 'Wheels of Hope' tour.

Day 1

Long flight, Atlanta to Frankfurt, Germany. Next flight into Zagreb filled with smokers, puffing throughout. The air is thick. Tough to take a breath. Put my jacket over my head, and fall asleep until finally touching down in Zagreb.

Years later, Craig Shewmake and I have a conversation. He has a vivid recollection of the flight into Zagreb. "Normally I wouldn't mention a plane ride as a memory but this one was like no other for me. After all my concerns about the safety of going to Bosnia—so shortly after the war—I suddenly realized I might not even make it there, when the captain turned off the 'No Smoking' sign. We were seated in the last few rows of the plane and you could just see this cloud billowing towards us like a Saharan Desert storm. I am pretty sure every single person on that plane smoked three packs of cigarettes in the time it took us to reach altitude. Visibility was down to three rows of seats. I was totally expecting, almost wishing, for the oxygen masks to drop from the ceiling. After an hour flight, head covered with shirt and jacket for survival, our flying hookah finally touched down. We made it, and I think only one of my lungs partially collapsed."

We're greeted by International Medical Corps (IMC), Leland Montell, and our interpreter—a Croatian named Marin. Jet-lagged and dog-tired we drive another good distance to an upscale resort near Lake Plitvice.

I'm struck by the surrounding waterfalls. There's over a dozen working at once, cascading into a south-sea-looking lagoon. The emerald pools are numerous, deep, luscious, and transparent. I eye its crystal-clear, sand bottom and fix for a moment on my beachy youth and upbringing. We're all byproducts of our fifteen-year-old selves.

Waterfalls and fond memories aren't enough to erase the sights of our initial drive in Bosnia. House after house are covered in bullet holes. Generational family homes used as target practice in a carnival of blood and bone.

Everything needs to stop.

It does not.

I sleep twelve hours.

Day 2

Wake up early, and travel in a convoy of vehicles to the city of Bihac. After a two-hour drive we arrive in the small city along the beautiful Una River. Along the way we witness more devastation and bullet riddled homes, stores and community buildings.

The war looks like it's fought in the neighborhoods. I can only guess exactly what went on.

Neighborhood warfare.

Marin is our driver. He speaks good English, and instantly feels like a comrade and friend. He attempts to explain the conflict in ways I'm able to understand. Through these initial teaching moments, I realize just how protected I am in the good ole U.S. of A. and how spoiled I am for the blessings I take for granted. Unaware of the world around me, I live my sissy life.

We rest at a lovely coffee house perched on the Una River. The Una is known for its trout. I imagine myself on its banks or in my boat, and for a moment escape to a place of peace and understanding. The stillness of fishing; my steady always.

Wheels chewing pavement towards the next game/contest is always a mixed, emotional bag. Sometimes light and chatty, led by a storyteller, spinning tall tales of embarrassment or conquest. Other times, a bumping mix of bass driven, measured melodies. Then there's the big game silence and solitude—athletes, coaches, and staff visualizing the best version of themselves during big moments. The air hangs stiff and heavy.

Today is different altogether. Sitting shotgun, listening to Marin, it's easy to forget the NATO-led security in lead and rear vehicles, but what's undeniable are the lasting images: a single brick wall standing, ascending to a roof that isn't there; bricks neatly knocked out of third story houses—a firing point for deadly snipers; panoramic balconies missing adjoining roofs; clean, white sheets and colorful children's clothes, hanging from a second story clothesline, surrounded by hundreds of bullets holes that missed kill targets; farmers imagining crops to market minus devastated barns and blown-to-smithereens tractors.

The opposite of inspiring, cynically rests beyond each turn and every bend in the road. We arrive at the gym.

The place is full of folks: a couple thousand, exciting and palpable.

The team we play is new. They've spent only six months together and are made up of novice, war veterans. The crowd is boisterous and encouraging of their team. We chose to pull back, keep the game within range and not embarrass the veterans before their home crowd. We coast to a 57-42 win in the first game of the 'Wheels of Hope' tour.

We leave and have a late lunch at the Hotel Sedra. The Una River again provides a backdrop to scenic, vista views.

I eat in fifteen minutes and am ushered to a press conference with the town's Mayor. It's a long-winded affair, in a smoke-filled room with no ventilation. I'm reminded how basketball-crazed this region of the world is as we're repeatedly told we're going to lose the upcoming game.

We leave directly for the game. I eye the Una River one last time.

The old and aging venue holds historic relevance. We're told, not only is this where wheelchair basketball is first played in the country but also the home of its first international games. We are excited to see and feel what's ahead of us.

The irony is the inaccessibility of the place. We need to be lifted and carried up steps to the playing floor. It's a small, Cracker Box of a gym. A Bosnian version of Hoosiers. There must be 500 people in a space for a hundred. Standing room only and wall-to-wall basketball fanatics. Young kids and teenagers hanging from climbing ropes along the four walls. The court's defined, not by lines but by people. When we chase balls into the crowd, they give us a turbo push back onto the floor, yelling and screaming with a second-to-none sporting passion.

Before the crowd packed the old venue.

I always love the energy and subtleties of a big game in a hostile environment. This is something altogether different and entirely new.

I have a bad feeling. We're prime for some home cooking from the local referee. The thickness of the Mayor's voice, "You're going to lose," echoes in my thoughts too often.

Two of the Bosnian stars show up late for the game. Upon their arrival the fans erupt and begin chanting their names. They are beloved. Impressive.

The game is a thriller and the crowd maintains its frenzied, hanging from the rafters, volume throughout.

They jump on us for an 8-2 early lead.

I hit a 3-pointer, from deep, at the half-time buzzer to put us up five.

Suzie and Tiana, keep their nerve, and play well.

Craig Shewmake has his own memories of the game. "We pull up and the gym is up this huge hill with several sections of stairs. It's snowing slightly and I'm thinking this is going to be a chore. Nope. Suddenly dozens of people come down, lift us on all sides of our chairs and carry us up the hill. Unreal. I am talking to one of the guys helping out and mention, 'there wasn't much lighting on the streets.' He replies, 'We had to cut the power to certain sections to get it to the gym'. Can it get more surreal than this? Then we enter the gym. WOW! This place is the size of the basketball floor, with a few feet of out of bounds real estate. You can maybe fit 100/200 people in there comfortably standing. There had to be well over a thousand people and closer to two. The lines of the court are the people's feet. The kids are literally hanging from the rafters. Being focused on what's going on 'inside the lines,' I usually have no clue what the crowd is doing while performing. This was just the opposite. I was paying more attention to the crowd than I was to the game. It was really a great experience, where everyone involved seemed to have a wonderful time."

We win, 59-51. It's a memory game for a lifetime. The environment and meaning of why affects us all in a way we hadn't imagined before. We are becoming passengers on a ship steered by the human spirit.

The gold medal game in the Barcelona Paralympics is my go-to sporting memory, but I've never played a more meaningful game than the one tonight.

Back to the hotel. Beers and beds.

Day 3

Zero-dark-thirty. It's too early. I wake up on the road to Zenica and it's still only seven in the morning. What's supposed to be a five-hour trip, is seven with snow and icy conditions. Zenica isn't far from Sarajevo. I remember the 1984 winter Olympics in Sarajevo. A country, and community dedicated to sport and hosting the world.

I'm brought to tears listening to Marin explain the complicated conflict. The road is littered with blown up houses and buildings. We talk for close to six hours. I turn towards the window when I feel the water-works building.

Marin tells me of Serbian neighbors forcing one another to rape the wife of Bosnians next door. If he won't go through with it, he'll be killed and a different neighbor is forced to do the raping. They do this to scramble the thinking and legacy of the community. The thinking is, when folks move back home, they'll be unable to co-exist. Once friends, but now mortal enemies by horrible, despicable acts of systemic, mass rape. I'm shaken to my core and offended with a newfound depth of mankind's deeds.

He explains, as the miles of destruction litter my mind, the complexity of war and devastation. I'm at the limit of how much more I can take in but to look out the passenger window takes on new levels of despair.

Muslim vs Serbs, Serbs vs Croats, Bosnians vs Serbs. Frontlines, with as many as five different groups fighting—and killing one another, at times unable to tell one from another—friend or foe. As a soldier, Marin is injured from an exploding landmine and its rocketing shrapnel.

Marin is a great man, with a happy, soulful spirit.

Another press conference at another hotel. We're again told we are going to lose, as the Zenica team is the best in Bosnia. There's a fire in my belly. I'm excited for the challenge before us. Bring it.

Another good crowd and better yet, a welcoming huge floor.

Our team speed is superior and jump on them 12-4, and lead by 12 at half. I pick up three phantom fouls and am to the bench at [the] five-minute mark in [the] first half. I hate the bench, not playing whilst others take space on a floor that is rightfully mine. I admire my teammates keeping the game close with rugged, determined play.

At the nine-minute mark in the second half, Team Bosnia, or Zenica ties the game at 46. The crowd erupts. There is singing and chanting.

I re-enter the game dripping with confidence. I know we will win once I get going. We do, 69-61.

We can't get out of [the] venue fast enough. The snow keeps the heatless venue frigid. I play with long-johns.

That night has too many beers but we have a blast laughing, and trying to speak with our lost-in-translation Bosnians.

The long day ends with a one-person capacity elevator ride to my room and blessed solitude.

Day 4

Tremendous, 6 a.m., sunrise out the hotel room window: snow capped mountains, bird of prey beneath the clouds, and river below. By eight, we're on the road to Tuzla, the third largest city in Bosnia.

Along the journey, we take a country roadside break. Lots of Wheel Heads needing to pee. David Gerletti, our baby-faced referee from Pasadena, California, slips away without folks noticing. He's attracted to the burned-out tank off the road. We hear Marin. He's loud and serious.

Yelling in Gerletti's direction, Marin barks, "Get out of there. Back here. Now."

Our concerned group all urge David to get back to the safety of the team.

I hear Craig Shewmake, "Hey, Dave, what's the reason we are on this little tour?"

Dave answers, "Land mine awarrrrrrr-uh-ness."

The 50-yard walk back to the roadway and the safety of our vehicles is tense and magnified. Gerletti walking the longest plank of his life.

Our scenic roadside breather turns serious and life-threatening; again, exemplifying our Americanness and naivety.

The rest of our two-hour drive is a constant reminder of devastation and despair. Each new approaching city [is] an upside-down landscape of before and after: bombed out bridges, burnt buses, bunkers with soldiers manning tanks, automatic weapons, and NATO-led peacekeeping vehicles.

The good guys and bad guys are a fading and fine line.

Still, the arrival in Tuzla is powered by humor and laughter. Marin, Babs, Craig and Alan cracking hilarious jackpots. Keeping it light works when surrounded by wretchedness, and misdeeds.

Hotel Tuzla is the nicest so far with larger (almost American size) bathrooms and English-speaking television. The remote fails to work and I am reminded again, just how spoiled I am.

Another lunch and reception outline the routine of why we're here. Today's home-town sponsor is a brewery. The team is happy.

We teach a clinic for [the] local Tuzla team before [the] anticipated, nationally televised evening game. The schedule is beginning to take its toll. I imagine what it's doing to the rest of the group.

The game begins. The crowd is early, ready, and loud. European community fans are an example of synchronized mayhem. They love their sport and home-grown personalities. We present a new performance basketball chair in the pre-game ceremony. The crowd erupts with sincere gratitude. The volume of it all gives me goosebumps.

I know I'm where I am supposed to be.

I look down the line at my weary, yet enabled compatriots and appreciate them completely. We again face the Bosnian national team. They've taken to following us from town to town. Overconfident and flat, we manage to get to halftime tied at twenty-nine.

We'd beaten the same group the night before as I sat [on] the bench in foul trouble. Tonight, free from the foul calls, I don't get it done. We only score 12 points in the second half to lose 49-41. We play poorly and not as a team. The Bosnian team beat a USA team on national television. Initially disgusted, I begin to understand what this game means to the Bosnians and their disabled veterans. We are destined to fulfil the mission of this tour, and tonight, watching the Bosnians celebrate with tons of national pride on national TV, is our role to play.

Still, I hate it.

We played so poorly, and didn't play team ball. After dinner and beers, we met, and discuss our play (or lack of it), and our problems with one another. These are the times when teams bond or begin to fall. We agree the loss is deserved.

Tiana Tozier remembers that night in a more recent message:

"Entering the dimly lit banquet room, Kiley is handed the microphone as we take our places. I watch him intently. Kiley, more than anyone I know, hates losing, but in typical Kiley fashion he rises to the occasion."

"'Congratulations,' he says addressing the Bosnian team. 'You played an excellent game and provided thousands of Bosnians the opportunity to view wheelchair basketball at its best.'"

"After restating our trip's mission, Kiley is sure to pivot, reminding all, 'It's just one game. We play again tomorrow.'"

"Rolling over and placing his arm around my shoulders, Kiley gives me a wry, cocky grin and says, 'See T, sometimes even when you lose, you win.'"

Day 5

Wake to find that my phone [call] home last night tallies a hundred bucks. With all the emotion of yesterday, I needed time with Sandy and the kids. The twenty-five-minute call pisses me off initially, but I'm quickly over it. Who am I to whine after speaking to my healthy, safe, and cherished loved ones?

Our travelling road show loads its mountain of gear: sport chairs, day chairs, bags, balls, cameras and the mammoth bag of candy we distribute to children after our games. The once-175-pound canvas bag of refined sugar and textured chocolate has certainly dwindled but the joyful smiles of happy children, with their fists full of sweets, is a lasting one.

The roads to Sarajevo are, in one turn of the head: snowcapped, mountain switchbacks—each curve and deep turn, a wonder of death-defying engineering and brave driving. The opposite turn, a reload of diminished dreams; traversing hundreds and hundreds of houses that used to be, before all the bullets and .50-caliber shells. I cannot properly digest what my eyes see.

Sad but true.

Marin drives like a champion whilst continually pointing out the front lines. Only a person with intimate knowledge can understand the complex military objectives that damn near destroys his homeland. Every time he makes light, or cracks a joke, I am amazed.

I can't say enough just how oblivious Americans are. One click of the remote, and a warring struggle like this, is gone—and so are we. We move to our next indulgence without a concept of how the world truly burns. Heartbreaking.

Every city except Zenica has to survive battles, takeovers, and disarray. Country roads are an epicenter of brutal killings. Land mines are everywhere blowing apart innocents and kids with equal, arbitrary ease.

It's 11:15 a.m. We arrive in Sarajevo.

I miss my family and love them more.

Marin points out a home, where one shell killed a family of eight: Mother, father, grandma, grandpa, son-in-law and their children. He then tells us the average income for Sarajevo residents is 60 to 80 dollars a month. Small beater cars litter the streets as others limp along.

We run the Sarajevo streets in our convoy of three, modern, Toyota Land Cruisers.

Above us, the city's high rises are skeletons of the buildings they used to be. Holes the size of Volkswagens scatter the different buildings' architecture and crumbling foundations. All the windows are blown out. Its glass litters floors and ledges. There are gravesites inside Sarajevo's Olympic Stadium.

Holiday Inn, here we come. Two hundred bucks a night, with .50-caliber, bullet-hole artwork.

Outside the Holiday Inn, Sarajevo.

Pizza for lunch.

Hour and a half nap.

For a brief period, I feel like I'm back home—a fine hotel, friendly food, and the needed space for myself.

Then, I'm reminded, I'm not. From my room I can see a walkway where blankets run along a path, hung by rope, so folks can move during daylight hours without being gunned-down by snippers from the surrounding hills; called 'Sniper Alley.'

The game against Bosnian team is massive. Our energy and willingness to play for one another is attacked and taken away from us last night. Tonight's different. Tied at half at 29, it's their turn to only score 12 second half points. We put a whoopin' on them and cruise to a 61-41 win.

Everyone's happy. The gap between performance and potential is tightening.

Day 6

A game with Sweden is arranged. They're young, fresh and fast; and it's obvious to me in warm-ups we're about to see a full-court press. Breaking a press is a tough, artful grind of ball handling, crossing-off defenders, outlet passing, and finishing with speed. When the factors sync up, points come in uncomplicated bunches and the majority of looks are high percentage layups.

The Swedes press. We're down 31-22 in a sluggish, first half.

Half way through the second half we're up six and have them thinking twice if they can stay with us throughout. Worn out, and fighting exhaustion, we hand them the game. We should have won. We should have won that damn game.

Our schedule is non-stop, vitally worthwhile, but gruelling. Earlier in the day we take a donation of clothes to Sarajevo orphanage.

Many of the people we met at [the] orphanage, as well as on the streets, see the nationally televised game in Tuzla. These are the nuggets of human exchange that continually spark the group towards the next clinic, press conference, unfamiliar hand grab or high five, and ultimately our next basketball game. This is our role and currency. We're luckier for it.

The difference between gratitude and guilt is drawn within a delicate, thin line. I can't escape how easy my life is back home. Futile attempts to compare the two lands inevitably come to a halt when I eye the rubble and concrete foundation of what was divine and charismatic. It's like I'm a lifeforce spirit amongst the blaze burning what's devout and holy. Today, I speak to an orphan. His entire family is killed in war. The salt in my eyes is constant.

Losing to the Swedes is humbling as an American.

Perspective is forever as a human being.

Day 7

As tired as one may be, some nights aren't meant for rest.

In the hustle of another smoky, stuffed-air, Holiday Inn reception, I hear a familiar voice. It's Chip Turner, a tennis playing, Southern California friend and photographer. We both played Open division in the early days of Wheelchair Tennis. Chip also represented the USA in the 1988 Seoul, Korea, Paralympics. These days he's a war photographer, working on a book. He's seen us on television and makes the trek to Sarajevo to shoot our game and share some laughs. Just when the world is so immense, dastardly, and full of rage, it becomes smaller and more like home. Such a surprise and twist of fate. Chip and I stay up most the night laughing, sharing stories of mutual times, and of course the atrocities of what is now Bosnia; but as long as we keep talking, sharing exaggerated tales of shared friends—I feel home, or as close to home as this place allows.

As soon as I close my eyes, I am drilled awake. We're due at the airport by 5 a.m. to play an afternoon game against the Croatians in Zagreb. Word is the Croats are a tough out. Our whirlwind schedule is dominating our psyche. Faces are long and eyes, red deep.

I wonder if we have enough juice for another game?

The high-altitude airport proves spooky and scary in the cool, morning mist.

The SFOR, our NATO buddies, are our military safety escort. This group helps us feel secure during an unsecure time. I am drawn to the two Americans: Lieutenant Colonel and Sergeant Major by rank and nation, but I'm also impressed by the Greek led NATO forces. The longer the tour continues the more I value this group. They're deciding if they might drive to Zagreb.

Hoping for a comfy jet, we instead fly in a cramped propellor plane with low visibility. The one-hour flight from Sarajevo to Zagreb is tense, bumpy, and full of fidgety apprehension. It's 9:15 in the morning at the Zagreb airport. I am wiped out.

Wanting to sleep—like it's my job—I instead do one last press conference. The good folks here are excited to have us. I focus on the surroundings, trying to stay sharp. The beer in the cola vending machine peaks my maladjusted interest.

Our game is televised on Croatian television. We've seen many of our opponents previously on tour. We should win. We are confident. We lose.

Down six at half, we're taken aback, as the crowd is hostile and angry towards us. Our exhaustion is a rallying point as we begin a comeback. We're behind 15, with 6 minutes to go. The atmosphere is hysterical, wild, and close to being out of control. I hit four straight 3-pointers. We press them full court. We cut the lead to four. We get no closer, but the game is a donnybrook and crazy exciting.

The SFOR drive the six-hours to see our last game and see us off. Meant the world to us all.

Post-game brewery reception hits the mark. Great food, and good feelings pouring out of us all. Everyone associated fell in love with people on tour, and our last night, with these happy, boisterous Croatians, drinking beer in massive mugs is the celebration everyone in the room deserves.

I can't help it. It's early. I excuse myself to call my wife and kids.

Then, I sleep.

Day 8

Airport terminals, trains, tubes and sandwiches are the incurable, uncorrectable major chord in the blues of international, sport travel.

Some do their brave, chatty best, to be a decisive spark in the irrefutable fact that we're almost there. At least we have each other. A cheeky vodka drink in the shadows, but only one—any buzz falls a far reaching second to the ball-ache of pissing on airplanes. Onto a discarded USA Today and a scan of sports pages, followed so intently when living my selfish rendering of who I think I am. I have changed. There is no doubt.

*Others tap out. Point **A** to point **B**. Sit. Plant. Headphones. Disconnect from utter exhaustion, consuming thought, movement, and exchange. The emotional* *malady that only a lover's hug, or young daughter's neck squeeze can remedy. I am done—and I am done without the pretense of caring what anyone thinks.*

Sporting, airport zombies, post-event, mainlining coffee. If I wasn't one so often, I'd take pity. We're so glaring, pronounced, and exposed. The endorphins down-sliding into pools of depression, simmering below and beneath the surface.

I haven't processed the joy of Bosnia. I push the hurt somewhere deep and boiling. How do I explain how I feel? Is it too much for my kids? I can't stay busy. The sterile, grey walls of the airport tap into my superball of emotions; bouncing wildly into the crevices of what's light and dark. I am awakened, but I am delirious.

No accidents.

No coincidences.

I read my trip journal, turning the pages. Shrapnel of words and sentences missing, then hitting its mark. I will try to explain and perhaps then I can make sense of why? Why war? An emotional discharge is building.

I hear his words, "This war was so dirty, and I don't think this war happened anywhere on earth like here in Bosnia." He tightens his grip on his wheels. "Because the Yugoslav army used all their forces against the Muslims and Croats here in Bosnia. We were without guns, tanks, and other things that we needed for this war, but anyway, we didn't lose. I don't wish for anybody, on this earth, to have the same thing."

Salt. Eyes. Again. Where's my sunglasses?

For just a second, I close my eyes.

There is love waiting at baggage claim: Sandy, Justin, and Danielle.

Bosnia shows me who I am and what I shall become.

It's not enough to be known for baskets, assists, championships, or gold medals.

Does God care?

Doubt it.

Who did I really help?

Will I continue on this path?

Will I play a role in the lives of newly injured kids?

What about adults?

God is talking.

Am I finally listening?

As a *'convenient'* believer, my spirituality works within horizontal planes. Spiritually awoken, I reach the vertical.

The air is thin.

PEACE THROUGH CHRIST & HOOPS

I can do all things through Christ who strengthens me.
— Philippians 4:13

I'm in seek mode. There is an expansion in the tumbling thoughts rebounding through my thinker. Since returning home from Bosnia, there's been a massiveness and a wrecking ball of weight to my state of mind. I'm simultaneously grateful and troubled. Immortality is a myth. The price to pay is one's mortality. Measures taken to remain alive are extraordinary. Measures taken to slay, slaughter, and dismember are even greater.

I'm unable to reboot or whitewash the images of a war-torn Bosnia. I'm indebted that ours is the side of peace, decency and rehabilitation. What we help kick-start lasts to this day. Disability sport in the Bosnia region is robust. Landmine awareness in Herzegovina and Bosnia is prevalent. Still, I am uneasy with my place in things. We parachute in for ten days and do our thing. We are just as quick to parachute back out. Home. Safety. Comforts.

I stare at Lake Norman, hoping that some shift of wind or faraway rainbow might give me a hint of insight or understanding of my most common thought since returning home. *Why?*

I'm looking for a sign.

The atrocities and war crimes of Bosnia are emotional and nonstop. I'll work my way through it, all but the experience has me over its knees.

I turn to Chaplain Mark Iacono. He works at the new job. In a sense he's in charge of *Faith* at the Charlotte Institute Rehabilitation Center. Before leaving for Bosnia, we have many conversations. I see a light in him that attracts. He never puts his beliefs on me. He listens. He shares. He treats me how I treat newly injured patients. Listen to their story, find a common ground, and let them know the unimagined possibilities of a new path.

In North Carolina the presence of God is abundant. There is a global faith and regional rule to the corner sanctuaries that adorn the landscape. North Carolina has modern, even opulent churches as well as free-standing, evangelical houses of worship built before the Civil War.

The question looms. How can I understand God? What must I do to live a spiritually-driven life?

In the fourth grade my mom, a devout Catholic, enrolls me at St. John the Baptist grammar school. I'm an altar boy. I don't act like one in the classroom. I'm physically disciplined. The nun's weapon of choice is called a Pointer.

When they tire of slapping me with their Pointer, I instead kneel for an hour or two in the far corner at the base of the Virgin Mary. The floor is hard, tiled, and does a number on my knees.

I believe in God but that is where it ends. From Grammar school through high school, I do not have what is called, 'a relationship with my creator.'

After my spinal cord injury, of course, I pray. Lying in the hospital bed, my 'foxhole prayers' go something like, *"God, if you would just let me have my legs back; I will commit to you for eternity."* My other greatest-hits prayer includes, *"Just let me have kids. I can handle the paralysis."*

I rub my leather Jesus necklace around my neck before closing my eyes.

A warm, evening breeze off the lake snaps me back into the now. It's time to be bold. I ask God to be part of my day and decisions.

It's been almost twenty-five years since the solitude of hospital beds and all its unintentional awakenings. It's my turn to be the light for others.

I hear Sandy calling the kids to dinner.

I turn and follow.

A SECOND BOUNCE

Start where you are. Use what you have. Do what you can.

— Arthur Ashe

*Randy Snow and I go undefeated for two straight
seasons sponsored by Team Quickie.*

I find the bag in a faraway corner of the garage. It's behind a stack of two wheelchair frames and a pile of Spinergy wheels. I feel the strings. Not great but good enough. There are three rackets inside the red Wilson bag. I've yet to unzip the other half. The space for towels, change of clothes, and an assortment of tennis odds and ends. I'm leary a pair of dirty socks from the 90s might pop out and assault me. I brush off a layer of dust before shaking the contents of the bag. It's an awakening. In a sense, I'm rattling an enjoyable and energetic time in my life back to a modern-day reality.

A few weeks prior, I agreed to compete in the tournament. Not sure why? Not sure how my mid-fifties body is going to react to multiple days of chasing down balls, hitting serves, and several hours of North Carolina summer sunshine.

I have a quick hit with Justin. He's a good player and keeps the ball in my strike zone. I feel the ball coming off my strings. Muscle memory kicks in. I start to come over the top of my forehand and move Justin around the court. He's a good son and continues to not move his old man around too much. My backhand is a continued slice. Find the ball out in front, lead with the bottom edge of the racket and drive through the shot with my lead shoulder. I work my way to the net and begin hitting balls out of the air. Juice hits with pace. I volley balls back at him before pasting a couple in the corners. Some overheads, fifteen minutes of serves, and I'm as practiced as I'm going to be at this point. I declare myself ready.

I haven't played a tennis tournament in over a decade-and-a-half, but damn the torpedoes.

Working my way to the third best player in the world throughout the 80s and into the 90s still brings a sense of extreme accomplishment.

Wheelchair tennis and I quickly fall for one another. The early days are fun-filled times traversing Southern California freeways and coastlines in search of new opponents and quality facilities. Vibrant characters like Jeff Minnebraker, Jim Worth, Chip Parmelly, Chip Turner, Dan Lachman, Russell Serr, Jim Black, and John Chambers are the colorful backbone to an emerging SoCal lifestyle. We have eight to ten players gather and play for hours. We'd rotate courts depending on who wins and loses.

It all happens under the protective umbrella of the National Foundation of Wheelchair Tennis and its founder Brad Parks. With his vision and guidance, the above hodgepodge of accomplices is corralled into a newfangled collective of personalities and talent to drive adaptive tennis forward.

Brad gets us on the phone and suddenly we're mixing it up with Hollywood celebrities and sporting superstars. We'd play doubles exhibition matches. The up/down affairs are great fun. We have tales of playing with/against Beau Bridges, his father Lloyd Bridges, Bo Derek, Martina Navratilova, Pete Sampras, Stefan Edberg, Andre Agassi, Lindsey Davenport, and so many more.

I'd always make sure to rifle one at the celebrity/pro at the net. Let them know I mean business. It's the early to mid-eighties, and those in attendance are taken—shocked even—at the athleticism and skill displayed by the Wheel Head players.

Then Brad has us on international flights playing up/down exhibition matches at professional tournaments with top-ranked players. It's a glorious time.

I develop my game. I believe I can be a national champion. Just need to apply my tested and true method of success. Work harder and better than everyone else. The timing of tennis works. It's the off season for basketball. Adding a tennis component to the summer mixes nicely with my track and road race training.

There is no 'off' switch when my mentality of being the best coincides with opportunity. I am working with precision and drive to be my absolute finest.

Tournament play picks up increased momentum in the 80s. Southern California is the hub with weekend tournaments throughout the summer. Northern California begins hosting events in Chico, Sacramento, Grass Valley, and San Francisco. There are also tournaments in Fresno and San Luis Obispo. In the far west of Hawaii an annual tournament highlights the talents and aloha of its increasing players.

Wheelchair tennis is bursting onto an ever-inflating scene.

I'm no country club player. In fact, I am the opposite. Tank top or shirtless, headband or hat on backwards and with a bravado of Ille Nastase or John McEnroe, I am more street court hustle than the tendered and manicured sensitivity of paying-to-play at the local country club.

The first generation of Wheel Head tennis players are a crew of trickeries and mischief. Ringleader and founder of the sport, Brad Parks has his hands full rounding up the merry pranksters. One of the first and biggest sponsors the NFWT wins over is Carta Blanca beer. Good times for everyone. At a regional event in Eugene, Oregon, all the beer goes missing. There are a few likely culprits. I have strong suspicions who the thieves are. The tournament director lets it be known if the beer is not returned the tournament will be cancelled. After hours, a green Volkswagen bus pulls up to the venue and unloads a dozen-odd cases of Carta Blanca at the tournament's adjoining swimming pool and clubhouse.

The tournament is a success and opens the door to many new players in the Pacific Northwest.

I'm content helping trail the path for adaptive tennis. I'm surrounded by memorable personalities tapping into genuine stoke and love for chasing a fuzzy, yellow ball. We photograph well, have something to say, and we all add a personal component that wheelchair tennis handsomely builds on. It's also outlandishly fun.

Brad Parks is my nemesis on-court during this initial time. His big serve, blistering forehand, and tendency to never let up frustrate me into the beyond. We play over a hundred pick up matches. I just can't beat him. It drives me crazy. My game is one of speed, chasing everything down and next level chair skills. If I'm able to get to the net, I can use my length and ability to hit into the corners of the court. Brad knows this. He keeps his ground strokes deep. He hits with pace. He dominates any short balls on his side of the court. He wears you down and makes you pay for any mental or physical lapse.

I love all our times on the tennis court. It's easy to see, experience, and feel that Brad and wheelchair tennis are on the cusp of something big.

"When the mind is free of any thought or judgement, it is still and acts like a mirror. Then and only then can we know things as they are," Timothy Gallwey.

Gallwey's book, The Inner Game of Tennis, *is either in my bag, next to the bed, or on my desk at work in my early days of competitive tennis. Published in 1974,* The Inner Game of Tennis *and its pages help me focus on the process, build belief in myself and most importantly to enjoy the moments of competition. These times are precious.*

I hire a coach. There's a greater number of quality players on the tournament circuit. Most notably, Randy Snow from Texas and Rick Slaughter from Nashville, Tennessee. Both play as ranked juniors before traumatic accidents have them playing from the chair. There are increased numbers of players out of Florida, Texas, and the Midwest adding to bigger draws and more rounds to navigate through before semifinals and finals are even an option.

My coach moves to Northern California. I'm not above hopping on a plane to spend a few days under his tutelage. I'm learning the nuances of the game: constructing and building points, finding angles, consistently returning serves with depth above all else, serving into the body as a weapon, adding the drop shot to help shorten points and aggressively using my forehand to open up the court.

I start taking the odd match off Brad. I refuse to lose to players ranked beneath me. I am a dependable semi-finalist in any event I play in. My rackets are sponsored and with continued success, I eventually take on the look of a top-ranked tennis player with the latest tennis garb.

At Casa Colina, I organize the first-ever prize money tournament at the Claremont Racquet Club. Winner takes home fifty bucks whilst the finalist pockets twenty-five. Have to start somewhere. In a couple years, I host the first "International Invitational" in the South Bay of Torrance. Men and women from the U.S., Canada, Australia, and various European countries attend. Winners take home thousands of dollars. Players are smothered in gear: Vuarnet sunglasses, Alpine car stereos, gifted clothing, and straight up cash.

I am still the third best player in the world and half of the best doubles tandem on the globe with Randy Snow. Still, I am unsettled with my place in things.

There are three players, during my day, that have better tennis skills than I. They are Brad Parks, Randy Snow, and Rick Slaughter. They are the big dogs. Frenchman Laurent Giammartini is the first European to begin winning consistently on our shores. I play him less than a half a dozen times but outlast his tremendous shot-making with regularity. It wouldn't be long before German Kai Schramayer and Australian David Hall adds a true, worldwide appeal to the game. Both are lifelong champions.

Brad and Randy stack up many wins against me. I continuously get to the U.S. Open semifinals with a consistency that allows me to keep a top five ranking throughout my playing days. Then, face either Brad, Randy, or Rick Slaughter.

One year, I am up 5-3 on Randy in the third set of the U.S. Open semifinal. It's my time. Randy goes on to win four straight games. His legend is fabled and undying. I experience his metal up close and with a pulse that steamrolls. I didn't play badly in those last four games; I just didn't play spectacular enough. I play too safe. Everyone roots for Randy. You're not just playing him; you're trying to overcome the will of everyone in his massive circle. I can still hear Shorty Powers, Randy's number one fan, yelling, "Boom" with each passing shot or service ace.

I inch my way to the net to shake hands. A painful tennis tradition. I'm ready to either burst into tears or enter into a fit of rage that will follow me for a lifetime. Instead, I shake his hand firmly. No limp wrist, soggy noodle exchange with the greatest that ever played the game. Randy's eyes simply say, 'Sorry, dude. This is what I do.'

I am able to take Randy a total of five times in tournament play. Yes, I've counted. I wonder, though, if Randy didn't become somewhat bored in the exercise of winning. Put him at a regional or community event and you get Randy looking for a hill to climb or a situation to work through. These situational plays don't always pay off for him. These lesser events are valuable touch tone experiences when it's time to win a major or Paralympic gold.

Brad Parks and Ricky Slaughter, on the other hand, never let up.

Brad's the stingiest player (in practice or tournament play) that I've ever gone up against. Rick looks to embarrass you with a multitude of spins, forehand drives, and his cocky demeanor. I take my lumps against both.

I beat Brad twice in tournament play. Probably played him over 30 times with ranking points and trophies on the line. I have one of those, "it's all going right days," in the finals at Nashville, Tennessee, and go on to a 6-2, 6-4 championship victory. I keep the ball, with the score on it as a keepsake. The ball sits in my office to this day. I also beat him at a bigger scale tournament in Palm Desert. I only remember the victories because he is such a tough guy to beat.

There's a new major tournament in New York. It's on the hallowed grounds of Flushing Meadows and a sight of one of the Grand Slam's four majors. The advancement of our sport is blatant and obvious. I'm playing on the same courts as the greatest pros ever. I beat Randy Snow in the first semifinal. It's an unforgettable moment. I train like a beast prior to the event. I absorb Randy's eventual run of games with a steely resolve and a confident run of my own. Slaughter beats Parks in the other semifinal. The stage is set.

"Most people think of poise as calm, self-assured dignity, but I call it 'just being you.' When we have poise, we're not acting, faking, or pretending. We're not trying to be something we're not, nor are we attempting to live up to others' expectations," John Wooden on Poise, fourth tier on the Pyramid of Success.

The finals at Flushing Meadows. Home to the United States Tennis Association. I find calm confidence.

I refer to the book next to my bedside, "The player of the inner game comes to value the art of relaxed concentration above all other skills. Fighting the mind does not work. What works best is learning to focus in it," Timothy Gallwey, The Inner Game of Tennis.

I am prepared to take on the well-trained Rick Slaughter and the superlative test of a major tournament finals like never before.

I win in straight sets.

Did I just win a major?

My first.

My only.

I'm part of the club.

I'm playing in my basketball chair. Don't know where my tennis chair has gone or to whom I probably gave it. I watch a couple of the top seeds warm up. They have the strokes but lack consistency. Their grips are extreme. Keep the ball low. Don't allow the space to come up and behind the ball. Time to be an annoying human backboard. Focus more on depth than angles.

Most importantly, have fun in the process of figuring it all out.

I work my way through the draw. The Charlotte tournament pulls in some of the top players in the deep south as well as the northeast. Early on, I simply stay patient. These new crops of players are overly aggressive. Keep enough balls in play and their unforced errors begin to outweigh any winners.

During changeovers, I visualize the ball on my strings, sense the feeling of hitting it square and pure. My right hand begins to take on a soreness. An aching pulse. I eliminate any notion of arthritis or any old guy malice. Pushing with a racket in your dominant hand is an art. I haven't been a tennis artist for over a decade and a half. Stay the course. Deal with the annoying discomfort. Drink some water. Get back out there.

I eye Justin. He's seen his old man do this so many times. I appreciate that he's here. We nod at one another and share an inner chuckle.

I lose the next game and the first set. I'm playing the top seed from New York. He hits a big ball and is driving me to the corners of the court. I'm able to chase down his driving shots but too often I'm hitting the ball back short, before the service line and New York is easily putting my short shots away.

Second set, I make the decision to move New York around the court. Drop shots to the backhand side, lobs and three-quarter pace arching shots force him to create his own pace. New York begins spraying shots well wide of the sidelines. I take the second set.

I'm now in a dogfight. New York is finding his groove. The third and deciding set is a battle of wills. The body feels good. We've both adjusted to the other's adjustment. All match, I've been spinning my serve in. Putting the ball in play and starting the point. I flatten a couple first serves. The increased pace gets him out of rhythm. I get some vital, easy points.

His unforced errors begin to mount. I'm back to using the lob before intentionally hitting the ball short and daring him to hit it by me. I'm pulling out some old and trusted tricks. I get back one. Then another. His driving and excessive forehand snaps the top layer of the net—the tape. The ball falls back onto his side.

Game. Set. Match.

It's rewarding winning a tennis tournament well into your fifties.

I meet New York at the net. I've always remembered how gracious Randy acted during his many wins. He makes losing hurt a little less.

We shake hands. Our eyes meet.

"Guy, you've played this game before. You have. Haven't you?"

"Back in the day," I answer. "Back in the day."

I will never pick up a racket again.

MY OPENING FAREWELL

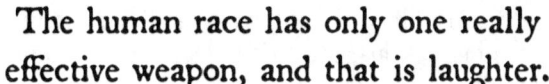

The human race has only one really
effective weapon, and that is laughter.

– Mark Twain

We're a band. Our chords, leads, beats, and original riffs dominate the scene for over forty years. There are quality session players joining us along the way. Their added notes and phrasing are vital in the definition of us. There are an array of producers and money people also. Each a trigger and accomplice for what we shall become, collectively and independently.

Together, we're pure comedy. One zinger after another. A one-upmanship that extends boundaries and personal identity or scope.

The four of us are on Lake Caddo in a town named Uncertain. It's one of Shorty's bass fishing tournaments. The Texas event is heaving with Wheel Heads living the adventures of the outdoors. It's Shorty's dream come true. His hard work and relationship-building make it so.

Shorty brings in Frank to be the evening's emcee. There's a colossal fish fry and awards ceremony. Frank is put on this earth to make people laugh. His theatre background is a prevalent tool he practices, sharpens, and performs throughout; either onstage for admiring audiences or in situations with his buddies. Tonight is both. Beware.

Frank is the lone, able-bodied member of the band. He's not just a member but also our invaluable roadie. He can pack a truck with three Wheel Heads, frames, and tires in a couple minutes.

Frank takes to the stage in sunglasses and a cane. He's a blind man in a sea of wheelchairs, crutches, and prosthetics. Instant laughter. Absurdity. I turn to Randy and Shorty. It's going to be a wild ride. Frank stumbles about before finding the mic. He starts peppering the crowd:

"What do fish say when they hit a concrete wall? Dam."

He then makes his way to a group of men next to the stage. His cane banging the frames of their chairs. His head bobs like Stevie Wonder on the piano. He takes a beat. He breathes in deep, "Welcome ladies."

The place erupts. I lean into Randy. I feel Shorty slapping then pushing on my shoulder. We laugh until we cry. He's just getting started.

"Why did the fish get kicked out of school? Sea-weed."

Shorty, Randy, and I are his targets for the next ten minutes.

You need tough-skin to be in our band. We trade barbs without a second thought. We're good at pushing one another. One can be an irritant to another. We cross over the line of decorum in making a point, finding a punchline, or boosting our magnified egos. We're brothers. We've earned the right to give and get grief.

Randy Snow, Michael Shorty Powers, and Frank T. Burns. Never once does it cross my mind, I'd live my life without them. The three catalysts of change steer my thinking, and then my actions, towards what's better and more progressive for our sporting subculture. The previous pages speak to this.

It's Randy and I competing against, with, and always for our beloved country. During competitions, all over the world, we're roommates. We both believe in the vitality of visualization. We plaster positive slogans all around the room. I go in the bathroom and lift up the toilet seat. Randy—being Randy—places a slogan, "Let it rip."

The levity and ease Randy brings to high-pressure moments and events transcends. The laughter we share lasts. There's clarity and a healthier perspective.

We're teaching a tennis clinic in Japan. We then hop a jet to Hawaii for a tournament. We rent a "hot rod" Lincoln Continental convertible. Careening down the pineapple roads of Kauai, rock tunes blaring, singing out loud and off key, we pull into our five-star resort for the week. I lose to Randy in the final. Again. However, I do catch the biggest fish later in the week. We celebrate eating sushi on our way back to the docks. Winning.

When Randy's involved there's going to be stories. Some of which are left better off the page. Our times are legendary. I've never known a more welcoming soul on planet earth. A champion of the underdog he routinely goes out of his way to bring the shyest or most awkward out of their cocoon. God gives Randy this big chest in order to house his big unselfish heart. A normal body cannot handle such a heart—he makes us all feel important.

To know Randy is to know Shorty. With one comes the other. Both are Texas born and bred. They eventually end up living down the street from one another. As discussed throughout, Shorty's passion is the outdoors and all its offerings. He takes us all along for the nature-loving ride of the outdoorsman until we are one.

There's a video for Shorty's induction into the Texas Freshwater Hall of Fame. Shorty's running a fishing camp for a couple dozen juniors. He exits the comforts of his bass boat for the swampy waters of Lake Caddo. A couple kids have spotted a water snake.

Randy's image and voice tells the story, "He swims like a creature and approaches this snake."

Shorty, staring down the aquatic creature, "I get my eyes down on the water. I know he has to come up."

"All of a sudden there's a splash and water is going everywhere," continues Randy. "There's a snake tail and a paralyzed limb flying, and Shorty's head pops up…"

"I take it and stick his head in my teeth so he can't bite me; and I can swim. He starts slapping his tail against my head. The kids are all freaking out…"

Randy adds, "Here's a guy, [who] doesn't care what people think. He wants people to touch the scales and feel its teeth."

Looking into the camera, Shorty concludes, "Guess I've been the Snakeman ever since."

This is the audaciousness that keeps me at Shorty's side. Be it the Dusty Ole Road of Mt. Guadalupe or my modern-day administering of his Turning Point Outdoor Adventure Program. We all owe people whose dreams are bigger than anyone else's. This is Shorty. It's like he says, "Deal with it. Get on with life."

Shorty turns this Southern California city boy into a true outdoorsman. I now share the message he so vividly dreamt.

Randy, Shorty, and Frank. Three Main Street gunslingers, firing joy and opportunity to all they cross paths with. All three pass way too early. It's not about how, when, or why. All you need to know is a lot of the blood on these pages is theirs.

Every time I ponder the glorious notion of saying no. I think of my bandmates. They set the stage for us to continuously display our talents.

Frank, I have succeeded your position as Chair of the NWBA, Hall of Fame. I didn't want to at first. It feels like I've worked my shift. All you've done for me. Any milestone in my life and you're there. Your Chicago banter still echoes in me. You should see our HOF jackets.

Shorty, Turning Point and Lake Caddo will always be a celebrated priority. You once said about the program you created, "I've influenced enough of them; they should be able to handle it when I'm gone." Done.

Randy, any time I want to dismiss or not reach out because of any of my biases, I stop. I take a breath. Recalibrate. I do what you do. I turn around. Offer my hand. Look him/her in the eye. I bring a welcoming smile and begin again.

These days, I still take to the stage—it's just what I do after six decades of advocating. I'm a solo act but damn, I miss the rhythms, beats, and notes of my bandmates.

DNA

I am no match for the Chevy Apache truck.
I wake up in a full-body cast.
Feet to chest.
There's also a cast on my broken arm.
Insult to injury.
My nose itches.
I bang my arm-cast across my chin.
Use your one good limb.
The only one left.
Immense pain.
I cry out for all to hear.
There's an injection.
The first hit isn't free.
I'm paying with everything that I am.
I feel the morphine in my veins.
It feels like high tide.
There's a rush beginning in my toes.
I feel advanced.
Beyond my years.
I'm ten years old.
I can't remember my times tables.
More pain.
Its path is swift and snakes skyward.
Relief.
Nirvana.
A manufactured state of grace.
Numbness transitions to contentment.
Sleep.
It happens quickly.

Or does it?
A comfortable confusion reigns.
I missed morphine day at school.
Do the other fourth-graders know about this?
Another nurse.
Another needle.
There it is again.
It's to my head quicker.
The warming trails less than before.
I fight to stay awake.
Enjoy the comfort zone.
Cosiness without the blanket.
A home run without swinging the bat.
Without wanting.
I sleep.
The pain hums to be heard.
A bass drum in the distance.
The train is approaching down the tracks.
It's another forty-two minutes to go.
I know how to read the fourth-grade clock.
Fourteen minutes to recess.
Twelve minutes to the first baseline jumper.
School is basketball.
Nothing else.
Forty-one minutes to go.
I exaggerate my pain.
Mom springs into action.
There's a nurse beside the bed.
There's an additional moan to my anguish.
There's the needle.
Another injection.
Nurse and needle ringing true.
I'm Pavlov's dog.
There's no bell but I'm assuredly the slobbering hound.

I'm forty-five years old and competing on the world's stage again. It's been six years, with a two-year suspension and a fistful of hard-to-swallow humble pie jammed down my gullet, but I am back. I'm wearing the USA logo across my chest for all to see. It has to be this way. There is no way the stench of Barcelona is my swan song to the international game I love so deeply.

It's 1998 and the Gold Cup (World Championship) is in Sydney, Australia. The United States is coming off a disappointing bronze medal showing on our home turf and the Atlanta Paralympic *Games*. I sit out in Atlanta. It takes a full Paralympic cycle to recalibrate. My failed drug test, the effort involved fighting it, and my internal spark to compete again are an undeniable recipe to tell a new and different story.

Time steamrolls. In the 1992 Paralympics, I am the captain and lead the team in minutes played. The game goes through me. This is what I am accustomed to for over two decades. At the Sydney, Gold Cup, I come off the bench and play the role of a steadying calm amongst the chaos. I have never come off the bench my entire career. The newer breakout performers are Paul Schulte, Will Waller, and Mel Juette. Their production, chair skills, and defensive attention to details are undeniable. They play the fast pace collegiate style coached at the University of Whitewater, Wisconsin, the University of Illinois, and the University of Texas, Arlington. The college game, with its triple-switching defenses and read and react, match-up offences are a fundamental pillar of any elite game played today.

Head Coach Dan Byrnes chooses a younger version of the team. The writing is on the wall. I'm not about to go down without a fight.

My Barcelona teammates Tim Kazee and Trooper Johnson gobble up much of the rest of the playing time on offer. Both are crucial to the success of the team but none more than Trooper in the gold medal game against (yes) the Dutch. In the 61-59 win for the United States, Trooper leads the team in scoring and assists. He finishes 8 for 11 from the free throw line for a total of 18 points. In a little over 14 minutes, I knock down 4 of 6 shots.

Trooper Johnson earns it. I'm proud of him. He puts in more work than anyone. I have a front-row seat to his superlative preparation. He belongs on the world's stage.

My competitive drive and ego never waver. It doesn't matter, I'm in my mid-forties and have sat out a complete four-year cycle. I want to be on the floor and in the midst of the action.

In '98, I also have a competitive and technological advantage. Quickie and I introduce my signature sports chair, the Allcourt. We introduce the world to the first-ever ratchet, click-strap. My center of gravity is superior to the rest of the team and certainly our opponents. My chair spins 360s after 360s with little effort. The snowboard click strap, above my knees and across my thighs, connects me to the chair like never before. I'm able to turn without touching my hand-rims. Advantage me. Will Waller nicknames the chair, the HoverCraft. No one quite knows what they're taking in just yet. Little do they know they're actually witnessing the largest paradigm shift in the history of sport chair technology. Click-straps are used by most all players to this day. The advancement has lifted our game with increased performance, athleticism, and connection to the designs beneath us. The Dave Kiley Allcourt, fully adjustable, signature chair goes on to lead the market in sales for close to a decade.

It's the semifinals against Australia. Aussie fans are a handful. Belligerent, beers in hand, and vocal throughout; their Aussie-Aussie-Aussie, Oi-Oi-Oi chants dominate the sounds and vibe of the action. Australia is also defending gold medal champions. Their improbable Paralympic trek in the 1996 Atlanta Games is led by the brash, outspoken, and extreme talent of big man, Troy Sachs. The gold medal champs don't lose a single game in their historic run.

The arena is stuffed with green and gold clad fans. There's the energy of a rock concert. We jump on them early. I enter into the game and hit a couple shots. I kiss a couple off the glass. I defend like my existence depends on it. My teammates are feeding off my effort and execution. I hit a couple more in transition. The team knows I'm hot. They feed me the ball. I'm processing in real time whilst all around me is the hectic squall of rowdy fans, twitchy decisions, and whistle-happy referees. I'm in the zone for the last time. I just don't know it yet.

I play every minute like it's my last.

Our talent depth wears down the Sachs-reliant Aussie squad. Our balanced attack and scoring prevail. In just over eighteen minutes, I lead the team in scoring with 14 points. I hit all four of my free throws. Trooper finishes with 13 points.

I'm awarded Man of the Match in our 64-46 victory over the home team. I'm fully aware my tournament MVP days are behind me. The collegiate programs are churning out fully prepared performers. There are more coming.

Accepting my award, I take an extra beat to eye my teammates and surroundings.

In high school, I share a car with my brother Jeff. Our Volkswagen bug is a prized possession. I add wider tires to the back end and flare the fenders. The VW is a loud, beefy ride and speaks to an early seventies car culture.

I'm working the evening shift in the meat department of Alpha Beta grocers. I'm an apprentice butcher and making good money for a teenager. Uncle Ted pulls the right strings. He's high-up in the supermarket food chain and secures the job for his nephew.

After work, I eye a crew of coworkers in a semicircle conversing and sharing beers. I join in. Two beers later it's time to head home. Rain begins to fall. There was a light but steady mist earlier in the day. I jump on Highway 55 heading south and towards the coast. The jobsite in Santa Ana borders Costa Mesa. I can take the side streets home. I take the quick ride down the Highway instead.

The oversize tires hydroplane. I feel the backend fishtailing before ending up down an embankment. The cops are there within minutes. There are no empties in my car and with hardly a buzz, I hope for the best—A quick wench out and I'd be on my way. No dice. Instead, the patrolman calls my dad. I'm underage and the cop probably thinks he's doing me a favor. He tells my dad he suspects I've been drinking.

During the ride home, I get an earful. It's a fearful ride. Dad has had far more than a couple with the boys from work. His volume increases. With each hand gesture, I'm expecting a slap or punch. He's livid. How does the patrolman not sniff out the real drunk? Once he parks the car in the driveway, it's on.

We begin rolling around on the front yard. I've learned how to keep him at a distance with my length. I have greater reach and fend off most blows. I feel his fists into my forearms as I cover up. He's a bulldog and doesn't stop attacking. I'm wrestling against his superior power but also in contrast to the man I am developing into. I am not him. Will never be him. This infuriates. The way to live through these tussles is the art of defending without attacking. The next couple minutes intensify. I'm not his son right now. I'm the latest in his path of rage. He lands one against my ear. Adrenaline. Anger. I have to get to my feet. A neighbor's headlights pass by. I'm able to push off his lower back. He takes his hands off me for a second. That's all it takes. I spring to my feet before scurrying to the front door and then my bedroom. I stare at the doorknob with fearful terror. I hear mom trying to calm him down. I'll be awake throughout the night. I must get out of here. This is not my home.

It's the last time I wear a USA jersey, after four-decades, with its red, white, and blue threads across my patriotic chest.

The Paralympic Games of 2000 in Sydney, Australia, are spectacular. It's a glamorous and thoughtful production of worldwide sport. Attendance is high, the village modern, and food consummate fuel for elite athletes. I compare and contrast the world class sporting experience to the cross-country road trip Ed and I endured in the seventies. Both events crown the best the world has to offer. That's undisputed. My gold medals, and 100-meter world record, garnered in 1976, and the Toronto Games, are not any less joyful. In fact, there's a naïve, youthful delight to roughing it across the country and coming out on top. I'm not sure if there is a deeper, more enlightening sporting reminiscence than the days driving back to California with Ed Owen. The idealistic memory transcends, but let's be clear, it also sucked. In Toronto, we slept in barracks, ate crap food, had sloppy uniforms, and the crowds were mostly family and event volunteers.

In twenty-four years of international competition, I live through the bare-boned, well-intentioned games of Toronto and Stoke Mandeville. It's a snail's pace, incremental journey that perseveres past politics, lack of funding, and spotty leadership.

I take time in Sydney: to wander the village, take an extra minute with conversations, thank the volunteers, eye the venue, the markings of the court and watch intently the path of the ball and flight. Such an unpretentious task. A ball and two goals. Such a wondrous path inside the yellow brick road of basketball and sport.

The romantic notions end there.

We lose to the Dutch in the semifinals by a point. A parting gut punch from Gert and his boys. In pool play we lose to Canada by 13 points. They're led by the legendary tandem of Pat Anderson and Joey Johnson. The Canadians win gold in 2000. They win the next 3 of 4 Paralympic championships in their historic run.

Curtis Bell and I, once the standard of dominance for the United States, are anchored to the bench. I receive a bit more playing time than Curtis but, for the first time, I feel my confidence slipping into the void of time and usage. Head Coach Dan Byrnes uses me sparingly and minus any defined role. His love of the college game and new school approach bend my spirit into a question mark of tactics and decisions. Entering into Sydney, I'm hopeful for a role similar to the World Championships two years prior. A role of relevance. It's not in the cards.

Leading up to the Sydney Paralympic Games the coaching staff put together a one-on-one tournament throughout the team. I advance through one side. Paul Schulte comes through the other. The training camp tournament has the OG's (old guys) lined up on one side of the court and the youngbloods on the other. I'm 47. He's 20. The youngbloods outnumber us considerably. Coming through my side of the draw is work. I'm feeling the pain.

I know I have to slow it down. Paul (or Pablo as I nickname him) has lightning speed. I relentlessly back him down into the paint. He's so athletic and likes to tilt on two wheels. This allows him to close space and get into my shooting periphery. I wait for him to eventually land back on all four wheels and shoot over him. Our teammates yell and jeer. The smack talk is deep. I think I hear them placing bets. Pablo shoots from deep. He's trying to undo me with his three-point shooting. It's his undoing. I beat the heir to the USA national team throne.

These are the memories I bank. Curtis and I win a separate training camp, 2-on-2 tournament. Statement made.

In the bronze medal game, the score is tied with just over 24 seconds remaining. Great Britain calls a timeout directly after Trooper's breakaway layup ties the game.

Our defense presses full court and keeps GB away from its goal and beyond the three-point arc. Our five-spot or baseline defender gets beat. A pinpoint pass leads to an easy look for GB. Will Waller helps from the weak side and gets a hand up in the shooter's face. He misses the bunny layup. There's less than five seconds remaining. Waller gets the rebound. He hits Eric Barber with the outlet pass. Barber hits Schulte with a pass at the half court line. With under a second, Pablo lets it fly from 35 feet. He has forward momentum. GB defender Jon Pollack puts a hand in Pablo's face. His shot is pure. Nothing but net. The bronze medal is ours.

What a blessing.

Getting old in the game I love.

Such a gift.

World Champs, 1998.

'The DK look.'

Mel Juette, an inspiration and example of a street fighter.

After 'The Shot.'

Goodbye at center court.

My mom and fan.

"Take the wheel," I say to Sandy.

I'm driving. An enormous jolt of electric pain pulsates and radiates in my left leg. My entire body wrenches and tightens up. I am incapacitated.

On a good day, the pain is always there. On a bad day, it's 24 to 36 hours in the emergency room. These attacks happen three to four times a year. It's not until the early 2000s that I have a life altering, successful surgery at Craig Hospital in Denver, Colorado. My leg pains are forever put to rest.

When dealing with my leg pains, I mostly white knuckled it. I take on the pain. There are times when fellow Wheel Heads witness my episodes and offer what's in their satchels as a form of relief. They offer without hesitation. If the pain is severe enough, I might take them up on their offer. The variables of responsibility, sport and family are always a consideration.

Doctors are liberal with Valium. Many Wheel Heads are prescribed Valium (a benzodiazepine) for recurrent spasms or a way to deal with prolonged isolation. The abuse of Valium is quite real in our subculture. Klonopin (also a benzodiazepine) is used to knock me out when the pain is too much. When I leave emergency rooms, Klonopin is the prescription of choice for most emergency room doctors.

I don't seek these pain meds. I seek relief.

Around 1986, I stop drinking alcohol. I even explore the odd AA (Alcohol Anonymous) meeting. I'm not ready for the 12 steps. I don't want a sponsor. I want to keep my drinking in check as thoughts of my father and the Kiley male lineage creep into my ever-expanding thoughts on the subject. I eliminate alcohol from the equation for ten years.

I smoke pot. I smoke a good bit of it. Ask any teenager growing up in the late-sixties/early-seventies, on the coastline of sunny Southern California, and we will all nod our head with an affirming 'yes' to either dabbling or being regular marijuana smokers. I play hide and seek from Sandy when I can. She knows. Always has. Her gift is the patience to let me figure things out on my terms. This process takes. She has a subtle cunning that I admire. If it's raising our two children or working with me through the obstacles of life, having her by my side is the partnership required for any successes.

I don't make it easy for her, the family, or myself.

After seventeen years working at Casa Colina and creating a world class adaptive sports and recreation program, we decide to begin again in Charlotte, North Carolina. It's an exciting time, full of new realities and possibilities. Even though the Casa job is a dream come true, the days are routine and predictable.

It's a benchmark time in the history of our family. The spark of change sweeps through our cores.

It's the spring of 1996. I pack up my Suburban for the April cross-country trek. The family will fly out after the kids finish school in June. The new job involves an impressive and friendly moving package. Sandy's Land Cruiser and all our belongings are transported to North Carolina. Even the expense of flying our two dogs, Magic and Barkley, is covered.

My plan is to drive north and ski: Mammoth Mountain, the many resorts of Lake Tahoe, and then head east and ski the steepest descents of Park City, Utah, and Jackson Hole, Wyoming. My ear-numbing, Alpine Stereo rides shotgun. Music, always the truest of comrades, pumps troughout. There is a smoke-on-the-water and fire-in-the-sky singalongs that power the Suburban down the road. I'm travelling solo but hardly alone. Possibilities and a new direction help steer the wheels.

The alcohol is gone. In its place, I've become a full-blown pothead. I don't realize this is what alcoholism does. It searches for something else to abuse and dominate your life.

I roll along with nothing to keep me in check. I ski the double black diamond runs of Mammoth and Lake Tahoe baked—stoned to the bone. I put trusty California in the rearview mirror before visiting good friend and teammate, Mike Schlappi, and his wife in Salt Lake City. After a lovely time, I take to the highway and get high all over again. I'm skiing expert runs, loading all my gear on and off mountains and blowing minds. The marijuana is part of my winning equation.

After the heavenly sights of skiing Park City, Utah, it's time to traverse to Jackson Hole, Wyoming. A sleepy mountain town with rustic cowboy lodging. I lay my head to rest. The next morning one thing is perfectly clear: Jackson Hole is a steep mother of a mountain. Its steepest regions are a measuring stick for any expert skier. After a couple warm up runs, I take to the task. I see a gaggle of able-bodied skiers contemplating their descent.

I learned long ago, waiting at the top only makes the descent scarier and steeper.

One of them eyes me up and asks, "Are you lost?"

"Not even," I reply.

I hear a chuckle. I ski past the group and drop in on the near vertical chute. I execute the vital first couple turns and ski to the bottom without stopping. I never look back.

That night, I call Sandy and the kids. It's our routine. They want to know where I've been and what I've seen. It's the highlight of my extended days on the road. My wife is sacrificing, yet again, to manage the move. I miss her and the kids.

I arrive in Charlotte a week after departing Southern California. The last few days of the journey, I make hay, driving ten hours a day, towards my new destination and impending home. The weed and thumping rock tunes passing the time. Spring is in full swing. There is nothing like the Carolinas as the dogwoods, tulips, buttercups, and azaleas are in bloom.

I'm given an apartment in the 'old money' section of Charlotte near the Charlotte Institute of Rehabilitation. I contact my new employer. I'm eager to get the ball rolling and make an impressive start with everything new.

I'm told to meet with Employee Health.

"What is Employee Health," I ask.

"It's to get your drug test done."

Coach John Wooden once said, "A coach is someone who can give corrections without causing resentment."

I understand completely what a tall task awaits me as I agree to coach the USA women's national team for the 2010 World Championships and 2012 London Paralympic Games. The responsibility is immense. I take it on with all I have.

It all starts in 2004 with a call from Mo Phillips. Mo is the Head Coach of the USA men's team. He asks if I'd like to join his staff. I have no real aspirations to coach at the elite level. I've witnessed and lived the behaviors of athletes at the highest levels. We can be real jerks at times. Still, the request intrigues me.

I attend the Paralympic Games of Athens, Greece, as an Assistant Coach. We lose to Great Britain in the quarterfinals and finish a miserable seventh place. The hook is set. I can do this.

Mo Phillips is not coming back for the next cycle of national team play. I apply to the High-Performance Committee led by Dan Byrnes (my coach for the 2000 Sydney Games). I hear nothing back. Odd. I hear I'm not selected from someone who is privy to the decision but has no official capacity. I get on the horn to Brynes and register my disappointment and protocol questions. After a back and forth, he tells me I need more experience in my coaching history. My ego tells me otherwise. My ego rarely tells the truth.

I am asked to take a team of 19-and-under young women to Australia to compete in a 23-and-under men's tournament. We take our lumps competing against men. I feel a better fit with the women's national team program. I then head a USA women's national team for the Osaka Cup in Japan. The team is spirited but raw. We finish second. In 2009, Head Coach Jim Glatch asks me to join his USA men's 23-and-under staff. The team is due to compete in Paris for its World Championships. The USA team goes undefeated in the tournament and are crowned 23-and-under World Champions.

The Worlds are in Birmingham, England, 2010. The ebbs and flows of the USA women's team can be dramatic at times. Personal decisions, playing time, and training methods are constant topics of conversation. The ladies are back-to-back Paralympic gold medalists. They are empowered, elite, and speak their mind. It's been twenty-four years since the USA women have been world champions. There's a gorilla to get off our back.

Leading up to Birmingham, England, and Worlds, I work all angles of creating an environment of fellowship. More than anything, I want the team to be at peace with one another. Gripes with myself or any of the staff is common enough to work through or past. Their need to support one another is the constant that cannot be compromised. The egos of the veterans need to align with the rising strength of the team's younger players. There are bonding exercises off the court, evening cookouts in my backyard, pontoon boating excursions, and jet ski options offered from a Lake Norman friend of mine. I even hire a limo ride for the team to an exhibition game at a filled-to-capacity Lake Norman High School. It feels like things are coming together.

The staff of Matt Buchi, Margaret Stran-Hardin and Miles Thompson relate to our mission and the individual arcs of the athletes. Matt is a next level tech-guy. Jeff Downes (nicknamed Details) is an extraordinary Team Leader. Physio Jen Brown tends to the ailments, existing injuries, and aches of a team trying to win it all.

We are undefeated heading into the finals. An upstart Becca Murray is quickly turning into one of the best mid-range shooters I've ever witnessed. Her work with Christina Ripp on the wing guarantees open look after open look. Veterans like Sarah Castle, Steph Wheeler, Natalie Schneider, and Carlee Hoffman are the constants we lean into. The newer input of Desi Miller, Darlene Hunter, and Becca Murray are the next generation's top performers. Low-point players Mary Allison Milford, Caitlin McDermott, and Jennifer Chew round out a stellar squad. Then there's Andrea Woodson-Smith: big, strong, and built for special occasions.

The final with Germany seesaws back and forth. It's the first time in the entire tournament, a team is able to break down our defense. We put more pressure on the ball. The turnovers come in bunches. The Germans adjust. The game is tight.

With under a minute to play, Christina and Becca execute a pick and roll. We go up a point. The pass is money and Becca's finish is never in doubt. The Germans call timeout. I sub in A (Andrea Woodson-Smith). The Germans run a similar pick and roll. Andrea rotates over and blocks the shot. She gathers the loose ball. The Germans foul. It's their only play. Andrea's blocked shot cements the game.

A proud group of American women, highly decorated, do what hasn't been done for 24 years—win a World Championship gold medal.

It's a moment in time to cherish.

1998 World Champs.

Becca Murray.

USA staff from left to right: Matt Bushi, Jen Brown, Margaret Stran-Hardin, myself, Jeff Downes and Miles Thompson, author of **Wheel Head**.

The air from my body leaves my lungs. I stare into the distance. Might be a minute. Might be a second. I'm a lost soul, in the midst of an epic flameout, for all to see.

I mumble, "Okay," into the telephone. "I'll be there."

I hang up. The sinking words, "It's to get your drug test done" have me anchored and sinking. Talk about not seeing this one coming. I feel like the spindly-legged spider caught in the drain of the shower, drowning and circling before a certain and untimely demise.

Casa Colina never drug tests. I'm not in California anymore, am I? I am oblivious. I am the fool on the hill for all to see. I've spent the last week smoking pot traversing the United States. Marijuana stays in your system for a month. I do know that.

I call a friend in Charlotte and ask for his advice. It's an embarrassing and nervous conversation. I reiterate to him the obvious. I've quit my job over 2,400 miles away, sold our home, and the family is due to arrive in a couple weeks' time. This is a point of no return situation.

Time calms my disastrous nerves. There is a pre-drug test. I find a health food store and purchase a gallon of 'Pee Tea' to go with the pre-test. I choke down the 'Pee Tea' with a vigor reserved for frat boys and keg beer. It works. The pre-test comes back negative. Success.

Time is my biggest ally. I need to buy a bit more before my appointment with Employee Health and the determining drug test. I tell the job I have a small pressure sore from the cross-country drive. I have an extra week to stew and pour more of the 'Pee Tea' concoction down my gullet.

Somewhat relieved but hardly confident, I show up for my Employee Health appointment. Everything is on the line. The drug test is on Friday. My first day on the job is Monday. The weekend is a bender of thoughts, possibilities, half-truths and what-ifs I beat myself up pretty good. I deserve it. I eye a clock slowly inching forward, a second at a time.

It works. I pass the test. I swear off my billowing path of dry goods. I maintain my career and reputation. What a disaster it could (might have) been.

It's not long after my initial time in North Carolina that I pick up the drink again. The blaze of the booze against the cool of its cubes is always there. I tuck it in a faraway corner for ten years. The forgotten and dusty luggage of my past.

I tell Sandy my desire to drink again. I present it to her as a revelation. A realization that I have the maturity and experience to successfully consume again. Her concern registers but I'm confident I can compartmentalize my desires.

"It's all good. It will be fine," I assure her.

My first venture back into the biosphere of drinking should be all the examples I need.

I head into a sports bar alone. I order two pitchers of beer.

"You can't order two pitchers of beer," I'm told.

"Why not?" I ask.

"It's against the law."

Perturbed and annoyed, I take a beat. "Make it one then."

The server doesn't miss a beat. I'm just another trigger-finger drinker on the verge of something new and old. I finish the first pitcher of grog and order another. I'll show all those that ever doubted my place as a successful drinker.

The next morning, I have a world class hangover. I'm a toilet hugger the rest of the day. I call in sick to work my first week on the job. There's a warning sign above my head buzzing in red neon. I pay it no heed. I carry on with my new life strategy.

I'm what's called a 'functioning drunk.' For the next fifteen years, I build an adaptive sports program that serves Wheel Heads like this region has never seen. We build our dream home in Mooresville, North Carolina. The kids are raised in a safe and friendly environment minus: fence-lines, gated windows, over-developed neighborhoods, and random violence. Our plan has come together.

I'm living the life reserved for romantics and idealists. We are the American Dream in vibrant, true-to-life, living color. The devilish parrot on my shoulder seeks more.

The first time I combine pain meds with beer it's game-on.

The buzz is warm and sociable.

I feel it in my ears and lips.

The pills are running low.

I'll play up the leg pains to doc.

He'll phone a script into the pharmacy.

Another pill and long pull of cold beer.

Reminds me of my first morphine injection.

That's over five decades ago.

How long are you going to play this card?

Face those times?

Do the work?

I pop another from the trusty cooler.

I tell myself; I am doing the work.

Keep driving.

The Patron awaits in the garage.

High-end tequila is a refuge to what ails.

Its sips hurry things along.

Even warmer.

A more outlandish subtle buzzing in my being.

Finally rest.

Or am I at the dinner table?

It's getting hard to tell.

I try to stop. I make positive adjustments. I substitute cheap vodka for the expensive tequila. I'm all in on the 'harder to smell' myth. I tell myself repeatedly I have an extreme willpower. Look at all I've overcome and persevered through. My willpower doesn't have the—will or power—to surrender to my disease.

I still love basketball and performing on its canvas, but I find myself checking the clock. When is this training session going to end? I have a couple iced down beers, vodka, and a pain pill or two for the ride home. Soon, it's going to be time to get my buzz on.

The times coaching juniors pull me in all sorts of sideways directions. I'm never impaired in anything I do with them. Like the adults, my time is after we've done the sports thing. The afterhours of responsibility. The kids look up to me. They are inspired by me; but here I am hiding this dark side of everything they think I am. The conflict of self runs deep. The more I feel this turmoil, the more I numb myself to my ballooning deficiencies.

I avoid mirrors.

I cannot look at myself.

The gold medals at the World Championships in 2010 tick a massive box. The veteran, world class performers have back-to-back Paralympic golds; and now a first ever World Championship gold. This shifts the landscape. The USA Women's Paralympic Basketball Team is transitioning. Gone are Stephanie Wheeler, Christina Ripp, and Carlee Hoffman. All starters. All studs. All moving into their future selves.

I make a call.

Lorraine Gonzalez leaves the team prior to Worlds to take care of a family matter. I want to gauge her interest in coming back. She agrees. I know her return to things will take some massaging with certain members of the team. Lorraine is a physical player that plays with an edge. When dialed in, she's a valuable piece to the puzzle.

We also add Alana Nichols and teenage phenom Rose Hollermann to the mix. The squad is good, with the potential to be excellent. Becca Murray, Desi Miller, and Natalie Schneider can all score in bunches.

In the lead up to the 2012 London Paralympic Games our exhibition games are one-sided. Gonzalez can defend and score. We have a formidable pressing line-up. The women beat the world's top teams abroad and on home soil.

It doesn't work out with Lorraine. She misses a training camp. The hows and whys are less important than the disappointing fact that together, Lorraine and I, cannot find a robust enough common ground to come together on. As a team, we make the decision. We move on, again, without her. Such a talent. Within the fallout, I lose a friend but understand completely there is a line that friendship cannot cross when coaching at the highest level.

The London Games are world class. Sir Philip Craven, President of the IPC and board member of the London Olympic and Paralympic Games, has everything to do with the integration of the games into the city.

In pool play we lose to the Germans by six. They're led by low-pointer Annika Zeyen's finishing and mid-range shooting. We also go down twenty to China before mounting one of the biggest Paralympics comebacks I've ever been a part of. With the improbable win against China, we finish second in our pool.

We defeat a stubborn Canadian team by twelve in the quarterfinals.

The semi finals against Australia are a street fight. The defensive battle between two like-minded teams. We miss shots we've been making all tournament. In the final eight minutes of the game, we are 1 for 6 from the free throw line. Still, it's a fight. Dez Miller knocks down a shot with under thirty seconds to play. Australia leads 40-39. Our defense only gives up two points in the last eight-and-a-half minutes of the game. We foul the Aussies and send them to the line for two shots. It's Desi's fifth. A smart, selfless play from her. She has fouled out. I look down the bench and motion to teenager Rose Hollermann. She knows it's her time.

Australia misses both free throws. Becca gets the rebound and outlets to Darlene Hunter. Darlene sees Rose and delivers a pass against Australia's constant full court pressure. Rose passes to Alana Nichols across the half court line. Alana finds Natalie Schneider just outside the paint. With fourteen-seconds on the clock Natalie dribbles away from the pressure and towards her teammates streaking down the floor. She bounce-spins back towards our goal. The move isolates Rose in the post. She flashes to the goal. Natalie delivers the pass. It's on the money. With 4.2 seconds on the clock, Rose is in the shooting position. She lets it go. She gets hit. The front end of her chair absorbs the hit but lifts a wheel off the ground. There's no call. Her shot hits the heel and slides off the left side of the rim. With 1.9 seconds remaining, Alana gets the rebound and makes the putback layup.

We win the game.

There's a whistle.

Why is there a whistle? The officials call a shot clock violation and claim Rose's shot never hit the rim. It hits the rim twice.

The staff and I are chasing down the referees. I am about to go Bobby Knight on them. They're gone into the labyrinth hallways of London's O2 Arena.

We have video proof of our victory. It's plain as day. We sequester the tournament committee. Everyone in the room knows we won the semifinals against Australia, but no one has the power to right the wrong. In 2012, there are no table reviews.

The next day we play for the bronze medal against the Dutch. We lead early. The Dutch, coached by (yes) Gert Jan van der Linden, are led by the emerging talent of Mariska Beijer. They dominate the second half and win going away.

The Dutch are hungry. They're at the beginning of a winning run of consistency that lasts the next twelve-plus years. With everything that happened the day before, we're unable to get the stink of it all behind us.

The sinking disappointment of London lasts to this day. What is the top of the mountain two years previous, is now replaced with an overriding deepness of pain and the unjust agony of defeat.

The job at the Charlotte Institute of Rehabilitation is a constant merry-go-round of personalities and administrators. The higher-ups that initially hire me have my back. The budding workplace relationships are equating into North Carolina as a disability sport destination. The revolving door of administrators and head doctors is constant. I get along with them all. They're supportive of me and our recreation and sports programming.

Until the latest, new-guy. New-guy is from the north. He knows most everything there is to know about most everything. He calls me out on my relationship with Quickie and my signature, All-Court chairs stacked in the storage closet for people to use. What he calls a 'conflict of interest,' I call an inexpensive way to get the newly injured into the possibilities of sport and health. I am able to purchase the sports chairs at a tremendous discount through my Sunrise Medical connections.

The new guy makes it personal. I'm tired of the constant stress his self-serving leadership puts on me.

He wants me to resign. I tell him to grow a pair and fire me. He obliges.

Life changes in that instant. The big paying job. The hour-plus drive each way subtracted. The space to do what I've only dared to imagine is now upon me. It's possibilities are a persistent question of how and when.

I become a professional speaker. I chase gigs like musicians track down studio time. It works. There's a dependable flow of engagements across the globe. The land and real estate deals I've been sitting on, pay off. The Quickie All-Court is selling across the globe. The quarterly, royalty checks flow. The parents of Charlotte area junior athletes break away from the new-guy and form Abilities Unlimited. They reach out. I'm coaching basketball again without missing a season, game, or practice.

These days, Abilities Unlimited is a charitable machine and an example for disability sports organizations across the country.

It's 2005. I am my own man. I am not encumbered with office politics, cutthroat back-stabbers, status-climbers or know-it-alls; I have something wonderful to say—jive fakers. It is all quite real.

I don't have more free time but I certainly have greater time with myself. Sandy is making good money as a dental hygienist; and with the kids in school, the late mornings and early afternoons are mine alone.

A drunk alone is in bad company.

What is a contained brush fire, slowly but most assuredly growing and building into an inferno of out-of-control flames. I am unchecked and building a tenacious, devoted tolerance to the opioids and the accompanying drink.

Time does not heal. Time infests my body and thoughts. The work and creation of building all things David Kiley intoxicates in its own way. I play it straight. The rush of speaking to a crowded ballroom, coaching a team, or working a Turning Point weekend on Caddo Lake is my newest life's work. It deserves my fullest attention. I deliver.

Alone. Things change drastically. I happily chase everything that isn't there with another pull and swallow of all that's advertised to help us change the way we feel. The process of unmanageability takes time. It's claws scratching the prospect of normalcy. Its regrets are constant.

Over and over, I ask for God's help. Please lead me beyond my self-destructive ways. Left to my own devices, I'm full of broken promises and disingenuous relationship arcs. I have a first-class, bulletproof window seat on the crazy train leading to the boils of hell. Each day, I bury my secrets deeper. I isolate and lie to myself that today I'm living a tolerable life.

I have to change.

Can I change?

Do I really want change?

On my basketball team is a good friend. I know he attends AA (Alcoholics Anonymous) and is a recovering alcoholic. I reach out to him. I need help. He gives me a list of AA meetings in the area and says he'll go with me. The disease festering inside me tells me it will never work. It tells me not to do the work. It tells me, I am better than the weak-minded, lost souls in the rooms of AA: revealing secrets and speaking in excruciating truths.

I begin the process of surrendering. Finally. It's 2011. It's overdue.

The previous summer, the USA women won gold. We are world champions. I am at the helm. To get home feels good. Being home also allows me the space needed to return to my manufactured highs. The juxtaposition has me on tilt. The thoughts pinging through me are dangerous. The empty Bud Light cans stashed in the garage trash are piled high. The vodka is in the garage freezer. The pills stashed in the pouch of my chair.

I cannot imagine my life with or without drugs and alcohol. This is the dilemma. I attend my first AA meeting. I'm worried about my image. I keep my head down. The bill of my ball cap is pulled down over my indigent glances of the room. I see my teammate. He has been sober for more than a decade. His self-confidence exudes. I eye my shoes constantly. The rare instances I lift my head: I see a neighbor, a water-skiing buddy and a couple from church. I am not prepared to see folks that I know, and more importantly, know me. I am not ready to humble myself. My ego and family-man persona are broken-glass fragile. I am living a false bravado. It feels like my manhood is fading into a blistering and faraway desert sun.

When the meeting concludes, my water-skiing buddy gives me a book. It's the Big Book. The Alcoholics Anonymous publication explains the twelve-steps needed to live a fulfilling sober life. Its pages speak of "love and tolerance" for others that do not share my views. I get home and throw the thing in the corner of the closet. I spend the next couple months in the throws and darkness of continued addiction. The near misses are constant.

I'm driving past the church of my initial AA meeting. There's a bloody Mary in the travel mug. I'm reminded of all the faces I don't ever want to meet there. I'm better. I am stronger. Bam. There's contact with an oncoming car. My driver's side mirror is gone. It shakes me. I pull off the two-lane country road and try to pull myself together. It doesn't take. My nerves are frayed. I am a mess of a man.

This is my bottom.

Stop. Stop. Stop.

Jails, institutions, or death. These are my options if I carry on.

I call my teammate and sober living friend. I tell him I've been living a new low. Please help me. He assures me, "AA doesn't shoot its wounded."

Getting sober is the greatest and hardest thing I've ever done. My relationship with God blossoms and intensifies. Without him, my higher power, I'm still a drunk and addict. Alcoholics Anonymous allows me to etch a better design for living. Sobriety is far more than quitting drinking and drugging. It teaches me to change the man behind the bottle. If I don't change, I'm just the same guy, minus the nonsense.

God is first. Sobriety is second. My beloved family receives the best me only when I prioritize God and sobriety. Anything I put before God and sobriety, I will lose. Fact.

I chose to live the dream. The obsession of a drink and drug has been lifted. I can go into far more detail here. There's a whole other book on the outrageousness involved with using; and then life-affirming tales of living life without substances.

Albert Einstein once famously said, "Insanity is doing the same thing over and over and expecting different results."

Another more spiralling form of insanity is doing the same thing over and over, and knowing exactly the result. This is me. This is the loop of behavior I continue to function in. If I don't stop this destructive pattern of behavior, a circle of chaos will feed upon itself, gather momentum, and be my undoing.

The program of AA forces me to deal with my childhood decisions. I treasure the morphine and Demerol injections as a recovering ten-year-old. I chose to be black-out drunk in an accident that devastates family members, changes the course of my life and leaves me paralyzed. Everything that happens that day is on me.

Of course it is?

It's obvious.

Right?

Not for this guy; not for someone who is predisposed with the alcoholic gene. None of this comes to the surface until I'm sober. It's only then that I can deal with my childhood and my collision course with my alcoholic father.

My hope is that my honesty may help someone else navigate through and past the land mines of addiction. I am vulnerable before you right now. These revelations might be a shock to some. For others it might be a chance to say, "I thought so." Either way, I feel relief and freedom.

Living sober reminds me to love my father. A good man with a horrible disease.

I have changed only for today. Tomorrow, I will have to earn it all over. I am living the version of myself that God intended for all to see. I am a good man. I can be counted on. I engage with family and friends every day. I serve others relentlessly. My grandchildren have never seen me lift a Bud Light or any other alcoholic drink to my lips.

I have put enough tomorrow's together that I'm currently over thirteen years sober. It's promised it can be this way. A thorough and honest working of the 12-steps makes it so.

I remind myself constantly that to keep this gift, I must give it away.

THE HALL OF HALLS

It's amazing. Life changes very quickly,
in a very positive way, if you let it.

— Lindsey Vonn

Awards are the byproduct of winning.

Recognition is the distinction of conquering times.

Records, titles, championships, MVP's and gold; the apex of competitive greatness.

These things come in forms of relief—an exhale to the thought that someone/something might triumph besides me. Accolades can be a bother. It's an unnatural, manufactured halt to the ebbs and flows of competition: the action of sport. The stage can dilute the fellowship of a team. It's a shadowy, fickle spotlight that inflates as quickly as it diminishes. I like it best, with my teammates—Kool and the Gang's "Celebration" reminding us what's obvious and repeated. Traversing the room, the boys are howling like coyotes. I open my arms to another welcoming teammate and the unspoken shimmering gleam that we not only did it, but we collectively banded together.

Simple. Direct. Just look at the scoreboard. This is my sweet-spot. Secure and validated. I lean into the full-throttle-mindset and ethics of outworking others. These are the skill sets the Great One, Ed Owen, instilled.

It's difficult to embrace the adulation—compliments make me itchy. I internalize/visualize every all-tournament, MVP, championship, and top of the podium accolade as if they were mine, made only for me. This brashness manifests itself in the sizzle, shine, and next level in all my performances.

In sport, I'm often the youngest version of myself. I'm still the gangly kid in awe of Pistol Pete Maravich. The Pistol once said, "Shooting is nothing. Anyone can shoot. The charge is putting on a show for the crowd."

There's a reason Pistol Pete is my 12-year-old guy, like there's a profound reason my 12-year-old self penetrates my being to this day.

The recognition and appreciation of others can work distressingly opposite. Once I receive the moment of accomplishment, I instinctively deflect. I want to be somewhere else and someone different. My story is less about the game-winning assist, final leg of a world record relay, or breakneck, top-speed of a downhill run conquering fear and time. It's about what I say, how I look, and if I remembered to thank all the sponsors.

411

The Great One left this out of his playbook. He knew I'd need to figure this one out myself.

I get the call.

It's Sarah Hirshland on the line.

Since the nomination process a couple weeks back, my mind's been awash in memories; a sometimes subtle—sometimes overriding—film trailer of my days competing in elite sport.

Do I really matter?

Will they remember me?

Did I fight the good fight?

Do I really have a legacy after I'm gone?

I think of Cruz, Lucas, Lily, and Jace. I see their faces against our backyard and the clear North Carolina sky. My kid's children with grandma and grandpa for the afternoon.

She gets right into it, "I know I'm a couple days early, but ……"

Sarah Hirshland, the Chief Executive Officer of the United States Olympic and Paralympic Committee (USOPC) is a heavy hitter. The most powerful woman in sport is on the line. The hairs on my arm tingle. I remind myself to breathe.

If I don't receive this, I'll be mortally wounded.

"It's my honor…"

I'm unable to hear much else. I tell myself no tears. I keep it together. I'm not sure how many times I say 'thank you' but it's constant.

When we hang up it hits me. I'm entering the United States Olympic and Paralympic Hall of Fame. I'm overwhelmed. I intuitively jump from bed to my Per4max chair. I race to the front room to share my excitement with my number one fan—Sandy.

"I'm in. I'm in."

I reach for her.

"I'm in the Olympic/Paralympic Hall of Fame."

She leaps from the couch. We share a long, joyful embrace. We wrap ourselves in the journey, celebration, heartache, reward, agony and most of all—sacrifice.

I've earned my way into elite sports legacy.

Randy Snow is in. Candace Cable is in.

I'm in.

It's no accident I hang with the driven, I-can-do-anything type competitors. Their examples are major ingredients in my successes.

Today, they're all foremost, but in a determining and influential way I also realize, today is mine.

I am in.

Thirteen Paralympics medals:

9 Gold—3 in Basketball—1976, 1988 & 1992

         2 in Alpine Skiing—Super G & Giant Slalom

         4 in Track—100, 800, 1500 & 4X100 Relay

2 Silver—Alpine Skiing—Downhill and Slalom

2 Bronze—Basketball—1980 & 2000

I'm unprepared for the magnitude of each passing moment since The Call.

It's a lifetime's work. When I ponder my Wheel Print through the landscape of sport, I can honestly say I've never chased or imagined any Hall of Fame distinction. Especially this one. Something this big can't be sought. It comes when it comes. Like Randy and Candace, I know my Wheel Print begins in earnest as I stay the course and continue to serve others. This is the only way to reach such a hallowed ground.

I'm due to enter the same Hall as legends Muhammad Ali, Joe Frazier, Teresa Edwards, Rafer Johnson, Peggy Fleming, Sugar Ray Leonard, Mary Lou Retton, Wilma Rudolph, Mark Spitz, and the 1992 Dream Team led by Magic Johnson, Michael Jordan, and Larry Bird to literally name only a few.

I am about to be inducted in the same class with Billie Jean King, the Paralympic 2002 Sled Hockey Team, Michael Phelps, Muffy Davis, Natalie Coughlin, Trischa Zorn Hudson, the 1976 Women's 4X100 Swimming Relay Team, Gretchen Fraser, Lindsey Vonn, Mia Hamm, Michelle Kwan, Roger Kingdom, and Pat Summitt.

When you're younger your ego tells you, 'No one will ever forget you.'

The years pass. I'm pushing 70 years of age and the nagging realization is, 'Everyone gets forgotten.'

The Olympic/Paralympic Hall of Fame distinguishes what easily could have been erased through time. When you're attached to the Olympic rings it all changes. There's only one way for a disabled athlete to be associated with the Olympic rings, and the Hall of Fame is it.

This is the pause—the reflection—in my faraway gaze.

The Olympic rings represent the globe. It's obvious. The tremendous and transformative reach that sport has throughout the planet. The rings were created by Pierre de Coubertin in 1912 and represent the five inhabited continents of the world. The Olympic motto, '*Citius, Altius, Fortius*'—faster, higher, stronger—is adapted by the International Olympic Committee (IOC) in 1894.

In contrast, the Paralympic logo was created in 2019. It's not distinguishable in meaning and clarity of disability sport. Its three backwards, Nike looking swooshes represent the three most popular colors in participating countries' national flags.

It's a reach. The Olympics is the big brother to mom's, later-in-life pregnancy, and birthing of a promising, albeit pestering Paralympic sibling, seeking unconditional love and dependent allegiance.

I'm a breathing, living case study: the weird, shabby uniforms of the 70s and 80s, absolutely no financial compensation for travel, training, equipment, camps, medical expenses, sport psychology, meals, and most importantly medals.

In 1984, Curtis Bell and I—the team's two most accomplished athletes—sat out the 1984 Paralympics in protest to the team's lack of funding. The NWBA, an all-volunteer organization at the time, lacked the professionalism and motivation to secure the needed monies to properly fund and prepare Team USA. I eventually find a sponsor and present a $25,000 check to the team. Curtis and I hold our ground and don't participate. Team USA doesn't twin a medal. Should have been gold.

In 1975, the Para Pan American games are held in Mexico City. I'm entered in track events and am playing basketball. The Para Pan Am Games qualify the Americas for the Paralympics, but in a slightly strange twist, I am also competing in a slalom course for wheelchairs. The event is just as it sounds with various curbs, ramps, 180-degree spins and rollers to navigate against the clock. Make a mistake and time is added on. Best time wins.

About halfway through my run an official sounding voice yells, *'Stop. Stop. Stop.'*

I stop.

What is this?

I look towards an official to see what's happening. He throws up his arms. He's as confused as I am. There's laughter and building cackle to the boisterous, Latino crowd. More laughter. I eye the culprit in the crowd. The one that yelled, *'stop.'* I charge the rat bastard, looking to do damage. I'm held back. My anger boiling, I make a last-ditch effort to break away. My shoulder length, blonde hair is covering my eyes, ears, and mouth. I clear my locks so I can see. I eye the guilty party and his hyena friends, before fingering them half-a-peace sign. The event is over for me. No way of recovering. The officials of the event do nothing. I exit. Just before leaving the crowd's building jeers, I give them one more nonverbal gesture.

I'm tagged with the nickname Custer for the rest of the games.

This kind of thing doesn't happen in the Olympics or Olympic qualifying events. Audience shenanigans and Mickey Mouse events like the obstacle course are obsolete. Even so, I am content as a living conduit between what was, and the current day professionalism, of what is.

I experience the Paralympics from 1976 through 2012 as an Athlete and Head Coach. Thirty-six years is enough time to fall in—and out—of love with the process, people, practices, and professionalism of everything Paralympic. The longest journeys require perspective. The kind that only the gift of health and time can ultimately answer. I'll always be the kid competing against his brothers and the Costa Mesa "no goods" on the block. Not that much changes when the block became the world and the neighborhood flimflam became the world's best.

Since my nomination into the USOPC Hall of Fame (thank you Darlene Hunter), my thoughts are of nostalgia, hope, and legacy.

Will it ever happen?

The phone rings.

After flying first class into Colorado Springs, a blacked-out—secret service-looking—SUV awaits our arrival. Instantly, my bearings reboot to the moment. Colorado Springs sits a mile above sea level. My heightened seven senses are justified.

I've been here many times. As an athlete or coach, the Olympic Training Center has been my destination to prepare for the red, white, and blue. Now, I'm on the other side of town. I am preparing for something altogether wondrous and life-shifting.

Colorado Springs rests within the southern regions of the Rocky Mountains. A radiant brilliance is on full display. A thriving city nestled within nature. Its aging, brick infrastructure is a distinct contrast between thriving city life and its surrounding wilds: cave tours, rafting, ziplining, and Pikes Peak are all a drive away. The region is also a strategic United States military staple with the Air Force Academy and a Division 1 university.

So much on offer, yet also a mere backdrop to the job at hand. The United States Olympic and Paralympic Hall of Fame is consuming me. The speech. My look. Legacy. History. Mortality.

I need help. I know just the guy.

Matt Scott is an original and invests in the details of his look, almost as entirely as he invests in his scintillating skill sets on the basketball court. Matt is one the first to earn real money playing wheelchair basketball professionally. He's earned double Paralympic basketball gold medals. His worldwide appeal in the sport is second to none. One of the sharpest tools in his box is his dapper and cutting-edge fashion sense.

Matt Scott.

I get him on the line. He is taken aback and appreciative that I've come to him. He's my only choice. USOPC Hall of Fame is not an *aw-shucks* moment. I don't want to be another guy in a chair squirming into a Men's Warehouse, ninety-nine-ninety-nine, suit off the rack.

As expected, Matt speaks succinctly about the details of *looking good.* A future Hall-of-Famer in his own right, he grasps what I'm after. He sends an example of a cravat and pocket square to accent my custom suit. What he forgets to tell me is the difficulty in tying the thing. The look is a departure for me, and one of a Sir or Lord. After about an hour on YouTube, I come closer to strangling myself than tying the thing. After another call to my fashion coach, it's decided I go with a tie-ring, just below the Windsor knot.

Later in the day, I traverse our top-notch hotel in need of an afternoon coffee drink. The Mining Exchange is an historical, 5-star facility. A Grand Piano sits in the lobby amongst timeless, leather armchairs. Exposed brick and marble countertops are a consistent theme.

Down the hall from the elevator, I see her. A blonde stunner demanding attention. It's Lindsey Vonn. A fellow inductee and Olympic champion. In short, one of my fav' downhill racers. We exchange some words. There's an important realization. We are contemporaries biding hotel time before the big night.

Inclusion comes in all forms.

Pistol Pete Maravich, long passed, yet ever an inspiration to my inner 12-year-old's life's journey, sits with me. We are quiet. I eye the expansive, clear window from the coffee café into the world of Colorado Springs.

By myself, but never alone, I sip my coffee. His words are like my own, "Character never quits; and with patience and persistence; dreams do come true."

Friday, June 24th—the year, 2022.

Six decades in elite sport. I know I have the credentials but still cannot believe I am here. The significance is staggering.

Six NWBA, Final MVP's. The most ever. ***Pales in comparison.***

Our 1976 relay team—all Californians, fastest in the world and recorded setting foursome. Amazing, youthful, future-is-here-now moment. ***The minor leagues***.

The speed of alpine skiing. The edgy velocity of skilfully and consistently saving hundredths of seconds at a time to another gold, another podium. The USA Ski Team needs overall medals. I enter all four competitive disciplines and deliver the needed medals. ***Doesn't come close.***

Then there's the rings.

The inclusion of the *P,* in the USOPC is monumental but also a long time coming. It's easy to speak to inequities. I champion the fighting spirit it takes for equal payment, uniforms, and access to sports sciences in the USA, Paralympic movement. I live it firsthand.

I'm a dinosaur. I remember Bob Beamon. The 1968 Olympics in Mexico City and Beamon breaking the long jump record by nearly two feet. Mark Spitz winning seven gold medals in the 1972 Olympics. Spitz breaks seven world records. Peggy Fleming, Dorothy Hamill, Shirley Babashoff, Sugar Ray Leonard, Edwin Moses, and Bruce Jenner.

The Olympic rings are personal. It's Jim McKay. The thrill of victory. The agony of defeat. It's decades of televised history on continuous display. It's politics.

Tonight (and forever), I am alongside all the greats. No, I am one of the greats. They are also beside me.

Prior to the inductions, we (the inductees) gather in the Miracle on Ice room. I sit beneath the Lake Placid scoreboard. The 1980 Winter Olympics. The greatest, worldwide, sporting upset—in all of humankind as my backdrop, I ponder the whole shebang.

I need to stay in the moment. I eye my wife.

I owe this to Sandy—my partner in life. The sacrifice and love she gives is not always easy. Matter of fact, I don't know any other woman who could have done what she did. My life now—and long before—should have been dedicated to her. It is now.

I've always shared with Sandy my words when it comes to speeches or talks. She's my sounding board. She's my muse. I coyly keep the speech to myself. I want her to feel the in-the-moment, intense selfless knowledge that without her, none of this is possible.

I'm the twelfth of fourteen Hall of Fame induction speeches. My jersey number throughout my basketball career has always been 12.

In front of me is Roger Kingdom: 1984 & '88 gold medalist in the 110-meter high hurdles. His world record of 12.92 seconds stands from 1989 to August of 1993. I am on my proverbial heels. Still, I introduce myself. He notices my tie-ring. Conversation starter.

"Next time, I'm wearing one of those things," he remarks.

I think of Matt and his sage fashion advice before noticing a monster ring on Kingdom's finger. I ask him *what the story* is behind the thing? He sheepishly smiles and tells me it's his 2019 Super Bowl ring he earned with the Tom Brady-led Tampa Bay Buccaneers. He's the team's speed coach. The conversation puts me at ease. We end up having dinner together with his wife and daughter, prior to the induction ceremony. The stunning ring, with its hundred-plus diamonds is passed around the table. In fact, during Lindsey Vonn's speech she references Roger's ring. She dares the USOPC to create one of their own for past, current, and future inductees.

I can hardly eat as I know what is about to follow.

I'm breathing shallow breaths.

My athlete muscle memory kicks in. Deep breaths put nerves in their place. I remember the teleprompter has my three-minute speech in big, bold letters. The sound of the evening is impeccable. The bass pounds into my chest.

It's my turn.

I take the stage.

My twelve-year-old self is at it again. I scream a ***Whoo-hoo*** through the speakers and into the Colorado Springs night.

I carry on.

I am one of the oldest inductees tonight, but I promised myself I would act the youngest.

I am so PROUD, Humbled, and Honored for this distinction and Induction. This Class of 2022 is as powerful as anyone could ever dream.

I am very grateful that my wife Sandy is here with me to share this moment. She deserves a Gold Medal and Induction to the HOF. We were married with 2 wonderful children through all my Paralympic experiences, Worlds and National Championships and the list goes on and on. Sandy and my kids sacrificed so much for me. I was gone all the time. I am so blessed to have you by my side, Sandy. I love you forever and our grandchildren are our greatest next step together.

My DNA was stamped to be an athlete by the third grade and basketball had become my everything. Everyone gets their drive from someone else. My mom, at 90, is still a competitive ninja, playing bridge 3 times a week.

My drive came from her.

I was hit by a car riding my bike to school as a 10-year-old and my knees were shattered. I had numerous surgeries/arthritis and cortisone injections by the eighth grade and through my playing days at Mater Dei High in Santa Ana. I couldn't and wouldn't stop. Right out of high school, came a blessing disguised as a tragic Spinal Cord Injury. God had His plan for me. It included a wheelchair for these broken knees. The chair became my wings to do what I was born to do and that was to play ball. Not only ball but any sport.

I have achieved much but in the end medals and awards are small compared to helping others achieve their dreams and improve lives. I think God will be pleased!

This is the Hall of Halls. The best athletes in the world live under this roof and I am one of them. I am in Heaven! Many posted and commented "what took so long to get in?" My response simply, "It's right on time."

For each person and company who supported and sponsored me, I am in your debt. Dromos Agency, thanks for your support. For every person, coach and player who drove me to do more, I am grateful.

To the USOPC, thank you for integrating the 'P' into the acronym of inclusion. USOPC.

It was never about what I lost as an adaptive athlete but was always about what I gained.

I'm moved to tears numerous times by others' induction speeches. I pray not to cry during my delivery—which I'm famous for doing. I want the audience and livestream viewers to hear my words; not be clouded by my emotions. When I look at Sandy and tell her, *"I'll love you the rest of our lives,"* I feel the salty waterworks mounting. I keep it together.

Moving across the stage, I shake Mike Tirico's hand. He's seen and announced it all. Such a pro.

I'm filled with joy of an undescribed type. A first ever mountain top experience—like a lion who growls over his kingdom.

My God will be pleased.

I will be remembered.

I did fight the good fight.

I do matter.

My God, wife, kids, and grandkids tell me so; and that's all that matters.

Lindsey Vonn, Michael Phelps, and Sandy/Michelle Quan.

Ish Tanyeri and her husband, Zach Falk, have become like family. Ish is the founder of Dromos Agency, the only athlete representation agency exclusively for Paralympians, and I was her first client. Today, Team Dromos proudly represents 10 Paralympic athletes, 7 of whom are headed to the Paris 2024 Paralympics as I write this. I am deeply grateful for Dromos Agency and the friendship that has grown from this partnership.

A DAY IN THE LIFE OF MIMI & POP

2-11-2024

I've dreamt of being a grandfather
from the day I was loved by mine.

— DK

It's a dream.

It's a prayer.

The dream afternoon with my grandfather. I'm on his lap and we're cutting grass together on his John Deere mower. Afterwards, on the drive home, we pull over and share time with a couple slushies. I can still smell the cut grass amongst our clothes, fingers, and boots. Its scent is the fragrance of sunshine, South Dakota, and a simmering Saturday afternoon.

The mornings my grandfather takes me fishing. The river behind his house is full of catfish. It's wandering waters full of memorable casts and catches. We bring the catfish up the bank and to grandma's kitchen. She fries the fish to a perfect crisp deliciousness. A smell, I spend a lifetime searching to replicate.

My mother's father gift to me. Everlasting memories forever inside and vivid in a landscape pushing over 70 years of life. Crisp recollections amongst a litany of forgotten times.

The answered prayer of first Justin, and then Danielle. Our children of this earth. My seed to this world. We watch as they mature into adults, figure their way in the world, fall in love and parent their own. Their children are our grandchildren. A tale told a trillion times, but only once in the story of us.

We embrace it.

When they are here, there is no plan. Life unfolds and happens. It is innocence, magic, crazy, controlled chaos, and total exhaustion. There are tender hugs, sweet kisses, and joy-filled memorable moments of belly laughter and silliness. Crocodile tears happen when things don't go as planned or one of them gets rough with the other. Like sponges, they always want to know and learn more by asking relentless questions.

We are Mimi and Pop. To everyone else in the world we are Sandy and Dave. When the world bends farther, more to perfect, we are Pop and Mimi.

From the other room, I hear, "I can do it myself, Mimi."

Then I hear, "I need help Mimi."

Everything is laced with love.

I return my grandfather's gift to me. I teach Cruz and Lucas how to fish when they're five years old. They're seven now. I eye their first cast like my grandfather eyed mine. The river behind their house. The pond down from ours. They catch their first fish. The amazement of something entirely new emits from their eyes and beaming smiles. I take too many photos. Everyone asks me to stop.

Our granddaughter, Lily, watches intently but wants nothing to do with the fish flopping on the end of the line. She's a princess. Lily likes her fish on a plate and with a side of crunchy potatoes. Lily is full of sugar and lots of spice… AKA…'Lily Pepper.' I ask her to give me kisses. She, without hesitation, says, "no" emphatically and runs away with a screaming shrill and mischievous laugh.

Jace is three. He unknowingly awaits his turn for the milestones ahead. He loves his Mimi. She never takes a moment away from engaging with him (or the other three). It's one of the most beautiful things I have ever seen.

Cruz and Lucas make their first baskets on the backyard court. A one-of-a-kind venue resting above our 8-acre pond. Who knew my selfish motives to house a home basketball court would serve such a larger purpose. I see Jace's future, his legs bent, pushing upward with everything he has. The ball is in flight. He watches with his saucer eyes as the ball falls through the net.

It's later in the afternoon. Our children will be around shortly to gather theirs.

From our bedroom, I yell throughout the house, "Pillow fight."

I hear footsteps scampering towards the room. Sounds like a small herd of ponies. I'm atop the bed. Ready for action. The fun doctor in all his glory. A pile of pillows surrounds me like a cushy fortress. A giant pillow fight ensues. I take a couple to the kisser. I retaliate with a tickle. Then another. Laughter. Uncontrolled hilarity.

It's a prayer.

It's a dream.

Mimi and Pop's bundle of blessings.

EPILOGUE

TILL THE WHEELS FALL OFF

Age is a Vicious Culprit.
— Dr. Bal Moore

It's a weekend requiring me to play six games. Basketball tournaments are my triumph above all others. I play all the marching minutes of each contested game. The chase of the ball is always stronger than the mounting fatigue.

Challengers, disguised as substantial competitors, are able to keep up early. As the match gets deeper and closer to the finish line, I reveal to them my Lion's endurance and chase of the hunt. Game over.

Within the first five minutes of contests, I get the best folks have to give. I am the others' measuring stick. They all have much to prove. "Put him in his place," they say to one another. They pump each other up like gladiators before the Lion. Misguided whims. Misplaced animosity. Love the game as much as I do. That's the lightning rod. That's the only place to begin.

It's early in my career. The old-guard standouts of the Midwest, Texas, and Florida are constantly testing me. They want an up close, personal, snapshot of myself in a compromised and adverse situation. It's dirty. It's what I'm used to.

How will I react?

What is my pain threshold?

I chase down Ed's outlet hook pass. The fifty-foot bomb lands just beyond me. Hand-speed and overdrive is needed. I find another gear. So does the defender. I pass him and have a greater reach. I stretch for the ball with both hands. The defender knows I'm vulnerable and clips my big wheel behind the axle. He knows exactly what he's doing. I am cannonballed from my chair (no strapping in the 70s); a 'flying squirrel' as we call it. I prepare for the landing. Reach and roll. Bad idea. The in-the-moment strategy has me potentially landing on my face. Adjust. I reach out with both hands; fingers spread like webbed duck feet. Both wrists absorb the fall and malice of my opponents' frustrations. My left wrist and then elbow, crack like eggs before the frying pan. I land with the thud of waves upon rocks. Adrenaline has me straight back into my chair with a prolonged reach and impending lift. Where is he? I find him. I hit his chair with the front end of mine. Both his back wheels lift from the ground. I want to pulverize him. My small brain is on tilt. I raise my right fist daring him to make a move. Teammates and the referees calm me down.

Decades later the above villain and I are proudly photographed together at a Hall of Fame induction ceremony. All water beneath the proverbial bridge.

Getting old with a spinal cord injury is the greatest test I refuse to fail. *"It's still early days,"* I keep telling myself.

I am living within Grand Funk Railroad's "Mean Mistreater."

I have a hellbent passion for being the best at everything.

I play tennis until I'm third best in the world. I don't miss a single basketball season, much less a game. The top players have tennis backgrounds. I'm competing against guys that would have been pros except for some dramatic/ tragic lack of judgement or river card of bad luck. My game is chasing down balls, keeping the ball deep and wearing down my opponents both physically and emotionally. I hit hundreds of thousands of overheads, serves, backhands, and forehands. Each serve slowly but surely, taking a precious nanosecond away from my shoulder life and function. My preparation and practice are the only reason I can hang with the best.

Brad Parks offers up twenty bucks if I can climb a 12-foot high, chain link fence. He just won the tournament and is feeling lively. Tennis players love a side bet. I pull myself up the fence with the strength of my upper body. Game on. Pay up. The descent down hits hard on everything I own. It's not worth the inevitable pain. Twenty bucks is pitiful for such a feat. Should have got a hundred off the guy.

In the 80s, I use a self-propelled Briggs & Stratton lawn mower. I cut my Southern California grass from my wheelchair. I push whilst it pulls. I feel like I can do anything. I love to blow my neighbor's mind. This is my problem. This is my eventual curse. The cumulative effect of my choices won't be known until the wheels begin to falter and fall off.

I learn to surf again at the age of sixty-three. As the king of Pipeline and dear friend, Jerry Lopez says, "When in doubt, paddle out." The risk/reward of surfing is wonderfully life-changing with a heavy underwater, human washing machine, price to pay.

In the summer of 1990, I tear the ligaments in my wrist. Team USA is in Belgium. It's World Championship time. I sit out the semifinal. It feels like there's hundreds of angry, sharp pins, plunging into my wrist, hand, and forearm. It's near impossible to sleep, much less focus on the specifics of a gold medal basketball game. Finals day, I'm in the starting line-up. I avoid making eye contact with our physio. There's nothing good to come from this exchange. During pregame warmups, I keep my distance from all staff and continually let my teammates know, "I'm good."

The salt in the wound is the championship game loss to the French. I'm hurt and unable to overcome the level needed to win a gold medal game. I am used to being a force that cannot be reckoned with. This is what I am accustomed to.

An operation on my wrist awaits.

That same winter, I compete in the 1990 National Alpine Ski Championships. I'm the event favorite. I catch an edge out of the starting gate. It happens in slow motion and in the bat-of-an-eye. I'm not close to top speed. I fight not to fall. I need to travel at breakneck speed to recover. I can't give up. I dig in with everything I have on my outrigger beneath me. Slowly, my arm gets behind me and my mono-ski. I have no choice now but to fall over and directly onto my right shoulder. The one with previous damage. My shoulder is leveraged perfectly for immediate dislocation. Within seconds, the adrenaline of competing and racing succumbs to pain and shock of dislocating my right shoulder and tearing my labrum. I scream like a wounded hyena. My helmet muffles the piercing sound of agony. Course volunteers and starting gate keepers must be wondering, *what the hell?* It doesn't look so bad. I can't get up. I scream relentlessly in absolute pain. I'm lying on my dislocated shoulder with all my weight. I begin the process of being lifted in the dreaded 'basket' and hauled from the mountain. Every skier's worst nightmare.

I am a wounded Lion.

My shoulder is burning for weeks prior to the race. I don't know what it is. I find out later it's a small tear in my shoulder. Muscle imbalance is the culprit. I've always kept maximum strength in my big, Venice Beach muscles but not in the smaller, stabilizing muscles. These muscles keep the shoulder girdle in balance. This is a classic oversight for Wheel Head athletes in the 80s and 90s. We push forward and those muscles get big and full of strength. It's imperative to push backwards or lift small weights in specific motions to keep the shoulder girdle balanced to protect injury and dislocation.

Lesson learned?

Somewhat. Two more shoulder surgeries await.

My pride and joy is my bass boat. It's where I recalibrate. I watch the wind on water and feel at peace. It's also where I race around at 65mph, from spot to spot, searching for the '*big one.*' It's an explicit form of competition. It's the 2013 Paralyzed Veterans Association (PVA) Bass Fishing Tournament. I'm heading towards the weigh-in. There's a chance my partner and I can place and be in the money. The rough waters launch the boat into the air. The motor leaves the water. I have a gorilla grip on the steering wheel. My eyes go huge when the thousand-pound motor re-engages with the water. The wrench of my grip rips everything I own in my shoulder. I tear my labrum, bicep tendon, and rotator cuff all in one unforeseen, airborne moment. Surgery and a brutal rehabilitation are in my immediate and long-term future.

In 2018, at 65 years old, I stop playing basketball. It's certainly time to call it quits, but I also want to eliminate the risk of any further injuries. I get hurt all the time. I'm well known for having to play through pain. There's a big difference between being injured versus playing hurt. I've been playing hurt for about the last forty years. I stop water skiing and snow skiing. Prudent decisions but also ones that eliminate mighty moments with nature. Like many Wheel Head seniors I know, time with nature is the newest gold medal standard.

My fitness is paramount: weights, cardio, and repeated preventative work on the small muscles in my shoulder are a sustained priority. I never stop working and maintain an elite level of fitness.

In 2020, without warning or incident my right shoulder begins to have significant pain. My trusty doc schedules an MRI. An MRI is the first indicator things are about to go sideways. The imaging test reveals another rotator tear. A third surgery on my shoulders. There's talk of a potential shoulder replacement. A road neither myself nor my doctor is keen to go down. The surgery is put off for a few months due to COVID protocols. My shoulder pain intensifies.

I tell myself the surgery will get me strong again. Just like the previous two. Not this time.

The therapy sessions and home health visits are tough going. My quality of life is slipping. The most mundane and routine tasks require assistance. This is a process I can only describe as an inhumane form of recovery. I gut through it all. The parrot on my shoulder constantly voicing, "Never again. Never again."

These days the cortisone shots are happening twice a year. Shoulder replacement is a possibility. We put it off with another injection. I've traded in my beloved Ford F150 truck for an SUV to make things more manageable. I struggle to hold a cup of coffee away from my body. It hurts to reach across the stove to season the fish caught earlier today. I aggravate my shoulder brushing my teeth. Typing on the computer. Texting. Opening the cap of the hot sauce bottle.

It all hurts.

If I don't laugh, I'll cry.

I keep a smile on my face.

The arthritis in my right shoulder disallows a full recovery from my latest surgery. Cumulative overuse. I cannot recover from a shoulder that has nothing left to recover from. More chatter about a full shoulder replacement.

My price to pay for trying to be the best at everything.

I'm a Wheel Head over fifty years in one of these things. Half a century pushing towards the edge of what's imagined and what's next. This change upon me is inevitable. I will adapt. It is what I've always done. I reach out to my peers. They're in the same boat of overuse and abuse, aging bodies over compensating for what's been mangled or lost.

It's a street fight.

I have to fish. It's that simple. I love it. The transfers from the boat deck to the fishing seat take an intense focus. What was an afterthought before might now take a couple attempts. I'm adapting a step-up system to make the transfer less of a do-or-die scenario.

Another hit to my stout ego. I'm realizing ego is an enemy to the passage of time, pestering me to fade. I proclaimed to the world long ago. The poster says it all, *'I will not fade away.'*

I push four miles a day. I am still the Lion. It's a routine that keeps me atop my bass boat, fitting in lifelong clothes, and dancing with the endorphins I need and crave. Each day, I take on my version of heartbreak hill. My head is down. I am on top of my wheels. I power push with torque. I work with the same effort and passion Ed Owen instilled in me six decades ago.

I get to the top. There's a call. It's someone from the NWBA Hall of Fame Committee. They have questions that need answering.

I take the call.

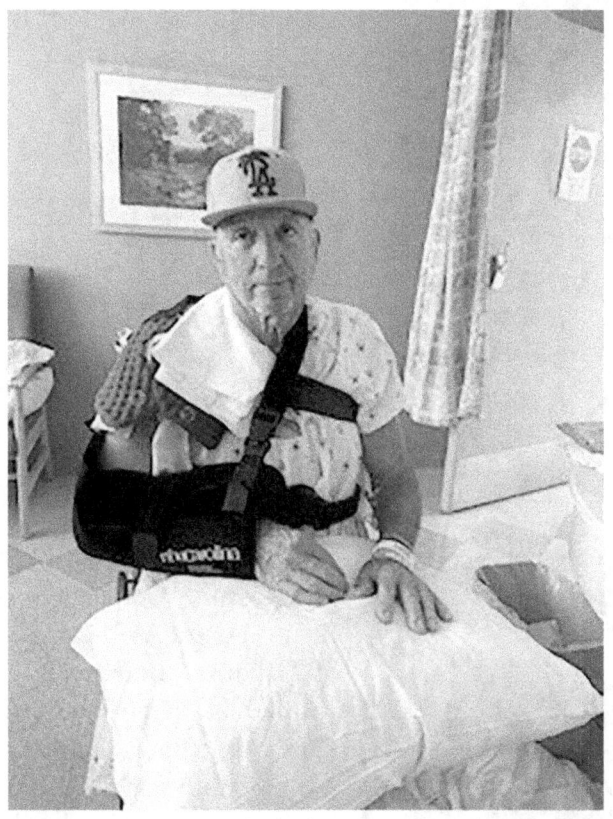

Oh, too familiar. The price of it, and would not change a thing...

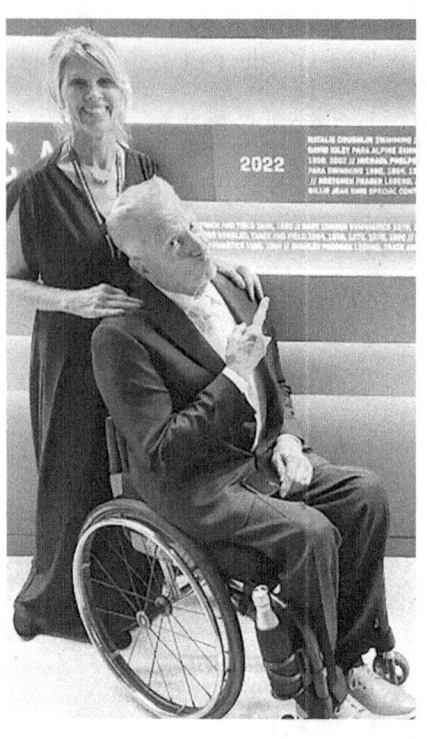

David Kiley is a Paralympic gold medalist in three sports (Wheelchair Basketball, Alpine Skiing, and Track and Field), and is a member of the U.S. Olympic and Paralympic Hall of Fame, Class of 2022, and the National Wheelchair Basketball Hall of Fame, Class of 2000.

Check out DK's "The Wheel Print Podcast"
available on Apple, Spotify, and YouTube.

Miles Thompson holds a Bachelor of Arts in English from the University of Alabama. A Southern California native, Thompson lived twenty-years in the deep south and the Heart of Dixie. He coached within disability sport for four decades at the Lakeshore Foundation in Birmingham, Alabama, the University of Alabama, and abroad in England with Great Britain and the Women's Paralympic Basketball team. His writing credits include a confessional book of poems, *The Loneliest Man in Chinaski County.*
These days Thompson lives a bike ride away from the beach back in Southern California. With his wife, the duo run a small business, but most days can be found chasing waves and the perfect tide.

www.ingramcontent.com/pod-product-compliance
Lightning Source LLC
Chambersburg PA
CBHW060851120626
46553CB00001B/41